LYLE PRICE GUIDE
TO
CHINA

ANTHONY CURTIS
Lyle Publications / A Perigee Book

A Perigee Book
Published by The Berkley Publishing Group
200 Madison Avenue
New York, NY 10016

While every care has been taken in the compiling of information contained in
this volume, the publisher cannot accept liability for loss, financial or
otherwise, incurred by reliance placed on the information herein.

TONY CURTIS (Editor)   ANGIE DEMARCO (Art Production)
EELIN McIVOR (Sub Editor)   CATRIONA DAY (Art Production)
ANNETTE CURTIS (Editorial)   DONNA RUTHERFORD

The Putnam Berkley World Wide Web site address is
http://www.berkley.com

Library of Congress Cataloging-in-Publication Data

Curtis, Tony, 1939–
  Lyle price guide to China / Anthony Curtis.
    p.   cm.
  "A Perigee Book."
  Includes index.
  ISBN 0-399-52310-3
  1. Pottery—Collectors and collecting—Catalogs.   I. Title.
 NK4230.C79   1997
 738'.075—dc21   97-12649
                                   CIP

Printed in the United States of America

10 9 8 7 6 5 4 3 2 1

PRICING POLICY
The prices given in this book are principally those which the item fetched at a
recent sale at the auction house indicated. In a few cases, however, where a
suitable example has not come up at auction, prices have been upgraded in line
with inflation and current auctioneer's estimates.

LYLE PRICE GUIDE
TO
CHINA

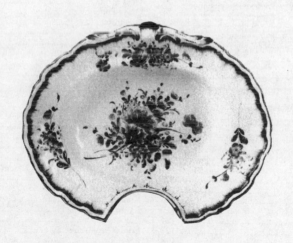

CONTENTS

CHINA

ACKNOWLEDGEMENTS

AB Stockholms Auktionsverk, Box 16256, 103 25 Stockholm, Sweden
Abbotts Auction Rooms, The Auction Rooms, Campsea Ash, Woodbridge, Suffolk
Academy Auctioneers, Northcote House, Northcote Avenue, Ealing, London W5 3UR
James Adam, 26 St Stephens Green, Dublin 2
Jean Claude Anaf, Lyon Brotteaux, 13 bis place Jules Ferry, 69456, Lyon, France
Anderson & Garland, Marlborough House, Marlborough Crescent, Newcastle upon Tyne NE1 4EE
Antique Collectors Club & Co. Ltd, 5 Church Street, Woodbridge, Suffolk IP12 1DS
The Auction Galleries, Mount Rd., Tweedmouth, Berwick on Tweed
Auction Team Köln, Postfach 50 11 68, D-5000 Köln 50 Germany
Auktionshaus Arnold, Bleichstr. 42, 6000 Frankfurt a/M, Germany
Barber's Auctions, Woking, Surrey
Bearnes, Rainbow, Avenue Road, Torquay TQ2 5TG
Biddle & Webb, Ladywood Middleway, Birmingham B16 0PP
Bigwood, The Old School, Tiddington, Stratford upon Avon
Black Horse Agencies, Locke & England, 18 Guy Street, Leamington Spa
Boardman Fine Art Auctioneers, Station Road Corner, Haverhill, Suffolk CB9 0EY
Bonhams, Montpelier Street, Knightsbridge, London SW7 1HH
Bonhams Chelsea, 65–69 Lots Road, London SW10 0RN
Bonhams West Country, Dowell Street, Honiton, Devon
Bosleys, 42 West Street, Marlow, Bucks SL7 1NB
Michael J. Bowman, 6 Haccombe House, Near Netherton, Newton Abbot, Devon
Bristol Auction Rooms, St John Place, Apsley Road, Clifton, Bristol BS8 2ST
British Antique Exporters, School Close, Queen Elizabeth Avenue, Burgess Hill, Sussex
Butterfield & Butterfield, 220 San Bruno Avenue, San Francisco CA 94103, USA
Butterfield & Butterfield, 7601 Sunset Boulevard, Los Angeles CA 90046, USA
Canterbury Auction Galleries, 40 Station Road West, Canterbury CT2 8AN
Central Motor Auctions, Barfield House, Britannia Road, Morley, Leeds, LS27 0HN
H.C. Chapman & Son, The Auction Mart, North Street, Scarborough.
Chapman Moore & Mugford, 8 High Street, Shaftesbury SP7 8JB
Cheffins Grain & Comins, 2 Clifton Road, Cambridge
Christie's (International) SA, 8 place de la Taconnerie, 1204 Genève, Switzerland
Christie's Monaco, S.A.M, Park Palace 98000 Monte Carlo, Monaco
Christie's Scotland, 164–166 Bath Street Glasgow G2 4TG
Christie's South Kensington Ltd., 85 Old Brompton Road, London SW7 3LD
Christie's, 8 King Street, London SW1Y 6QT
Christie's East, 219 East 67th Street, New York, NY 10021, USA
Christie's, 502 Park Avenue, New York, NY 10022, USA
Christie's, Cornelis Schuytstraat 57, 1071 JG Amsterdam, Netherlands
Christie's SA Roma, 114 Piazza Navona, 00186 Rome, Italy
Christie's Swire, 2804–6 Alexandra House, 16–20 Chater Road, Hong Kong
Christie's Australia Pty Ltd., 1 Darling Street, South Yarra, Victoria 3141, Australia
A J Cobern, The Grosvenor Sales Rooms, 93b Eastbank Street, Southport PR8 1DG
Cooper Hirst Auctions, The Granary Saleroom, Victoria Road, Chelmsford, Essex CM2 6LH
The Crested China Co., Station House, Driffield, E. Yorks YO25 7PY
Cundalls, The Cattle Market, 17 Market Square, Malton, N. Yorks
Clifford Dann, 20/21 High Street, Lewes, Sussex
Julian Dawson, Lewes Auction Rooms, 56 High Street, Lewes BN7 1XE
Dee & Atkinson & Harrison, The Exchange Saleroom, Driffield, Nth Humberside YO25 7LJ
Garth Denham & Assocs. Horsham Auction Galleries, Warnsham, Nr. Horsham, Sussex
Diamond Mills & Co., 117 Hamilton Road, Felixstowe, Suffolk
David Dockree Fine Art, The Redwood Suite, Clemence House, Mellor Road, Cheadle Hulme, Cheshire
William Doyle Galleries, 175 East 87th Street, New York, NY 10128, USA
Downer Ross, Charter House, 42 Avebury Boulevard, Central Milton Keynes MK9 2HS
Dreweatt Neate, Holloways, 49 Parsons Street, Banbury
Hy. Duke & Son, 40 South Street, Dorchester, Dorset
Du Mouchelles Art Galleries Co., 409 E. Jefferson Avenue, Detroit, Michigan 48226, USA

CHINA

Duncan Vincent, 1 Station Road, Pangbourne, Berks RG8 7AY
Sala de Artes y Subastas Durán, Serrano 12, 28001 Madrid, Spain
Eldred's, Box 796, E. Dennis, MA 02641, USA
R H Ellis & Sons, 44/46 High St., Worthing, BN11 1LL
Ewbanks, Burnt Common Auction Rooms, London Road, Send, Woking GU23 7LN
Fellows & Son, Augusta House, 19 Augusta Street, Hockley, Birmingham
Finarte, 20121 Milano, Piazzetta Bossi 4, Italy
John D Fleming & Co., The North Devon Auction Rooms, The Savory, South Molton, Devon
Peter Francis, 19 King Street, Carmarthen, Dyfed
Fraser Pinney's, 8290 Devonshire, Montreal, Quebec, Canada H4P 2PZ
Galerie Koller, Rämistr. 8, CH 8024 Zürich, Switzerland
Galerie Moderne, 3 rue du Parnasse, 1040 Bruxelles, Belgium
Geering & Colyer (Black Horse Agencies) Highgate, Hawkhurst, Kent
Glerum Auctioneers, Westeinde 12, 2512 HD's Gravenhage, Netherlands
The Goss and Crested China Co., 62 Murray Road, Horndean, Hants PO8 9JL
Graves Son & Pilcher, 71 Church Road, Hove, East Sussex, BN3 2GL
Greenslade Hunt, Magdalene House, Church Square, Taunton, Somerset, TA1 1SB
Halifax Property Services, 53 High Street, Tenterden, Kent
Halifax Property Services, 15 Cattle Market, Sandwich, Kent CT13 9AW
Hampton's Fine Art, 93 High Street, Godalming, Surrey
Hanseatisches Auktionshaus für Historica, Neuer Wall 57, 2000 Hamburg 36, Germany
William Hardie Ltd., 141 West Regent Street, Glasgow G2 2SG
Andrew Hartley Fine Arts, Victoria Hall, Little Lane, Ilkely
Hauswedell & Nolte, D-2000 Hamburg 13, Pöseldorfer Weg 1, Germany
Giles Haywood, The Auction House, St John's Road, Stourbridge, West Midlands, DY8 1EW
Muir Hewitt, Halifax Antiques Centre, Queens Road/Gibbet Street, Halifax HX1 4LR
Hobbs & Chambers, 'At the Sign of the Bell', Market Place, Cirencester, Glos
Hobbs Parker, Romney House, Ashford Market, Ashford, Kent
Holloways, 49 Parsons Street, Banbury OX16 8PF
Hotel de Ventes Horta, 390 Chaussée de Waterloo (Ma Campagne), 1060 Bruxelles, Belgium
Jacobs & Hunt, Lavant Street, Petersfield, Hants. GU33 3EF
P Herholdt Jensens Auktioner, Rundforbivej 188, 2850 Nerum, Denmark
Kennedy & Wolfenden, 218 Lisburn Rd, Belfast BT9 6GD
G A Key, Aylsham Saleroom, Palmers Lane, Aylsham, Norfolk, NR11 6EH
George Kidner, The Old School, The Square, Pennington, Lymington, Hants SO41 8GN
Kunsthaus am Museum, Drususgasse 1–5, 5000 Köln 1, Germany
Kunsthaus Lempertz, Neumarkt 3, 5000 Köln 1, Germany
Lambert & Foster (County Group), The Auction Sales Room, 102 High Street, Tenterden, Kent
W.H. Lane & Son, 64 Morrab Road, Penzance, Cornwall, TR18 2QT
Langlois Ltd., Westway Rooms, Don Street, St Helier, Channel Islands
Lawrence Butler Fine Art Salerooms, Marine Walk, Hythe, Kent, CT21 5AJ
Lawrence Fine Art, South Street, Crewkerne, Somerset TA18 8AB
Lawrence's Fine Art Auctioneers, Norfolk House, 80 High Street, Bletchingley, Surrey
David Lay, The Penzance Auction House, Alverton, Penzance, Cornwall TA18 4KE
Gordon Litherland, 26 Stapenhill Road, Burton on Trent
Lloyd International Auctions, 118 Putney Bridge Road, London SW15 2NQ
Brian Loomes, Calf Haugh Farm, Pateley Bridge, North Yorks
Lots Road Chelsea Auction Galleries, 71 Lots Road, Chelsea, London SW10 0RN
R K Lucas & Son, Tithe Exchange, 9 Victoria Place, Haverfordwest, SA61 2JX
Duncan McAlpine, Stateside Comics plc, 125 East Barnet Road, London EN4 8RF
McCartneys, Portcullis Salerooms, Ludlow, Shropshire
Christopher Matthews, 23 Mount Street, Harrogate HG2 8DG
John Maxwell, 133a Woodford Road, Wilmslow, Cheshire
May & Son, 18 Bridge Street, Andover, Hants
Morphets, 4–6 Albert Street, Harrogate, North Yorks HG1 1JL
Neales, The Nottingham Saleroom, 192 Mansfield Road, Nottingham NG1 3HU
D M Nesbit & Co, 7 Clarendon Road, Southsea, Hants PO5 2ED
John Nicholson, 1 Crossways Court, Fernhurst, Haslemere, Surrey GU27 3EP

CHINA

Onslow's, Metrostore, Townmead Road, London SW6 2RZ
Outhwaite & Litherland, Kingsley Galleries, Fontenoy Street, Liverpool, Merseyside L3 2BE
Phillips Manchester, Trinity House, 114 Northenden Road, Sale, Manchester M33 3HD
Phillips Son & Neale SA, 10 rue des Chaudronniers, 1204 Genève, Switzerland
Phillips West Two, 10 Salem Road, London W2 4BL
Phillips, 11 Bayle Parade, Folkestone, Kent CT20 1SQ
Phillips, 49 London Road, Sevenoaks, Kent TN13 1UU
Phillips, 65 George Street, Edinburgh EH2 2JL
Phillips, Blenstock House, 7 Blenheim Street, New Bond Street, London W1Y 0AS
Phillips Marylebone, Hayes Place, Lisson Grove, London NW1 6UA
Phillips, New House, 150 Christleton Road, Chester CH3 5TD
Andrew Pickford, 42 St Andrew Street, Hertford SG14 1JA
Pieces of Time, 1–7 Davies Mews, Unit 17–19, London W17 1AR
Pooley & Rogers, Regent Auction Rooms, Abbey Street, Penzance
Pretty & Ellis, Amersham Auction Rooms, Station Road, Amersham, Bucks
Harry Ray & Co, Lloyds Bank Chambers, Welshpool, Montgomery SY21 7RR
Peter M Raw, Thornfield, Hurdle Way, Compton Down, Winchester, Hants SC21 2AN
Rennie's, 1 Agincourt Street, Monmouth
Riddetts, 26 Richmond Hill, Bournemouth
Ritchie's, 429 Richmond Street East, Toronto, Canada M5A 1R1
Derek Roberts Antiques, 24–25 Shipbourne Road, Tonbridge, Kent TN10 3DN
Rogers de Rin, 79 Royal Hospital Road, London SW3 4HN
Russell, Baldwin & Bright, The Fine Art Saleroom, Ryelands Road, Leominster HR6 8JG
Rye Auction Galleries, Rock Channel, Rye, East Sussex
Schrager Auction Galleries, 2915 N Sherman Boulevard, PO Box 10390, Milwaukee WI 53210, USA
Selkirk's, 4166 Olive Street, St Louis, Missouri 63108, USA
Skinner Inc., Bolton Gallery, Route 117, Bolton MA, USA
Soccer Nostalgia, Albion Chambers, Birchington, Kent CT7 9DN
Sotheby's, 34–35 New Bond Street, London W1A 2AA
Sotheby's, 1334 York Avenue, New York NY 10021
Sotheby's, 112 George Street, Edinburgh EH2 2LH
Sotheby's, Summers Place, Billinghurst, West Sussex RH14 9AD
Sotheby's Monaco, BP 45, 98001 Monte Carlo
Southgate Auction Rooms, 55 High St, Southgate, London N14 6LD
Spink & Son Ltd, 5-7 King St., St James's, London SW1Y 6QS
Michael Stainer Ltd., St Andrews Auction Rooms, Wolverton Rd, Boscombe, Bournemouth BH7 6HT
Mike Stanton, 7 Rowood Drive, Solihull, West Midlands B92 9LT
Street Jewellery, 5 Runnymede Road, Ponteland, Northumbria NE20 9HE
Stride & Son, Southdown House, St John's St., Chichester, Sussex
G E Sworder & Son, 14 Cambridge Road, Stansted Mountfitche, Essex CM24 8BZ
Taviner's of Bristol, Prewett Street, Redcliffe, Bristol BS1 6PB
Tennants, Harmby Road, Leyburn, Yorkshire
Thomson Roddick & Laurie, 24 Lowther Street, Carlisle
Thomson Roddick & Laurie, 60 Whitesands, Dumfries
Timbleby & Shorland, 31 Gt Knollys St, Reading RG1 7HU
Truro Auction Centre, Calenick Street, Truro TR1 2SG
Venator & Hanstein, Cäcilienstr. 48, 5000 Köln 1, Germany
T Vennett Smith, 11 Nottingham Road, Gotham, Nottingham NG11 0HE
Duncan Vincent, 92 London Street, Reading RG1 4SJ
Wallis & Wallis, West Street Auction Galleries, West Street, Lewes, E. Sussex BN7 2NJ
Walter's, 1 Mint Lane, Lincoln LN1 1UD
Wells Cundall Nationwide Anglia, Staffordshire House, 27 Flowergate, Whitby YO21 3AX
Woltons, 6 Whiting Street, Bury St Edmunds, Suffolk IP33 1PB
Peter Wilson, Victoria Gallery, Market Street, Nantwich, Cheshire CW5 5DG
Wintertons Ltd., Lichfield Auction Centre, Fradley Park, Lichfield, Staffs WS13 8NF
Woltons, 6 Whiting Street, Bury St Edmunds, Suffolk IP33 1PB
Woolley & Wallis, The Castle Auction Mart, Salisbury, Wilts SP1 3SU
Worthing Auction Galleries, 31 Chatsworth Road, Worthing, W. Sussex BN11 1LY

CHINA

The word 'china' does not, surprisingly enough, come from the country of the same name, but from a Persian word which sounds like 'chini', and means porcelain. It was originally incorporated into English in the 17th century as 'cheney'.

If the term did not come from China, however, the product most certainly did, so it is perhaps inevitable that the word should have become adapted to conform.

The ceramics of China were the ideal to which every other country and civilization aspired. From earliest times their influence had filtered west through Mesopotamia and the Middle East, reaching Europe in a diluted form when the Moorish armies conquered Spain in 711. They brought with them the secrets of what was to become known as Hispano-Moresque ware, by which the majolica of Italy was further inspired in the 15th and 16th centuries.

It was the Dutch East India company, however, which brought the first examples of real Chinese porcelain back from the East in the early years of the 17th century, and it would be difficult to overestimate the reaction when the new material burst upon Europe. Nothing like the brilliance of the blue, the sparkling white and the depth of the red and green of late Ming polychrome had ever been seen before, and at once everyone started trying to reproduce these hard, translucent, breathtaking pieces. Here again it was the Dutch who chalked up one of the earliest successes, with their blue and white delft ware.

It was not until the early years of the following century that Böttger discovered the secret of true porcelain for Augustus the Strong at Meissen, and from then on the stage was set for truly dazzling developments in Europe. It is interesting to note, however, how the influence of the original Chinese inspiration lingered on. Almost every 18th century factory produced its blue and white ware, while Chinese and oriental motifs remain a hugely popular decorative theme right to the present day.

The race to reproduce real porcelain had meant that china had become an enormous international status symbol and factories everywhere benefited from royal and aristocratic patronage, leading examples being Vincennes-Sèvres in France, Capodimonte in Italy, and of course, Meissen itself.

The enthusiasm was not confined to the rich and ruling classes, however, and factories were soon turning out pieces for the middle classes and finally the 'masses' as well.

It is this scale of production which helps to make china the vast, varied and fascinating collecting field it is today, for it is possible to make delightful collections of everything from famille verte to fairings, from Sèvres to Staffordshire, from Ming to mustard pots. There is something to appeal to the taste and pocket of everyone.

Nor is it necessary to go far into the distant past to begin a worthwhile collection. One of the most popular fields is Doulton figures, of which over 200 are in production today. Pieces by contemporary potters too, such as Hans Coper and Lucie Rie are now fetching huge sums, while those of their junior disciples are also attracting increasing attention. There are of course the stars, Meissen, Ming, Wedgwood etc., which are forever fixed in their firmament, but others are rising (and, occasionally, falling) all the time. Clarice Cliff, for example has enjoyed a period of unprecedented popularity of late, while such names as Poole and Moorcroft are becoming more and more sought after. (If embarking on a collection from a 'fashionable' field, it is worthwhile ensuring that it is one which you like for its own sake and not just for its potential investment value. That way, if fashions later change, you at least have something which it gives you pleasure to own. That, at the end of the day, must be the real criterion for the serious collector.)

This book is designed to assist the amateur and professional alike in distinguishing and determining the current value of a huge range of pieces. The examples have been carefully selected to provide a representative sample of each factory or potter's output, with a description and prices recently paid. It also contains short accounts of what is often the fascinating history of individual factories, together with useful hints on dating their output and identifying fakes. All in all, it provides an indispensable reference work for anyone interested in any branch of the china collecting field.

AMERICAN

Pottery has been a thriving American tradition from earliest times, and examples by native Americans are a prominent feature of every sale of Red Indian wares. Among the white settlers, the traditional pottery of the United States was redware, which was produced from the time of the earliest settlers in just about every town and village. It was only really supplanted by stoneware in the 19th century, due to persistent fears that the lead oxides which gave it its color could be poisonous.

During the 19th century such firms as Norton and Fenton and the United States Pottery Co at Bennington had been turning out commercial wares, but, with the exception of the Chelsea Keramic Art Works, founded in 1866, art pottery as such did not exist in the US before 1879. The Centennial Exhibition of 1876 may possibly have acted as a touchstone for the development of a decorative pottery industry. In any case Ohio became a principal center for the production of such wares, with six potteries opening in Cincinnati alone in the next ten years.

Carl Walters pottery rooster for Stonelain, high glaze with decoration in maroon and black on white ground, impressed marks, 11¹/₈in. high.
(Skinner) $288

Ernst Wahliss Art Nouveau pottery plaque, with portrait of an appealing young couple holding musical score, 21 x 18in.
(Skinner Inc.) $2,600

An important pair of Tucker and Hulme porcelain 'vase' shape pitchers, Philadelphia, dated *1828*, initialed and dated *JWM.LM 1828*, 9¹/₂in. high.
(Sotheby's) $27,600

Clewell Ware bronze clad Pottery vase, Canton, Ohio, original copper red to verdigris patina, 7in. high.
(Skinner) $748

A brown-glazed earthenware pitcher, American, probably 19th century, molded in two parts in the form of a human head, 10¹/₂in. high.
(Christie's) $3,450

Vance faience vase with molded mermaid decoration, Ohio, circa 1905, with repeating figures and fish (some chips and roughness), 12½in. high. (Skinner) $285

Cowan Pottery table lamp, Rocky River, Ohio, circa 1925, gloss Chinese blue glaze on high relief form, impressed mark, base 12½in. high.
(Skinner) $345

AMERICAN

Catalina Pottery vase, California, lavender glaze, flaring rim, ink stamp mark, 6in. high.
(Skinner) $402

Scheier pottery charger, hand-thrown plate glazed mauve and brown with central geometric panels, 14½in. diameter.
(Skinner) $880

North Dakota Art pottery vase, dated *1953*, in squat globular form with pink floral design, signed *Lebacken*, 7½in. high.
(Eldred's) $385

An Omega earthenware vase by Roger Fry, covered in a finely crackled white tin glaze with yellow ocher and blue abstract decoration, circa 1914, 16.5cm. high.
(Christie's) $2,000

Stang Pottery figural bird, Trenton, New Jersey, gloss translucent glazed in shades of blue, green and brown on white clay body, 7¼in. high.
(Skinner) $300

An incised and cobalt-decorated stoneware harvest jug, New York, 1805, decorated on the obverse with incised floral vine below a fish, the reverse with a Masonic apron, inscribed and dated *J. Romer, 1805*, 7in. high.
(Christie's) $6,050

A glazed earthenware bank, George A. Wagner Pottery, Pennsylvania, 1875–1876, in the form of a Staffordshire poodle with coleslaw mane, 6½in. high.
(Christie's) $1,495

Matt Morgan Art Pottery scenic plaque, Cincinnati, circa 1883, Limoges style slip decorated scene with swallows, clouds and bamboo, 11½in. diameter.
(Skinner) $518

A fine Union Porcelain Works white parian 'Poet's Pitcher', Greenpoint, New York, 1879–88, designed by Karl L. H. Müller, 8⁹/₁₆in. high.
(Sotheby's) $4,312

AMERICAN

CHINA

Early 20th century pottery pitcher, New Hampshire, 8¼in. high.
(Skinner Inc.) $240

Five Rockwell Kent 'Salamina' ceramic plates, designed in 1939 for Vernon Kilns, Vernon and Los Angeles, brown stamp marks, 16¾ x 9½in. diameter.
(Skinner) $546

Spongeware umbrella stand, late 19th/early 20th century, 21in. high.
(Skinner Inc.) $480

An American market teabowl and saucer, circa 1795, each piece enameled with a three-masted ship at sail flying an American flag from her stern, blue enamel and gilt star borders.
(Christie's) $1,210

A five-piece Picard China Co. porcelain breakfast set, decorated with the 'Aura Argenta Linear' design, artist signed by Adolph Richter, circa 1910-30.
(Skinner Inc.) $640

American Encaustic Tiling Co. Ltd., figural of a woman with urn, New York, W. J. Griffiths, inscribed artist's signature, firm's paper label, 11¼in. high.
(Skinner) $747

A green-glazed incised earthenware pickle jar, attributed to Lucius Jordan, Washington County, Georgia, late 19th century, 15in. high.
(Sotheby's) $1,100

Rare Shawsheen Pottery teapot, Billerica, Massachusetts, Mason City, Iowa, circa 1911, incised stylized decoration in slate blue and green panels on mottled green ground, 10in. wide.
(Skinner) $805

A glazed earthenware 'Face-jug', attributed to Norman Smith, Bibb County, Lawley, Alabama, circa 1930, with strap handle, 10in. high.
(Sotheby's) $2,640

AMERICAN

Important pottery vase, by Fritz Wilhelm Albert (1865–1940), circa 1906, 14½in. high. (Skinner Inc.) $25,000

Overbeck Pottery bowl, matt frothy white and green glaze, inside decorated with mustard and red-brown glaze, incised *Overbeck 5-3*, 5¾in. diameter. (Skinner) $1,200

Parian pitcher, America, 19th century, with figures of George Washington in relief, 10in. high. (Skinner Inc.) $960

Double handled pottery floor vase, probably Zanesville Stoneware Co, Ohio, early 20th century, 18½in. high. (Skinner Inc.) $200

Six-piece tea set attributed to Dreamacre Pottery, by George F. Frederick, Vineyard Haven, Martha's Vineyard. (Skinner) $600

A cobalt decorated and incised jug, America, early 19th century, decorated with incised figure of standing bird, 15½in. high. (Skinner Inc.) $1,250

Causton Ernest Soper's stoneware bank, Fort Edward Pottery, Fort Edward, New York, dated *February 27, 1883*, 7in. high. (Sotheby's) $8,625

Adelaide Robineau porcelain vase, Syracuse, New York, circa 1912, spherical form with white crystalline glaze, 4¾in. high. (Skinner) $5,500

Anna pottery snake jug, with four snake heads and lower torso of man, with initials *A.M.A.B.* and *C2WK Anna ILL 1881*, 9in. high. (Skinner Inc.) $2,900

CHINA

Byrdcliffe Pottery bowl, Woodstock, New York, blue and white glaze, impressed mark, 1¾in. high, 3¾in. diameter. (Skinner)　$500

An American teapot and cover, of swollen cylindrical form, commemorating the New York World's Fair, 18cm. high. (Christie's)　$240

Wheatley pottery bowl, Cincinnati, Ohio, circa 1900, relief decorated with open petaled flowers and leaves, 7½in. diameter. (Skinner Inc.)　$800

A glazed earthenware bank, George A. Wagner Pottery, Pennsylvania, 1875–1876, in the form of a Staffordshire spaniel, glazed in yellow with green and brown daubs, 6½in. high. (Christie's)　$1,093

Important Union porcelain Heathen-Chinee pitcher, Greenpoint, New York, 1876, the relief of Bill Nye, knife in hand, attacking Ah Sin for cheating at cards, 9⅝in. high. (Skinner Inc.)　$3,200

American Belleek landscape vase, Ceramic Art Company, Trenton, New Jersey, handpainted by J. H. Schindler, late 19th century, 12¼in. (Butterfield & Butterfield)　$690

Grotesque pottery jug, America, late 19th/early 20th century, carved into a devil-like mask, 19in. high. (Skinner)　$650

Scheier Pottery bowl, 1941, wide mouth on tapering cylindrical form, relief decorated with repeating figures, flowers, and the sun, 8¾in. diameter. (Skinner Inc.)　$2,100

Porcelain pitcher, American China Manufactory, Philadelphia, circa 1830, each side decorated with floral bouquets, 9½in. high. (Skinner Inc.)　$2,160

14

AMERICAN INDIAN POTTERY

The nomadic lifestyle of many groups of Native Americans meant that they have left few durable artefacts. Pottery, however, is one, and one which has an enthusiastic following among collectors. As might be expected, most examples come from the more settled farming tribes of the Southwest, such as the Hopi and Navajo. The decoration is often very fine, and its stylized nature appeals to modern taste.

Laguna/Acoma polychrome pottery jar, painted in a single elaborate design band of repeated and complementary feather and plant motifs, 10¼in. high.
(Butterfield & Butterfield)

$862

Mimbres black-on-white pictorial pottery bowl, depicting a long-legged water fowl with elongated sinuous neck, a fish dangling from its bill, 10in. diameter.
(Butterfield & Butterfield)

$4,600

Hopi polychrome pottery jar, Frog Woman, the white-slipped vessel painted in a panel style, showing various bird and feather motifs, 10½in. high.
(Butterfield & Butterfield)

$2,070

San Ildefonso Blackware pottery plate, Maire, painted in a large scale repeat feather pattern within a triple perimeter band, 11in. diameter.
(Butterfield & Butterfield)

$2,160

San Ildefonso pottery jar of hemispherical form, painted on the body, lip and both sides of top, in black on red, 11¼in. high.
(Butterfield & Butterfield)

$10,000

Zia polychrome pottery jar, with traditional arches framing a pair of roadrunners, 9½in. high.
(Butterfield & Butterfield)

$690

Santa Clara Blackware pottery jar, Christina Naranjo, carved to depict an Avanyu below a rim band of parallel linear devices, 9¼in. high.
(Butterfield & Butterfield)

$1,326

Acoma polychrome pottery jar, the flaring sides with connected stepped and fine-line diamond lozenges, checkered diamonds within, 12in. diameter.
(Butterfield & Butterfield)

$2,587

15

Acoma pottery olla, circa 1920, with black, white and orange stylized decoration, 6in. high. (Eldred's) $275

A finely decorated Hopi Placca pottery bowl. (Skinner) $800

Southwestern polychromed jar, Acoma, 13¼in. diam. (Skinner) $1,450

A Zuni pottery jar, decorated in brown and red on a white ground, 27cm. high. (Phillips) $2,250

American Indian contemporary San Carlos design Apache vase by Manna, 17in. high. (Du Mouchelles) $480

Southwestern polychrome pottery jar, Zia, 14in. diam. (Skinner) $2,250

A 19th century Santa Ana polychrome jar, 12in. diam. (Skinner) $3,600

San Ildefonso blackware pottery plate, Maria/Popovi, the shiny black surface with a repeat feather pattern within three encircling bands, 14in. diameter. (Butterfield & Butterfield) $5,600

Santo Domingo pottery olla, circa 1910, black and white geometric decoration, 11in. high. (Eldred's) $480

16

AMPHORA

The Amphora Porzellanfabrik was established at Turn-Teplitz in Bohemia to make earthenware and porcelain. Much of their porcelain figure output was exported.

The mark consists of three stars in a burst of rays over *RSK* (for the proprietors Reissner & Kessel).

An Amphora Turn-Teplitz bowl, designed by Riessner, Stellmacher & Kessel, painted on the obverse with the bust of a woman in pink, blues, green and purple, 10¼in. wide.
(Bonhams) $900

An Amphora pottery figural vase, surmounted on the shoulder by a large figure of a cockerel, painted in shades of brown, 43cm. high.
(Christie's) $1,328

Austrian Amphora mirror with stylized Art Nouveau figure, 1910, 13in. high.
(Muir Hewitt) $450

Reissner Stellmacher and Kessel for Amphora, portrait vase, circa 1900, 10⅝in. high.
(Sotheby's) $2,851

An Amphora polychrome-painted pottery group modeled as a Bedouin tribesman astride a camel, 19in. high.
(Christie's S. Ken) $400

Amphora glazed earthenware vase, early 20th century, in gold glaze with green and violet iridescence, 13½in. high.
(Butterfield & Butterfield) $1,265

An Amphora oviform earthenware jardinière, painted with geese walking in a wooded landscape, 8½in. high.
(Christie's S. Ken) $600

A large Amphora earthenware vase, modeled in full relief with a proud cockerel standing before reeds, painted overall in greens and blues, 16in. high.
(Bonhams) $750

ANSBACH

Forty years after faience production began, in 1758, Johann Friedrich Kaendler, who was possibly a relative of the Meissen modeler, helped the then margrave Alexander of Brandenburg to establish a porcelain factory at Ansbach, which continued in production until 1860.

Their wares show little originality and tended to follow Meissen, Nymphenburg and particularly Berlin styles pretty slavishly. The figures in particular closely resemble those produced at Berlin, though Ansbach pieces can be distinguished by their lightweight, elongated bodies and half-closed eyes painted in red. Groups were also made based on plays written by the margrave's wife, and show lovers, hunters or allegories set against architectural arbors.

Marks, where they exist, show the shield of the Arms of Ansbach, impressed, showing a stream with three fishes. Tablewares are sometimes marked with an *A*, sometimes with a shield or the Prussian eagle.

An Ansbach bullet-shaped teapot and cover with a dog's head spout and foliate scroll handle, painted in puce camaieu with bouquets of flowers, circa 1770, 7.5cm. high.
(Christie's) $2,363

An Ansbach faience hexagonal vase, circa 1730, manganese L mark, of baluster form, decorated in a brilliant famille verte palette with two panels each with two birds, 11in. high.
(Christie's) $72,900

A rare Ansbach group of three putti probably symbolic of Summer, two small boys seated with wheatsheaves and a little girl standing, 10.5cm., circa 1765–1770.
(Phillips) $1,520

An Ansbach arbor group of lovers, the lady seated holding a nosegay, her companion standing beside her, circa 1770, 25cm. high.
(Christie's) $24,000

An Ansbach baluster coffee-pot and a cover, painted with two birds perched in branches flanked by scattered sprigs of puce flowers, circa 1770, 18.5cm. high overall.
(Christie's) $1,600

An Ansbach chinoiserie plate painted in colors with a Chinese pheasant perched on a branch, probably Johann Georg Forch, circa 1755, 24.5cm. diam.
(Christie's) $2,560

An Ansbach arched rectangular tea-caddy and cover painted with men fishing from a rock and in a boat before a village and distant mountains, circa 1775, 12.5cm. high.
(Christie's) $2,400

ANTIQUITIES

One of the greatest fascinations of ceramic antiquities must surely be the fact that they were created by the hands of someone living thousands of years ago, and that, despite the innate fragility of the medium, they have survived. That said, the fact that many examples can be picked up for hundreds rather than thousands of dollars is all the more amazing. One would pay more for a black plastic comb belonging to Elvis, and one can only ask why?

An Apulian Red-Figure knop-handled patera on a stepped ring base, Greek South Italy, later 4th century B.C., 15¹/₂in. diameter.
(Bonhams) $3,220

Mochica figural pottery vessel, circa 200–500 A.D., the rectangular base surmounted by a fierce looking human head, having long fangs, 8³/₄in. high.
(Butterfield & Butterfield) $715

A Daunian double askos, the handle joining the necks, both with strainers to restrict pouring, Greek, South Italy, circa 3rd century B.C., 7¹/₂in. high.
(Bonhams) $570

Mayan polychrome pottery cylinder vase, circa 550–950 A.D., painted allover in a repeat panel pattern of bat face profiles, 8in. high.
(Butterfield & Butterfield) $770

A large Apulian black-glazed bell krater with red-figure decoration of a seated nude female gazing into a mirror, Greek South Italy, late 4th century B.C., 12¹/₂in.
(Bonhams) $2,000

A Campanian Red Figure bell krater attributed to the Capua Painter, with added details in white, Greek, South Italy, 360–330 B.C., 7⁵/₈in.
(Bonhams) $1,170

A buff-colored Messapian ornamental nestoris or torzella, umber decoration on the body, late 5th century B.C., 11¹/₄in. high.
(Bonhams) $332

An Apulian black-glazed hydria decorated with the draped standing figure of a winged Nike, early 4th century B.C., 11³/₄in. high.
(Bonhams) $4,000

CHINA

19

ANTIQUITIES

A Palmyran ribbed pottery bag-shaped amphora with two small handles at the neck, 1st century B.C./A.D., 20in. high.
(Bonhams) $406

A finely potted stemless kylix, black-glazed with added red-painted decoration, Red Swan Group Apulia, South Italy, mid-4th century B.C., 8¼in. diameter.
(Bonhams) $775

A West Iranian buff-colored pottery bridge-spouted vessel with rope-twist handle, 8th–7th century B.C., 5½in. high.
(Bonhams) $655

An early Lucanian Red-Figure bell krater attributed to the Pisticci Painter, circa 440–420 B.C., 14in. high.
(Bonhams) $12,880

Veracruz seated pottery figure, circa 550–950 A.D., with legs crossed and hands to the knees, 14½in. high.
(Butterfield & Butterfield) $1,980

A Mycenaean stirrup vessel, the piriform body swelling at the shoulder and tapering to the foot, 1400–1200 B.C., 8¾in. high.
(Bonhams) $2,340

A sizeable Cypriot bichrome ware amphora, the neck decorated on either side with two panels, a four-leaf flower in each, Iron Age, 10th-8th centuries B.C., 21in.
(Bonhams) $2,400

An Orientalizing black-figure Greek amphora, the upper body decorated on side A with a centrally seated female Sphinx, a lion standing before her, 6th century B.C., 12¾in. high.
(Bonhams) $3,750

A Lucanian Red-Figure bell krater, showing Nike carrying a timpanum facing a youth carrying a thyrsus with his right hand, Greek, South Italy, 360–340 B.C., 12¼in. high.
(Bonhams) $3,432

An Etruscan hollow terracotta head of a female wearing a diadem and earrings, circa 4th-3rd century B.C., 9in.
(Bonhams) $830

A circular terracotta antefix with the facing head of Medusa, snakes surround her face, 4th-3rd century B.C., 9in. diameter.
(Bonhams) $1,200

A Hellenistic terracotta female head with an ornate crown of rosettes, circa 2nd-1st century B.C., 4in.
(Bonhams) $522

A rare Cypriot terracotta model mortuary house, the entrance door secured by two bronze pins (not original), Hellenistic, late 4th-3rd century B.C., 6³/₄in.
(Bonhams) $1,500

A Byzantine square terracotta tile showing a leaping jackal in relief within a box, circa 5th–7th centuries A.D., 10¹/₄in. high.
(Bonhams) $455

A Campanian terracotta antefax showing in relief the facing head of a bearded satyr, Greek, South Italy, circa 4th century B.C., 8¹/₄in. high.
(Bonhams) $750

An Etruscan terracotta antefix, molded in relief with a female head within a shell-like niche, circa 6th–5th centuries B.C., 9³/₄in. high.
(Bonhams) $1,170

A Roman terracotta relief fragment showing a winged siren playing the twin pipes (auloi), circa 2nd–3rd century A.D., 5in. high.
(Bonhams) $1,092

An Etruscan hollow terracotta head of a youth with prominent ears and short hair, the eyes incised, 4th-3rd century B.C., 11in. high.
(Bonhams) $780

A Greek terracotta protome of a female, both hands raised to her breasts, Rhodes, mid 5th century B.C., 12in. high.
(Bonhams) $1,500

An Etruscan terracotta hollow head of a curly-haired youth, 4th-3rd century B.C., 7½in.
(Bonhams) $900

A Roman terracotta actor's mask of a woman, her hair swept back off her face, 2nd-3rd century A.D., 7¾in. high.
(Bonhams) $960

A Greek fragmentary terracotta female bust with archaic features, her centrally parted and dressed hair beneath a stephane, South Italy, circa 5th-4th century B.C., 7in. high.
(Bonhams) $990

A Cypriot bichrome ware amphora, the neck decorated on either side with two panels, Iron Age, 10th-8th centuries B.C., 14in.
(Bonhams) $764

A sizeable terracotta head of a woman wearing a polos head-dress, her curly-hair decorated with rosettes and wearing earrings, Greek, South Italy, circa 4th-3rd century B.C., 10½in.
(Bonhams) $975

A Boeotian buff-colored terracotta seated female figure, the hollow body of flattened form with fully modeled head and arms, circa 600–550 B.C., 6in. high.
(Bonhams) $1,288

A Boeotian terracotta figure of a tall-necked horse and rider (one arm missing), both with black linear decorations, mid 6th century B.C., 6¾in. high.
(Bonhams) $886

A Syro-Hittite terracotta jar, the body decorated with multiple stylized figures, Syria, circa 2000–1500 B.C., 3¾in.
(Bonhams) $1,061

ARITA

Porcelain first appeared in Japan when the discovery of kaolin nearby in 1616 led to the establishment of a ceramic center in Saga prefecture, Hizen, which came to be known as Arita. Early Arita was painted in grayish underglaze blue and primitive red and green enamels. Enameled and blue and white wares with paneled decoration in the later Ming style were brought to the West by the Dutch from the 17th century onwards, often through the port of Imari. Kakiemon and Nabeshima wares were also made at Arita, and production continues there to the present day.

A pair of Arita models of carp, decorated in iron-red and black enamel, gilt and underglaze blue, late 17th century, each approximately 19cm. high.
(Christie's) $2,390

An Arita model of a cat, 19th century, seated with head turned over its left shoulder and right paw raised, 24cm. high.
(Christie's) $2,600

An Arita blue and white pear-shaped tankard and silver cover decorated overall with peonies issuing from rockwork, late 17th century, silver mounts later, 20cm. high.
(Christie's) $3,657

A group of three Arita models of a cockerel, hens and stands, late 17th/early 18th century, decorated in iron-red, black, aubergine and yellow enamels and gilt.
(Christie's) $14,750

An Arita blue and white coffee urn with elaborate engraved Dutch silver mounts, the urn decorated with a ho-o bird on rockwork, late 17th/early 18th century, 33cm. high.
(Christie's) $6,975

An Arita blue and white tureen and cover decorated with six shaped panels depicting sprays of peony and chrysanthemum among rockwork, late 17th century, 31cm. diameter.
(Christie's) $12,000

A pair of ormolu-mounted Arita vases and covers, each with domed cover surmounted by a karashishi above a pierced C-scroll and foliate collar, the porcelain 17th century, 31in. high.
(Christie's) $29,130

An Arita blue and white vase decorated with three shaped panels containing peonies among rockwork, divided by lotus sprays, late 17th century, 41.5cm. high.
(Christie's) $13,475

ARITA

A large Arita jardinière, the wide flattened rim with panels of birds, horses, ships and temples, mid 19th century, 75cm diam.
(Christie's) $2,639

A pair of Japanese Arita vases, 12in. high.
(Dockree's) $725

An Arita model of a hare, seated on rockwork decorated in iron-red, green, brown enamels and gilt, early 18th century, 22cm. high.
(Christie's) $13,800

A rare Arita octagonal blue and white vase decorated with scholars and attendants in a boat on a river, late 17th century, 52cm. high.
(Christie's) $12,000

Two rare Arita blue and white ewers in the Kakiemon manner of Islamic form, each decorated with birds among branches of bamboo, late 17th century, 28.5cm. high.
(Christie's) $31,559

A rare Arita blue and white drug jar of European form, decorated with a horned satyr's head, mid 17th century, 27.3cm high.
(Christie's) $35,190

An Arita kraak style foliate rimmed blue and white dish, bordered by panels of Buddhistic emblems and flowers, late 17th century, 43.5cm diam.
(Christie's) $1,760

A pair of Arita blue and white baluster jars overlaid with gold and colored lacquer decoration, the porcelain painted overall with flowering peonies and foliage, 26¹/₂in. high.
(Christie's) $9,250

An Arita blue and white charger painted with a central roundel enclosing the letters *V.O.C.*, surrounded by two Ho-o birds, late 17th century, 14¹/₂in. diameter.
(Christie's) $22,500

ARITA

A fine Arita blue and white charger, the central roundel with a lady fanning herself, late 17th century, 59cm. diameter.
(Christie's) $12,458

A pair of large Arita porcelain vases, painted with various shaped panels of birds, flowers and landscapes, 141.5cm. high.
(Bearne's) $2,025

An Arita blue and white jardinière depicting a three clawed dragon amidst scrolling clouds, late 17th century, 37cm. diameter.
(Christie's) $2,194

An Arita blue and white oviform Jar, decorated with two birds on rocks flanked by flowering plants, late 17th century, 27.5cm. high.
(Christie's) $3,680

A pair of Arita blue and white deep dishes decorated with pomegranates in finger citron, the reverse with branches of peaches, late 17th century, 35cm. diameter.
(Christie's) $12,150

An Arita blue and white pear-shaped tankard with loop handle decorated overall with peonies issuing from rockwork, late 17th century, 21.5cm high.
(Christie's) $1,495

A pair of Arita models of dogs decorated in iron-red, black enamels and gilt with irregular piebald, each seated with its mouth agape, late 17th/early 18th century, each approx. 41cm. high.
(Christie's) $115,000

An Arita blue and white choshi (wine pitcher) in the Kakiemon style decorated with a continuous scene of flying ho-o birds, late 17th century, 22cm. high.
(Christie's) $2,743

A pair of large Arita blue and white bottles decorated with buildings in mountainous landscapes beneath a band of foliate design, late 17th century, 44.5cm. high.
(Christie's) $22,250

ASHTEAD POTTERY

The Ashtead Pottery was established in 1923 by Sir Laurence and Lady Weaver to give employment to disabled ex-servicemen. It produced tableware, nursery novelties and figures, at first in white glazed earthenware. Painted landscape decoration and linear designs were introduced later, and the figures, usually in white glazed earthenware with touches of color, are characterised by garlands of flowers painted in bright blue, yellow, maroon, light green and yellow. The original workforce of 14 had risen to 30 by 1925, and the pottery continued in business until 1935.

The mark is usually a printed tree, with *Ashtead Potters*.

'Wembley Lion', an Ashtead pottery figure modeled by Percy Metcalfe, covered in an orange glaze, 18cm. high.
(Christie's) $207

'Summer', an Ashtead pottery figural group by Joan Pyman, modeled as the Season holding a spray of flowers, 35cm. high.
(Christie's) $900

Three of five Art Deco Ashtead pottery wall plates.
(Phillips) $480

'Shy', an Ashtead pottery figure modeled as a young girl seated on a pedestal draped with a garland of flowers, 15¼in. high.
(Christie's S. Ken) $1,200

An Ashtead advertising plaque, for the Ideal Home magazine, molded in relief with ballet dancer, 6in. high.
(Christie's S. Ken) $240

A pair of Ashtead pottery bookends designed by Percy Metcalfe, each modeled as a seated cherub with doves at his feet, 18cm. high.
(Christie's) $320

An Ashtead lamp base, of ovoid form molded in relief on each shoulder with the head of gazelle, 11in. high.
(Christie's S. Ken) $400

AULT POTTERY

William Ault (b. 1841) was an English potter who worked in Staffordshire before going into partnership with Henry Tooth in 1882 to open an art pottery at Church Gresley, Derbyshire. In 1887 he opened his own pottery near Burton-on-Trent, where he produced earthenware vases, pots, pedestals and grotesque jugs.

The painted decoration of flowers and butterflies was often executed by his daughter Clarissa. Between 1892-96 Christopher Dresser designed some vases for Ault, which he sometimes covered in his own aventurine glaze. Between 1923-37 the firm traded as Ault and Tunnicliffe and thereafter became Ault Potteries Ltd.

Marks include a tall fluted vase over *Ault* on a ribbon, or a monogramed *APL*.

An Ault vase, designed by Dr. Christopher Dresser, with curling lip continuing to form two handles, streaked turquoise glaze over dark brown, 18cm. high. (Christie's) $1,600

An Ault pottery vase, designed by Christopher Dresser, the footed bun shaped body with four applied masks, facsimile signature, 32cm. high. (Phillips) $760

An Ault pottery vase, designed by Christopher Dresser, the vessel of broad double-gourd form, glazed in streaked green and manganese brown, 27.5cm. high. (Phillips) $2,265

An Ault pottery vase, possibly designed by Christopher Dresser, molded on each side with a stylized fish face, 18cm. high. (Sotheby's) $635

An Ault pottery bottle vase, designed by Dr. Christopher Dresser, the bulbous lobed base with slender neck, covered overall with an ox blood glaze, 9in. high. (Bonhams) $240

An unusual Ault Pottery pouring vessel, designed by Christopher Dresser, of compressed globular shape with two pouring spouts, 28cm. wide. (Phillips) $3,850

An Ault pottery vase designed by Dr. Christopher Dresser, with swollen cylindrical neck, the shoulder applied with four goat's head masks, 26cm. high. (Christie's) $1,007

BAYREUTH

This German faience factory was established in 1714 by Johann Kaspar Ripp. Their output consisted of brown glazed (or, much more rarely, yellow-glazed) pieces with baroque style patterns in silver and gold, a hazy blue faience and also white faience resembling porcelain which was much used for armorial dinner services. All the usual South German shapes were made, as well as some which were less common, such as butter dishes in the form of birds, logs, and fruit, and some unappealing jugs in the form of top boots.

The painters most associated with Bayreuth during the factory's most productive period between 1728-44 are Dannhöfer and von Löwenfinck. Löwenfinck was particularly noted for a group of famille verte dishes, trays and tankards. Dannhöfer was responsible for a characteristic group of items, decorated with black and red baroque arabesques reminiscent of the Du Paquier period at Vienna. After 1744, production tended more towards utility wares with the painting restricted to blue. By the 1760s hard paste porcelain was being made and this output continued in the 19th century, together with stoneware and creamware. Marks before 1728 were irregular, though between 1728-44 *BK* (Knöller period) in blue with the painter's initials was used. In fact Bayreuth marks are among the most informative with regard to date. From 1745-47 we find *BFS* (for Fränkel and Schreck). From 1747-60 *BPF* (Pfeiffer & Fränkel) and post 1760, *BP* (Pfeiffer).

A German faience Stein, probably Bayreuth, pewter mounts inscribed *AFW* and *CCW*, 1773, ball finial, 11in. overall.
(Bonhams) $720

A mid 18th century Bayreuth two-handled oval basket, the pierced basket work sides with yellow lined lattice work, 25cm. wide.
(Christie's) $3,200

A Bayreuth glazed brown stoneware teapot and cover, circa 1730, the pear-shaped body decorated in gilding on either side with a cluster of three blossoms and foliage, $5^{11}/_{16}$in. high.
(Sotheby's) $1,380

A Bayreuth glazed red-stoneware coffee-pot and cover, the curved square spout issuing from a dolphin's-head mask and joined to the body by a convex bridge, circa 1725, 18.5cm. high.
(Christie's) $12,936

A Bayreuth faïence blue and white plate, 1730–40, painted with two birds perched on a bowl of fruit and foliage within foliate lappets, $8^3/_4$in. diameter.
(Sotheby's) $805

A Bayreuth faience Hausmalerei famille rose baluster teapot and cover, painted in the manner of Adam Friedrich von Loewenfinck, in the delft dore style with indianische Blumen issuing from rocks, circa 1740, 18.5cm. wide.
(Christie's) $12,800

BELLEEK

The Belleek porcelain factory was established in 1863 in Co. Fermanagh, Ireland, by David McBirney and Robert Armstrong, and continues in existence today. Its production is characterized by the use of parian covered with an iridescent glaze, and its wares consist principally of ornamental and table wares, such as centerpieces, comports, ice buckets etc. Belleek is especially noted for its frequent use of naturalistically molded shell forms, perforated decoration and woven basketwork effect.

The early impressed or printed mark from 1863–80 consisted of a crown above a harp, while later versions had a wolfhound seated alongside a harp over *Belleek*. After 1891 *Ireland* or *Co. Fermanagh* was added to comply with the McKinley Tariff Act.

Belleek porcelain teapot with decorative handle, bird's head spout, hand painted overall with rushes and reeds with gilding. (Jacobs & Hunt) $165

Belleek 2nd black mark 'Imperial conch shell' vase, 10 x 8in., resting on coral branches, green tint edge. (Du Mouchelles) $1,000

A pair of Belleek candlestick figures of a boy and girl basket bearer, 22cm. high. $7,200

A mid 19th century Belleek porcelain honey pot and cover in the form of a beehive, 14.5cm. high. (Spencer's) $720

A Belleek partially glazed Parian bust of Clytie, after the sculpture by C. Delpech, the young woman with wavy hair and off the shoulder dress, 28.5cm. high. (Phillips) $1,188

A fine Belleek circular basket, the looped rim applied with opalescent twig handles and sprays of lily-of-the-valley, 23.5cm. diameter. (Bearne's) $1,120

A Belleek pottery mug printed in green with the factory mark of a hound and a harp before a tower above the legend *Belleek* inscribed on a scroll, First Period, 4¼in. high. (Christie's) $100

BELLEEK

A Belleek porcelain three strand circular basket and cover, the finial formed as a large spray of flowers, buds and leaves including a rose, shamrock and daisy, early 20th century, 10in. diameter.
(Christie's) $2,159

A Belleek second period Neptune pattern tea service, comprising teapot, six cups, six saucers, sugar bowl and milk jug.
(James Adam) $589

A Belleek teapot, the compressed globular ozier pattern body boldly applied with fantastic eagle spout to each side, 6¹/₂in. diameter.
(Lawrence) $1,031

A Belleek vase modeled as a nautilus shell upheld on coral branches above a circular-section base, Second Period, black printed mark, 8³/₄in. high.
(Christie's) $399

An attractive and unusual Belleek porcelain coffee service, the shell molded body painted in polychrome enamels with a landscape.
(Spencer's) $1,216

A second period Belleek china mask jug vase, with applied encrusted flowers and raised on spreading base with scroll feet, 12¹/₂in. high.
(James Adam) $515

A late 19th century Belleek circular basket, with woven three strand base, looped rim applied with a trail of intricately modeled roses and thistle heads, 22cm. diameter.
(Peter Wilson) $556

Two Belleek flower vases of flared trumpet form, each applied with tulips and tulip buds above circular-section bases molded with stiff-leaf borders, First Period, black printed marks, 9in. high.
(Christie's) $465

A First Period Belleek shaped circular tray from a 'Chinese' pattern tea service molded in relief with a dragon chasing a pearl, printed black mark and registration lozenge for 1872, 15¹/₄in. diameter.
(Christie's) $1,101

BENNINGTON

Bennington is the name often, and erroneously, given to American Rockingham ware in general. The Vermont town had two potteries; the smaller was a stoneware factory belonging to the Norton family (operated 1793–1894) while the larger belonged to Christopher Fenton (called the US Pottery Co from 1853), who produced many different wares, from yellow and Flint Enamel, to parian ware and porcelain.

THE EDWARD NORTON CO.
BENNINGTON, VT.

A flint enamel poodle, Lyman Fenton & Company, Bennington, Vermont, 1849-1858, with fruit basket in mouth, applied coleslaw mane and ears, 8¼in. high.
(Christie's) $2,070

Bennington Pottery Rockingham pitcher, ribbed pattern, 1849 mark, 8in. high.
(Eldred's) $165

A flint enamel pitcher and washbowl, Lyman Fenton & Company, Bennington, Vermont, 1849-1858, the pitcher with ribbed body and circular faceted foot and squared handle, 12½in. high.
(Christie's) $2,070

A pair of green-mottled flint enameled pottery lions Bennington, Vermont, 1849-1858, covered in a mottled green, rust and cream glaze, 9½in. high.
(Sotheby's) $7,475

A four-gallon salt-glazed and decorated stoneware crock, 'J. Norton & Co., Bennington, VT,' 1859–1861, with everted neck above applied lug handles, 17in. high.   (Christie's) $1,120

Two gallon Bennington stoneware jar, circa 1855, 13¾in. high.
(Skinner) $1,450

Pair of porcelain cottage vases, attributed to Bennington, mid 19th century, 8¾in. high.
(Skinner) $460

Large Toby pitcher, possibly Bennington, Vermont, 1849, seated gentleman with tricorn hat, 10¾in. high.
(Skinner) $360

BERLIN

Berlin ceramics date back to the late 17th century, when from 1678 faience and red earthenware was produced. In 1763 the factory came under royal patronage when Frederick the Great purchased it to become the Königliche Porzellan Manufaktur, and production turned to hard-paste porcelain. From the end of the First World War it became known as the Staatliche Porzellan Manufaktur in Berlin. Throughout its existence it has continued to produce fine table-ware with high quality painted decoration, though various designers have also pursued contemporary trends. During the late 19th century, for example, its wares were often characterised by elaborate glaze effects under oriental influence, as seen in the work of H Seeger. Notable figures were designed by Scheurich and in the early years of this century tableware was also produced to Bauhaus designs.

A Berlin, Royal Works pair of oval porcelain plaques, painted with half-length portraits of 18th century ladies, 17.8 x 12.8cm.
(Bristol Auction Rooms)
$1,485

A 19th century KPM cup and saucer, the cup decorated with an armorial, the saucer with dedication and dated *16th September 1861*.
(Academy) $565

A pair of Berlin fayence red lacquer beaker-vases with flared rims, decorated in enamels, Funcke's factory, circa 1720, the lacquer circa 1800, 50.5cm. high.
(Christie's) $6,417

A Berlin (K.P.M.) porcelain cup painted with a view of figures in a landscape before a town in the distance within gilt borders, mid 19th century.
(Christie's) $440

A good Berlin plaque, by F. Zapf, signed, painted with a lady standing seductively in a shady grotto, 26 x 40.3cm., impressed marks.
(Phillips) $7,440

A pair of Berlin two-handled tazzas of krater shape, the exteriors painted to simulate black marble with white veins and red inclusions, circa 1810–1820, 6in. high.
(Christie's) $5,833

A finely painted Berlin plaque of Princess Louise, by F. Zapf, signed, the figure standing by a classical column, 25.9 x 40.5cm., impressed KPM and scepter.
(Phillips) $5,735

BERLIN

A Berlin oval plaque painted with a half length portrait of a girl in Greek national dress, impressed *KPM*., scepter and F5 marks, circa 1880, 26.5cm. high. (Christie's) $4,800

A Berlin casket and hinged cover in the form of a commode, the corners molded with foliate scrolls enriched in gilding and surmounted with two cherub heads on the front corners, blue scepter and iron red *KPM* and globe marks, circa 1895, 20³/₄in. wide. (Christie's) $11,500

A German plaque of 'The Interlude' late 19th century, depicting two gypsies, one playing the violin for his slumbering companion, signed J Schmidt, framed, 15 x 12in. (Christie's) $16,000

A Berlin ruby luster two-handled campana vase, finely painted in colors with an elaborate family tree of the House of Hohenzollern, circa 1820, 43cm. high. (Christie's) $17,700

A pair of Berlin rectangular plaques painted with head and shoulders portraits of young girls, each with long brown hair, signed *L. Schinnel*, impressed *KPM* and scepter marks, circa 1880, 12³/₄ x 10¹/₂in. (Christie's) $30,096

A Berlin campana-shaped gilt-ground two-handled vase painted with a broad band of garden flowers including roses, carnations, poppies, hydrangeas, delphiniums and nasturtium, circa 1810, 56cm. high. (Christie's) $12,800

A Berlin rectangular plaque of the three Fates, Clotho scantily draped and carding the thread of life, flanked by Lachtsis and Atropos, impressed K.P.M., circa 1880, 40.5 x 26cm. (Christie's) $10,000

A pair of Berlin rectangular plaques painted with head and shoulders portraits of young girls wearing early 17th century style dress, impressed KPM, circa 1880, 8¾ x 6in. (Christie's) $12,800

A large and finely painted Berlin plaque of the Holy Family after Raphael painted by Otto Wustlich, signed, 48.5cm. x 39cm., impressed *KPM* (Phillips) $15,200

33

BERLIN

A finely painted Berlin plate, the center painted with a view of the Palace of the Prince of Prussia in Berlin, 24.5cm., mark of scepter, orb and KPM.
(Phillips) $8,680

A Berlin porcelain plaque 'The Pursuit of Happiness' by R. Rossner, signed and inscribed, 10¼ x 16in., gilt frame.
(Andrew Hartley)

                             $6,512

A Berlin (later decorated) circular tureen, cover and stand, painted in the manner of Teniers with peasant revelers, the porcelain 18th century, the stand 17¼in. wide.
(Christie's) $1,553

A Berlin group of mythological figures modeled as Venus seated on a shell-molded plinth, a hunter seated beside her with his dog, on a mound base crisply molded, blue scepter mark, iron-red KPM and globe mark, circa 1880, 9in. high. (Christie's) $1,771

A pair of Berlin blue and white octagonal vases and covers, painted in the Oriental style with chinoiserie figures in landscapes (repairs to one neck), circa 1725, 44cm. high.
(Christie's) $6,400

A Berlin rectangular plaque painted by R. Dittrich, Wien with a portrait of Ruth, impressed KPM and scepter mark and letter H, Pressnummern 237 158, circa 1880, 9¼ x 6½in.
(Christie's) $1,771

A large Berlin rectangular plaque painted after Rubens with The Rape of the Daughters of Leucippus, impressed *KPM*, circa 1880, the plaque 15¼ x 13in.
(Christie's) $17,919

An attractive and well painted Berlin plate, painted in the center with a view of Das Rathhaus in Potsdam, 25cm., scepter and KPM in blue and orb in red, titled in black.
(Phillips) $4,030

A Berlin rectangular plaque painted by Wagner with Tannhäuser on the Venusberg, signed, impressed KPM and scepter mark, circa 1880, giltwood frame, 12½ x 13in.
(Christie's) $12,397

BERLIN

Round footed Berlin beaker vase painted after Bendemann and C. F. Sohn, with two girls at a well, circa 1837, 17.2cm. high. (Lempertz) $9,043

A very fine Berlin plaque by Carl Meinelt, painted after Rubens with seven naked children supporting a garland of fruit, signed with monogram, 36.5 x 52cm., impressed marks. (Phillips) $24,800

KPM porcelain plaque, depicting Christopher Columbus, impressed marks, 9 x 6in. (William Doyle) $3,680

A Berlin rectangular porcelain plaque painted after Murillo with Boys Playing Dice, impressed *KPM*, circa 1880, the plaque 11 x 8³/₄in. (Christie's) $5,119

A Berlin two-handled campana vase painted in the neo-classical taste, 1803-1810, 45cm. high. (Christie's) $14,400

A finely painted Berlin cabinet plate after a 17th century Dutch painting, with a lady seated and holding a small dog, 24.5cm., scepter and KPM in blue. (Phillips) $2,254

A K.P.M. circular two-handled tureen and cover, the sides painted in colors with loose bouquets and butterflies below molded drapery swags, the cover similarly decorated with a diamond pattern, with ball finial, 11in. diameter. (Christie's) $863

A Berlin classical group, representing Wisdom, with Athena standing supporting her shield flanked by winged putti holding attributes, 23cm. high, late 19th century. (Christie's) $392

A Berlin rectangular plaque painted with a young girl reclining on a couch in an interior before orange drapery and beside a box of scrolls, circa 1880, framed, 9¹/₄ x 6in. (Christie's) $3,425

BERLIN

A K.P.M. plaque of Königin Luisa, late 19th century, impressed marks, signed *Karu*, 11¹/₂ x 10in.
(Christie's) $6,400

A K.P.M. rectangular plaque of 'Clementine', late 19th century, signed *Von L. Schunzel* and *C. Kiesel*, 12⁵/₈ x 10³/₈in.
(Christie's) $7,600

A finely painted Berlin Easter egg, with a view of Werdesdie Kirche in Berlin, flanked by a house and with figures under a tree, 6.5cm. high.
(Phillips) $4,800

A Berlin rectangular plaque painted with a portrait of Princess Louise descending a stone staircase, impressed KPM and scepter mark, circa 1880, 9¹/₄ x 6¹/₄in.
(Christie's) $2,985

A pair of Berlin two-handled porcelain vases and covers, of inverted baluster form, each painted with scenes of lovers in 18th century costume, late 19th century, 15in. high.
(Christie's) $1,450

A Berlin rectangular plaque painted by Back with a portrait of a young girl, artist's signature, impressed KPM and scepter mark, circa 1880, 9¹/₂ x 6¹/₄in.
(Christie's) $8,500

A Berlin rectangular plaque of Judith finely painted in half-profile, signed H. Sch., impressed scepter and *KPM* marks, incised numerals, circa 1880, 53 x 29cm.
(Christie's) $19,200

A Berlin cabinet plate, the center painted with huntsmen in 17th century dress, with their game around a table within a gilt border, incised 16 for 1816, 24.5cm. diameter.
(Christie's) $1,600

A Berlin rectangular plaque painted by R. Dittrich with a portrait of Ruth in the cornfield's, artist's signature, circa 1880, 19 x 11¹/₂in.
(Christie's) $9,200

BERLIN

A K.P.M. plaque of Christ in the Temple, late 19th century, impressed marks, 17 x 14¹/₂in. (Christie's) $4,400

An interesting and finely painted Berlin cabinet cup and saucer, painted with a view of Windsor Castle. (Phillips) $2,400

A KPM plaque, late 19th century, depicting Europa and the Bull at the water's edge with attendant maiden and two figures in the distance, 9 x 11in. (Christie's East) $6,400

A Berlin rectangular plaque painted by G.L. Schinzel after C. Kiesel with a bust-length portrait of a young girl facing right, her dark-brown hair en chignon, impressed *KPM*, circa 1880, 12³/₄ x 10¹/₄in. (Christie's) $8,765

A pair of Berlin armorial oval gold-ground tureens, covers and plinths with linked scroll handles, painted in colors with two putti supporting bronzed swags of fruit hung from satyrs' heads, circa 1820, 45.5cm. wide. (Christie's) $40,000

A Berlin rectangular plaque painted in Vienna by Fr. Wagner with Gute Nacht, a young girl holding a pewter chamberstick and shading the glow of the candle with her left hand, circa 1880, 13 x 7³/₄in. (Christie's) $4,145

A Berlin porcelain plaque painted with the head and shoulders of a Neapolitan peasant boy, after the original by Richter, 30.5cm. by 24cm. (Bearne's) $6,000

A very good Berlin porcelain plaque, depicting courtiers in a garden setting, possibly Marie Antoinette, 13³/₄in. diameter. (John Nicholson) $4,500

A finely painted Berlin plaque of 'Die Neapolitaner', a head and shoulders portrait of a young girl in pensive mood, 24.5cm. x 18.5cm. (Phillips) $7,200

37

BESWICK

Beswick are perhaps best known for their highly glazed equestrian and animal figures and for their legendary flying duck wall plaques, which typify 1930s design, and yet were not launched until 1938. James Wright Beswick and his son set up their pottery in Longton in the 1890s and by 1930 employed 400 workers. After the war their expansion continued, until they sold out as a thriving concern to the Royal Doulton Group in 1973.

In addition to their figures, Beswick also made facemasks, vases, cottage ware and salad ware, together with statuettes of such popular figures from literature as Rupert Bear, Alice in Wonderland and Beatrix Potter characters. Their prewar mark is usually *Beswick Ware Made in England,* with its postwar counterpart *Beswick England* in block letters.

BESWICK ENGLAND

Beswick Ware Atlantic salmon, pattern No. 1233, 9in., English, 20th century.
(G. A. Key) $130

Beswick model of a cougar, pattern No. 1702, white polychrome glazes, 12in., English, 20th century.
(G. A. Key) $154

Beswick, graduated set of three seagull wall plaques, numbered 658/1/2/3, introduced 1938, withdrawn 1967.
(Peter Wilson) $101

Beswick character jug, molded with Shakespearean figures within a castle, entitled on the base *Hamlet, Prince of Denmark,* 8in. high.
(G. A. Key) $93

A Beswick Pinto horse, (tail hanging loose), 6¹/₄in. high.
(Dee, Atkinson & Harrison)
                             $30

Beswick, 15th century knight in armor on horse, no number, should be 1145, introduced 1949, withdrawn 1969.
(Peter Wilson) $608

A Beswick Green Woodpecker, No. 1218, 8¹/₂in. high.
(Dee, Atkinson & Harrison)
                             $107

BÖTTGER

It was J F Böttger's discovery of red stoneware and porcelain in 1708–9 which gave Augustus the Strong's Meissen factory a lead in porcelain production which it did not lose until after the Seven Years War some fifty years later. Böttger's success as an arcanist was not equalled by his success as a business man, however. He remained under Augustus's close eye almost until his death, and it was not until after that event that the factory reached the period of its true greatness and prosperity.

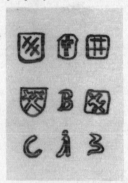

A Böttger Hausmalerei Schwarzlot silver-mounted teapot and cover, painted in the Seuter workshop at Augsburg with travelers in rocky wooded landscape vignettes, circa 1725, 13cm. high.
(Christie's) $8,021

A Böttger white bust of an infant modeled by Paul Heermann with his head turned to his left and with curls around the hairline, circa 1719, 13cm. high.
(Christie's) $28,934

A Böttger cream-pot, cover and stand, painted in the manner of J. G. Mehlhorn, the cream-pot with everted rim and scroll handle, circa 1725, the stand 7¼in diam.
(Christie's) $35,420

A Bottger red Steinzeug hexagonal tea caddy and cover molded with alternating panels of birds in trees issuing from terraces, circa 1715, 12.5cm. high. (Christie's
(Christie's) $44,000

A Böttger Hausmalerei Schwarzlot and Silbermalerei silver-mounted baluster coffee-pot and cover decorated at Augsburg in the Auffenwerth workshop, stenciled luster *GL* monogram, circa 1725, 18.5cm. high.
(Christie's) $24,024

A Böttger Hausmalerei teabowl and saucer painted in the manner of Johann Philipp Dannhofer, with an Oriental woman among shrubs, circa 1725.
(Christie's) $1,961

A Böttger flared beaker painted with a continuous shipping scene with boats, quays, river islands and trees, circa 1720, 3¼ in. high.
(Christie's) $2,834

BOW

The Bow factory was one of the most prolific of the mid 18th century and concentrated mainly on producing 'useful' tablewares in blue and white.

Very few pieces dating from before 1750 survive, and these are mainly painted in vivid famille rose colors against a grayish paste. A selection of items were also produced unpainted but with relief decoration in imitation of Fukien blanc de Chine. The 'quail' pattern derived from Japanese Kakiemon ware is also especially characteristic of the factory as are other exotic bird patterns and botanical designs.

Blue and white production falls broadly into three periods. The first, 1749–54, saw the production of thickly potted, heavy wares painted in a vivid cobalt blue. Decoration was often in the Chinese style with a slightly blurred appearance.

During the middle, and most successful period, from 1755–63, a wide range of products were made, especially sauceboats, center-pieces, mugs, bowls etc. These were less thickly potted, often in powder blue, and favorite designs are 'Image', 'Jumping Boy', dragon, and a harbor scene, all still showing a very strong oriental influence.

From 1764 quality declined both in terms of opacity and painting. Sauceboats and plates remained a speciality, but were now much less elaborate, and after 1770 production fell considerably.

A pair of Bow figures of Harlequin and Columbine, after the Meissen Commedia dell'Arte models, 11.5cm. high.
(Phillips) $1,440

A rare Bow star-shaped dish painted in blue with floral sprays within a jagged blue border, 6in. wide.
(Bonhams) $360

A pair of rare Bow models of small green parrots perched on flower-encrusted cross boughs, the green plumage with black markings and orange patches on the wings, 11.4cm.
(Phillips) $2,720

A Bow figure of the Doctor wearing blue hat, pale-pink cloak, his flowered jacket edged in yellow and blue breeches, standing with his left hand raised, circa 1755, 16cm. high.
(Christie's) $5,200

A pair of Bow porcelain tubs filled with bouquets of flowers painted in a bright palette, circa 1760, 8¼in. high.
(Christie's) $1,980

A Bow saucer painted in blue with a heron by a bridge in an Oriental-style landscape, 4⅝in. wide.
(Bonhams) $375

BOW

A Bow model of a squirrel with bushy tail, seated erect nibbling a nut held in its right paw, 1758–60, 20.5cm. high. (Christie's) $3,200

A pair of Bow porcelain figures modeled as a lady and gentleman in exotic costume, circa 1760, 5¼in. high. (Christie's) $898

A Bow model of a cockerel standing on a mound base, with red comb and wattles, 11cm. high. (Phillips) $576

A rare Bow Commedia dell' Arte group of Scaramouche and Isabella seated side by side beneath a flowering tree, 29.5cm. (Phillips) $5,200

Two rare Bow models of kestrels perched on flower-encrusted tree trunks, the birds with red heads, and mostly green plumage with touches of blue, purple and red, 14.5cm. (Phillips) $3,680

A Bow figure of Harlequin holding his slap-stick beneath his right arm, wearing a black mask and feathered hat, circa 1756, 16cm. high. (Christie's) $3,200

A small Bow model of a monkey, also an adaptation from the chinoiserie group, holding a flower in its paw, 5.7cm. (Phillips) $480

A pair of Bow porcelain candlestick bases modeled as seated cherubs beside bocages, circa 1760, 5¼in. high. (Christie's) $518

A Bow candlestick fountain-group modeled as a gallant and his companion flanking a grotto, 24cm. (Phillips) $1,600

BOW

A Bow model of a dismal hound
seated on an oval base applied
with a flower spray and edged
with puce scrolls, 8cm. high.
(Phillips) $2,080

An extremely rare pair of Bow
white 'Lisard candlesticks' after
Chinese Fukien originals,
18.5cm. high.
(Phillips) $3,360

A rare Bow octagonal deep
plate, printed in sepia/purple
after Robert Hancock with a full
version of 'L'Amour', 22cm.
(Phillips) $1,705

A pair of Bow figures of
musicians, circa 1762, he in
flowered breeches, his
companion in a flowered skirt
playing a zither, 6¾in. high.
(Christie's) $1,923

A Bow sparrow-beak jug,
painted in famille rose palette
with a Chinese lady and a boy
flanked by tables set with vases
of flowers, 9.5cm.
(Phillips) $438

Two Bow figures of a youth and
companion, he standing before a
tree-stump playing the bagpipes, his companion holding a
posy, circa 1760, 15cm. high.
(Christie's) $2,817

A Bow white squat baluster
bowl and cover with loop
handles, applied with prunus
sprigs, the cover with branch
finial, circa 1752, 13cm.
diameter.
(Christie's) $3,544

A pair of Bow figures of a monk
and a nun seated on stools, their
habits in white, black and puce,
rosaries on the base, 10cm. and
12cm.
(Phillips) $960

A Bow pierced circular basket
painted in the Kakiemon palette
with The Quail pattern, the
border with a band of iron-red
foliage, circa 1758, 18cm.
diameter.
(Christie's) $1,409

BOW

A Bow octagonal plate painted in blue with the 'Golfer and Caddy' pattern, 22cm., pseudo Chinese character marks. (Phillips) $949

A pair of Bow models of songbirds, each perched on a woody stump applied with brightly colored leaves and flowers, 9cm. (Phillips) $1,085

A pair of Bow uncolored three-shell salts, each modeled as three scallop shells upheld on shell-encrusted coral branch bases, circa 1753, 5in. wide. (Christie's) $941

A pair of Bow figures of dancers after the models by J.J. Kändler, he standing before a tree-stump wearing a pale-yellow hat, his blue-lined white jacket applied with blue bows and ribbons, circa 1758, 19cm. high. (Christie's) $5,513

A Bow blue and white pierced circular basket painted with a version of The Pinecone and Foliage pattern, circa 1765, 17cm. diameter. (Christie's) $931

A pair of Bow figures of a sportsman and companion, he standing before rockwork with a gun and a hound at his feet, his companion standing before a tree-stump, circa 1756, 17.5cm. high. (Christie's) $1,407

A rare Bow octagonal plate painted in colors in Chelsea Hans Sloane style with a botanical specimen surrounded by floral sprigs, 20cm. (Phillips) $4,015

A pair of Bow porcelain figures of nuns, each seated reading from books, the text headed 'Of Purgatory' and 'Of Absolution', 12.5cm. high. (Bearne's) $1,209

A Bow white large shell salt, circa 1755, the bowl formed as a deep scallop shell on a base of shell-encrusted coral, 7⅝in. wide overall. (Christie's) $920

BOW

A Bow candlestick group of 'Birds in Branches', modeled with two yellow buntings perched in a flower-encrusted tree, 24cm.
(Phillips) $1,360

A pair of Bow figures of grape sellers, circa 1762, both seated on scroll molded bases with baskets of grapes, circa 1762, 13cm. high.
(Phillips) $912

A Bow group of a gardener and companion modeled standing, wearing a tricorn hat and yellow coat, circa 1765-70, 24cm. high.
(Christie's) $640

A Bow figure of a dancer, the boy holding the remains of a garland and standing in pastel clothing with typical opaque sky-blue detail, 5$^{3}/_{4}$in. high, circa 1755–60.
(Tennants) $1,309

A Bow botanical octagonal plate painted with a specimen spray of pink flowers and buds and with scattered butterflies and insects, circa 1758, 23cm. wide.
(Christie's) $4,145

A Bow figure of a cook wearing a white turban, a pink-lined blue jacket with gilt seams and buttons, white blouse and pale-yellow striped breeches, circa 1756, 17cm. high.
(Christie's) $5,700

An attractive Bow polychrome cream boat, the fluted sides enameled with floral sprays detailed in black, the interior with floral and leaf sprigs, 4$^{1}/_{4}$in. long, circa 1765.
(Tennants) $400

A pair of Bow figures of Harlequin and Columbine, after the Meissen Commedia dell'Arte originals, both standing in dancing attitude, 13.5cm. high.
(Phillips) $2,240

A Bow triple-shell sweetmeat stand modeled as three shells resting on a bed of shells and seaweed, 6$^{3}/_{4}$in. wide.
(Bonhams) $1,200

A Bow mug of cylindrical shape with a grooved loop handle and heart-shaped terminal, 5⅝in. high, circa 1770.
(Bonhams) $750

A pair of Bow white models of birds, perched on conical bases applied with leafy branches, the birds with long tail feathers, 10.8cm.
(Phillips) $1,600

A rare Bow fountain chamber-candlestick group with simulated water spouting from a mossy mask and overflowing the basin below, 7¼in. high, circa 1765.
(Tennants) $560

A Bow fountain group modeled as a shepherd and shepherdess wearing simple 18th century dress, flanking a fountain, circa 1765, 21cm. high.
(Christie's) $1,280

A Bow botanical octagonal plate painted with a spray of guava and with a caterpillar, scattered butterflies and insects, circa 1758, 24cm. wide.
(Christie's) $3,454

A Bow figure of Columbine in a dancing pose with her right hand raised to her puce-lined pale-yellow hat and holding a slap-stick in her left hand, circa 1760, 15.5cm. high.
(Christie's) $2,560

A Bow blue and white silver-shape sauceboat, circa 1755, of hexafoil outline, painted with an Oriental pattern of pagodas among trees, 18cm. wide.
(Christie's) $358

Two Bow figures of a putto, circa 1762, both standing scantily draped with a wreath of flowers, one holding a dog and the other a posy, 13cm. high.
(Christie's) $1,255

An attractive Bow group of a monkey with young, the mother seated and eating a fruit, 6.8cm.
(Phillips) $1,320

A Bow figure of Euterpe by the Muses Modeler, her pink-lined dress painted with flowers and with pale-yellow drapery, 1750–52, 16cm. high.
(Christie's) $2,954

A pair of Bow porcelain figures of a sheep and a ram with orange markings, 13cm. high.
(Bearne's) $1,109

A fine Bow sweetmeat figure of a Turkish lady seated and holding a flower-painted shell dish edged in puce, 16.5cm. high.
(Phillips) $2,040

A pair of Bow figures of a shepherd and shepherdess, he leaning against a flower-encrusted tree-stump playing the clarinet, she in a dancing pose with a recumbent lamb at her feet, circa 1770, 18.5cm. high.
(Christie's) $1,409

A pair of Bow white busts of Mongolians, she with her hair plaited, he with a moustache and pointed beard, circa 1750, 27.5cm. high.
(Christie's) $80,000

A pair of Bow figures of a youth and companion, he seated on a tree-stump, his seated companion with a basket of grapes on her lap, circa 1762, 14cm. high.
(Christie's) $1,950

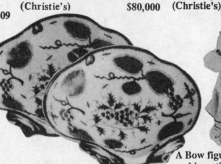

A Bow figure of Kitty Clive in the role of 'The Fine Lady' from Garrick's farce 'Lethe', standing holding a spaniel beneath her right arm, circa 1750, 25.5cm. high.
(Christie's) $14,767

A good pair of Bow blue and white shell pattern dessert dishes, the triple lobed bowls decorated with fruiting vines and insects, 7½in., circa 1760.
(Canterbury) $763

A Bow figure of a girl emblematic of Autumn from a set of the Seasons, bare-footed and seated holding a basket of grapes, wearing a yellow hat with puce ribbon, circa 1760, 13.5cm. high.
(Christie's) $817

CHINA

BRANNAM

Charles H Brannam (1855–1937) worked as a potter in Barnstaple, Devon, at first making kitchenware and ovens. From 1879 he started making art pottery, known as Barum ware, usually of brownish clay with simple designs in white slip, mostly in the form of small jugs and vases. His work is usually signed and dated.

C. H. BRANNAM LTD.

C. H. BRANNAM
BARUM DIXON

BRETBY

The Bretby pottery was founded in 1883 at Woodville, Derbyshire, by Henry Tooth and William Ault. They made jardinières, bowls, jugs, vases etc. first in earthenware decorated with colored glazes and applied with flowers and insects in light colored clay.

William Ault struck out on his own in 1887, but Bretby continued, making 'carved bamboo' ware, and, from 1912 onwards, Clantha ware, which was decorated with geometrical designs on a matt black glaze. Art pottery was made until 1920.

BRISTOL

Hard paste porcelain production began in Bristol in 1770, when William Cookworthy removed his factory there from Plymouth, as a place with a stronger potting tradition. Mugs, sauceboats, bowls, creamboats, coffee cups and pickle leaf dishes were among the items produced, and it is in fact often quite difficult to tell Plymouth from early polychrome Bristol. Most Bristol blue and white ware is marked with a cross in underglaze blue.

Brannam Barum Ware puzzle jug, of bulbous form, the body having an incised fish and inscription against a deep green glaze, dated 1906, 13cm. high. (Peter Wilson) $108

A Brannam twin-handled vase by Frederick Braddon, the handles formed as open-mouthed and scaly dragons, 23.7cm. high. (Phillips) $240

An unusual pair of Bretby Pierrot figures, pattern No. 2700, 11½in. high. (Dee, Atkinson & Harrison) $283

A Bretby tobacco jar and cover, inscribed 'Nicotiank', 16.5cm. high. $120

A Bristol globular teapot and cover with ear-shaped handle, Richard Champion's Factory, circa 1775, 16cm. high. $2,400

A Bristol white figure of a girl symbolic of Autumn, standing and holding a large basket of fruit on her left hip, 37cm., probably John Toulouse. (Phillips) $1,120

47

BRITISH

The British pottery tradition before the industrial period is rooted in the medieval use of tin glazed earthenware. This was often manufactured in monasteries, such as the Cistercian pottery of the 16th century, and was the direct forerunner of the Staffordshire slipwares of the succeeding centuries, which were to form the mainstream of English potting development.

The first inspiration towards refinement came, in England as elsewhere, when the Dutch brought back the first examples of Chinese porcelain. English delft, though never in the same class as its Dutch counterpart, was made at Liverpool, Bristol and elsewhere, painted in very high temperature colors, with little overglaze enameling.

In Staffordshire, the call for a more delicate ware was answered by the development of a fine saltglazed white stoneware, and then Wedgwood's creamware, which, with its numerous imitators, soon achieved a worldwide market.

18th century English porcelain was distinguished by its variety of composition, ranging from the French style soft-paste type made at Derby, Chelsea and Longton Hall, to the soapstone pastes favored at Worcester, Caughley and Liverpool and the hard paste varieties of Plymouth and Bristol, while it was the bone ash type pioneered at Bow which was to become the standard body.

No English factory enjoyed the royal patronage which so often fostered their European counterparts, and most were short lived. Inspiration, however, did not fail, and throughout the 19th century, English potters continued to make wares ranging from simple cottage and luster ware to the fine porcelains of Worcester, Derby and Spode.

A rare Thackeray Turner bowl, the interior with three entwined mythical beasts in the center, 14½in. diameter.
(Bonhams) $747

A Maw yellow and green luster baluster vase painted with flowers and foliage, dated 1899, 31cm. high.
(Christie's) $167

Joseph Holdcroft dark-blue-ground jardinière of shaped cylindrical form, molded in relief with a continuous frieze of three birds, circa 1870, 10in. high.
(Christie's) $629

A Walton type group of lovers standing before a flowering bocage, the man wearing a brown cap, the woman wearing a plumed hat, circa 1820, 7in. high.
(Christie's) $447

A Wileman & Co 'Intarsio' vase, designed by Frederick Rhead, Celtic style foliate bands, the neck with flowers, 8¾in. high.
(Bonhams) $598

Frank Brangwyn for Wilkinson Ltd, painted by Clarice Cliff, painted plaque, 1932–3, 17½in. diameter.
(Sotheby's) $2,138

BRITISH

Dog shaped vase by Flaxman,
1930s.
(Muir Hewitt) $32

Hancock's Ivory ware Galleon
plate with shaped edge.
(Muir Hewitt) $80

Booths hors d'oeuvre dish
decorated with a stylized country
scene.
(Muir Hewitt) $270

A tin glazed pottery spouted
posset pot and cover, the
bulbous vessel with two strap
handles supporting perched
birds, 11in. high, English, early
18th century.
(Tennants) $32,400

A pair of Herculaneum urn
shaped vases, having caryatid
winged handles, printed
Herculaneum and Liverpool
ribbon mark, circa 1835, 12in.
high.
(Woolley & Wallis) $1,970

An H. & R. Daniel blue-ground
oviform jug, painted with a view
of Teddesley Hall, the reverse
with a gentleman dressed in a
coachman's uniform in
conversation with a peasant
woman, circa 1835, 23cm. high.
(Christie's) $5,475

Honiton jug designed by
Collard.
(Muir Hewitt) $120

Miniature vase with elf
decoration.
(Muir Hewitt) $40

Stylized dog, 1930s, decorated
with red spots.
(Muir Hewitt) $55

Samuel Lear blue and white Jasper Ware Stilton dish and cover with figures in classical relief, impressed mark, circa 1877–86, 8¹/₂in.
(G. A. Key) $375

A pair of fine 19th century porcelain boy and girl figures, each carrying baskets, 13¹/₄in. high.
(Dee, Atkinson & Harrison) $643

An H. and R. Daniel presentation jug attributed to William Pollard, of baluster shape with gilt leaf-molded lip and handle terminals, 22.5cm.
(Phillips) $435

A rare David and John Philip Elers red stoneware mug, circa 1695, the slip-cast cylindrical body mold-applied on the front with a flowering branch in relief between two borders of lathe-turned horizontal reeding, 4in. high.
(Sotheby's) $8,625

A pair of pottery book-ends in the form of little girls sitting under sunhats, holding a camera and a rose, 5³/₄in. high, with the William Goebel crown mark.
(Christie's S. Ken) $400

A Jessie Marion King christening mug, for 'Adam', Eve with a spinning wheel, inscribed *When Adam delved and Eve span who was then the gentleman*, signed, circa 1921, 3in. high.
(Christie's) $748

An attractive early English 'blue dash' tulip charger painted with a blue and yellow tulip flanked by green leaves and other blue and red flowers, 34cm. diameter.
(Phillips) $1,105

A pair of Davenport two-handled baluster vases, circa 1835, each with gilt handles molded as swan heads, 19³/₈in. high.
(Christie's) $5,750

An earthenware teapot decorated with croquet theme, English, late 19th century, white ground overglazed pink and decorated with transfer printed geometric cartouches, 7in. high.
(Sotheby's) $480

BRITISH

English earthenware vase of globular baluster form, the slightly flared neck incised with foliate designs and buds, base signed *W.W.*, 4¹/₂in. high. (G. A. Key)　　$30

British Art pottery jardinière, decorated with flowers and foliage on yellow ground, circa 1920–6, 9³/₄in. high. (G. A. Key)　　$208

A Donyatt earthenware puzzle jug, incised with birds, utensils and a poem, covered in a cream glaze splashed with green, 18.5cm. high. (Bearne's)　　$649

An Ewenny pottery yellow glazed commemorative plaque, with high relief male portrait bust inscribed in raised capitals: *Reverend Edward Matthews of Ewenny, Born 1813, died 1892; A.D. 1913*, 8¹/₄in. (Peter Francis)　　$910

A pair of Joseph Holdcroft majolica jardinières with two female mask handles, the dark-blue grounds molded in high relief with swags of flowers suspended from bosses, impressed marks, circa 1865, 9¹/₄in. high. (Christie's)　　$2,302

A dated pottery tyg and cover attributed to South Wiltshire, in mottled brown glazed pottery, inscribed around the rim *Drink wp yower drink be war of the fox*, initials *KM/C* and date *1672*, 25cm., circa 1672. (Phillips)　　$8,360

A very interesting bell-shaped mug, painted in blue with a Chinese fenced landscape incorporating a small house, 13cm., probably Vauxhall or Gilbody. (Phillips)　　$576

A pair of English porcelain cylindrical pink-ground ice-pails and covers with pinecone finials, painted in colors with shaped panels of figures wearing 18th century dress, 19th century, 14¹/₂in. high. (Christie's)　　$1,683

A William Brownfield plaque, handpainted with ducks and riverbank landscape, signed with initials, date to reverse *9/88*, 26cm. diameter. (Peter Wilson)　　$201

Stylized porcelain dog, 1930s, 2½in. high. (Muir Hewitt) $15

Flaxman running hare, 5in. wide, 1930s. (Muir Hewitt) $45

J.H. Cope & Co. wall mask, 6in. high, 1930s. (Muir Hewitt) $150

A large stoneware vase by Janet Leach, swollen cylindrical form with inverted rim, brown glazed body beneath mottled speckled olive green with wax resist 'scars', 35.2cm. high. (Christie's) $2,009

A Portobello model of a recumbent doe, circa 1810, with raspberry markings edged in black, on a mound base splashed in brown, 3¾in. high. (Christie's) $550

A rare Vauxhall vase, painted in colors with a bouquet of flowers and smaller sprays, gilt foot rim, 4⅛in. high. (Bonhams) $1,440

A majolica spill-vase group of a squirrel seated on its haunches nibbling a nut beside a hollow tree-trunk, circa 1870, 4¼in. high. (Christie's S. Ken) $170

Fine tobacco leaf charger, 18th century, the interior painted overall in vivid shades of yellow, green, turquoise, blue, brown and iron-red with gilt-edged overlapping leaves, 15in. wide. (Butterfield & Butterfield) $7,700

A cylindrical commemorative vase bearing the emblems of the Houses of York and Lancaster under a crown, 8½in. high. (Christie's) $480

BRITISH

Amusing dog-shaped pottery container.
(Muir Hewitt)   £32

Humpty Dumpty teapot, 1930s.
(Muir Hewitt)   £170

1930s honeypot with bee finial.
(Muir Hewitt) $30

An Astbury 'Fair Hebe' pearlware loop-handled jug molded in relief with a young man offering his sweetheart a bird's nest, circa 1790, 5½in. high.
(Christie's) $1,162

An English porcelain blue-ground plate, the center painted with figures on a shore and in a boat in a landscape, circa 1830, 9in. diameter.
(Christie's S. Ken) $240

An English majolica tobacco-jar and cover in the form of a pug dog, glazed in shades of brown and with a pink interior, circa 1860's, 8in. high.
(Christie's S. Ken) $596

An earthenware plate decorated to a design by Marcel Goupy, painted in red, black and blue, 12½in. diameter.
(Christie's S. Ken) $180

A finely painted English 'Honeysuckle Group' box, the cover painted with a man in classical dress reading the hand of a young lady, her friend at her side, 9.5cm. wide.
(Phillips) $1,485

A Pountney's 'Bristol Pottery' bowl, painted by George Stewart in Wemyss style with pink flower sprays, 17cm. diameter.
(Allen & Harris) $46

BRITISH

An Edwardian blue Jasperware biscuit barrel, the cover with acorn knop finial.
(Dee, Atkinson & Harrison) $85

A 19th century pottery sugar bowl, printed in black and decorated in colors with two scenes of a cricket match, 5¹/₂in. diameter.
(Bonhams) $330

A rare Sabrina ware vase of pear shape, decorated with fish swimming among seaweed, 14cm., date code for 1931.
(Phillips London) $195

An English ironstone vase and cover twin-handled, the handles modeled as grotesque beasts, enriched allover with a dark-blue-ground painted in gilt, 19in. high, circa 1825.
(Christie's) $866

After Privat Livemont, Johnson, Walker & Tolhurst Ltd, as retailers, large pot and cover with girl with yellow roses, 1901, the cover with the head and shoulders of a young girl, stamped with maker's mark, 7.5cm. diameter.
(Sotheby's) $2,422

A rare and interesting Absolon-decorated double-handled cup and cover titled *A Trifle from Yarmouth* in puce above a vignette of two ladies in a governess cart drawn by a spirited horse, 10cm.
(Phillips) $1,522

An early earthenware jug by David Leach, with ocher glaze over dark brown slip decoration, impressed *DL* seal, 7³/₄in. high.
(Bonhams) $184

A Yorkshire pottery model of a horse, wearing a molded bridle, saddle cloth and surcingle, 15cm. high. (Henry Spencer) $3,200

A Fowler's phrenology head, the cranium printed with the areas of the sentiments, the base with maker's label and title, 11¾in. high.
(Christie's) $1,120

BRITISH

Victorian stoneware teapot and cover of globular form, inscribed in black *What About A Dish of Tea*, 7in. high.
(G. A. Key) $42

A large blue and white pottery meat dish, printed with the 'Hospitality' scene of a farmer's wife offering food to a lame traveler, 52.4cm. wide.
(Bearne's) $1,311

Ridgways triangular shaped cheese dish and cover, 'Old Derby' pattern, circa 1890, 8in. high.
(G. A. Key) $225

Hummel wall mask, young girl wearing a deep blue hood, naturalistically painted face, the back incised with crown mark and *heindl*, circa 1935/49, 10½in.
(G. A. Key) $151

A pair of tiles designed by George Frampton, with molded decoration, one depicting the profile of the God of Music, the other the God of Poetry, circa 1900, 30 x 15.1cm.
(Christie's) $295

A Bovey Tracey blue and white pearlware tea caddy of rectangular form, the head and shoulders of putti on the corners, 13.2cm. high, circa 1800.
(Bearne's) $742

A Turner caneware urn-shaped fluted teapot and cover, circa 1790, with lion finial and bail handles, the shoulder enriched in blue, 6¾in. high.
(Christie's) $1,380

A pottery charger painted by Nellie Blackmore with a view of the ship the Harry Paye, by Arthur Bradbury, 15in. diam.
(Christie's) $938

Early English cylindrical mug, printed en grisaille with alphabet pattern hands and letters in square frames, late 18th/early 19th century, 2½in.
(G. A. Key) $120

BRITISH

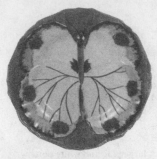

Willow Art china vase with enameled American Indian design, 6in. high.
(Muir Hewitt) $135

Hancock's butterfly plate, 1930s.
(Muir Hewitt) $100

Art Deco vase with stylized decoration, 8in. high, 1930s.
(Muir Hewitt) $83

A magnificent circular tin glazed earthenware vase by James Tower, of flattened form, the surface highly ribbed and patterned, black and white, 21in. high.
(Bonhams) $4,771

1930s stylized cottage teapot and milk jug.
(Muir Hewitt) $105

Deco jug with stylized floral decoration.
(Muir Hewitt) $45

A figure of a child in a plumed hat seated on the back of a deer with iron-red fur markings, 10in. high.
(Christie's S. Ken) $469

A Wincanton manganese-ground dish, circa 1745, with iron-red flowers in a vase, the rim with wheat sheafs alternating with fleur-de-lis, 13¼in. diameter.
(Christie's) $1,540

Hancocks ivory ware cottage jug, 1930s, 7in. high.
(Muir Hewitt) $70

BRITISH

1930s budgie vase in green and fawn.
(Muir Hewitt) $70

Biscuit barrel, 1930s, with floral decoration.
(Muir Hewitt) $75

Burleigh ware jug with parrot handle, 8in. high, 1930s.
(Muir Hewitt) $115

Stylized elephant bottle, 1930s, 7¹/₂in. high.
(Muir Hewitt) $45

Set of six 1950s liqueur bottles in the form of a jazz band.
(Muir Hewitt) $195

A Glasgow (Delftfield) polychrome slender baluster vase and cover painted in a Fazackerly palette, circa 1760, 44cm. high.
(Christie's) $17,336

A Crimean group of an officer and his companion, seated either side of a fire place surmounted by a wall clock, circa 1855.
(Christie's S. Ken) $852

A Brown, Westhead, Moore & Co. majolica group of two kittens, one climbing up the front of a lady's boot, the other chasing a ball of wool, circa 1880's, 6¹/₄in. high.
(Christie's S. Ken) $894

A pearlware portrait bust of John Wesley, painted in colors, on a shaped socle, inscribed to the reverse *W. L., Oct. 26 1822*, 12in. high.
(Christie's) $751

BRITISH

A very rare Lunds Bristol coffee cup, painted in blue with a version of the 'Union Jack House' pattern, 5.5cm.
(Phillips) $4,896

Oval egg dish and cover, the lid applied with hatching egg and three chicks, over a cream basket weave base, 8¹/₂in.
(G. A. Key) $196

A Christian sauceboat with scroll handle, painted in blue with chinoiserie landscape panels, 8cm.
(Phillips) $475

A Jackfield sparrow beak baluster jug, the black glazed body inscribed on one side in gold *Succefs to Admiral Nelson*, 18.3cm. high.
(Bearne's) $536

A pair of large treacle glazed models of spaniels both wearing collars and name tags around their necks, 43cm.
(Phillips) $1,920

A very rare documentary toby jug of Fiddler type, inscribed *J. Marsh, Folley*, 27.5cm., the head a replacement made in bell metal. $3,680

Blue and white hand basin, decorated with foliate border and alternate panels of floral sprays and lattice work, by Brown Westhead Moore & Co., 19th century, 30in. wide.
(G. A. Key) $400

A pair of Compton Pottery stoneware bookends, each trefoil form with relief decoration of a butterfly, on semi-circular base, circa 1945, 12.2cm. high.
(Christie's) $197

An English porcelain foxhead stirrup cup with gilt collar inscribed *Tallyho*, with bright eyes and pricked ears, 13cm.
(Phillips) $1,280

BUFFALO

The Buffalo pottery was established in 1903 for the express purpose of making promotional free gifts for a soap firm in Buffalo, New York. They developed to produce also mail order gifts and then began to make advertising ware for other firms.

From there they progressed to tableware and in 1908 introduced a range with an olive green base, transfer printed and hand-decorated with hunting scenes, which was marketed as Deldareware.

Art Nouveau influence was apparent in Emerald Deldareware, which was introduced in 1911, decorated with Doctor Syntax subjects. Porcelain was also produced from 1915, marked *Buffalo China*. Most products were marked *Buffalo Pottery* and, until 1940, were also dated.

Buffalo Pottery Deldare Ware jardinière and stand, Buffalo, New York, W. Foster and W. Forrester, 1908 and 1909, Ye Lion Inn, stamp marks, jardinière 9in. high.
(Skinner) $3,450

Buffalo Pottery Deldare Ware pitcher, Buffalo, New York, J. Gerhardt, 1909, 'The Fallowfield Hunt', 6in. high.
(Skinner) $403

Set of six Buffalo Pottery Deldare Ware 'Ye Lion Inn' mugs, Buffalo, New York, N. Sheehan, J. Gerhardt, B. Willow, 1909, 3¾in. high.
(Skinner) $460

Buffalo Pottery Deldare pitcher, 'The Great Controversy' signed *W. Foster*, stamped mark, 12in. high.
(Skinner) $500

Buffalo pottery Deldareware water pitcher, *Ye Old English Village*, 10in. high.
(Eldred's) $523

Two Buffalo Pottery Deldare Ware bisque plates, Buffalo, New York, 1909, 'Ye Olden Times', one with partial decoration, 9¼in. diameter.
(Skinner) $172

Buffalo Pottery Emerald Deldare vase, stylized foliate motif in shades of green and white on an olive ground, 8½in. high.
(Skinner) $800

BURLEIGHWARE

Burgess & Leigh evolved from the firm of Hulme & Booth in 1877, when the other partners retired. It moved to a new factory at Middleport, Burslem in 1889, and on the death of R.S. Burgess in 1912, passed entirely into the hands of the Leigh family, who still own it today.

They produced domestic and ornamental wares, many with underglaze prints, but some also hand painted, tube-lined, or lithographed.

Burgess & Leigh are perhaps best known for their 'flower' jugs of the 1930s, which appeared in various forms such as Squirrel, Harvest, Highwayman, etc., the subject forming the handle, with appropriate decoration on the body. Many of these were designed by Charles Wilkes. Later additions to the range included Butterfly, Village Blacksmith, Coronation, Tally-ho and Sally in our Alley, and a range featuring sporting characters was also produced. They came in various sizes and colorways, some with matching plaques.

Burleigh ware Harvest jug, 8in. high, 1930s.
(Muir Hewitt) $85

Burleigh ware miniature parrot jug, 3½in. high, 1930s.
(Muir Hewitt) $85

A Burleigh Ware bowl with fluted rim, pattern 4133, painted with stylized flowers and foliage in shades of green, yellow, orange and blue, 27cm. diameter.
(Christie's) $271

A Burleigh Ware character jug, modeled as Winston Churchill in naval dress, 13cm. high.
(Christie's) $325

Burleigh ware luster jug with squirrel handle, 8in. high, 1930s.
(Muir Hewitt) $110

A Burleigh toby jug, modeled at Winston Churchill, in full riding attire, straddling a bulldog, 28cm. high.
(Christie's) $1,302

Burleigh ware Pied Piper jug, 8in. high, 1930s.
(Muir Hewitt) $210

BURMANTOFTS

Burmantofts is the name given to products from the pottery of Wilcock and Co, which was established in 1858 in Leeds. Initially terracotta earthenware was produced, but after 1880 they also made a hard buff colored high fired earthenware with a feldspathic glaze, which became known as Burmantofts faience. This was used to make tiles and, from 1882, art pottery. Their output included vases, bowls, jardinières and figures, covered in colored glazes and showing oriental or Middle Eastern influence. Other decorations in the range included underglaze designs trailed in slip, painted or incised and copper and silver luster was also used on dark colors. From 1904 they reverted to specializing in terracotta.

Marks include the name in full or the monogram *BF*.

A Burmantofts faience vase of squat ovoid form applied with two strapwork handles, painted in the Persian manner, 19cm. high.
(Christie's) $724

A Burmantofts Persian pattern vase, the globular vessel painted with large blue and mauve flowers, 23cm. high.
(Phillips) $589

BURMANTOFTS
FAIENCE

BＦ B

BURSLEY WARE

A pair of Burmantofts faience grotesque vases, each modeled as a three-legged animal with bumpy skin,23cm. wide.
(Christie's) $310

A Burmantofts faience vase, of swollen cylindrical form, incised with a sunrise country scene, painted in colors, 28.5cm. high
(Christie's) $387

A Bursley Ware vase designed by Frederick Rhead, decorated in the 'Trellis' design, 31cm. high.
(Christie's) $251

Pair of Charlotte Rhead Bursley ware vases, circa 1925, 7in. high.
(Muir Hewitt) $700

Charlotte Rhead plate with floral decoration, Bursley ware, 1940s, 12¹/₂in. diameter.
(Muir Hewitt) $420

CANTON

There is a reference which suggests that earthenware cooking vessels were made in Kuangtung (Canton) as early as the T'ang dynasty (618–906). The dating of what has come to be known as Canton stoneware is, however, very difficult. It is certain they go back at least to late Ming times, and they are still made and exported in large quantities.

Canton ware is usually dark brown at the base, varying to pale yellowish gray and buff with a thick smooth glaze which is distinctive for its mottling and dappling effect. The color is often blue, flecked and streaked with gray green or white over a substratum of olive brown. Sometimes brown tints predominate, but it is the blue toned ware which is most highly prized.

Very large jars, vases etc. were made for outdoor use, sometimes with elaborate applied work, and incense burners, water pots etc. were also made in form of small animal figures.

Workshops at Canton decorated porcelain in the famille rose style for export, as well as the 'Canton enamels' painted on copper.

A pair of Canton porcelain famille rose vases mounted as lamps, late 19th century, each of tapering quadrangular shape, 25.7cm. high. (Sotheby's) $6,325

19th century Cantonese toilet jug with brilliant enamel decoration in the famille-rose palette, 11in. high. (G. A. Key) $147

Pair of unusual Canton enamel and ivory figures of foreigners, first quarter 19th century, each portrayed as a kneeling Dutchman, 20in. high overall. (Butterfield & Butterfield) $90,500

A Canton porcelain 'Rose Medallion' hexagonal garden seat, late 19th century, painted in famille-rose enamels with three rows of panels depicting Mandarin figures, 18³/₄in. high. (Sotheby's) $3,737

A Canton famille rose jug and cover, the ovoid body painted with figures in a pavilion, 11¹/₄in. high, 19th century. (Bonhams) $1,760

A pair of unusual Canton vases, applied with writhing dragons below an everted rim, the body brightly painted with processions, 63.5cm. high. (Bearne's) $1,500

Canton porcelain teapot, decorated in typical colors with panels of figures, birds and butterflies, 19th century, 7in. high. (G. A. Key) $100

CANTON

Shaped Canton shrimp dish, 19th century, typical Canton scene, diam. 10¼in.
(Skinner) $400

Pair of Canton blue and white tea caddies, China, mid 19th century, hexagonal shape, with lids, 6in. high.
(Skinner Inc) $6,400

Late 18th century famille rose Canton enamel circular segmented supper set formed as eight fan-shaped dishes, 18in. diam.
$1,600

A Cantonese garden seat, of barrel shape painted all-over design of flowers, fish and birds in famille rose enamels, 19in. high, on ebonized wood plinth.
(Russell, Baldwin & Bright)
$865

A pair of 'famille-rose' cache pots and stands, Qing Dynasty, Canton, 19th century, the upright sides painted with ladies in pavilions, 27.5cm. high.
(Sotheby's) $4,410

A Cantonese porcelain large vase and cover of inverted baluster form, with four mask lugs, decorated in famille rose et verte enamels, 42cm. high.
(Spencer's) $770

A large Canton punchbowl, Qing Dynasty, mid-19th century, painted in 'famille-rose' enamels, the interior painted with an extensive figurative frieze, 51.5cm. diameter.
(Sotheby's) $7,486

A pair of Cantonese vases with enameled polychrome decoration, circa 1830, 90cm. high.
(Hôtel de Ventes Horta)
$7,138

An ormolu-mounted Canton famille rose bowl, the interior and exterior painted with panels of figures, flowers and birds, late 19th century, 20in. high.
(Christie's) $5,485

CANTON

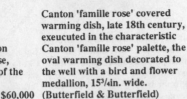

A rare famille rose Canton enamel large baluster vase, Qianlong seal mark and of the period, 18½in. high.
(Christie's) $60,000

Canton 'famille rose' covered warming dish, late 18th century, exeucuted in the characteristic Canton 'famille rose' palette, the oval warming dish decorated to the well with a bird and flower medallion, 15¾in. wide.
(Butterfield & Butterfield)
$1,210

A famille rose Canton enamel and gilt-bronze model of a jardinière, the knobbly bonsai tree with gilt branches, set with metal and hardstone leaves and blossoms, 58cm. high.
(Christie's) $5,907

A pair of massive Canton famille rose baluster vases, 19th century, each applied with two gilt dragon handles at the waisted neck, 89cm. high.
(Christie's) $6,199

A massive Canton enamel temple tripod incense burner and cover, raised on monster-mask legs and fitted with box-section upright bracket handles, Qianlong seal mark, 110cm. high.
(Christie's) $20,000

A pair of ormolu-mounted Chinese (Canton) baluster vases, each with everted lip and scrolled handles, 19th century, 27in. high.
(Christie's) $12,400

A famille rose Canton enamel gilt-bronze mounted vase, blue enamel Qianlong mark and of the period, the pear shaped body delicately enameled with a wide blue scrolling foliage band, 9in. high.
(Christie's) $4,800

A famille rose Canton enamel shell shaped basin, Qianlong, decorated in the interior with a trefoil lappet of peony, lotus and hibiscus sprays, 15¼in. wide.
(Christie's) $4,000

A fine famille rose Canton enamel slender baluster vase, ruby enamel Qianlong seal mark and of the period, delicately decorated with three cartouches of lady immortals standing among turbulent waves, 9⅜in.
(Christie's) $28,387

CAPODIMONTE

The Capodimonte factory near Naples was established by King Charles III in 1742 to make soft-paste porcelain of the French type.

It was not until 1744, however, after numerous failed attempts, that Gaetano Schepers managed to produce a paste which was suitably 'white and diaphanous' and which achieved a brilliance to rival Meissen.

The most famous modeler at the Capodimonte factory was Giovanni Caselli, a former gem engraver and miniature painter. Figurines were among the earliest output of the factory, but snuff boxes, tea services and scent bottles were also made. The small objects were often mounted on gold or silver gilt, and the fine floral decoration was usually painted in finely drawn hair lines.

In 1759 Charles acceded to the throne of Spain, and the factory closed. He set up again at Buen Retiro, but the quality of products produced there is generally inferior to their Capodimonte antecedents.

A Capodimonte (Carlo III) group of fisherfolk, modeled by Giuseppe Gricci, circa 1750, 17.5cm. wide.
$16,000

A Capodimonte (Carlo III) shaped gold mounted snuff box, the porcelain circa 1755, 8.5cm. wide.
$1,600

A pair of Capodimonte (Carlo III) coffee cups and saucers, painted by Giovanni Caselli with equestrian figures and warriors, circa 1750, blue fleur de lys marks.
(Christie's) $32,000

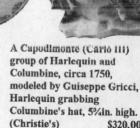

A Capodimonte (Carlo III) group of Harlequin and Columbine, circa 1750, modeled by Giuseppe Gricci, Harlequin grabbing Columbine's hat, 5¾in. high.
(Christie's) $320,000

A Capodimonte group of a youth riding a mastiff modeled by Giuseppe Gricci, the youth in peaked pale-pink cap with gilt bow, 1755–1759, 17cm. high.
(Christie's) $7,200

An extremely rare and finely painted Capodimonte candlestick base of triangular shape, modeled by Gaetano Fumo and Giuseppe Gricci, 18.5cm. high.
(Phillips) $2,500

A Capodimonte (Carlo III) group of an artist painting the portrait of a lady, modeled by Giuseppe Gricci, she with gilt choker, in puce and white bonnet, 5¾in. high.
(Christie's) $70,000

MICHAEL CARDEW

Born in 1901, Michael Cardew was a pupil of Bernard Leach. His earliest products from his Winchcombe Pottery, dating from the 1920s, consist mainly of slip-decorated earthenware for domestic use, often with sgraffiato decoration. He later experimented with tin-glazed earthenware and in 1941 went out to teach at Achimota College in Ghana. Following the closure of the college in 1945 he opened a pottery on the Volta river, producing stoneware often decorated with African inspired motifs. He returned to this country in 1948 and at Wenford Bridge began making light colored stoneware, often with brushed decoration, before returning to Africa to work for the Nigerian government in 1950, establishing a training center at Abuja. He died in 1983.

An important and fine stoneware bowl by Michael Cardew, banded with vertical lines alternate with abstracted pattern, impressed MC and Wenford Bridge seals, 12¼in. diameter.
(Bonhams) $2,500

A fine Winchcombe Pottery earthenware cider flagon by Michael Cardew, covered in a mottled dark olive-green glaze with bands and panels of pale brushwork decoration of a deer and foliage, 39cm. high.
(Christie's) $689

An earthenware oviform jug by Michael Cardew, impressed MC and Winchcombe Pottery seal, circa 1930, 22.6cm. high.
(Christie's) $640

An oval earthenware slip decorated dish by Michael Cardew, the interior covered in a dark toffee-brown glaze with trailed mustard-yellow slip, circa 1930, 21cm. wide.
(Christie's) $280

An earthenware open bowl by Michael Cardew, with trailed dark brown slip over a vivid green and ocher glaze, circa 1930, 13¾in. diameter.
(Bonhams) $2,202

A Wenford Bridge stoneware tea-pot by Michael Cardew, unglazed, red-brown brushwork decoration of pairs of fish within linear bands, 15cm. high.
(Christie's) $383

An earthenware bowl by Michael Cardew, cream with brown slip-trailed lines, impressed *MC* and Winchcombe Pottery seals, 10½in.
(Bonhams) $710

CARDEW

An earthenware two-handled motto tankard by Michael Cardew, impressed MC and Winchcombe Pottery seals (circa 1930), 10.1cm. high. (Christie's) $400

A stoneware casserole and cover by Michael Cardew, Wenford Bridge seals, circa 1970, 32cm. diam. (Christie's) $800

An earthenware coffee pot by Michael Cardew, covered in a pale brown glaze over which pale yellow, stopping short of the foot, 14.8cm. high. (Christie's) $480

An earthenware dish, by Michael Cardew, impressed MC and Winchcombe Pottery seals, circa 1930, 35.1cm diam. (Christie's) $960

An earthenware jug by Michael Cardew, covered in a translucent brown glaze over a mottled lime green and olive brown glaze, 25.6cm. high. (Christie's London) $320

An earthenware inscribed platter by Michael Cardew, decorated by Henry Bergen, Winchcombe Pottery seals, 42.7cm. diam. (Christie's) $2,250

An Abuja stoneware oil jar by Michael Cardew, with screw stopper, covered in a mottled olive-green glaze, impressed MC and Abuja seals, circa 1959, 33cm. high. (Christie's) $960

A stoneware globular casserole by Michael Cardew with tall neck, two lug handles and a concave cover with knob finial, circa 1975, 20.7cm. high. (Christie's) $520

An earthenware cider jar by Michael Cardew, the top half with green slip drawn through to brown, Winchcombe Pottery seals, 14¹/₂in. high. (Bonhams) $568

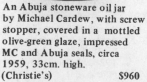

CARDEW

A small earthenware jug by
Michael Cardew, impressed MC
and Winchcombe Pottery seals.
12.4cm. high.
(Christie's) $200

An earthenware motto jug,
by Michael Cardew, circa
1925, 18cm. high.
(Christie's) $1,200

An earthenware coffee pot
and cover by Michael Cardew,
impressed MC and Winchcombe
Pottery seals, circa 1933, 17cm.
high. (Christie's) $510

A stoneware charger by
Michael Cardew, covered in an
oatmeal glaze, the interior with
olive green glaze and combed
waved bands through to
oatmeal glaze, 34.3cm. diam.
(Christie's London) $760

A Winchcombe Pottery
earthenware pitcher by Michael
Cardew, with applied strap
handle, covered in a translucent
brown glaze beneath yellow
ocher, with bands of brown
decoration, 28.3cm. high.
(Christie's) $394

A stoneware bowl by Michael
Cardew, the interior with
incised decoration and blue
and brown brushwork of a
bird amongst grasses, MC and
Wenford Bridge seals, 24.5cm.
diam. (Christie's) $1,200

An early earthenware
Winchcombe jug by Michael
Cardew, with a band of painted
swirls, ocher and brown, 9in.
high.
(Bonhams) $587

A stoneware stemmed bowl,
by Michael Cardew, with
crescent lug handles, circa
1975, 17.1cm. high.
(Christie's) $240

An earthenware slip-
decorated rhyme tankard
by Michael Cardew, circa
1926, 13.7cm. high.
(Christie's) $640

CARLTON WARE

Carlton was born out of the partnership of J. F. Wiltshaw and H. T. Robinson, who got together in 1890 to operate out of the Carlton Works in Stoke on Trent. Robinson bowed out of the enterprise some twenty years later, and the firm then remained in the hands of the Wiltshaw family until the late 1960s, when it became part of Arthur Wood & Son (Longport). It finally ceased production in 1989. From the first, Carlton ware was noted for the enormous range and versatility of its designs, from luster items destined for the luxury end of the market, down to what can most kindly be described as kitsch.

At the top end, items were produced to the highest standards, with rich luster glazes, fine gilding and stylized Jazz Age decorative motifs being applied to such classical shapes as footed bowls, ginger jars, and the like.

Carlton's embossed floral ware proved highly successful from the mid 1920s, and in 1928 print and enamel decorated china tableware was introduced.

A Carltonware service decorated in polychrome enamels, coffee pot 20.4cm. high. $1,230

One of a pair of Carltonware vases, 21cm. high, and a tray, 25cm. wide.
(Christie's) $960

A pair of Carlton Ware book ends, each modeled with a Britannia figure standing with shield and serpent against a triangular back, 18.5cm. high.
(Christie's) $184

Oviform vase with dark gray ground simulating nightfall, signed by E. F. Paul, with Kate Greenaway style fairies design, 230mm. high.
                    $960

A Carltonware vase with polychrome decoration on a mottled purple and white ground, circa 1930, 26.7cm. high. $400

Graduated set of three Carlton Ware Guinness advertising toucans, carrying foaming tankards on their beaks, inscribed *My Goodness My Guinness*, painted in colors largest 10in.
(G. A. Key) $174

A Carlton Ware ovoid ginger jar and cover, printed and painted in colors and gilt with exotic trees on a blue spotted ground, 28cm. high.
(Christie's) $435

CARLTON WARE

A large Carlton ware two handled punch bowl, molded and painted on one side with King Henry VIII and Cardinal Wolsey on the other. (Bearne's)　　　$600

Carlton ware shell cruet, 1930s. (Muir Hewitt)　　　$75

A Carlton ware orange ground bowl boldly decorated with flowers and multi-patterned quarter circle motifs, 9½in. diam. (Christie's)　　　$240

Standard Carltonware vase of pale blue ground with tube lined floral decorations on primary colors, also blue inside the vase, 165mm. high.　　　$160

A Carltonware Keg Bitter advertising figure modeled as Shakespeare holding a quill and book, painted with naturalistic tones, 27.5 cm high. (Christie's)　　　$280

A Carltonware oviform ginger jar and cover, painted with clusters of stylized flowerheads and bold geometric bands, 31cm. high. (Christie's)　　　$2,000

Carlton ware enameled vase with mallard decoration, 6in. high. (Muir Hewitt)　　　$127

Carlton ware salad dish and strainer, 7in. wide, 1930s. (Muir Hewitt)　　　$65

An hexagonal vase with chinoiserie decoration, 17.5cm. high.　　　$200

CARLTON WARE

Vibrant lustrous red 'Rouge Royale' leaf, one of a series introduced after 1930, 220mm. long. $48

A light red shaped vase with multi-colored duck in flight, 240mm. high. $360

Carlton ware Australian design salad bowl and servers, 8in. diameter. (Muir Hewitt) $75

Carltonware Guinness advertising lamp, the support formed as a toucan adjacent to a glass of stout, the base inscribed, painted in colors, 16in. (G. A. Key) $390

Carlton ware luster jug with gilt loop handle, the body painted and gilt with stylized floral and fan decoration, 5in. high. (Prudential Fine Art) $180

A Carlton ware ginger jar and cover, with gilt colored chinoiserie decoration depicting temples and pagodas, 31cm. high. (Phillips) $465

A Carltonware plaque painted in gilt, orange, blue, green and white with wisteria and exotic plants, 15½in. diam. (Christie's) (Christie's) $400

A Carlton ware twin-handled boat shape bowl on splayed cylindrical column painted with an exotic bird of paradise, 23.5cm. high. (Phillips) $285

A Carltonware ginger jar decorated with flying birds in gilt clouds on a mottled blue ground, 8½in. (Russell, Baldwin & Bright) $114

CARLTON WARE

A highly unusual Carlton ware ceramic butter dish depicting a well proportioned couple in horizontal embrace, 26cm. across. (Phillips) $720

A Carlton Ware vase and cover, covered in a lustrous orange glaze, decorated in gilt and polychrome glazes with Egyptian figures and motifs, 31.5cm. high. (Christie's) $1,707

Carlton Ware ceramic cruet set in the form of a mushroom with pepper, salt and mustard pot.
(Muir Hewitt) $75

Deep red jug with gold handle and sea-green interior, one of the famous birds series, featuring fantastic and mythical birds, 295mm. high. $360

Carlton Ware stylized dog in shades of brown, with ribbed body, 1930'.
(Muir Hewitt) $83

Egyptianesque jardiniere with frieze decoration and hieroglyphics on a blue ground, 160mm. high. $1,600

A fine Carlton Ware scenic vase with shaped handles, 7" tall.
          $83

A Carlton Ware ginger jar and cover, covered in a mottled blue glaze, with gilt and polychrome enamel decoration of a heron in flight, 26cm. high.
(Christie's) $766

Carlton ware vase with raised oak leaf decoration, 8½in. high.
(Muir Hewitt) $112

CARTER STABLER & ADAMS - THE POOLE POTTERY

The history of this famous pottery began in 1873, when Jesse Carter set up in business in Poole, Dorset. He was joined by his sons Ernest, Charles and Owen, and they engaged the services of the distinguished designer, James Radley Young, in the early 1900s. It was Young who developed the glazes which have come to characterize the output of this factory. These are in the delft style, the glaze and decoration being fired on to the biscuit body, the result being a matt, silken effect. In 1913 the silversmith, Harold Stabler, and his wife Phoebe, joined the company, which by now was supplying Heal's, Liberty and an eager American market. John Adams and his wife Truda completed the team in 1921, on their return from South Africa.

At this time the pottery was hand thrown and hand decorated, and included earthenware in simple shapes for table use and stoneware painted boldly and sketchily in clear, fresh colors. Many of their painted designs were by Truda Adams, and featured floral motifs based on Jacobean and peasant embroidery patterns, presented in a highly stylized form. They also produced strongly Art Deco designs throughout the 20s and 30s. The company kept going with a skeleton staff during the war, and business built up again in the subsequent period. From 1963 it was known officially as the Poole Pottery, and was taken over in 1971 as a unit within the Thomas Tilling group.

A pottery oviform jug, shape no. 304, painted by Marjorie Batt with bluebirds and foliage in typical colors, impressed *CSA Ltd* mark, 5in. high. (Christie's S. Ken) $400

A Carter Stabler Adams pottery dish, possibly a design by Erna Manners, painted in mauve, green and blue with stylized leaves and scrolling tendrils, 37.8cm. diam. (Phillips) $285

The Bull, a pottery group designed by Phoebe and Harold Stabler, modeled as two infants astride a bull in ceremonial trappings of swags and garlands, impressed *CSA* mark, 13in. high. (Christie's) $4,000

A terracotta twin handled oviform vase painted by Ruth Pavely with bluebirds and foliage between contrasting borders, impressed *CSA Ltd.* mark, 6½in. high. (Christie's) $1,120

A pottery vase, decorated with scrolling flowers and foliage, in typical colors on a white ground, impressed *CSA Ltd.* mark, 7in. high. (Christie's S. Ken) $240

A terracotta plate painted by Anne Hatchard with a green spotted leaping gazelle amongst fruiting vines, impressed *CSA* mark, 12in. diam. (Christie's) $1,440

CASTEL DURANTE

Castel Durante, in the province of Urbino, is the birthplace of two of the outstanding figures concerned with Italian maiolica, Nicola Pellipario, the master of maiolica painting, and Cipriano Piccolpasso, who wrote the definitive work Li'tre libri dell'Arte del Vasaio.

The earliest Castel Durante wares can sometimes be attributed to the painter and potter Giovanni Maria, who specialized in grotesque and trophy borders around deep-welled plates containing beautifully drawn heads of girls or youths.

Even in Pellipario's earliest works the pictorial painting style is fully developed. In 1519, he painted the d'Este service for the wife of the marquis of Mantua, where every dish and plate, in addition to heraldic arms, bears a different subject from Classical mythology, often taken from slightly earlier woodcuts.

Pellipario left Castel Durante about 1527 to join his son in Urbino.

A shallow dish, Castel Durante, circa 1525, attributed to the 'In Castel Durante' painter, painted in muted blues, greens, yellow and ocher on a cream ground with Vulcan Forging Cupid's Arrows, 11³/₈in. diameter.
(Christie's) $68,500

A Castel Durante majolica dish decorated with a portrait of a warrior and inscribed *Gallafrone*, circa 1520, 8³/₄in. diameter.
(Christie's) $46,838

A Castel Durante portrait dish boldly painted with an almost full face portrait of 'Faustina Bella', her hair coiled and braided with a white bandeau, 23cm., circa 1540.
(Phillips) $19,200

A Castel Durante wet-drug jar with short yellow spout and wide strap handle, named for *S. ABSINTII* on a yellow rectangular cartouche, circa 1570, 21cm. high.
(Christie's) $4,800

An interesting small Castel Durante dish with sunken center painted with a coat of arms of a standing figure of a negro inscribed *V: Sapes: Forts*, 17cm. diameter.
(Phillips) $850

A Castel Durante squat drug jar painted with the naked Fortune arising from the waves on the back of a dolphin, circa 1580, 23.5cm. wide.
(Christie's) $28,500

A Castel Durante tondino with a central yellow and ocher foliage mask inscribed *PACIFICAB* on a ribbon above reserved on a blue ground, circa 1525, 22cm. diameter. $6,800

CASTELLI

Castelli, in the kingdom of Naples, owes its fame to the maiolica made there from the late 17th century onwards, principally by the Grue and Gentili families. They produced a style which is rich in architectural detail, with borders adorned by flowers and putti, the main colors being buff, yellow and a greenish brown.

The original stylistic inspiration is generally thought to have come from Carlo Antonio Grue (d. 1723), whose four sons, Francesco Antonio, Anastasio, Aurelio and Libero continued the tradition until the death of the last in 1776.

Few factory marks were used, but the artists frequently signed their work, enabling accurate attributions to be made.

Two Castelli wall plaques painted in colors with coastal landscapes, 18th century, 20 x 28cm.
(Kunsthaus am Museum)
$2,158

A Castelli portrait wet-drug jar of 'Orsini-Colonna' type and baluster form, with a strap handle and dragon's head spout, early 16th century, 25.5cm. high.
(Christie's) $17,825

A Castelli rectangular plaque painted with Pan being comforted after the musical contest with Apollo seated, circa 1725, 28cm. square.
$1,600

A maiolica charger painted in the Castelli style with a scene of a Sybil in a rocky wooded landscape, within a border of masks within stylized geometrical ornament and cherubs at play, circa 1880, 20in. diameter.
(Christie's) $506

A Castelli plate painted with two women washing clothes in the river, buildings and mountains in the background, 17th century, 18cm. diam.
(Christie's London) $440

A Castelli rectangular plaque painted by Saverio Grue with Joseph sold by his brothers to the Midianites, circa 1770, 32.5 x 23.5cm.
(Christie's) $10,800

A Castelli armorial circular dish, the center painted with equestrian figures hawking, circa 1720, 40.5cm. diam.
(Christie's) $8,800

CASTELLI

A Castelli armorial plate painted in the Grue workshop with a traveler and companion riding a horse and a donkey, circa 1720, 24cm. diameter.
(Christie's) $4,000

A Castelli oval plaque painted by Saverio Grue with St. Francis, circa 1730, 38cm. high.
(Christie's) $6,400

A Castelli plate painted in yellow, brown, manganese, ochre and blue with seven blonde cherubs entwined, 23.5cm. diameter.
(Phillips) $2,380

A Castelli campana vase, probably painted by Liborio Grue, circa 1740, 41.5cm. high.
(Christie's) $2,400

A Castelli rectangular plaque painted with the Meeting between St. John and the Infant Christ, circa 1690, 30 x 40cm. $2,800

A Castelli large vase of campana form painted in colors and gilt, circa 1720, 41cm. high.
                    $2,560

A Castelli armorial plate by Aurelio Grue, after a print from the Hunt Series by Antonio Tempesta, yellow and brown line rim, circa 1725, 29cm. diam.
(Christie's) $21,600

A Castelli oval dish painted by Ed. Foiviteau with a fierce Roman battle scene with combatants attempting to cross a river by an arched bridge with a burning town in the distance, perhaps 1857, 19³/₄in. wide.
(Christie's) $1,899

A Castelli tondino saucer painted in the Grue workshop in shades of green, yellow and blue with a scene from the Biblical legend of 'Cain and Abel', mid 18th century, 7¹/₈in. diameter.
(Christie's) $5,732

CAUGHLEY

Around 1772 Thomas Turner established his factory at Caughley in Shropshire. Turner had been manager at Worcester, and had trained as an engraver under Robert Hancock. He persuaded Hancock to join him in his new venture, and set out to rival the Worcester production of blue printed porcelain. He was so successful that by the 1780s Caughley was completely dominating the market, making mass produced, affordable wares in simple shapes with very elaborate decoration.

Turner then dealt his rivals a further blow by persuading their chief decorators, the Chamberlains, to set up on their own, and having done so, they gilded blue and white Caughley wares, and also made enamel pieces to order for Turner.

Turner countered elaborate Chinese patterns with transfer printing, and it is often claimed that he was the first to introduce the celebrated Willow pattern. The factory made a wide range of attractive shapes, including sauceboats, mugs, creamboats, pickle leaf dishes and bowls, as well as a number of small items, such as spoontrays, asparagus servers and egg drainers. Miniature tewares were very common and were produced in two patterns, one printed and one painted. These are very sought after today.

Both Caughley and Worcester used a number of the same transfer prints, but some are unique to Caughley, notably that commemorating the erection of the Ironbridge at Coalbrookdale in 1779.

Painted Caughley wares tend to be earlier than the more common printed pieces.

Some later printed wares were enhanced with gilding, but this tends now to detract from their value.

Caughley porcelain dessert dish of square form, decorated with a blue weir pattern, circa 1790, 8in. wide.
(G. A. Key) $361

Caughley porcelain milk jug, leaf molded with blue and white floral patterns and mask lip, English, late 18th century.
(G. A. Key) $240

A Caughley blue and white teapot and cover and four cups and saucers printed with the 'Pagoda' pattern, within gilt rims, circa 1785.
(Christie's) $597

An early Caughley teapot and a coffee pot, the coffee pot printed with the 'Three Flowers' pattern, thinly glazed base, 13cm.
(Phillips) $323

Caughley blue and white porcelain coffee can, painted with chinoiserie scene, crescent mark, 2¹⁄₂in., English, circa 1775–90.
(G. A. Key) $225

A Caughley coffee pot of baluster shape, printed with 'The Fisherman' pattern, 9½in. high. (G. A. Property Services) $320

CAUGHLEY

A Caughley 'pickle' leaf, printed in blue with the 'Fisherman' pattern, 3¹/₂in. long. (Bonhams) $300

An important Caughley loving cup, printed in blue with a view of the Iron Bridge, 11.7cm. (Phillips) $6,000

An early Caughley coffee pot and cover, of plain pear shape with unusual scroll finial, 17cm. (Phillips) $452

A fine Caughley blue and white eye-bath, 1785–95, with a scroll-molded lozenge-shaped bowl and baluster-form stem above a fluted oval foot, 2¹/₈in. high. (Sotheby's) $1,725

A Caughley porcelain cabbage leaf molded jug, with rotund body and slant eyes to the mask spout, 22.5cm. high. (Henry Spencer) $480

A very rare Caughley pounce pot or sander of 'hour glass' shape with conical top and foot, printed with hexagonal cell borders and flower sprigs, 7.8cm. high. (Phillips) $651

A Caughley shanked sugar bowl and cover painted with landscapes within gilt circular cartouches, circa 1792, 12cm. diam. (Christie's) $480

A rare Caughley inkwell of waisted drum shape with a separate central well fitting within four holes for quills, 9.75cm. diameter. (Phillips) $995

A Caughley trefoil dessert dish, with a scroll molded handle, painted in blue with 'chantilly sprigs', 7¹/₂in. diameter. (Bonhams) $180

CAUGHLEY

A Caughley custard cup, with a scrolled loop handle, printed in blue with the 'Willow Nankeen' pattern, 2in. high.
(Bonhams) $300

A Caughley asparagus server, printed in blue with the 'Fisherman' pattern, 2³/₄in. long.
(Bonhams) $375

Fluted porcelain Caughley teapot and cover, printed in blue with a temple pattern, circa 1790, 5¹/₄in. high.
(G. A. Key) $373

A fine Caughley blue and white cabbage-leaf jug, dated *1783*, molded around the ovoid body with overlapping leaves and on the fluted neck with a border of leaves and caillouté, 8⁵/₈in. high.
(Sotheby's) $2,760

A Caughley cream-jug painted with the Badge of George IV as Prince of Wales, enclosed by the crowned Royal Garter and motto within a blue dot and gilt cartouche, circa 1790, 14cm. wide.
(Christie's) $1,360

A Caughley leaf-molded inverted baluster mask-jug painted with sprays of flowers amongst scattered sprigs, circa 1785, 7¹/₂in. high.
(Christie's) $1,122

A Caughley fable-decorated plate painted in shades of gray with the fable of the Wolf & Crane, titled to the reverse, circa 1795, 8¹/₄in. diameter.
(Christie's) $759

A very rare Caughley inkwell with separate liner, of spreading circular shape with sloping shoulder pierced with four holes for quills, 9.5cm. diameter at the base.
(Phillips) $1,705

A Caughley egg drainer, printed in blue with the 'Fisherman' pattern, leafy handle, 3⁷/₈in. long.
(Bonhams) $330

CHALKWARE

This was particularly popular in the United States during the 18th and 19th centuries and was originally imported from Europe, before indigenous production began in the 1760s.

It was essentially an imitation of more expensive pottery and porcelain figures of animals, birds, and personalities of the day, made in plaster of Paris.

Sometimes these could be slip molded in in plaster of Paris and coated inside with heavier plaster to add weight. Cottage form lamps were also made in this medium.

A painted chalkware lamb with ewe, Pennsylvania, mid 19th century, with red, yellow, black and green details, 7in. high.
(Christie's) $480

Chalkware spaniel with original paint, 19th century, 5in. high.
(Eldred's) $150

Chalkware reclining stag mantel ornament, 16in. high.
(Skinner) $172

Pair of chalkware dogs on rectangular bases, 19th century, 5in. high.
(Eldred's) $200

A 19th century painted chalk ware cat, America, 10¾in. high.
(Skinner) $1,200

A large figural chalkware Cheshire cat, Pennsylvania, 19th century, with a gold painted body and smoke-decorated stripes, 14¾in. high.
(Christie's) $10,925

Late 19th century painted chalkware horse, 10in. high.
(Christie's) $480

A molded and painted chalkware figure of a Poodle, Pennsylvania, mid 19th century, on a red and green rectangular base, 6½in. high.
(Sotheby's) $575

CHALKWARE

Paint decorated chalkware cat, 19th century, 7¼in. high. (Skinner) $920

A pair of molded and painted chalkware figures of deer, probably Pennsylvania, mid 19th century, 9¾in. high. (Sotheby's) $1,437

Antique hollow chalkware spaniel, 8in. high. (Eldred's) $357

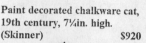

A figural chalkware mantle garniture, Pennsylvania, 19th century, the hollow molded figure depicting a stylized group of fruit, vegetables and foliage, 13¼in. high. (Christie's) $1,093

A pair of late 19th century painted chalkware doves, American, 11½in. high. (Christie's) $800

A painted and smoke decorated molded chalkware cat, probably New England, 19th century, the seated figure of a cat painted yellow and black with smoke decoration, 15in. high. (Sotheby's) $4,312

A molded and painted chalkware group of 'Kissing' doves, mid 19th century, perched side by side on a circular socle with molded feather detail, 5¾in. high. (Sotheby's) $500

Rare pair of chalkware dogs, original paint and in good condition, 19th century, 8in. high. (Eldred's) $275

A painted chalkware cat, Pennsylvania, 19th century, the hollow molded figure painted white with red-painted stripes, 10½in. high. (Christie's) $1,725

CHANTILLY

The Chantilly porcelain factory was founded in 1725 by Louis Henri de Bourbon, Prince du Condé, under the direction of Cicaire Cirou. The Prince was an avid collector of Arita pottery and set his factory to manufacture this type of ware. The unique feature of Chantilly is its glaze, which in contrast to the usual transparent lead glaze of soft paste porcelains was an opaque white tin glaze such as that used in the production of faience. The use of this precluded underglaze decoration, but was ideal for painting in the delicate colors of the Kakiemon style typical of Arita ware.

These Japanese designs were exquisitely painted, sometimes from the original and sometimes from Meissen copies, which they excelled both in quality of shape and decoration. After the death of the Prince in 1740 Kakiemon styles were abandoned, and a year after the death of Cirou in 1751 disaster struck the factory in the form of a Royal edict forbidding the manufacture of porcelain for a period of 12 years at any factory other than Vincennes, which was the particular pet of Louis XV and Madame de Pompadour.

While the edict was not, in fact, strictly enforced, Chantilly now abandoned the use of tin glaze in favor of a transparent lead glaze which revealed an attractive cream colored body. Over the next few years most decoration was done in camaieu (monochrome). Favorite styles were crimson cupids after Boucher and the use of a border of diapered quatrefoils in blue enamel.

Typical of the Cirou period is the red hunting horn mark, while later pieces carry a blue horn, often more crudely drawn and sometimes accompanied by *Chantilly*.

A 1870s Chantilly dish with gros bleu ground and a central gilt cartouche depicting, in puce, a chateau by a lakeside, 24cm. across.
(Phillips) $400

A Chantilly green ground two handled pot pourri, the waisted campana body applied with swags of flowers, circa 1750, 19cm. high.
(Christie's) $9,200

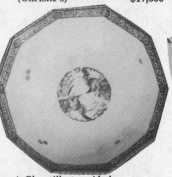

A pair of Chantilly white wolves naturalistically modeled seated on their haunches looking to left and right, with ferocious looking teeth, pricked ears, long curly coats and bushy tails forming the bases, circa 1740, 21cm. high.
(Christie's) $17,000

A pair of Chantilly seaux à verre, circa 1745, painted in pale in colors with a gallant and companion in an arbor trapping game in a landscape, 4½in. high.
(Christie's) $8,020

A Chantilly ten sided Kakiemon bowl, the interior with a roundel composed of two ho-ho birds, circa 1735, later French gilt metal mounts by A. Risler & Carre, Paris, 26cm. diam.
(Christie's) $2,560

A Chantilly 'Kakiemon' lobed beaker painted with stylized magnolia and chrysanthemum branches issuing from rockwork, circa 1745, 2¼in. high.
(Christie's) $783

CHARLOTTE RHEAD

Charlotte Rhead, who, with Clarice Cliff and Susie Cooper, is one of the famous 'Pottery Ladies', was a gentle, unassuming soul who was taught to draw and paint at home by her father, Frederick Rhead. Her childhood was dogged by ill health, but she was able to attend the Fenton Art School with her younger sister Dollie. Thereafter she worked for various factories as a tube-liner and enameler, until her father set up his own business at the Atlas Tile Works, and both girls joined the family firm.

This venture was sadly short-lived and in 1913 Charlotte moved with her father to Wood & Sons, where he had been appointed Art Director. The vividly colored pieces which she produced for them are sometimes marked *Lottie Rhead Ware*.

In 1926 she moved to Burgess & Leigh, where she introduced tube-lining, a tricky process whereby liquid clay or 'slip' is squeezed from a rubber bag through a glass nozzle on to the surface of an item, rather as icing is piped onto a cake. She produced many designs for Burgess & Leigh, such as Florentine, Sylvan, Garland and Laurel Band, her favourite motifs remaining fruit and flowers, still effected in bright colors but in rather more subtle juxtapositions. In 1931, she moved to A.G. Richardson at Tunstall, where she produced such superb designs as Rhodian, Byzantine, Persian Rose and Golden Leaves, all marked with a tube-lined *C. Rhead* on the base.

She returned to Woods in 1942, where, despite failing health, she produced over a hundred new designs before her death in 1947.

Charlotte Rhead Art Deco vase, 5½in. high. (Muir Hewitt) $320

Charlotte Rhead vase, Crown Ducal in stepped Aztec design, 7in. high. (Muir Hewitt) $300

A pair of Charlotte Rhead Crown Ducal pottery wall plaques, tubelined in brown and decorated with orange flowers and scattered blue and red flower heads, 14in. diameter. (Spencer's) $320

Charlotte Rhead vase with stylized tube lined floral decoration, 1930s, 12½in. high. (Muir Hewitt) $540

Crown Ducal Charlotte Rhead jug, signed *C. Rhead*, 1930s, 9in. high. (Muir Hewitt) $320

Charlotte Rhead vase, 1930s, Bursley ware, 8in. high. (Muir Hewitt) $480

CHELSEA

The new Chelsea factory, founded in the 1740s, was largely inspired by Nicholas Sprimont, a Huguenot silversmith from Flanders, and it was probably the first of the six or so soft paste factories which sprang up in England by 1750.

Early Chelsea products were very attractive, highly translucent and based on glass ingredients. Pieces from this period often carry an incised triangle and have a strong affinity with Sprimont's silverwork, with particular emphasis on shellwork and scroll motifs.

The next, or Raised Anchor Period (1749–53) saw the porcelain becoming more opaque as less lead was used. Figures are now more usually colored, this often being done in the London studio of William Duesbury.

By 1752 a painted Red Anchor Mark was becoming common, and this Red Anchor period, which lasted until about 1758, saw the apogee of Chelsea figure modeling. Table wares still showed oriental and Continental motifs while a new development was the manufacture of handsome vegetable and animal tureens and stands.

The final Gold Anchor period shows a departure towards the opulent and the elaborate, with colored grounds in the Meissen and Sèvres style, and figures in ornate bocages and flowery backgrounds. There was much gilding, and rich color often came to disguise inferior modeling.

By 1770 Chelsea had passed into the hands of William Duesbury of Derby, and by 1784 porcelain manufacture was concentrated there. The brilliant history of Chelsea was over.

A pair of Chelsea flowersellers with open panniers, wearing florally painted and colored clothes, 15cm. high. (Phillips) $2,210

A Chelsea teaplant coffee-pot, with spirally molded brightly colored teaplants, 1745-49, 13.5cm. high. (Christie's) $8,200

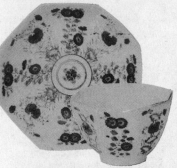

A Chelsea octagonal teabowl and saucer, in Kakiemon style, painted in red, blue and turquoise with chrysanthemums and carnations, the bowl 8.2cm. diameter. (Phillips) $589

A pair of Chelsea figures of pilgrims, circa 1798, each with one arm outstretched and a staff in the other hand, their clothes applied with scallop-shell badges, 10¼in. high. (Christie's) $5,244

A pair of Chelsea groups of gallants and companions emblematic of the Seasons, Winter and Spring, circa 1765, about 35.5cm. high. (Christie's) $13,816

A rare Chelsea Kakiemon style leaf dish, with an exotic bird in display and another perched on a prunus branch, raised anchor period, 8½in. long. (Tennants) $7,200

CHELSEA

A Chelsea fable-decorated silver-shaped plate painted in the manner of Jefferyes Hammett O'Neale with the fable of The Fox and the Monkey, circa 1752, 22.5cm. diameter.
(Christie's) $26,884

A pair of Chelsea figures of street vendors, both standing on heavily scrolled and pierced floral encrusted bases, 25cm., gold anchor marks.
(Phillips) $1,085

A Chelsea 'Hans Sloane' botanical lobed plate painted with a yellow tulip, fern, lilac, a caterpillar and insects, circa 1756, 25cm. diameter.
(Christie's) $4,726

A Chelsea kakiemon lobed and flared beaker painted in a vibrant palette with a Ho Ho bird perched on pierced turquoise rockwork, circa 1750, 7cm. high.
(Christie's) $3,650

A fine pair of Chelsea sunflower dishes, each yellow flower partially obscured by a leaf growing from a stalk handle, 23cm., red anchor mark, circa 1755.
(Phillips) $5,230

A Chelsea white chinaman and parrot teapot and cover modeled as a grinning figure of Budai, his loose robe open to reveal his protuberant stomach, 1745–49, 17.5cm. high.
(Christie's) $48,000

A Chelsea 'Hans Sloane' botanical plate painted with a branch of fruiting mulberry and with a leaf-spray, butterfly and insect, circa 1756, 24cm. diameter.
(Christie's) $5,840

A pair of Chelsea groups of gallants and companions emblematic of the Seasons, gold anchor marks, circa 1765, 33cm. high.
(Christie's) $12,478

A Chelsea 'Hans Sloane' botanical soup-plate painted in a vibrant palette with a large puce fritillary and a spray of small blue flowers, circa 1756, 23cm. diameter.
(Christie's) $15,543

CHELSEA

A Chelsea bowl with slightly flared rim, painted with five naked iron-red putti, one with a basket of grapes and another with a bunch of grapes, circa 1755, 15.5cm. diameter.
(Christie's) $4,750

A rare Chelsea bough pot, of fluted semi-circular shape bound by a central simulated ribbon, 18.5cm. wide, unmarked, red anchor period.
(Phillips) $1,163

A Chelsea silver-shaped oval dish with molded thumbpieces, painted in a vibrant Kakiemon palette with a red tiger looking up towards a sinuous red-scaled dragon, circa 1750, 25cm. wide.
(Christie's) $14,600

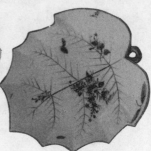

One of a pair of Chelsea finger bowls painted in colors with flower sprays and scattered springs including a striped tulip and rose, 7.5cm. high.
(Phillips) $2,380

A pair of Chelsea sweetmeat-figures modeled as a lady holding a fan and a gentleman, their clothes elaborately painted and enriched in gilding, circa 1760, 19.5cm. high.
(Christie's) $5,526

A Chelsea strawberry-leaf dish with incised vein markings enriched in puce, painted with a loose bouquet and with scattered flowers and foliage, red anchor mark, circa 1756, 22.5cm. long.
(Christie's) $1,575

A Chelsea 'Hans Sloane' botanical soup-plate painted in a vibrant palette with a spray of magnolia and with scattered butterflies and insects, circa 1756, 23.5cm. diameter.
(Christie's) $12,953

A Chelsea group of Harlequin and Columbine standing hand-in-hand in a dancing pose before a tree-stump applied with flowers, circa 1760, 17cm. high.
(Christie's) $4,800

A Chelsea lobed circular shallow dish painted with a loose bouquet and with scattered flowers and insects beneath a brown line rim, circa 1753, 26.5cm. diameter.
(Christie's) $1,674

CHELSEA

A Chelsea salt of compressed oval form, painted with scattered flowerheads and ladybirds, the interior with a moth and similar flowerheads, circa 1745, 8cm. wide.
(Christie's) $9,000

A Chelsea botanical pierced oval dish, the center painted with pale-pink cistus and with scattered moths, insects and a caterpillar, circa 1756, 31cm. wide.
(Christie's) $6,900

A rare Chelsea bough pot of tapering semi-circular shape molded with flutes and encircled by a simulated length of ribbon, 18cm. wide, circa 1756.
(Phillips) $730

A Chelsea white Chinaman teapot and cover modeled as a grinning figure of Budai, his loose robe open to reveal his protuberant stomach, 1745–49, 17.5cm. high.
(Christie's) $60,000

A pair of Chelsea figures of a shepherd and shepherdess, he leaning on a staff filling a satchel with wool, she with a garland of flowers over her shoulder, gold anchor marks, circa 1768, 28cm. high.
(Christie's) $4,922

A Chelsea mottled claret ground bucket shaped sugar bowl and cover painted with Oriental musicians, gold anchor mark, circa 1765, 11.5cm. diam.
(Christie's) $8,400

A Chelsea plate of Mecklenberg Strelitz type, the border with five shell-shaped panels of flower festoons between mazarine blue panels with exotic insects, circa 1764.
(Phillips) $1,426

A Chelsea billing doves box, modeled as two doves entwined with garlands of flowers and with a quiver of arrows between, inscribed on a ribbon cartouche *Sort* (sic) *tres heureux*, circa 1760, 6cm. wide.
(Christie's) $4,425

A fine Chelsea Plate, circa 1755, of 'Warren Hastings' type, painted in soft shades in the center with a floral bouquet, a large leaf sprig and eight scattered floral sprigs, red anchor mark, 9⁷/₁₆in. diameter.
(Sotheby's) $2,070

87

CHELSEA

A rare Chelsea model of a hound, modeled seated on an oval grassy base, wearing black collar, 5cm., red anchor mark. (Phillips) $2,580

A Chelsea asparagus tureen and a cover naturally modeled as a bunch of asparagus enriched in puce and green and tied with chocolate-brown ribbon, circa 1755, 18.5cm. wide. (Christie's) $5,120

A Chelsea figure of a monk seated on a stool and reading an open prayer book inscribed *Respice Finem*, 14cm. (Phillips) $2,160

A Chelsea melon-tureen and cover naturally modeled and enriched in yellow and green, the cover with curled branch finial with foliage and flower terminals, circa 1756, 17cm. long. (Christie's) $7,482

A pair of Chelsea figures of the imperial shepherd and shepherdess, he leaning on a staff held in his left hand, his companion holding a basket of flowers under her right arm, circa 1765, 34cm. high. (Christie's) $16,000

A Chelsea botanical octagonal teabowl and saucer, the teabowl with trailing blue convolvulus, the reverse and interior with two specimen flowers, circa 1753. (Christie's) $8,200

A finely painted Chelsea chocolate cup, both sides painted with views along the river Thames, gilt dentil border 'to rim, 6.5cm., gold anchor mark, circa 1765. (Phillips) $988

A pair of Chelsea mazarine-blue ground tapering square vases, the sides painted with Oriental figures with birds and parasols, the sloping shoulders with exotic birds, circa 1765, 31.5cm. high. (Christie's) $9,130

A Chelsea acanthus leaf moulded teapot and cover with bamboo molded handle, incised triangle mark, circa 1745-49, 12cm. high. (Christie's) $40,000

CHELSEA

A Chelsea cup and saucer with a pale yellow ground painted with purple tulips and green leaves.
(Bonhams) $928

A Chelsea fable-decorated octagonal teapot painted in the manner of Jefferyes Hammett O'Neale with a wolf barking at a boar, circa 1752, 10cm. high.
(Christie's) $4,400

A Chelsea Red Anchor period cauliflower tureen and cover, decorated in shades of green, 4¹/₂in. high, circa 1755.
(Tennants) $2,511

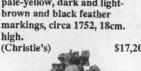

A Chelsea model of a little hawk owl, its head turned and with pale-yellow, dark and light-brown and black feather markings, circa 1752, 18cm. high.
(Christie's) $17,200

A pair of Chelsea blue ground lobed tapering oviform vases and covers with pierced gilt scroll handles and finials, gold anchor marks, circa 1765, 32cm. high. (Christie's London) $10,000

A Chelsea fluted baluster cream jug of silver shape, the scroll handle with elaborate foliage-molded scroll terminals, painted with a butterfly, an insect and scattered flowerheads, 1745–49, 12cm. high.
(Christie's) $14,400

A very rare Chelsea group of Mercury and Argus, the former seated before a tree playing a pipe and lulling Argus to sleep, 18.5cm.
(Phillips) $689

Two Chelsea eel tureens and covers naturally modeled with their bodies curled, their tails forming the handles, circa 1755, 18.5cm. wide.
(Christie's) $37,000

A Chelsea lobed beaker painted in a famille rose palette with a bird perched on a trailing branch pendant from blue rockwork, circa 1750, 7cm. high.
(Christie's) $6,800

CHELSEA DERBY

This term is used to describe wares made between 1770-84 at Chelsea after the factory was taken over by William Duesbury, and also at Derby during the same period. Such pieces tend to be very neo-classical in style and it is extremely difficult to tell the London examples from those made at the northern factory. The gold anchor was still used as a mark, as was a gold anchor and letter *D* combined, and a *D* beneath a crown, often in blue.

Pair of Chelsea Derby candlestick figures of a gallant and his companion, 6½in. and 6in. high, no nozzles. **$960**

A Chelsea-Derby figure of Diana, standing on a rocky, flower encrusted base, a stag at her feet (slight damage), circa 1770-5. **$1,040**

A Chelsea-Derby two-handled chocolate cup and saucer, painted with groups of flowers. **$400**

A pair of Chelsea Derby figures, Neptune and Venus and Cupid, on high rocky bases, 24cm. and 25cm. high. **$960**

One of a pair of Chelsea-Derby groups of Renaldo, Armida, Cephalus and Procris, 20cm. high, incised numbers 75 and 76 with the initials J. W. (Phillips) **$1,920**

One of a pair of Chelsea Derby custard cups and covers, interlaced A and anchor in gold, circa 1775, 3.1/8in. high. **$760**

A pair of Chelsea Derby figures of a youth and girl standing before a bocage supporting candle sconces, 29cm. high. **$1,120**

A Chelsea-Derby jardinière of 'U' shape, Chelsea style with fabulous birds on rockwork and in the branches of leafy trees, 17cm. high. (Phillips) **$1,600**

CHELSEA 'GIRL IN A SWING'

The relationship between the main Chelsea factory and the Girl in a Swing factory in the mid 18th century is not clear, but it seems certain that many workmen were employed there from Chelsea, and its guiding light was probably the jeweler Charles Gouyn.

The factory was noted between 1749–54 for its scent bottles, but also produced some rare figures, modeled in a unique and dainty style, as well as some dressing table ware. Often these have been attributed to Chelsea proper, but it seems likely that the two factories were entirely separate.

A 'Girl in a Swing' cream jug with brown twig handle, circa 1750, 8cm. high. $24,000

A Chelsea double scent bottle modeled as a parrot and a rooster, circa 1755, 7cm. high. (Christie's) $4,000

A 'Girl in a Swing' white candlestick group of Ganymede and the Eagle, circa 1750, attributed to Charles Gouyn's factory, St. James's, 7½in. high. (Christie's) $40,997

A 'Girl in a Swing' white Holy Family group after Raphael, the Virgin Mary wearing flowing robes seated on rockwork before a tree-stump, her left arm encircling the Infant Christ Child, circa 1750, 21cm. high. (Christie's) $51,700

A Chelsea figure of a Chinaman wearing a pink-lined yellow conical hat and long-sleeved white coat painted with iron-red flowers, his hands tucked in his sleeves, circa 1755, 11cm. high. (Christie's) $2,900

A Girl-in-a-Swing type seal, modeled as a seated chinaman, cross-legged on a cushion, playing a mandolin, circa 1755, 2.8cm. high (Christie's) $960

A 'Girl in a Swing' white group of Europa and the Bull, the nymph wearing draped robes seated on the back of the garlanded recumbent bull, circa 1750, 18.5cm. wide. (Christie's) $8,170

A 'Girl-in-a-Swing' scent bottle and stopper, circa 1755, modeled as Cupid seated on a tree stump holding doves, in contemporary case, 7cm. high. (Christie's) $6,238

CHELSEA KERAMIC ART WORKS

Alexander Robertson founded the Chelsea Keramic Art Works near Boston Mass. in 1872, in partnership with his brother Hugh and later his father James. They produced reproductions of Greek vases, ornamental plaques and tiles, often with decorations in high relief.

Shortly after 1876, Hugh introduced an earthenware with underglaze decoration in colored slip, which was marketed as 'Bourg la Reine' ware, and also turned to oriental glazes and designs. The firm failed in 1888, but a new company, the Chelsea Pottery, was established in 1891 in Chelsea, MA, after a group of Boston business men had come to Robertson's rescue. The new Chelsea works continued to produce art pottery, often covered in a crackle glaze in the oriental style. However, the humidity in the soil at the new site caused recurrent problems with steam in the kiln, and in 1896 this forced the removal of the firm to Dedham, where it became known as the Dedham Pottery. Chelsea Keramic marks include an impressed *CKAW*, or the name in full, with artist's marks also incised.

Late 19th century Chelsea Keramics Art Works pottery vase, Mass., 10½in. high. (Skinner) $2,800

Chelsea Keramic Art Works elephant vase, Hugh C. Robertson, circa 1880, angular 'metal shape' octagonal body with applied elephant head handles, 6½in. high. (Skinner) $495

A pair of Chelsea Keramic Art Works double handled vases, Massachusetts, circa 1885, blue-green and brown glaze, 6¼in. high. (Skinner) $480

Chelsea Keramic Art works pottery vase, flat oval form, handles at sides, blue and brown glaze, impressed mark, 13in. high. (Skinner) $287

Chelsea Keramic Art vase, applied white flowers on crimpled squat-form with butterscotch glaze, 5in. wide. (Skinner) $517

Late 19th century Chelsea Keramic Art Works square molded vase, 7½in. high, 4in. diam. $640

CHELSEA KERAMIC ART WORKS

Late 19th century Chelsea Keramic Art Works oxblood vase, 8¼in. high.
(Skinner) $880

Chelsea Keramic Art Works slipper, Massachusetts, circa 1885, mottled olive green and brown glaze, 6in. long.
(Skinner Inc.) $320

Chelsea Keramic Art Works vase, classical form in green glaze, impressed marks, 5in. high.
(Skinner) $250

Chelsea Keramic Art Works lamp base, Chelsea, Massachusetts, circa 1880, gloss translucent blue/green glaze on high relief floral branch decoration, 7¼in. high.
(Skinner) $173

A fine pair of Chelsea Keramic art pottery vases with blue-green glossy glaze, circa 1885, 11¼in. high.
(Skinner) $1,360

A stoneware carafe, underglaze painted in brown and green tones, narrow necked, oval body and beak spout, Hugh Robertson (Chelsea Keramic), circa 1900.
(Lempertz) $605

Late 19th century Chelsea Keramic Art Works pottery 'oxblood' vase, 8in. high.
(Skinner) $2,000

Chelsea Keramic Art Works vase, Massachusetts, late 19th century, with relief decoration of squirrels and oak branches, 12in. wide.
(Skinner Inc.) $1,400

Late 19th century Chelsea Keramic Art Works covered jar, Mass., impressed CKAW, 5½in. high.
(Skinner) $320

CHINESE

The antiquity of Chinese ceramics and their beauty and variety down the ages make their study and collection particularly attractive, and provide scope for every taste.

The earliest unglazed earthenware jars date from as early as 2,000 BC, but it was not really until the Han Dynasty (206BC–220AD) that finer techniques, especially the art of glazing had been definitively mastered.

The next truly great period was the T'ang Dynasty (618–906AD) when the pottery was characterized by a beautiful proportion and vitality. A lead glaze was revived, which was often splashed or mottled, and many decorative themes reflect Hellenistic influence.

It was during the Sung Dynasty (960–1279AD) that the first true porcelain seems to have been made, and this period too saw the production of some of the most beautiful shapes and glazes of all time. It also saw the beginning of underglaze blue painting, which was to be perfected during the Ming period.

During the Ming Dynasty (1368–1644AD) a more or less standardized fine white porcelain body was developed which acted as a perfect vehicle for brilliant color decoration. Glazes tended to be thick or 'fat'. Colored glazes too were introduced and used either together or singly.

The K'ang Hsi period (1662–1722) marked a further flowering of the potter's art, which continued under his sons Yung Cheng and Ch'ien Lung (Qianlong). The body by now consisted of a very refined white porcelain, thinly and evenly glazed, providing the best possible base for elaborately painted decoration sometimes in the famille rose, famille verte, or famille noire palettes.

A pair of Chinese green, yellow and aubergine-glazed buddhistic lions, seated on tall rectangular plinths with their opposite forepaws resting on a cub and a brocaded ball, 18in. high.
(Christie's) $1,049

An 18th century Chinese porcelain tankard, decorated in polychrome enamels with flowers and fruit beneath a scroll and diapered border, 19.5cm. high.
(Spencer's) $573

A pair of Chinese porcelain-mounted brass two-branch wall-lights, each with rectangular backplate with courtly scenes surmounted by a pagoda roof, 46cm. high.
(Christie's) $2,972

One of a pair of Chinese silver-shaped octagonal dishes, each painted in iron red and gilt, with peonies and chrysanthemums, 18th century, 12¼in. wide.
(Christie's)
(Two) $1,004

A pair of Chinese powder-blue ground blue and white rouleau vases, 18th/19th century, painted on the cylindrical bodies and necks with the "one hundred antiques", 17¾in. high.
(Christie's) $4,140

A Chinese Yixing teapot, 19th century, the large pouring vessel of bulbous form with thick, curved spout and domed cover, fitted with a bronze, hinged handle, 11½in. high.
(Christie's) $805

CHINESE

A Chinese porcelain jardinière, painted in bright famille rose enamels with rulers and their attendants, 35cm. high.
(Bearne's) $626

A pair of ormolu-mounted Chinese blue and white porcelain vases, each with ribbon-tied laurel wreath collar, 14¹/₄in. high.
(Christie's)
$7,535

A Chinese blue and white Fitzhugh-pattern barrel-shaped water jug and cover, with buddhistic lion finial, 18th century, 8in. high.
(Christie's) $1,089

Pair of Chinese porcelain baluster-form vases, each painted in underglaze blue with peacock amid exotic gardens, the domed lid topped by a rampant fu dog finial, height 36in.
(Butterfield & Butterfield)
$1,495

A pair of Chinese Guangdong figures of mythical three-legged toads, modeled with wide open mouths, seated on pierced wave-form bases, 11¹/₂ in. high.
(Christie's) $5,980

A pair of Louis XV style Chinese ormolu-mounted famille verte covered baluster jars, each with courtly maidens by a garden with fluttering butterflies, surmounted by a foo-dog finial, 29in. high.
(Christie's) $16,100

A Chinese guanyao-type crackle-glazed globular jar, 19th century, molded with two animal-mask fixed ring-handles, all under a thick widely crackled gray glaze, 12in. high.
(Christie's) $2,797

A pair of Wu Ts'ai porcelain joss stick holders, depicting guardian lions, one holding a brocade ball, the other a pup, 8in. high.
(Eldreds) $1,000

An ormolu-mounted Chinese armorial porcelain bowl, with lion-mask and ring-handles, with pierced and block-feet, the porcelain early 18th century, 11¹/₄in. wide.
(Christie's) $4,664

CHINESE

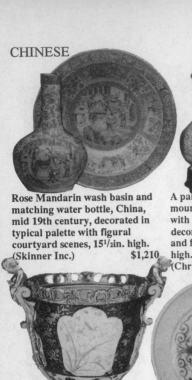

Rose Mandarin wash basin and matching water bottle, China, mid 19th century, decorated in typical palette with figural courtyard scenes, 15½in. high. (Skinner Inc.) $1,210

A pair of Chinese bronze-mounted porcelain lamps, each with baluster apple-green body decorated with a stylized dragon and fish, 19th century, 20¼in. high. (Christie's) $2,806

A rare Chinese teapot and cover, decorated in London, the reverse inscribed '57 Miles to London', a milestone inscribed 'XIV Miles from London', 16cm., 1750-1760. (Phillips) $1,200

An ormolu-mounted and parcel-gilt Chinese porcelain jardinière, the pierced floral and C-scroll rim above the tapering vase-shaped body, the porcelain late 17th century, 16½in. diameter. (Christie's) $5,741

A pair of 19th century porcelain plates decorated with phoenix and clouds on exterior and interior, six character Chia Ching mark on base, 6¼in. diameter. (Eldreds) $1,595

A magnificent Yuan blue and white jar, guan, painted around the globular body with an arching peony scroll comprising six blooms, circa 1340-50, 39cm. high. (Christie's) $800,000

A pair of gilt-decorated blue-glazed bottle vases, with vertical lines of shou character medallions joined by wan characters and surrounded by stylized bats, Guangxu six-character marks, 39cm. high. (Christie's) $5,244

A pair of Chinese blue and white ginger jars and covers, late 19th century, the baluster bodies decorated with figures within fenced gardens, 10in. high.(Christie's) $835

A pair of ormolu-mounted turquoise Chinese porcelain ewers, each with the water-cast everted spout above a paired set of two upright carp, the porcelain 18th century, 16¾in. high. (Christie's) $73,369

CHINESE

A Transitional blue and white jar painted with a dragon chasing a flaming pearl amongst clouds, the short neck with pendent stiff leaves, Shunzhi, 27cm. high.
(Christie's) $2,000

A Chinese blue and white porcelain platter, centrally painted with a busy lakeland scene, 14½in. wide, Qianlong, circa 1760.
(Tennants) $259

A fine underglaze-blue and copper-red garlic-head vase, Qianlong seal mark, the Buddhistic lion cubs pawing and playing with ribbonned brocade balls, 10½in. high.
(Christie's) $63,871

A Louis XVI ormolu-mounted Chinese porcelain vase decorated with bamboo shoots and shrubs and a bird on a light-blue ground, the porcelain Qianlong and repaired, 11½in. high. (Christie's) $11,000

A fine Transitional blue and white brush-pot, circa 1635, painted on the exterior with a scholar seated at a rootwood table shaded by a pine tree, 7⅛in. diameter.
(Christie's) $9,935

A blue and white stemcup, Qianlong seal mark, the flaring sides of the cup painted to the exterior with lanca characters divided by arches formed by lotus sprays, 3¼in. high.
(Christie's) $5,677

A fine and rare blue and yellow vase, early Qianlong, painted on the globular body with formal scrolling lotus, each flower-spray divided by kui dragons, all between bands of ruyi-heads, 10½in. high.
(Christie's) $70,968

A rare large Yuan blue and white bowl, circa 1350–60, the interior with a swimming carp between clumps of waterweeds, 11½in. diameter.
(Christie's) $176,000

A highly important large Geyao octagonal vase, Ba Fanghu, Song dynasty, the thinly-potted vase imitating an archaic bronze shape of oblong octagonal section, 10½in. high.
(Christie's) $1,480,918

CHINESE EXPORTWARE

The first Chinese Exportware was produced as a result of the presence of the Jesuit fathers, who established themselves there from 1600. About fifty years later pieces of porcelain began to appear decorated with crucifixes and the letters *IHS*. Later, religious scenes were painted, mostly on plates, but sometimes even on tea sets!

Heraldic ware was the first form called for from China in great quantities in the early 18th century. Great services were manufactured with decoration often in imitation of the silver they were to replace. Punchbowls and other utilitarian pieces followed, decorated with creditable reproductions of European paintings or illustrations of events. Figures in European dress were also attempted.

The factories which produced these were grouped at Ching te Chen and they were decorated mostly at Canton. Some pieces were also made in Fukien Province, which were characterised by their creamy white appearance. These were usually decorated in Europe and were known as blanc-de-Chine.

A pair of Chinese export figures of cocks, early 19th century, standing astride lustrous dark brown rockwork, 31cm. and 30.3cm. high.
(Sotheby's) $6,325

A Chinese Export blue and white small cruet pot and cover, mid-18th century, painted with flowering plants growing from the footrim, height 5¼in.
(Sotheby's) $920

A good pair of Chinese export fluted hexagonal wine coolers, circa 1765, painted with a duck in flight, 7¾in. high.
(Sotheby's) $9,775

A Chinese export blue and white ribbed ginger jar mounted as a lamp, early 18th century, 11½in. high.
(Sotheby's) $2,300

A Chinese Export blue and white circular soup tureen and cover, circa 1760, each with a whorl-patterned ground decorated with lotus blossoms, width 10¹¹⁄₁₆in.
(Sotheby's) $2,300

A fine pair of Chinese export peony-form water droppers, dated *1882* and *1883*, each lightly molded with peony petals delineated in black, 7³⁄₈in. long.
(Sotheby's) $3,162

A Chinese Export porcelain goose tureen and cover, 1765–85, naturalistically modeled with incised plumage delineated on the back and wings in black, brown, blue and green, 32.8cm. high. (Sotheby's) $28,750

CHINESE EXPORTWARE

A pair of Chinese export blue and white quatrefoil tea caddies and covers, 19th century, painted with two butterflies amidst peony, 20.1cm. high. (Sotheby's) $920

A Chinese export blue and white chamfered rectangular soup tureen, a cover and a platter, circa 1770, 36.7cm. and 22.1cm. long. (Sotheby's) $2,300

A Chinese export 'faux bois' shallow fish bowl, 19th century, painted on the interior with two cranes above two ducks, 40cm. diameter. (Sotheby's) $1,265

A Chinese export porcelain covered bowl, circa 1810, decorated in sepia with a bucolic figure leaning on a cow with a dog at his feet, 5³/₄in. high. (Christie's) $935

A fine Chinese Export mythological plate, circa 1745, painted en grisaille in the center with Juno seated in her chariot, diameter 9in. (Sotheby's) $920

A Chinese export 'Mandarin Palette' large cylindrical mug, circa 1785, loop handle with a gilt ruyi-head thumbpiece, 5⁵/₈in. high. (Sotheby's) $805

A Chinese Export circular basin, mid-18th century, painted with a brown-delineated gold crane perched on an underglaze-blue rock, diameter 15⁹/₁₆in. (Sotheby's) $690

A pair of Chinese export blue and white silver-shape oval platters, circa 1750, each painted in underglaze-blue with a box, a vase and a censer, 29cm. long. (Sotheby's) $1,035

A Chinese export 'Judgment of Paris' plate, 1745–50, the rim painted with alternating views of Plymouth Sound and the Pearl River, 23cm. diameter. (Sotheby's) $2,875

CHINESE EXPORTWARE

A Chinese Export circular soup tureen and cover, 1765–75, each piece painted in rose, iron-red, yellow and shades of green, width 11¼in.
(Sotheby's) $1,610

A Chinese Export figure of a seated rabbit, late 18th/early 19th century, naturalistically modeled with ears pricked back, height 5¼in.
(Sotheby's) $3,450

A Chinese export porcelain hot-water plate, early 19th century, decorated in polychrome with the arms of the state of New York, 11¼in. diameter.
(Christie's) $2,860

A pair of Chinese Export white-painted Chinese geese, each with repaired break to neck, 19th century, 25¾in. high.
(Christie's) $95,150

A matched pair of 18th century Chinese porcelain wine pots adapted with French ormolu mounts as pot pourri vases, on later oval bases, 14cm. high.
(Phillips) $4,760

A Chinese flambé baluster vase, with French gilt-bronze mounts, Paris, circa 1860, 76cm. high.
(Sotheby's) $6,296

A Chinese Export 'Tobacco leaf' pattern plate, 1770–85, painted with a green-centered rose and purple and yellow tobacco blossom, diameter 8¹⁵/₁₆in.
(Sotheby's) $1,725

A Chinese Export porcelain tankard, enameled with a medallion enclosing a half portrait of the Duke of Cumberland, height 6¼in., Qianlong period.
(Bonhams) $2,800

A Chinese Export armorial charger, circa 1745, painted in the center with the arms of Willey, diameter 16⁷/₁₆in.
(Sotheby's) $3,450

CLARICE CLIFF

The legendary Clarice Cliff was born in 1899 in, perhaps inevitably, Staffordshire, where she started work at 13 in one of the local potteries, painting freehand onto pottery.

Her formal training comprised a year, when she was 16, at the Burslem School of Art, and a later year at the Royal College of Art, where she studied sculpture . At 17, she had gone to work at the firm of A.J. Wilkinson, and she remained with them, and their subsidiary the Newport Pottery, for the next two decades, ending up as Art Director and marrying the boss, Colley Shorter, when she was forty.

During the 1920's she painted Tibetan ware, large jars painted with floral designs in bright colors and gold, and she also transferred on to pottery designs by such distinguished artists as Paul Nash and Laura Knight.

In 1928, however, she painted 60 dozen pieces of her own design to test the market at a trade fair. These proved so popular that by 1929 the whole factory was switched to producing her Bizarre ware.

Cliff's style is characterized by combinations of bright colors, such as orange, blue, purple and green, or black, yellow, orange and red. Her pieces are often angular in shape and strongly Art Deco in style. Major ranges, besides Bizarre, include Crocus, Fantasque, Biarritz and Farmhouse.

At the beginning of the Second World War, the factory was commandeered by the Ministry of Supply, and Wilkinson produced only a few white pieces. After the war, the market had changed and production was not resumed.

A 'Bizarre' Chahar wallmask, painted in colors, printed factory marks, 10½in. long.
(Christie's) $1,725

Clarice Cliff Inspiration double conical vase with hand written mark.
(Muir Hewitt) $1,087

A 'Bizarre' Bonjour teapot and cover, painted in bright colors on a yellow ground with scenes of a Slavonic peasant couple, 5in. high.
(Christie's) $1,625

A Clarice Cliff 'Bizarre' vase, shape No. 342, decorated in the 'Sliced Circles' pattern, painted in orange, green and black, 7¾in. high.
(Christie's S. Ken) $1,000

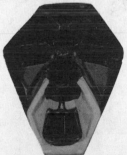

A 'Bizarre' grotesque mask designed by Ron Birks, painted in orange, red, yelow and black, 10½in. long.
(Christie's) $868

A 'Fantasque Bizarre' plate in the 'Farmhouse' pattern, painted in colors, 9in. diameter.
(Christie's) $521

CLARICE CLIFF

An original 'Bizarre' pentafoil rimmed vase, shape No. 361, decorated with overlapping triangles in shades of purple, green, orange, brown, and blue, 20.5cm. high.
(Christie's) $471

A pair of original 'Bizarre' squat candlesticks painted in colors with stylized leaves, 8cm. high.
(Christie's) $269

A Clarice Cliff twin-handled baluster vase, 'Bizarre', painted with a sunburst and geometric landscape between two broad orange borders, 11¹/₂in. high.
(George Kidner) $3,080

A 'Fantasque Bizarre' single-handled Lotus jug in the 'Orange Autumn' pattern, painted in colors, 30cm. high.
(Christie's) $1,262

A superb wall plaque by Clarice Cliff painted with a scene inspired by Diaghilev's costume design for The Ballet Russe. $13,600

A Clarice Cliff 'Coral Firs' single handled Lotus jug, brightly painted, the rim with brown, yellow and beige banding.
(Neales) $616

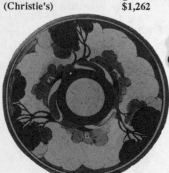

A 'Fantasque Bizarre' large ribbed wall charger, decorated in the 'Blue Autumn' pattern, painted in colors, 45.5cm. diameter.
(Christie's) $3,029

A rare miniature Clarice Cliff wall plaque molded as the head of a woman with red checkered scarf, 3¼in. high.
(David Lay) $360

A Clarice Cliff 'Orange House' pattern plate, painted with a stylized cottage and trees enclosed by orange border, 26.3cm. diameter.
(Phillips) $850

CLARICE CLIFF

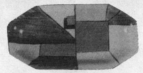

A 'Fantasque Bizarre' Bonjour preserve pot and cover decorated in the 'Windbells' pattern, painted in colors, 10.5cm. high.
(Christie's) $252

A 'Bizarre' octagonal sandwich set in the 'Cubist' pattern, comprising five sandwich plates and a tray, 29cm. wide.
(Christie's) $1,346

'Sliced Circle', a 'Bizarre' twin-handled lotus jug, painted in colors, printed factory marks, 29cm. high.
(Christie's) $6,795

A Clarice Cliff Applique-Lucerne lotus jug, painted with an orange roofed chateau perched on the side of yellow and green hills, 29.5cm. high.
(Phillips) $9,600

Clarice Cliff 1951 Teepee teapot with "Greetings from Canada" on underside.
(Muir Hewltt) $1,140

An 'Appliqué Bizarre' Conical jug decorated in the 'Lugano' pattern of farmhouse in alpine landscape, 9$^{1}/_{2}$in. high.
(Christie's) $6,400

A 'Bizarre' plate designed by Dame Laura Knight, the well printed and painted with three performing acrobats, 23cm. high.
(Christie's) $1,400

'Age of Jazz' a 'Bizarre' table decoration of two musicians in full evening dress playing piano and banjo, naturalistically painted, on rectangular base, 14.5cm. high.
(Christie's) $7,069

A 'Latona Bizarre' plate, painted in colors around a central medallion with overlapping half circles and stylized foliage, 26cm. diameter.
(Christie's) $539

CLARICE CLIFF

Twin handled Isis jug by Clarice Cliff, 10½in. high. (Muir Hewitt) $1,875

Clarice Cliff dish in 'House and Bridge' design, 10in. diameter. (Muir Hewitt) $930

A 'Bizarre' biscuit barrel and cover, shape No. 336, decorated in the "Swirls" pattern, 6½in. high. (Christie's) $760

Clarice Cliff 'Flora' wall mask, 15in. high. (Muir Hewitt) $2,565

A Clarice Cliff 'Inspiration Bizarre' stick stand, decorated in the 'Caprice' pattern, in shades of pink, lavender and blue on a turquoise ground, 24in. high. (Christie's S. Ken) $3,200

A 'Bizarre' Chippendale jardinière in the 'Crocus' pattern, painted in colors, 9¼in. diameter. (Christie's) $416

A 'Bizarre' single-handled Lotus jug decorated in the 'Lightning' pattern, painted in colors between orange borders, 11½in. high. (Christie's S. Ken) $4,400

A 'Bizarre' grotesque mask designed by Ron Birks, the features painted in panels of orange, yellow and black, 11in. long. (Christie's) $2,035

A Clarice Cliff 'Fantasque' vase, shape No. 358, decorated in the 'Trees and House' pattern, painted in colors, 8in. high. (Christie's S. Ken) $880

104

CLARICE CLIFF

Clarice Cliff conical bowl on foot in the Swirls design.
(Muir Hewitt)　$3,375

A 'Bizarre' Chester fern pot in the 'Swirls' pattern, painted in colors, 4in. diameter.
(Christie's)　$416

A 'Fantasque' mushroom vase, decorated in the 'Sunrise' pattern, painted in orange, green and blue, above orange banding, 5¼in. high.
(Christie's)　$560

A 'Bizarre' model of a laughing cat, after a design by Louis Wain, the orange body with black spots, and green bow tie, 6in. high.
(Christie's)　$1,525

A 'Fantasque Bizarre' ginger jar and cover decorated in the 'Blue Autumn' pattern, painted in colors with contrasting banding, 7¾in. high.
(Christie's S. Ken)　$1,600

A 'Fantasque Bizarre' cylindrical biscuit barrel and cover decorated in the 'Blue Autumn' pattern, 6¼in. high.
(Christie's S. Ken)　$560

A 'Patina Bizarre' spherical vase painted with red tree bearing blue and green foliage, under blue spattered slip, 6in. high.
(Christie's)　$1,400

A 'Fantasque Bizarre' Dover jardinière decorated in the 'Trees and House' pattern, rubber stamp mark, 8in. high.
(Christie's S. Ken)　$2,080

A 'Bizarre' wall mask modeled as the head of an exotic woman with blue ringlets and a cap of green foliage, 9in. long.
(Christie's)　$521

CLARICE CLIFF

A 'Fantasque Bizarre' globular vase, decorated in the 'Honolulu' pattern, painted in colors, 16cm. high.
(Christie's) $2,861

'Crocus', a 'Bizarre' duck egg cruet set, comprising: circular tray surmounted with a yellow duck, with six egg cups, 13cm. high.
(Christie's) $475

A 'Fantasque Bizarre' beehive honey pot and cover in the 'Trees and House' pattern, painted in colors, 9cm. high.
(Christie's) $320

A 'Fantasque Bizarre' Athens jug decorated in the 'Autumn' pattern, painted in colors, 20cm. high.
(Christie's) $286

A Clarice Cliff 'Bizarre' tankard coffee set for six in the 'Crocus' pattern, printed factory marks, height of coffee pot 18cm.
(Christie's) $535

A 'Bizarre' single-handled Lotus jug in the 'Luxor' pattern, painted in orange, green, lavender and blue between yellow borders, 30cm. high.
(Christie's) $2,020

A 'Fantasque Bizarre' plate in the 'Bobbins' pattern, painted in colors with blue dash border, 23cm. diameter.
(Christie's) $808

'Flora' a wall mask molded in relief in the form of a womans head with flowers and foliage in her hair, 35cm. high.
(Christie's) $1,760

A 'Bizarre' charger in the 'Oranges' pattern, painted in colors, printed factory marks, 45.5cm. diameter.
(Christie's) $4,575

CLARICE CLIFF

A 'Bizarre' Dover jardinière in the 'Summerhouse' pattern, painted in colors, 20cm. diameter.
(Christie's)   **$1,599**

A 'Bizarre' Bonjour teapot and cover designed by Eva Crofts, painted with a red breasted bird amongst flowers and trees.
(Christie's) $528

'Orange Roof Cottage', a 'Bizarre' Daffodil preserve pot and cover, 12cm. high
(Christie's) $680

A 'Fantasque' Archaic vase, decorated in the 'Broth' design, painted in green, black and red with corresponding banding, 25cm. high.
(Christie's) $2,693

A pair of Clarice Cliff teddy bear book ends decorated in the 'Red Flower' pattern, painted in colors, 6in. high.
(Christie's S. Ken) $6,800

A Clarice Cliff 'Fantasque Bizarre' vase, decorated in the 'Orange House' pattern, painted in colors, 20cm. high.
(Christie's) $752

An 'Appliqué' octagonal plate decorated in the 'Caravan' pattern, painted in colors, 11in. diameter.
(Christie's S. Ken)   **$3,850**

A 'Bizarre' Flora wallmask painted in shades of orange, yellow and black, rubber stamp mark, 14^{1}/$_{2}$in. long.
(Christie's) $1,630

An Appliqué 'Bizarre' charger in the 'Etna' pattern, painted in colors, remains of painted mark, 45.5cm. diameter.
(Christie's) $19,360

CLARICE CLIFF

A 'Bizarre' vase, decorated in the 'Applique Lugano' pattern, painted in colors with blue roof and orange sky, 8in. high.
(Christie's) $1,950

A pair of 'Bizarre' bookends, modeled as a pair of parakeets with green plumage on checkered base, 7in. high.
(Christie's S. Ken) $1,480

'My Garden' vase from the Bizarre range by Clarice Cliff, 5½in. high.
(Muir Hewitt) $202

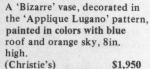

Clarice Cliff 'Lotus' jug, Secrets design from the Bizarre range, 12in. high, 1930s.
(Muir Hewitt) $2,850

A 'Bizarre' Stamford trio in the 'Tennis' pattern, painted in colors with red banding, height of teapot, 4½in.
(Christie's) $4,475

'My Garden' vase from the Bizarre range by Clarice Cliff, 7in. high.
(Muir Hewitt) $319

A Bizarre twin-handled lotus jug, in 'Autumn crocus' pattern, 29cm. high.
(Allen & Harris) $460

A pair of 'Bizarre' bookends, shape No. 406 decorated in the 'Honolulu' pattern, painted in colors, 6in. high.
(Christie's S. Ken) $840

'Age of Jazz', a 'Bizarre' table decoration modeled as two musicians in evening dress, rubber stamp mark, 6in. high.
(Christie's) $4,475

CLARICE CLIFF

A 'Fantasque' plate decorated in the 'Flora' pattern, painted in orange, yellow, green and black. (Christie's S. Ken) $360

A 'Bizarre' double bonjour candlestick in the 'Green Bridgewater' pattern, painted in colors, 5in. high. (Christie's) $868

A Bizarre 'orange roof cottage' cylindrical biscuit jar and cover, with wicker handle, 15cm. high. (Allen & Harris) $535

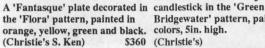

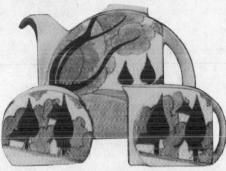

A 'Latona Bizarre' stepped circular vase in the 'Red Roses' pattern, painted in red and black, 18in. high. (Christie's) $4,859

A Clarice Cliff 'Fantasque Bizarre' Stamford trio decorated in the 'May Avenue' pattern, painted in colors, height of teapot 4$^1/2$in. (Christie's S. Ken) $4,000

A 'Bizarre' hexagonal baluster vase decorated in the 'Sunray' pattern, painted in colors between multibanded borders, 15in. high. (Christie's S. Ken) $3,680

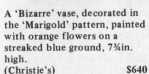

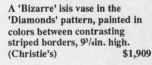

A 'Bizarre' vase, decorated in the 'Marigold' pattern, painted with orange flowers on a streaked blue ground, 7¾in. high. (Christie's) $640

A pair of 'Bizarre' cottage book ends painted with orange roof to cottage, green and yellow base, 5$^1/2$in. high. (Christie's) $2,603

A 'Bizarre' isis vase in the 'Diamonds' pattern, painted in colors between contrasting striped borders, 9¾in. high. (Christie's) $1,909

CLEMENT MASSIER

Clement Massier was a French artist potter who worked around the turn of the century at Golfe-Juan in the Alpes Maritimes. He produced a luster decorated earthenware, often embellished with plant motifs.

A large Clément Massier ceramic jardinière. (Christie's) $5,730

A Clement Massier art pottery vase, signed and bears impressed mark, 10in. high. (D. M. Nesbit & Co.) $480

A large Clement Massier porcelain urn, the dark green glaze decorated with gold colored leaves and polychrome enameled insects, 102cm. high. (Christie's) $5,200

A Massier art pottery jardiniere, sculpted to simulate ocean waves with a full-form nude woman perched amidst the breakers, 9½in. high. (Skinner) $3,200

A Clément Massier earthenware jardinière with a pedestal, decorated in relief with irises, the pedestal naturalistically molded with a heron among bulrushes, 38cm. diameter of jardinière. (Christie's) $560

Clement Massier art pottery vase, pinched oval clay body with handpainted decoration of two dragonflies among cat-tails and grasses, 7½in. high. (Skinner Inc.) $450

A massive Clément Massier jardinière, of irregular tapering form, decorated in an overall luster glaze of green, yellow, amethyst and amber, 56cm. high. (Christie's) $1,280

Clement Massier iridescent glazed pottery vase, decorated overall with sunflowers in tones of iridescent and flat yellow ocher, 14¼in. high. (Butterfield & Butterfield) $977

COALBROOKDALE

The Coalport or Coalbrookdale factory was established in Shropshire around 1796 by John Rose. Soft paste porcelain, sometimes in imitation of Chelsea, Swansea, or even Sèvres, continued to be made by his descendants until 1862. Around this time the factory passed into the hands of the Bruff family and in 1924 it was sold to Cauldon Potteries, moving to Staffordshire in 1926.

Pieces are often clearly marked *J Rose Coalbrookdale*, though some Chelsea pieces have an imitation blue anchor mark. Crossed tridents and *Swansea* are printed on red on imitation Swansea, and *RP* in crossed *L*s on imitation Sèvres.

C Dale
Coalbrookdale

JOHN ROSE & C°
COALBROOKDALE
SHROPSHIRE

Two Coalbrookdale vases and covers, circa 1830, one of ovoid shape painted with birds and fruit, the other circular, painted with birds and insects, 15 and 11cm. high.
(Phillips) $341

A pair of Coalbrookdale type pastille burners and stands, pear-shaped, molded and gilt with leaves and applied with flowers, circa 1835, 15.2cm. high.
(Christie's) $496

Pair of Coalbrookdale porcelain vases, mid-19th century, with handpainted floral bouquet, accented in gilt, (both handles showing breaks and repair) 15½in.
(Skinner Inc.) $800

A 'Coalbrookdale' garniture of one large and two smaller baluster form two-handled vases, all encrusted with flowers and leaves, 12in. and 11in. high.
(Bonhams) $325

A pair of mid 19th century Coalbrookdale porcelain vases of ovoid shape with flared wave pattern rim and rustic loop handles, 9in. high.
(Hartley) $465

Coalbrookdale porcelain handled ewer, mid 19th century, white ground with applied flowers, leaves and vines (minor flower and petal damage), 8in. high. (Skinner Inc.) $400

Pair of Coalbrookdale porcelain covered potpourri, mid-19th century, with scrolled leaf handles, pierced body and lid, 8in. high. (Skinner Inc.) $1,600

COALPORT

The Rose family established the Coalport Porcelain Works in Coalport Shropshire in 1796, and it remained in the family until the last member retired in 1862. In general, their output copied 18th century French and German porcelain, with decoration often in the Sèvres style. They employed some notable decorators, such as Jabez Ashton, who painted naturalistic flowers and fruit on large plaques, and James Rouse.

The business was declared bankrupt (1875-80) and then was acquired by Peter Bruff, who was later succeeded by his son Charles. They now turned out tableware decorated with landscapes of flower panels, or lightly decorated on pink and green grounds.

Parian and porcelain were used together for comports and centerpieces etc. and enameled jeweled decoration was used on tall vases, which were also painted with views or landscapes.

In 1924 the firm was purchased by Cauldon Potteries and in 1926 it the operation was moved to Staffordshire. It is still in existence today at Stoke on Trent.

There are numerous different marks from the various periods, usually in underglaze blue, either *C, S,* or *N,* in loops of monogram *CS,* or *Coalport AD 1750.* Later *England* or *Made in England* (from circa 1920) were added.

A pair of Coalport outside-decorated plates, the centers painted in a bright palette with country churches, circa 1810, 23cm. diameter.
(Christie's) $1,095

A pair of Coalport two-handled urns, painted with a continuous band of flowers on a richly gilt ground, circa 1810, 40cm. high.
(Christie's) $3,200

A pair of large Coalport pedestal jars and covers with ram's head handles, each painted by Frederick H. Chivers with grapes and peaches, 41cm. high.
(Bearne's) $1,389

A rare Coalport clockcase, circa 1835, boldly modeled in rococo tase with shells and scroll motifs, 34.5cm. high.
(Phillips) $2,340

A Coalport gold-ground two-handled 'jeweled' and reticulated vase and domed cover of baluster form, the body enriched with turquoise and gilt 'jewels' beneath a cream band at the shoulder, circa 1895, 10in. high.
(Christie's) $1,590

A Coalport taperstick and extinguisher, circa 1810, on a circular foot with ring handle, painted possibly in the Thomas Baxter workshop, 6.5cm. high.
(Phillips) $624

COMMEMORATIVE

Commemorative is the word used to describe the myriad objects made and decorated to mark some person or event of special significance, coronations, jubilees, battles etc.

The first china to be made in any quantities with such intention appeared in Stuart times, and delft of the period often bears royal names and portraits.

The arrival of Queen Victoria on the throne opened the floodgates for the manufacture of commemorative china. Her predecessors as rulers were more often lampooned than venerated, but Victoria changed the popular attitude towards royalty. China commemorating events in the reigns of William and Mary, George III, George IV and William IV are rare but pieces with pictures of Victoria and Albert were made in their thousands and enjoyed pride of place on the walls and mantlepieces of rich and poor up and down the land. Plates, tobacco jars, mugs, vases, pipes, teapots, doorstops and spill jars marked every event in the royal life. The china cost little to buy and proved so popular that the range spread to include political happenings, military displays, exhibitions and even famous crimes and criminals.

Obviously age and rarity play a large part in determining the value of any piece of commemorative china, but the whole field is an attractive one. It is possible to start a collection with very little outlay, and each piece, whether modern or older, has its own intrinsic interest, which can only increase as time goes by.

A Pountney's 'The Fiscal Pottery' commemorative tyg, painted by George Stewart in Wemyss style, circa 1905, 17cm. diameter.
(Allen & Harris) $323

A pearlware commemorative jug molded in relief with a bust-length portrait of the Duke of York in military costume, circa 1810, 8in. high.
(Christie's) $744

A rare pair of miniature Herculaneum coronation plaques, one puce printed with a floral cartouche enclosing the caption *God Save The King*, 3in. diameter, circa 1821.
(Bonhams) $4,400

An English porcelain flared cylindrical vase, with central rectangular panel painted with a colorful portrait of King George IV wearing ceremonial robes, height 6in., circa 1820.
(Bonhams) $2,240

A Read and Clementson pottery coronation mug, entitled *Victoria Regina* in bold capitals, together with the inscription *Proclaimed 20 of June 1837 Crowned June 28th 1838*, height 3¹/₂in.
(Bonhams) $1,920

An English pottery jug, molded and enameled with titled equestrian portraits of The Duke of York and Prince Cobourg, both in military attire, 6in. high, circa 1793.
(Bonhams) $880

A large white Luck and Flaw two-handled caricature loving cup formed as the head of Prince Charles, 20cm.
(Phillips) $120

A cylindrical pottery mug printed in colors with flags and inscribed 'G.R. *Peace of Europe signed at Paris May 30th, 1814'*, 11 cm.
(Phillips) $400

A bulbous jug with animal-headed handle, printed in puce with an unusual portrait of the young Queen Victoria, 18cm.
(Phillips) $250

A Dillwyn & Co. pottery plate, painted in bright enamel colors, the center printed in black with the seated figure of the young Queen Victoria, 20.5cm.
(Bearne's) $480

A pair of Whitman and Roth caricature figures of Gladstone and Disraeli, both standing on mottled turquoise and brown bases, 40cm.
(Phillips) $5,450

A Coalport plate printed in blue in commemoration of Captain Matthew Webb being the first person to swim the English Channel in 1875, 27cm.
(Phillips) $240

A black printed jug bearing portraits of William IV and Queen Adelaide, probably commemorating the Coronation in 1830, 14cm.
(Phillips) $240

A fine quality English biscuit figure of King William IV seated crossed legged on an elegant sofa, 11cm.
(Phillips) $480

A crisply molded jug of hexagonal shape, embossed with half length profile portraits of Victoria and Albert flanked by scrolling flowers, 15.5cm. (Phillips) $195

COPELAND

In 1833 William Copeland bought the Staffordshire firm of Josiah Spode, and it was in 1842 that Copeland and Garrett of Stoke on Trent first produced statuary in what came to be known as Parian ware. Its success was due to the large quantity of feldspar contained in the soft paste, and a firing process which allowed an unusually large quantity of air into the kiln. The result was a porcelain notable for its lustrous transparency and delicacy of molding. A second quality parian statuary, slightly different in composition, was produced in 1850, and became known as standard parian. It lacked the silky surface of the first, but could withstand repeated firings and could be decorated in colors and gold. Copeland's were also noted for a variety of tableware produced in porcelain and earthenware and often lavishly ornamented, together with handpainted tiles.

A variety of marks were used, bearing variations of Copeland and Spode. From 1970 the firm has traded as Spode Ltd.

A pair of Copeland parian porcelain busts of young women with flowers in their hair, representing 'Spring' and 'Summer', after originals by Louis Auguste Malempre, 32cm. high. (Bearne's) $1,102

One of a set of seven Copeland handpainted porcelain plates with pink, green and gilt borders enclosing a reserve decorated with floral sprays, 10.2in. diameter. (James Adam) $347

A Copeland blue pottery teapot, the sides decorated in royal blue glaze and with white pottery golfing figures in relief, 21cm. (Phillips) $780

A Copeland parian group, in the form of a young peasant man and woman seated on a rocky mound, 31cm. high. (Bearne's) $800

Copeland parian ware jug, scroll looped handle, heavily decorated in the neo-classical manner, 8in. high. (G. A. Key) $73

A large pair of Copeland vases, each painted by C. F. Hurten, signed, circa 1870, 19¾in. high. $4,350

An early Victorian Copeland Parian bust of Clytie, raised upon a waisted socle, impressed C. Delpech, 1855, 15in. high. (Spencer's) $528

COPER

Hans Coper (1920–1981) trained as an engineer in his native Germany, but fled to England in the late '30's. During the war, he met another refugee, Lucie Rie, and went to work in her studio. They started making ceramic buttons, then graduated to domestic ware and in the evenings Coper could experiment with his own designs.

His biggest 'break' came when Basil Spence commissioned two candlesticks from him for Coventry Cathedral. His work is now established among the foremost modern pottery with prices to match.

A large stoneware bowl by Hans Coper, with horse and rider sgraffito design, circa 1955, 36cm. diameter.
(Bonhams) $9,600

A fine black stoneware cup form by Hans Coper, made in three pieces, impressed *HC* seal, circa 1965, 6in. high.
(Bonhams) $10,000

A fine stoneware standing form by Hans Coper, the spherical body surmounted by a flattened oval form, circa 1970, 18.8cm. high.
(Bonhams) $12,000

An early stoneware goblet form by Hans Coper, manganese over a 'toffee' glaze, unglazed foot, impressed HC seal, circa 1952, 4³/₄in. high.
(Bonhams) $4,000

A rare cup form stoneware pot by Hans Coper, distinguished by two dark textured panels and two vertical incised lines, impressed HC seal, circa 1970, 6¹/₄in. high.
(Bonhams) $10,000

An important early stoneware 'thistle' form pot by Hans Coper, with diagonal texturing, impressed HC seal, circa 1958, 12¹/₄in. high.
(Bonhams) $10,800

An early stoneware goblet pot by Hans Coper, dark brown over a shiny 'toffee' glaze, the foot unglazed, circa 1952, 6in. high.
(Bonhams) $4,000

A superb stoneware 'egg-in-cup' form by Hans Coper, white with distinctive brown and bluish shading, impressed HC seal, circa 1975, 7³/₈in. high.
(Bonhams) $11,600

COPER

An important early stoneware bottle form by Hans Coper, brown with sgraffito revealing the cream body, 11in. high.
(Bonhams) $8,000

A stoneware shallow bowl by Hans Coper, the interior covered in a matt manganese glaze, the center carved with circular band, impressed *HC* seal, 17.5cm. diameter.
(Christie's) $3,200

A stoneware buff cup form by Hans Coper, on a conical base surmounted by a manganese disk, impressed *HC* seal, circa 1970, $6^3/_4$in. high.
(Bonhams) $2,160

An outstanding stoneware spade pot by Hans Coper, white with a deep manganese band at the rim merging into a textured surface, impressed IIC seal, circa 1966, $7^1/_4$in. high.
(Bonhams) $12,500

A rare 'tripot' by Hans Coper, three cylindrical, straight sided, attached pots on narrowing feet decorated with graffito lines, circa 1956, 8in. high.
(Bonhams) $8,000

A fine stoneware white pot by Hans Coper, the squared form on a drum base, hollowed impressions on both sides, impressed HC seal, circa 1975, 5in. high.
(Bonhams) $8,400

A stoneware vase form by Hans Coper, buff merging into brown towards the everted rim, with two vertical brown bands, circa 1958, 21cm.
(Bonhams) $5,600

A rare stoneware bell form pot by Hans Coper, the top third manganese merging into beige, circa 1963, 5in. high.
(Bonhams) $6,800

A highly important black 'discus' form by Hans Coper, incised rectangular form on one side and spiral on the other, circa 1962, 10in. high.
(Bonhams) $16,000

A fine stoneware 'Spade' form by Hans Coper, covered in a buff slip glaze with areas of blue glaze burnished to reveal matt manganese beneath, 31cm. high. (Christie's) $6,690

A 'cup and disk' stoneware form by Hans Coper, buff with dark brown disk, impressed HC seal, circa 1965. 4½in. high. (Bonhams) $4,400

A magnificent spade form by Hans Coper, the buff body with inlaid horizontal and spiraling lines, the whole surface varied in tones, circa 1972, 13¾in. high. (Bonhams) $17,433

A tall stoneware flattened tapering cylinder with spherical belly-form by Hans Coper on drum base, incised with spiral decoration, covered in a bluish-buff slip, circa 1968, 21.2cm. high. (Christie's) $12,800

An early stoneware shallow dish by Hans Coper, covered in a matt manganese glaze, the interior with carved abstract spiraling decoration through to a pitted translucent white glaze, circa 1950, 35.3cm. diam. (Christie's) $9,200

A wonderful oval cup form by Hans Coper, the upper part mottled with dark brown and deep orange, the cup mounted on a cylindrical base which rises to a point, circa 1972, 6¼in. high. (Bonhams) $27,525

A massive stoneware 'Thistle' vase, by Hans Coper, dimpled disk-shaped body with flared rim, on cylindrical foot, circa 1960, 45.6cm. high. (Christie's) $9,994

A stoneware bulbous form on a stem by Hans Coper, surmounted with a two-tone brown disk, circa 1965, 4½in. high. (Bonhams) $4,037

A handsome sack form by Hans Coper, with wide brown disk rim on circular neck, the buff body accentuated with brown texturing, circa 1974, 9⅜in. high. (Bonhams) $16,515

CREAMWARE

Creamware was developed by Josiah Wedgwood in response to the huge middle class demand for tableware which would be both durable and attractive. It was first introduced in 1761, at which time the glaze was not very resilient, and could be easily scratched. Nor could it withstand boiling water, which made it unsuitable for tea and coffee pots. By 1764, however, Wedgwood had solved all these problems. The final result was pleasing and modestly priced, and moreover was well suited to mechanical decoration.

It enjoyed immediate and lasting popularity. In 1765 Queen Charlotte commissioned a 60 piece tea service, which was so admired that Wedgwood was granted permission to call his new material Queensware, which name it has borne ever since. On the strength of such success, Wedgwood began using creamware for neo-Classical decorative items as well. Much creamware was sold without decoration or, in other cases, this was restricted to a simple border or pierced rims and lattice work. It was adaptable to all tastes, however, and lent itself to transfer printed scenes or painted decoration.

A pair of Staffordshire creamware models of birds, circa 1755, with green cresting and green, ocher blue and gray plumage, 8¹/₂in. high.
(Christie's) $143,000

A creamware teapot and cover, unusually decorated with a chintz design in polychrome printing heightened in colored enamels, 16cm.
(Phillips) $640

A pair of English creamware Dutch-decorated plates, 1775–85, each painted with 'Our Lady of Kevelaar', 9³/₄in. and 9¹⁵/₁₆in. diameter.
(Sotheby's) $1,265

A Staffordshire creamware bear-baiting group, circa 1770, the seated bear with brown muzzle and clasping a terrier to his chest, 10in. high.
(Christie's) $1,210

A Staffordshire creamware cauliflower tea-canister, circa 1765, naturalistically molded with overlapping green leaves beneath white cauliflower, 4¹/₈in. high. (Christie's) $460

A pair of Staffordshire creamware wall-pockets, circa 1765, of Whieldon type, molded with a pot of ocher and brown flowers with green trailing leaves, 9¹/₂in. high.
(Christie's) $7,700

An English creamware enameled jug, probably Leeds, dated 1771, the barrel-shaped body painted on the front with the inscription John and Martha Wheeler. 1771, 7¹/₈in. high.
(Sotheby's) $1,035

CREAMWARE

A Pratt creamware sauce boat in the form of a duck, painted in ochre, yellow, brown and green, 18.5cm. long.
(Bearne's) $1,040

A Staffordshire creamware figure of William III or the Duke of Cumberland, circa 1785, in blue cloak, green and blue armor astride a rearing brown charger, 14³/₄in. high.
(Christie's) $13,200

A Staffordshire creamware hexagonal teapot and a cover, circa 1755, with green crabstock handle and finial, 4in. high.
(Christie's) $5,500

A Staffordshire creamware toby-jug, circa 1780, of Ralph Wood type, modeled seated holding a frothing jug of ale and a beaker with a pipe between his feet, 9¹/₄in. high.
(Christie's) $1,100

A large creamware teapot and cover, probably Leeds, of oviform with reeded, double interlaced handles, 15.5cm. high.
(Phillips) $1,750

A Wedgwood creamware cylindrical mug, black printed with a design by Thomas Billinge of Liverpool showing a profile portrait of the young King George III, 6¹/₄in. high, circa 1793. $2,850

A creamware baluster coffee pot and cover with flower finial, printed in black with figures taking tea in a garden landscape, circa 1775.
(Christie's) $431

A Staffordshire creamware arbor group circa 1765, modeled as a couple in a covered arbor splashed in ocher, brown and green, 6in. high.
(Christie's) $71,500

A Staffordshire creamware model of a lion of Ralph Wood type, its mane splashed in manganese, on a pale-green mound base, circa 1785, 7cm. high. (Christie's) $800

CREAMWARE

A Staffordshire creamware teapot and cover, circa 1785, of Ralph Wood type, modeled as a brown elephant surmounted by a monkey seated in a green crenellated howdah, 11in. high. (Christie's) $28,600

A Staffordshire creamware 'Fair Hebe' jug, circa 1788, signed and dated *I. Voyez 1788*, 9¹/₂in. high. (Christie's) $1,540

A Staffordshire creamware oval two-handled reticulated basket and stand, circa 1760, of Whieldon type, 9⁵/₈in. wide. (Christie's) $6,050

An English creamware oviform jug with a loop handle, printed in black and colored with a satirical cartoon entitled *British Slavery* after James Gillray, circa 1800, 6¹/₂in. high. (Christie's S. Ken) $880

A Staffordshire creamware model of a parrot of Whieldon type covered in a bright-green glaze and with blue/gray beak, circa 1760, 16.5cm. high. (Christie's) $9,499

A Staffordshire creamware dated cider jug, printed in red with *The World in Planisphere* the reverse with *The Tythe Pig* and inscribed and dated *John Smallwood 1790*, 11in. high. (Christie's) $2,640

A creamware model of a recumbent lion, its head turned to the front, with pale-green mane and its coat splashed in brown, perhaps Yorkshire, circa 1790, 8.5cm. wide. (Christie's) $480

A Staffordshire creamware toasting cup, circa 1770, of Ralph Wood type, modeled as with the faces of Dr. Johnson and Boswell, 4in. high. (Christie's) $3,300

A Staffordshire creamware model of a swan, circa 1800, splashed in blue with brown beak and feathers, 3¹/₂in. high. (Christie's) $660

CREAMWARE

A good creamware teapot and cover, attributed to Cockpit Hill, of globular shape with crabstock handle and spout, 15cm. (Phillips) $1,395

A creamware fox head stirrup cup, with grinning expression, decorated in brown and buff glazes, 5in. long. (Spencer's) $504

A Staffordshire creamware punch-pot and cover, circa 1760, with strap handle, Buddhistic lion finial and crabstock spout, 8¹/₂in. high. (Christie's) $9,350

An English creamware enameled jug, dated 1791, the swelling body painted with two cottages with smoking chimneys, 8¹/₈in. high. (Sotheby's) $1,380

A pair of creamware copper luster curly dogs, Staffordshire, 19th century, with green decorations and copper luster highlights, 12³/₄in. high. (Christie's) $2,180

A pink luster creamware puzzle jug, printed with the word 'Reform' and flanked by bust portraits of Earl Grey, and Lord Brougham and Vaux, 17cm. (Phillips) $1,124

A Staffordshire creamware cylindrical tea-canister, circa 1765, with sprigged relief of a flower spray and mottled in green, yellow and brown glazes, 3⁵/₈in. high. (Christie's) $552

A creamware dated plate transfer printed by John Sadler with The Sailor's Return (minute rim chip at 1 o'clock), circa 1769, 24cm. diam. (Christie's London) $3,200

An English creamware wine-measuring jug, dated 1783, the pear-shaped body molded with a lady's-mask spout wearing a feather headdress, 6³/₄in. high. (Sotheby's) $2,645

CREAMWARE

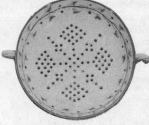

A Staffordshire creamware figure of Saint George and the Dragon, circa 1790, mounted on a green and brown spotted horse above the writhing dragon, 11¼in. high.
(Christie's) $1,150

A Staffordshire creamware four-sided teapot and cover, circa 1760, possibly by William Greatbatch, with a bust-length portrait of the King of Prussia and symbols, 5in. high.
(Christie's) $2,990

A creamware small two-handled egg poacher, circa 1774, with green leafy border, 4½in. diam. overall.
(Christie's) $403

A creamware toby jug and cover, the smiling man seated holding a jug of frothing ale, wearing dark-blue hat, his brown jacket with blue button-holes, perhaps Yorkshire, circa 1790, 25.5cm. high.
(Christie's) $1,137

A pair of Staffordshire creamware triple spill-vases of Ralph Wood type, each modeled as entwined green dolphins supporting three reed-molded vases, circa 1780, 19cm. high.
(Christie's) $1,181

A creamware bonbonnière, circa 1790, molded as a fashionable lady's head, the bottom enameled with a star with brown hair entwined with a ribbon, 3¼in. high.
(Christie's) $1,380

A Staffordshire creamware satyr mask cup, circa 1780, with loop handle splashed in brown, green and ocher, on a flaring foot, 4½in. high.
(Christie's) $368

An English creamware oval teapot and flattened cover with flower finial, painted in red and black with hearts joined by a ribbon above the motto *Love Unites Us*, circa 1765, possibly Derbyshire, 5in. high.
(Christie's) $1,193

A Staffordshire creamware cauliflower hot-milk jug and cover, circa 1765, with green foliate scroll handle, 6¼in. high.
(Christie's) $1,380

CRESTED CHINA

The greatest name in crested china was Goss but there were some 200 other makers who copied the lead set by William Henry Goss and his enterprising son Adolphus. The names of their British rivals include Arcadian, Carlton, Foley, Fords China, Grafton China, Macintyre, Melba, Nautilus, Podmore, Savoy, Shelley, Tuscan and Victoria. There were also foreign competitors who often made mistakes with British coats of arms.

Crested china boomed as a result of the enthusiasm for day trips and holidays that overtook the British public at the end of the 19th century. Trippers wanted a souvenir of their trip away from home and the perfect solution was a cheap little piece of china with the holiday town's coat of arms on it. Several subjects dominate the china manufacturers' output – the Great War – one of the more unusual items was a figure of Old Bill produced by Shelley; animals and birds; transport; memorials including the Cenotaph; statues; cartoon and comedy characters; sport and musical instruments. A cup and saucer was one of the most common items sold and, as a result today the price for such an item would be considerably less than for an Old Bill or a model of the Cenotaph. The rivals to Goss never took such fastidious care about their products as the trail blazers and their china is never as fine. However when buying crested china it is important to remember that imperfections of manufacture do not affect the price so much as subsequent damage.

Arcadian 'Jester on a spade shaped tray', 65mm. wide. $115

Arcadian 'Black boy holding pumpkin mustard pot with lid. $190

Savoy china fireplace 'Keep the home fires burning', 94mm. wide. $40

Carlton, 'Owl wearing black mortar board', 75mm. wide. $40

Willow art 'Old Curiosity Shop', 80mm. wide. $250

Carlton 'Laxey Wheel', 92mm. wide. $100

Arcadian 'Policeman holding truncheon', 106mm. high. $115

Carlton 'Trefoil Dish with five flags of the Allies'. $55

CRESTED CHINA

Carlton 'Black cat on settee', 80mm. wide. $55

Carlton 'Irishman in black hat with yellow pig', 90mm. wide. $250

Carlton Donkey inscribed 'Gee up Neddy', 110mm. wide. $70

Arcadian 'Drunkard leaning against a statue', 100mm. high. $210

Arcadian 'Black boy and girl on log', 80mm. wide. $135

Carlton 'Goose standing on a green base', 85mm. wide. $55

Carlton 'Jackie Coogan', 1920's cartoon character inkwell with lid, 73mm. wide. $80

Carlton fireplace with cauldron in the fireplace, 80mm. wide. $40

Arcadian 'Black cat in a boot', 61mm. high. $100

Arcadian 'Black cat climbing pillar box to post letter', 56mm. high. $115

Savoy china, 'Snail', 84mm. long. $55

Grafton, 'Child kneeling on beach with bucket and spade, 75mm. wide. $210

CRESTED CHINA

Gemma recumbent cow creamer, arms of Eastbourne. (Crested China Co.) $57

Grafton airfield tractor, arms of Leamington Spa. (Crested China Co.) $400

Grafton ambulance, arms of Falmouth. (Crested China Co.) $152

Arcadian black cat sailing yacht. (Crested China Co.) $200

Arcadian walking donkey. (Crested China Co.) $120

Arcadian black cat on wall with arms of Portsmouth. (Crested China Co.) $120

Arcadian milk basket. (Goss & Crested China Ltd) $30

Swan china bust of Ally Sloper. (Goss & Crested China Ltd) $60

Arcadian Black Cat radio operator. (Goss & Crested China Ltd) $150

Arcadian 'Mr. Pickwick' on horseshoe shaped ashtray base. (Crested China Co.) $152

Arcadian black boy in bath of ink, towel hanging at side, inscribed *How ink is made*, with arms of Torquay. (The Crested China Co.) $150

Carlton black cat on horseshoe dish. (Crested China Co.) $57

CROWN DEVON

The Crown Devon dynasty was founded by Simon Fielding, who in 1873 invested his savings in the Railway Pottery, Stoke on Trent, with his son Abraham as first apprentice and then partner in the Cresswell Colour Mill.

In 1878, with the Railway Pottery on the edge of bankruptcy, Abraham bought it out and increased its size fivefold by the time his father died in 1906. Abraham was in turn succeeded by his son and grandson. The trade name Crown Devon was introduced in 1913.

The factory was a major producer of items in the Art Deco style, many featuring stylized flowers and fruit set against a rich, dark background. Major ranges include the Mattajade (jade green plates with stylized floral patterns), the Mattatone (matt glazes with Cubist patterns) and Garden ware (decorated with highly colored flowers on a green, cream or yellow base). Musical novelties were also introduced and, from the 1930s, salad ware and figurines. Many figurines were the work of Kathleen Fisher, and were of an astonishing lightness and delicacy.

Throughout the succeeding decades, the factory moved with the times, continuing to adapt its products to current trends, despite a devastating fire which gutted it in 1951. It continued in business until 1982, when it became an early victim of the recession. Marks include *FIELDING*, impressed, and *SF & Co* printed with the pattern title.

FIELDING

Crown Devon ceramic dog with glass eyes, 4in. high.
(Muir Hewitt) $48

A Crown Devon coffee pot and cover painted with a geometric pattern of overlapping circles and diamonds, 19.5cm. high.
(Christie's) $117

A Crown Devon octagonal bowl with fluted rim, printed and painted in colors and gilt on a blue ground with a ferocious dragon among flowers, 23cm. diameter.
(Christie's) $240

A Crown Devon baluster vase of footed ovoid form with flaring conical neck, painted with figures in a pagoda landscape, 29cm. high.
(Christie's) $400

Crown Devon jug, 1930s, with floral decoration.
(Muir Hewitt) $48

Crown Devon lamp base with elaborate enameled oriental dragon design, 6in. high.
(Muir Hewitt) $315

CROWN DUCAL

Crown Ducal was a range manufactured in the 1930s by the A G Richardson factory in Staffordshire. It was decorated in the Art Deco style, notably by Charlotte Rhead who used the 'tube lining' technique. The result looks as if the decoration has been applied with an icing bag, as indeed it has!

A.G.R. & Co. Ltd.

Crown Ducal

Charlotte Rhead Crown Ducal Stitch pattern jug, 7in. high.
(Muir Hewitt) $112

Charlotte Rhead Crown Ducal vase in Persian rose design, 10in. high.
(Muir Hewitt) $300

Crown Ducal three handled vase with floral decoration.
(Muir Hewitt) $75

Crown Ducal wall plaque, 1930s, 12½in. diameter.
(Muir Hewitt) $120

Charlotte Rhead vase, 1930s, Crown Ducal, 8in. high.
(Muir Hewitt) $225

Charlotte Rhead vase, 1930s, Crown Ducal, 8in. high.
(Muir Hewitt) $315

Crown Ducal tea pot, 1930s, with floral design.
(Muir Hewitt) $60

Crown Ducal vase, 6in. high, 1950s.
(Muir Hewitt) $60

DAVENPORT

Davenport's Staffordshire Pottery was established in 1773 at Longport, and produced earthenware, ironstone china, and porcelain. In the 1880s, under John Davenport, many tea services were produced, with Japanese patterns. The firm was noted for its strong and durable wares, many of which were used aboard ships of the period. Porcelain plaques, decorated both in-house and by independent artists, were also made. Marks include *Davenport* painted in blue over an anchor, or, from 1850, a crown over *Davenport* and the address. The firm finally closed in 1887.

A Davenport shaped oval two-handled foot bath, printed with the 'Mosque and Fisherman' pattern.
(Christie's S. Ken) $2,700

Large Davenport kaolin ware soup tureen cover, blue and white bamboo pattern, English, mid 19th century.
(G. A. Key) $203

A pair of Davenport green-ground plates from the Royal Dessert Service made for William IV, the centers painted with a bouquet of rose, thistle, shamrock and leek, circa 1830, 25.5cm. diameter.
(Christie's) $6,400

A rare Davenport 'Drunken Sal' jug, the obese lady seated and wearing a pale salmon-pink dress with red and black markings, 31cm., 1836.
(Phillips) $2,030

A Davenport caneware wine cooler, molded in relief with a bust of Nelson, the reverse with naval trophies, 25.5cm., impressed mark.
(Phillips) $1,200

A rare pair of Davenport vases in Empire style, the ovoid bodies painted with panels of baskets overflowing with ripe fruit on marble tables, 28.5cm., circa 1820–1825.
(Phillips) $1,064

A Davenport stone china ice pail, liner and cover, with floral and bird decoration. $1,280

DE MORGAN

William Frend de Morgan (1839–1917) was an English ceramic designer, perhaps now particularly remembered for his tiles. His designs were much influenced by his friend William Morris and include, birds, fish, flowers and mythical beasts. He established his own pottery in Chelsea in 1872, producing his own tiles, and experimented with luster decoration in an attempt to reproduce the red luster of maiolica painted in Gubbio. He also designed dishes in cream earthenware decorated in red luster, and the Sunset and Moonlight suites decorated in gold, silver and copper. With Morris at Merton Abbey he continued to make tiles and dishes, and also established a factory at Fulham with Halsey Ricardo producing tiles and murals. He retired in 1905 and the factory closed in 1907.

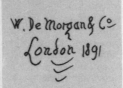

A William De Morgan eight inch tile forming part of the Fan pattern, painted with two stylised flowers.
(Phillips) $825

A William de Morgan Persian style pottery vase, Fulham period, painted by Jo Juster, 28.5cm. high.
(Phillips) $2,250

A William De Morgan two-handled vase, Merton Abbey Period, circa 1882–1888, painted with peacocks and Iznik flowers bordered with fish on a blue scale ground, 13³/₈in. high.
(Sotheby's) $6,820

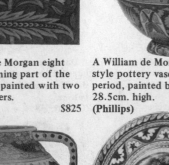

A good William de Morgan 'Persian-style' circular wall plate, painted by Charles Passenger, depicting in the sunken center, a pair of dolphins, encircled with stylized floral and scale borders, 43.5cm. diam. (Phillips) $7,837

A William de Morgan two handled baluster vase, decorated in green and purple with fruiting vines, the foot, handles and neck interior in turquoise, 27.3cm. high.
(Christie's London) $1,995

A William De Morgan ruby luster dish, painted with a scaly sea creature against a red and white ground of swirls and waves, 36cm diameter.
(Phillips) $1,736

A William de Morgan ruby luster vase, with cup neck and twin handles painted with a pelican and a crane against a background of scales, 19cm. high.
(Phillips) $2,000

An earthenware dish, possibly William de Morgan, early 20th century, painted in ruby luster with a winged dragon and a snake, 36cm. diameter. (Sotheby's) $980

A William De Morgan ruby luster vase, decorated with a young boy attacking a winged dragon, impressed *J. H. Davies*, 46.6cm. high. (Christie's) $3,000

A William de Morgan circular plate, painted with a central griffin-like creature and bordered by a frieze of birds, 22cm. diam. (Phillips) $1,193

A William de Morgan red lustre vase and cover, the white ground decorated in red, with three bands of stylized birds and beasts, with scolloped borders at rim and base, 33.6cm. high. (Christie's) $4,000

A Craven Dunhill & Co. metal mounted four tile jardiniere, each tile decorated with a design by William de Morgan, 21.2cm. high. (Christie's London) $1,120

A William de Morgan 'Persian-style' vase and cover, painted with foliate fronds in turquoise, blue and pale-green against a white ground, 36cm. high. (Phillips) $7,450

A William de Morgan red luster charger, the white ground with ruby luster decoration of a startled antelope with band of elaborate geometric patterns to rim, 29.6cm. diam. (Christie's London) $640

A William de Morgan ruby lustre twin-handled oviform vase, painted with scaly carp swimming in alternate directions, 37cm. high. (Phillips) $3,225

A William De Morgan 'Rose trellis' tile, painted with two yellow, brown and red flowers, 15.2cm. square, and three similar. (Bonhams) $517

THEODORE DECK

Theodore Deck (1823-91) was a pioneering French artist potter who worked first in Strasbourg and then in Paris, where he made ornamental earthenware which he decorated with scenes commissioned from painters. He was strongly influenced by near eastern styles, notably 16th and 17th century Persian and Isnik wares, in terms of styles and glazes. Byzantine influence is also evident in some of his work of the 1870s, where he used different colored glazes within raised outlines of the clay, sometimes with lavish gilding.

From the mid 1870s he experimented with stoneware and porcelain. Between 1887 and his death he was art director at Sèvres, where he introduced new underglaze colors and also fostered the use of stoneware for architectural use.

A Theodore Deck jardinière, painted in colors on a cream ground with birds and flowers, 41cm. diameter.
(Christie's) $620

A floral decorated vase by Theodore Deck, of baluster form with scroll handles at the neck, 44.25cm. high.
(Sotheby's) $1,445

Pair of polychrome earthenware vases by Theodore Deck, each enameled in vibrant colors with clusters of flowers, circa 1880, 24in. high.
(Sotheby's) $6,334

A small Theodore Deck bottle vase and metal stopper, late 19th century, molded in relief with Islamic style motifs under a turquoise glaze, 8½in. high.
(Sotheby's) $651

A Theodore Deck pottery jug, of globular form with cylindrical neck and loop handle, decorated with stylized Persian flowers, 20cm. high.
(Christie's) $666

A Théodore Deck earthenware vase, with short neck and everted rim, body flanked by a pair of molded mask and ring handles, 28.2cm. high.
(Christie's) $1,860

A pair of Theodore Deck footed hexagonal vases, painted in iron red and green on a celadon green ground with sprays of flowers and foliage, 33cm. high.
(Christie's) $1,000

DEDHAM

The Dedham Pottery was established in 1895, following the move of the Chelsea Keramic Art Works to Dedham Mass. under Hugh Robertson, who had succeeded his father as master potter at Chelsea. At Dedham, Robertson produced a crackle glaze on a heavy stoneware decorated with borders of bird and animal designs. Dedham Ware was made in forty eight patterns and proved very popular. Its mark is *Dedham Pottery* over a crouching rabbit.

A rare crackle ware pottery dish, by Dedham Pottery, modeled with a naked lady reclining, 4¹/₂in. long. (Christie's) $1,610

A 'lobster' crackle ware pottery breakfast plate, by Dedham Pottery, decorated in blue with two lobsters, 8¹/₂in. diameter. (Christie's) $863

Dedham Pottery oak block pitcher, unmarked, 6in. high. (Skinner) $863

Three Dedham Pottery chick pattern items, plate, exhibition sticker, blue stamp, impressed rabbit, 8½in. diameter, bowl and a child's mug, blue stamp. (Skinner) $1,725

Early 20th century Dedham pottery decorated crackle-ware vase, 7½in. high. (Skinner) $1,950

Dedham Pottery pond lily plate with scenic center, impressed rabbit, signed in center *HR,* 6in. diameter. (Skinner) $978

Dedham Pottery Stein, Massachusetts, early 20th century, rabbit pattern, impressed and ink stamped marks, 5¹/₄in. high. (Skinner Inc.) $225

A 'rabbit' pattern crackle ware pottery ashtray, by Dedham Pottery, decorated in blue in the rabbit pattern, 3⁷/₈in. diameter. (Christie's) $81

DEDHAM

An 'elephant' pattern crackle ware pottery child's mug, by Dedham Pottery, decorated in blue, 3in. high.
(Christie's) $4,025

A 'Crab' crackle ware pottery serving platter, by Dedham Pottery, decorated in blue with a single large crab and a bit of seaweed, 17⁵/₈in. long.
(Christie's) $3,220

Dedham Pottery Night and Morning pitcher, blue stamp, 4¾in. high.
(Skinner) $230

A 'lion' pattern crackle ware pottery dinner plate, by Dedham Pottery, the border decorated in blue in the tapestry lion pattern, 10¹/₈in. diameter.
(Christie's) $1,265

A 'rabbit' pattern crackle ware pottery No. 3 covered sugar bowl, by Dedham Pottery, the octagonal body molded with two handles, 6¹/₄in. high including cover.
(Christie's) $748

A crackle ware pottery dinner plate, by Dedham Pottery, the center painted in blue with a white terrier posed in a landscape, 9³/₄in. diameter.
(Christie's) $1,035

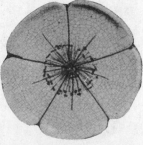

A 'rabbit' pattern crackle ware pottery covered egg cup, by Dedham Pottery, egg-shaped on shallow dish base, 4¹/₄in. high.
(Christie's) $1,265

A crackle ware pottery coaster, by Dedham Pottery, the small lobed dish painted to resemble a wild rose blossom, 3¹/₂in. diameter.
(Christie's) $173

Dedham Pottery experimental vase, Massachusetts, late 19th/ early 20th century, executed by Hugh C. Robertson, 6in. high.
(Skinner Inc.) $350

A rare 'elephant' crackle ware pottery paperweight, by Dedham Pottery, modeled as an elephant, painted with features in blue, 4in. high.
(Christie's) $6,670

A 'rabbit' pattern crackle ware pottery No. 1 creamer and No. 1 covered sugar, by Dedham Pottery, decorated in blue in the rabbit pattern, creamer 3¹/₂in. high.
(Christie's) $863

A rare crackle ware pottery ashtray, by Dedham Pottery, signed by Charles Davenport, modeled as the figure of a little boy urinating, 4⁷/₈in. high.
(Christie's) $920

A rare crackle ware pottery dinner plate, by Dedham Pottery, the blue border design of turtles alternating with clover, 10in. diameter.
(Christie's) $4,140

Dedham Pottery day/night pitcher, early 20th century, blue decoration on white craquelure ground, 5in. high.
(Skinner Inc.) $400

A 'tiger lily' crackle ware pottery bread and butter plate, by Dedham Pottery, the center decorated with white lilies against blue, 6in. diameter.
(Christie's) $1,610

Dedham Pottery mushroom pattern pitcher, blue stamp, impressed rabbit, 4¼in. high.
(Skinner) $1,150

A rare crackle ware pottery breakfast plate, by Dedham Pottery, the raised border decorated in blue with long-beaked ibis birds, 9in. diameter.
(Christie's) $1,265

A 'rabbit' pattern crackle ware pottery teapot, by Dedham Pottery, decorated in blue in the rabbit pattern, 5¹/₂in. high.
(Christie's) $1,380

DELFT

When Chinese porcelain arrived in the West, Europe was literally dazzled. Nothing of such beauty and brilliance had ever been manufactured there, and the indigenous pottery industries now had to compete with the flood of imports. Majolica had been made in small workshops throughout Holland by potters who were experienced yet open to new techniques. A result of this was delft, a decorated, tin-glazed earthenware, known elsewhere as faience. It first appeared in the early 17th century and the next 120 years were to see the steady development of both technique and quality. Majolica had been mainly multicolored, but delft was nearly all blue and white, imitating Chinese porcelain. Decoration too at first followed Chinese traditions, but later pieces saw innovative themes, such as the peacock jar, with a motif of two peacocks facing a central basket.

The finest period lasted until about 1730, when the seduction of enamel colors and the prettiness of porcelain began to sap the vitality of the medium.

A delft model of a cat, modeled seated, a mouse caught in its jaws, 19th century, 8½in. high. (Christie's) $783

A Delft oviform tobacco jar named for *Tabac d'Ollande* within an elaborate rocaille-scroll border, 18th century, 7½in. high. (Christie's) $599

A Southwark delftware white posset pot and cover, 1655–75, the compressed spherical body dimpled and molded with bosses, 6⅛in. high. (Sotheby's) $28,750

A tin-glazed earthenware Documentary triangular salt, Southwark, dated *1674*, painted on a white ground in shades of blue, green , turquoise and yellow, 5¾in. high. (Christie's) $16,100

A Brislington delft portrait charger boldly painted in blue, manganese and yellow with a portrait of a gentleman, probably King William III, 34cm. (Phillips) $6,916

A delft plaque, painted in blue, green, brown and ocher with a chinoiserie figure standing, holding a bunch of flowers, 24cm. high. (Spencer's) $322

A delft charger, the central dished circular section painted in underglaze blue with a European couple in a landscape, 34.5cm. diameter. (Spencer's) $314

DELFT, BRISTOL

A Bristol delft blue-dash Adam and Eve charger, circa 1670, both figures holding yellow fig leaves, 13in. diameter.
(Christie's) $4,950

A Bristol delft blue and white two-handled double-lipped sauceboat, circa 1760, decorated with stylized flowering branches, 8⁷/₈in. wide.
(Christie's) $2,860

A Bristol delft blue and white cylindrical mug with broad strap handle, circa 1730, 12cm. high. $1,600

A Bristol delft blue and white dated miniature shoe, the date 1721 beneath the sole (crack to front, slight chips), 10cm. long.
(Christie's) $2,000

A Bristol campana shaped vase with double rope twist handles and frilled rim, circa 1750, 6¾in. high. $3,850

A Bristol delftware polychrome Queen Anne portrait charger, circa 1710, the monarch wearing a blue and yellow crown and dress, holding a yellow scepter and orb, 13³/₈in. diameter.
(Sotheby's) $12,650

A Bristol delft plate, circa 1740, decorated with a manganese sponged plant in a blue pot, 8³/₄in. diameter.
(Christie's) $495

A Bristol polychrome posset pot and cover decorated in the Chinese style with flowers in red, blue and green, circa 1710-30, 9in. high. $5,450

A Bristol delft blue and white octagonal plate, circa 1770, decorated with a couple taking tea in a garden within a circular reserve, 8¹/₂in. diameter.
(Christie's) $3,850

DELFT, DUTCH

A Dutch delft figure of a horse, mid 18th century, cold-decorated with an iron-red muzzle, brown mane and tail, gold hooves, 8³/₄in. high. (Sotheby's) $1,380

A pair of fine Dutch delft polychrome figures of a lady and gentleman, on green washed bases with chamfered corners, 21cm. high. (Phillips) $8,500

A well-painted Dutch delft quintal vase with shield-shaped body painted in blue within a black outline, 21.5cm. (Phillips) $1,989

A fine and interesting Dutch delft polychrome plaque, of shield shape, spiritedly painted with a Chinese man standing upright on a galloping horse, in Kakiemon style, 33.5cm. (Phillips) $4,185

A pair of rare Dutch poly-chrome delft vases and covers, painted in blue with stags and does within yellow bordered panels, 32.5cm. (Phillips London) $3,200

A Dutch delft blue and white barber's bowl, circa 1780, boldly painted in the center with flowers and a stylized rock by a garden fence, 9¹/₁₆in. diameter. (Sotheby's) $690

A Dutch delft ovoid jar, painted after a Japanese Arita original with figures in a highly stylized landscape with willow and banana trees, 31cm. (Phillips) $1,705

A pair of Dutch delft doré cylindrical two-handled jardinières, circa 1710, with shell handles enriched in iron-red, each side painted in petit feu colors, with ladies playing go, 9¹/₂in. wide. (Christie's) $21,850

A Dutch blue and white delft cabinet in the form of a miniature armoire, the sides and doors painted with figures in gardens, 44cm. high. (Bearne's) $954

DELFT, DUTCH

One of a pair of Dutch Delft leaf dishes, blue VH/3 marks probably for Hendrick van Hoorn at the Three Golden Ash Barrels, circa 1765, 21cm. wide. **$4,800**

A Dutch delft model of a cow, the animal painted in colors with garlands of flowers, yellow horns and blue features, circa 1750, 22cm. wide. (Christie's London) **$1,350**

A Dutch delft royal portrait plate, painted in blue with a bust of King William III wearing a crown, flanked by the initials *K.W.*, diameter $8^{1}/_{2}$in., circa 1689. (Bonhams) **$1,280**

A Dutch delft figure of Harlequin standing holding a blue hat, wearing a suit enriched with blue, yellow green and iron-red lozenges and dots, circa 1720, 23cm. high. (Christie's London) **$4,500**

A pair of Dutch delft polychrome hounds, their coats splashed in manganese with their tails curled over their flanks and their ears flapping behind their heads, mid-18th century, 21cm. high. (Christie's) **$8,500**

One of a pair of Dutch delft tobacco jars, painted in blue with a negro with feathered head-dress and skirt, smoking a pipe, 26cm., 15th century. (Lawrence Fine Art) (Two) **$5,750**

A Dutch delft lobed dish painted in yellow, blue and green, the center with a man on horseback flanked by trees, circa 1700, 34.5cm. diameter. (Christie's) **$680**

Dutch delft tile picture of a cat, late 18th century, mounted in a wood frame, $12^{1}/_{2}$ x $17^{1}/_{2}$in. (Skinner Inc.) **$2,400**

A Dutch delft blue and white fluted dish, circa 1690, the center with a half portrait of William of Orange in crown and ermine robes, $9^{5}/_{8}$in. diameter. (Christie's) **$4,400**

139

DELFT, ENGLISH

Delft blue and white bulb bowl, England, circa 1750, 8½in. diameter.
(Skinner Inc.) $1,045

An interesting early English delft mustard pot, possibly Brislington, painted with a Chinese figure amidst trees, shrubs and rocks, 7.5cm. high.
(Phillips) $2,000

A very rare English delft flower holder, of tapering square shape, the sides painted in blue with leafy sprays, 10.8cm. wide.
(Phillips) $2,790

An English delft polychrome small flower-tub of flared square section, the sides painted in blue and iron-red with a trailing flower-spray, circa 1700, London or Bristol, 9cm. high.
(Christie's) $2,383

An English delft blue and white drinking vessel, modeled as a spurred boot, inscribed beneath the flared rim *OH. MY HEAD* above a wide blue band, Southwark, circa 1650, 17.5cm. high.
(Christie's) $21,659

An English delft dated octagonal powdered manganese-ground plate painted in blue with a central erotic scene of a lady and a gentleman in an interior, inscribed *I:G 1739*, probably Bristol, 8in. wide.
(Christie's) $7,474

One of a pair of attractive English delft 'bird' plates, boldly painted in the centers with a yellow and blue crane-like bird with red head, 22.5cm.
(Phillips)(Two) $1,920

A rare and important English delft wine bottle, inscribed in blue with the crowned monogram of Charles 1st, *CR, 1644, Wh. WINE*, 15.5cm. high.
(Phillips) $59,500

A English delft plate, painted in blue with a half portrait of George I wearing coronation robes and crown, diameter 8¾in., circa 1714.
(Bonhams) $19,200

DELFT, ENGLISH

Delft blue and white barber bowl, England or Continental, 13¼in. diameter. (Skinner Inc.) **$825**

A very rare and early English delft coffee cup or 'Capuchine', of bell shape with a turned central groove and a rolled loop handle, 6.2cm. (Phillips) **$3,100**

Delft blue and white bowl, England, circa 1760, inscribed in center *One Bowl More & Then* 10½in. diameter. (Skinner Inc.) **$1,760**

An English delft blue and white royal portrait plate, circa 1690, the centre with half-length portraits of William and Mary in crowns and court robes, 8⅛in. diameter. (Christie's) **$3,300**

A very unusual pair of English delft vases of baluster shape with spreading bases, painted in blue with massive stylized flowerheads. (Phillips) **$3,255**

An 18th century English delft small charger, with Fazackerly type decoration, the central circular panel painted with flowers and leaves, 31cm. diameter. (Spencer's) **$450**

An English delft blue dash polychrome 'Adam and Eve' charger, painted with the two nude figures flanking the green tree, 33.5cm. (Phillips) **$2,295**

An English delft blue and white mug, painted in a bright palette with flowering water-lily beside bamboo, circa 1750, perhaps London, 16.5cm. high. (Christie's) **$3,387**

An English delft farmhouse plate painted in yellow, red and blue with a cockerel amongst sponged manganese trees, blue line rim, 21cm. diameter. (Phillips) **$1,530**

DELFT, LAMBETH

A Lambeth delft dated armorial caudle-cup, dated *1657*, decorated with the arms of the Bakers' Company beneath the initials *M/AR*.
(Christie's) $71,500

A pair of Lambeth delft cups, circa 1700, decorated in iron-red, blue, green and ocher with a dancing Chinaman.
(Christie's) $4,180

A Lambeth delft blue and white bowl, circa 1740, with stylized floral decoration beneath a band of blue stylized leaves, 9in. diameter.
(Christie's) $2,860

A Lambeth delft blue-dash portrait charger, circa 1640, painted with Charles I in blue **armor astride a manganese rearing war horse**, 16¼in. diameter.
(Christie's) $99,000

A Lambeth delft blue and white posset-pot and cover, circa 1690, decorated in the 'Transitional' style with Chinamen seated in landscapes, 6¾in. high.
(Christie's) $6,600

A Lambeth delft charger, painted in green, orange, red and blue with a head and shoulder portrait of King George I, diameter 13in., circa 1714.
(Bonhams) $28,000

A Lambeth delft 'Persian blue' posset pot, encircled with white painted landscapes and seated Chinamen, 11cm. high, late 17th century.
(Bearne's) $14,994

A Lambeth delft salt, circa 1680, modeled as a seated boy with yellow hair, blue robe, yellow shirt, stockings and buckles holding an oval basin in his lap, 7¾in. high.
(Christie's) $165,000

A Lambeth delft plate, commemorating the Union of England and Scotland in 1707, with painted polychrome decoration, diameter 8¾in.
(Bonhams) $4,160

CHINA

A rare English delft coffee cup, possibly Liverpool, with an everted rim and a blue-dash loop handle, 5.5cm.
(Phillips) $1,500

A Liverpool delft blue and white slender baluster vase, circa 1750, 14½in. high.
$2,500

A delft blue and white flower brick, probably Liverpool, the rectangular top pierced with eight holes, 12.5cm. wide, circa 1760.
(Bearne's) $773

A massive Liverpool delft punch-bowl, circa 1760, the interior decorated in colors with a ship flying the Union Jack within a Fitzhugh-type border, 20in. diameter.
(Christie's) $10,450

A pair of Liverpool delft wall-pockets, circa 1770, modeled as fish in blue and green with iron-red spines, 8in. high.
(Christie's) $8,800

A Liverpool delft plate, circa 1760, of Fazackerly type decorated in colors with a yellow and blue bird, 9in. diameter.
(Christie's) $1,650

Liverpool delft wall-pocket of spiral form, lightly molded and painted in a Fazackerly palette with a bird perched on a flowering branch, circa 1760, 20.5cm. long.
(Christie's) $1,450

A Liverpool delft polychrome dish sketchily painted with a swan on a lake flanked by a willow tree, circa 1760, 33cm. diam. (Christie's London)
$1,500

An inscribed Liverpool delft puzzle jug, the rim with three spouts and hollow handle, circa 1750, 8in. high.
$3,700

A London delft blue and white two-handled beaker of flared form, painted with stylized flowers, circa 1720, 7cm. high. (Christie's) $545

An exceptional delft bottle, probably London, of rare mallet shape, painted in blue with a seated Chinese lady playing a dulcimer, 26cm. high. (Phillips) $5,550

An English delft polychrome miniature mug, painted in iron-red, blue and green with stylized shrubs and rockwork, London or Bristol, circa 1730, 5cm. high. (Christie's) $2,800

A London delft blue-dash royal equestrian portrait charger painted with King William III in ermine-edged blue robes and holding a scepter, riding a prancing stallion, circa 1690, 35.5cm. diameter. (Christie's) $8,170

A London delftware white salt, probably Southwark, circa 1675, the circular top with a hemispherical well and flat rim supporting three 'ram's-horn' scrolls, 4$^7/_8$in. high. (Sotheby's) $19,550

A London delftware blue and white posset pot and cover, 1670–90, the cylindrical body painted in a slightly runny blue with three Chinamen seated amidst shrubbery in a rocky landscape, 6$^{15}/_{16}$in. high. (Sotheby's) $7,475

A London delft blue and white royal portrait shallow circular dish painted with bust portraits of King William III and Queen Mary, circa 1690, 25cm. diameter. (Christie's) $4,726

A very rare and interesting London delft pierced basket, attributed to Vauxhall, of circular shape supported on three bun feet, 26cm. (Phillips London) $7,600

A London delftware polychrome plate, circa 1760, painted with a Chinaman seated amidst shrubbery, 9in. diameter. (Sotheby's) $920

A rare London delftware blue and white cup, 1655–75, painted around the ovoid body with the inscription *DRINCK ᵛ·ᵖ YOVR · DRINK · AND · SE · MY · CO[N]E*, 2³/₈in. high.
(Sotheby's)   **$14,950**

A London (Southwark) delft dated blue and white mug, with strap handle and molded with five bands of raised dimple ornament, 1653, 19cm. high.
(Christie's)   **$51,693**

A London delftware polychrome posset pot, 1680–1700, the cylindrical body painted in blue and manganese on the front with two chinoiserie figures, 5¹/₈in. high.
(Sotheby's)   **$1,725**

A rare early London delft baluster vase with slightly spreading foot, painted in blue with bold plant motifs and a butterfly, 29cm.
(Phillips)   **$800**

A pair of tin-glazed earthenware Documentary shoes, probably London, dated *1695*, each court shoe with a bow at the instep, 4⁷/₈in. long.
(Christie's)   **$8,625**

A London delftware blue and white octagonal pill slab, mid 18th century, painted with the arms and rhinoceros crest of the Worshipful Society of Apothecaries above a blue-ground scroll-edged cartouche, 12¹/₄ x 10¹/₄in.
(Sotheby's)   **$3,737**

A London delft plate, painted in manganese and blue, with a half portrait of King George III, diameter 9in. (chips to rim).
(Bonhams)   **$25,000**

A delft blue and white oval Royal portrait plaque of Queen Anne, blue E mark to the reverse, probably London, circa 1705, 23cm. high.
(Christie's)   **$19,000**

A London delft blue dash royal equestrian charger, painted with a monarch wearing a crown, and holding a baton, diameter 13¹/₂in., circa 1690.
(Bonhams)   **$29,000**

DELLA ROBBIA

The Della Robbia pottery was established in 1894 at Birkenhead by H. Rathbone and the sculptor, Conrad Dressler. It produced vases, bottles, jars, plates and dishes with sgraffito decoration and sometimes elaborate modeled relief with a strong Italian maiolica influence. The factory closed in 1901, but reopened and continued until 1906. Their mark consists of *Della Robbia* with a ship device and the decorator's initials.

A Della Robbia jardiniere, bulbous shape with incised and slip decoration of a scrolling foliate band between foliate rim and foot borders, 25.6cm. high. $1,000

A Della Robbia vase of swollen cylindrical shape with flaring cylindrical neck, incised Della Robbia mark and decorators' monogram, 22.2cm. high. (Christie's) $240

A Della Robbia two-handled vase, of bulbous cylindrical form with knopped neck, with incised Della Robbia mark and decorator's signature Enid, 34.8cm. high. (Christie's) $1,200

A Della Robbia twin-handled vase, decorated by Charles Collis, with eight circular medallions, each with a sea-creature whose long tail curls round on itself, 35.8cm. high. (Christie's) $1,120

A Della Robbia vase decorated by Charles Collis, with an incised frieze of running hounds against a background suggesting grassy slopes with trees, 32.5cm. high. (Christie's) $960

A Della Robbia twin-handled vase decorated by Liz Wilkins, with incised and slip decoration of daffodils framed within leafy border, 40.5cm. high. (Christie's) $886

A Della Robbia dish, with incised and slip decoration of a sea sprite riding a fish, covered with polychrome glaze, dated 1895, 26.2cm. diam. (Christie's) $640

A Della Robbia twin-handled terracotta vase by John Shirley, decorated on both sides with confronted peacocks, dated *1898*, 41.5cm. high. (Christie's) $1,421

DELLA ROBBIA

A Della Robbia bottle vase, designed by Charles Collis, with piped slip decoration of peaches and leaves covered in pink and turquoise glazes, 33.5cm. high. (Christie's) $560

A Della Robbia terracotta vase, incised with stylized flowers and foliage painted in brown, green and yellow, dated 1896, 23cm. high. (Christie's) $251

A Della Robbia two-handled vase, decorated by Annie Smith, of bulbous cylindrical form with knopped neck, dated 1895, 37.6cm. high. (Christie's) $400

A Della Robbia vase, with incised and slip decoration of two friezes of equestrian and Ancient Greek figures, 18.4cm. high. (Christie's) $320

A Della Robbia wall charger, the base incised DR with a sailing ship and artist's monogram, 47.5cm. diam. (Christie's) $640

A Della Robbia pottery vase, with marks of Chas. Collis, potter and sgraffito artist and G. Russell, Paintress, circa 1903/06, 11in. high. $320

A large Della Robbia two-handled bottle-vase and cover, decoration by Ruth Bare, date 1924, 53cm. high. (Christie's) $640

A Della Robbia twin-handled vase decorated by Charles Collis, with a broad decorative frieze of stylized Tudor Roses, 31.6cm. high. $1,120

A Della Robbia pottery vase by Roseville Pottery, signed with Rozane Ware seal, circa 1906, 8¼in. high. (Skinner) $1,000

DERBY

Porcelain making in Derby commenced around the mid 18th century and has continued there ever since. During the early period, from 1750 onwards, production concentrated mainly on figures, with the result that, in contrast to most other factories of the period, comparatively few 'useful' wares were made. Emphasis from the beginning was on decoration, which was always very fine, even if some pieces of the pre–1760 period appear rather primitive and thickly potted. When more functional pieces were produced these still had decorative themes, with openwork baskets, pot pourris and frill vases featuring largely in the output. Fine tea and coffee wares were often painted with Chinese figure subjects.

William Duesbury, the London porcelain painter, became a key figure from 1756. He bought the Chelsea factory in 1770 and finally moved to Derby in 1784, where he was succeeded by his son, William II, in 1786. By the 1770s a really perfect porcelain body was being produced at Derby, and the employment of superb landscape and flower painters as decorators ensured that the finished product was of a quality second to none. In 1811 the factory was purchased by Robert Bloor, and production continued until 1848. While the quality of the body declined somewhat during this period, that of decoration remained high, and the factory continued to specialise in Imari and Japanese styles. From 1848 a new factory was opened in King Street, Derby, which continued till 1935 and specialised in copies of earlier Derby pieces. A further factory opened in 1876, called Derby Crown Porcelain Co.

A pair of Derby figures of a boy with a Macaroni dog and a girl with a cat, on pierced scrolling bases, early 19th century, 6^{1}/$_4$in. high.
(Christie's) $1,393

A Derby coffee can, painted by Richard Askew, with a female figure, a sketch in her hand, seated by a classical style tomb, 6cm. high, 1794-98.
(Phillips) $3,700

A pair of Derby Crown Porcelain Co. vases and covers, the pale creamy-yellow ground decorated in gilding and silver with bamboo and other leafy branches, 40.5cm., date code for 1888.
(Phillips) $608

Derby 'Japan' pattern plate, third quarter 18th century, centrally painted with stylized floral and foliate forms in orange and dark-blue, 8^{1}/$_4$in. diameter.
(Butterfield & Butterfield) $1,000

A pair of impressive Derby ice pails and covers painted possibly by Robert Brewer, 24.1cm.
(Phillips) $3,040

Derby porcelain chocolate mug and cover, decorated in Imari style enamels, red painted mark, circa 1825, 4^{1}/$_2$in. high.
(G. A. Key) $340

DERBY

A Derby 'Dolphin Ewer' creamboat molded as a rococo shell design with a high scroll handle and entwined dolphins below the lip, 8cm. high.
(Phillips) $403

A pair of Derby candlestick figures of seated putto in loosely draped robes and crowned with flowers, circa 1760, 7in. high.
(Christie's S. Ken) $600

A Derby coffee cup, probably painted by William Billingsley, with roses within a gilt edged rectangular and circular-shaped panels, 6.8cm. high, circa 1790.
(Phillips) $1,550

A pair of Derby blue-ground two-handled vases and covers (Lebes Gamikos), circa 1770, painted front and back en grisaille with a dancing nymph, 9³/₄in. high.
(Christie's) $5,520

A Derby trout's head stirrup-cup naturally modeled and colored, the rim reserved and inscribed in gilt *THE ANGLER'S DELIGHT*, circa 1800, 10.5cm. high.
(Christie's) $1,969

A pair of Derby campana-shaped vases, the two gilt handles with satyrs' mask terminals, one vase painted with a bird among a display of flowers, the other with flowers, circa 1810, 17¹/₂in. high.
(Christie's) $3,281

A Derby coffee can and saucer, the can probably painted by George Complin, with a finch perched on a still life of fruit, 7.5cm. high, 1789-95.
(Phillips) $28,200

A pair of large Derby vases of rare elongated campana shape, with twin scroll molded handles painted with a bright Japan pattern, 34.5cm.
(Phillips) $2,170

Derby cream jug and saucer, third quarter 18th century, painted in rose camaieu, 2⁷/₈in. high.
(Butterfield & Butterfield) $800

DERBY

An attractive early Derby bell-shaped mug, painted with a bouquet of colored flowers and scattered sprigs, the rim edged in brown, 11cm.
(Phillips) $1,450

A pair of Derby groups, both of a cow with calf in front of a flowering bocage background, 16cm. high. (Phillips)
$760

A fine Stevenson & Hancock Derby plate, painted by W. Mosley, signed, with tulips, pink roses and other summer flowers, 8³/₄in. diameter.
(Neales) $631

A pair of Derby biscuit figures of a shepherd and his companion, probably modeled by J.J. Spangler, 24.5cm. and 26.5cm. high.
(Phillips) $2,720

A boldly painted Derby ice pail of 'U' shape with double scroll handles outlined in gilding, painted on both sides with a central exotic bird, 24cm. high.
(Phillips) $1,750

Two Derby figures emblematic of Europe and America, one in crown and flowing robes, the other dressed in colored feathers and carrying a quiver of arrows, 24cm.
(Phillips) $2,550

A Derby figure group of a gallant and his companion walking with their arms entwined, he in a pink jacket, she with a lacy mob cap, 16.5cm.
(Phillips) $2,160

A magnificent pair of Derby campana-shaped vases, probably painted by W. 'Quaker' Pegg, with a profusion of flowers, 33.3cm.
(Phillips) $6,902

A Derby figure of a reaper in a black hat, turquoise jacket and yellow apron with a scythe on his shoulder, circa 1760, 11¹/₄in. high.
(Christie's S. Ken) $760

DERBY

A Derby coffee pot and cover, painted in colors with flower sprays and scattered sprigs, 23cm.
(Phillips) $1,040

A Derby butter tub and cover, painted in colors with birds in branches and scattered butterflies and insects, 13.5cm. wide.
(Phillips) $1,275

A rare and early white Derby model of a pug dog, scratching its left ear with its hind leg, 9.5cm.
(Phillips) $1,440

A Derby group of Europa and the Bull and Leda and the Swan, painted in colors and gilt, 11¼in. high, circa 1765.
(Christie's) $2,547

A Derby cylindrical tankard painted with a landscape in the manner of George Robertson with a figure before a cottage by a stream titled to the base *Near Glasgow*, 5in. high.
(Christie's) $1,080

A pair of Derby bocage candlestick figures of Italian farmers modeled as a lady and gentleman, standing, each holding chickens, wearing 18th century dress, circa 1765.
(Christie's) $1,188

A Derby porcelain plate, the center painted with a castle by a lake within a blue border, inscribed *View in Wales*, 23cm.
(Bearne's) $320

A Derby baluster jug, painted by Richard Dodson, 17cm. high, crown, crossed batons and D mark in red. (Phillips)
                                     $2,550

A fine Derby dessert plate, painted with a border of roses and flower garlands, the center painted in puce with a Cupid, by Richard Askew, 21cm.
(Phillips) $1,129

DERBY, BLOOR

Robert Bloor began his career as a clerk to William Duesbury, and went on to become owner of the Derby porcelain factory until the onset of his insanity in 1826. Unfortunately the period was characterised by the production of much poor quality, transfer-printed bone china, decorated often in the Japanese style. Thomas Steele, Moses Webster and George Robertson were the principal painters of the period.

A Derby miniature teapot and cover of compressed form with a scrolling handle, applied with flowers on a green ground, iron-red mark, Robt. Bloor, 4¹/₈in. high, circa 1830.
(Christie's) $451

Bloor Derby porcelain sauce tureen and cover, Japan polychrome pattern with gilt work, circa 1820. (G. A. Key) $320

A Derby shoe-black group, modeled as a gallant, his shoes being polished by a maid, incised No. 81, Robert Bloor & Co., circa 1830, 18.5cm. high.
(Christie's) $1,120

A pair of Derby Mansion House dwarfs, wearing brightly colored striped and flowered clothes, Robt. Bloor & Co., circa 1830, 17.5 and 17cm. high. (Christie's) $3,200

A Bloor Derby porcelain jug, richly gilded with feathered scrolls and anthemion, possibly by Thomas Steel, 6¹/₄in. high, circa 1820.
(Tennants) $1,004

A pair of Bloor Derby figures modeled as 'Toper' and companion, typically modeled standing, 11cm. high, 19th century.
(Christie's) $755

A Bloor Derby jar with foliate handles, applied with a panel of flowers, together with a pair of similar flower encrusted vases.
(Bearne's) $1,600

A pair of colorful Bloor Derby figures, each seated, he sitting cross legged reading a book, she sewing, 15cm. high.
(Bearne's) $864

DERBY, DUESBURY

William Duesbury (1725-86) was a ceramic painter and entrepreneur who held controlling interests in the factories at Bow (1763), Chelsea (1770-84) and Derby (1756-86), where he was succeeded by his son William.

From the 1770s Derby specialized in making figures and fine cabinet ware. They employed fine flower and landscape painters, of whom William Billingsley was one.

Two Derby figures of John Wilkes and General Conway, Wm. Duesbury & Co., circa 1765. (Christie's) $2,250

A Derby baluster coffee pot and cover, painted with scattered cornflowers between gilt line rims, Wm. Duesbury & Co., circa 1785, 24.5cm. high. (Christie's) $960

A Duesbury & Kean Derby porcelain porter mug of cylindrical form, with 'S' shape handle, richly gilded with scrolls and anthemion, 4½in. high, circa 1810. (Tennants) $1,620

A pair of Derby turquoise-ground two-handled vases, covers and plinths, the oviform bodies painted in the manner of Richard Askew with putti at play with a dolphin, Wm. Duesbury & Co., circa 1775, 34cm. high. $5,450

A Derby (Wm. Duesbury II) botanical plate painted to the center with a spray of Blue Navel wort., possibly by William Billingsley, circa 1793, 9in. diameter. (Christie's) $661

A pair of Derby figures of a sportsman and companion holding guns and with satchels slung from their shoulders, Wm. Duesbury & Co., circa 1770, about 16cm. high. (Christie's) $4,935

A pair of Derby arbor musicians, he playing the bagpipes and his companion the mandolin, Wm. Duesbury & Co., circa 1775, 35.5cm. high. (Christie's) $10,400

A pair of Derby figures of blackamoor dancers, each holding a posy of flowers, he with his left hand on his hip, his companion holding out the edge of her cape, Wm. Duesbury & Co., circa 1758, 22cm. high. (Christie's) $3,741

DERBY, ROYAL CROWN

A further Derby factory, the Derby Crown Porcelain Co. had been established in Derby in 1876, and it continued after 1896 as the Royal Crown Derby Co. They specialized in the use of raised gold and strong ground colours.

It is still in existence today as part of the Doulton Group.

A jeweled and gilt Royal Crown Derby vase and cover by Desire Leroy, signed, of oval shape with double scroll handles, 11cm. high, date code for 1901. (Phillips) $4,838

A fine Royal Crown Derby dessert dish, the center painted by Albert Gregory, 22.3cm. diameter, date code for 1905. (Bearne's) $1,341

A Royal Crown Derby jeweled vase and cover painted by Albert Gregory, with pearl bordered panels of flowers and swags, 34.5cm., date code for 1911.
(Phillips) $7,740

A pair of Royal Crown Derby candlesticks, each baluster stem and candle sconce set on a shaped rectangular base moulded with dolphins, 1979, 26.5cm. high. (Bearne's) $680

A Royal Crown Derby two-handled vase and cover painted by Cuthbert Gresley, of campana form, painted with trailing blooms suspending swags of flowers, date codes for 1906, 22½cm. high.
(Christie's) $1,288

Royal Crown Derby 'Billy' Dean, flattened ovoid vase, painted with fishing smacks within a raised gilt scroll cartouche, date code for 1883, 3³/₄in. high.
(Bonhams) $480

A Royal Crown Derby dark blue ground plate painted by Edwin Trowell with a street scene in Bakewell, Derbyshire, 22.9cm. diam.
(Christie's) $1,460

A Royal Crown Derby campana shaped vase painted by William Mosley, signed, with vases and festoons of flowers in colors, 26.5cm., date code for 1903.
(Phillips) $3,064

DERUTA

The pottery industry in Deruta, Umbria, dates from the late 15th century. At that time wares in the usual high temperature colors were produced, together with some with metallic luster decoration. Some, too, were very distinctive in that, in order to achieve a 'near-flesh' tint, the enamel was scraped away to reveal the pinkish clay body, to which a clear lead glaze was then added.

Early 16th century Deruta luster is brassy yellow outlined in soft blue, often showing a nacreous iridescence. Later wares have a deeper tone, sometimes approaching olive green.

Large plates predominate as a form, with tin glaze on the front only and a colorless lead glaze on the underside. Some dishes and bowls with raised decoration were made using molds. Many of these feature a raised central boss, perhaps to fit the base of a matching ewer.

Reproductions of Deruta wares were made in the 19th century, notably by Ulysse Cantagalli in Florence. Most of these are marked with a blue cockerel.

A Deruta maiolica wet-drug jar painted in colors with a plain banner on a ground of grotteschi and foliage, 8¼in. high.
(Christie's) $1,362

A lustred armorial piatto da pompa, Deruta, circa 1520, lustered in blue and gold on a cream ground, the well with a Greek Sphinx with bared breasts supporting a stemma, 16⅝in. diameter.
(Christie's) $63,000

A Deruta blue and gold lustered dish, the center painted with a winged mythical beast with the naked torso of a woman and the lower part of a hoofed monster with a divided tail, circa 1525, 43cm. diameter.
(Christie's) $55,132

A large albarello, Deruta, dated 1501, painted in strong ocher, yellow, blues, greens and manganese on a cream ground, the front labeled for *Seme.Comvn*ᵍ below a female grotesque and above the head of a blackamoor, 12¾in. high.
(Christie's) $96,000

A Deruta figural salt, the bowl supported by four three footed winged caryatids on a square pedestal with four claw feet, early 17th century, 15cm. high.
(Christie's) $3,200

A Deruta documentary oviform drug jar with two serpentine handles, dated 1707, 32cm. wide.
(Christie's) $1,280

A Deruta Armorial dish painted in the center with a shield with a wide band in ocher on a dark blue ground, 38cm.
(Phillips) $6,175

DOCCIA

The Doccia porcelain factory, which flourishes today, was established in 1735 by Carlo Ginori. He produced a hard gray porcelain which was at first inferior to the output from Germany factories of the time, the wares being heavily potted, with spouts in the form of snakes and high domed lids. Many pieces were painted in underglaze blue, their grayish tone suggesting that they were fired at excessive temperatures.

From 1757 to 1791 Lorenzo Ginori was running the factory and introduced many improved materials and shapes, and a fine white hard-paste product was now being manufactured. In the early 19th century, the body included kaolin, and some fine egg-shell pieces, often decorated in blue and gold chinoiserie, were produced.

As well as tablewares, plaques and vases were produced from the beginning, which were finely modeled, the vases often decorated with full relief figures overpainted in the full enamel palette with gilding.

Figures were made in a hard gray paste with an unevenly applied glaze which often shows fine cracks. Early examples were mostly based on the figures of the Commedia dell'Arte, and are usually set on a simple square base, painted to suggest marble.

After about 1780, many were left white and these are usually arranged round a tree on a hollow rock-like base. These show the true spirit of the Baroque.

The factory mark, from the late 18th century, comprised a six pointed star in red, blue or gold. It is sometimes in Star of David form, and *Ginori*, *Gin* or *GI* is often found impressed on wares dating from the mid 19th century onwards.

A Doccia globular teapot and cover from the Isola Marana service, the branch handle with leaf terminals, circa 1749, 18cm. wide.
(Christie's) $36,047

A Doccia giltmetal-mounted oval snuff-box con basso relievo istoriato, the cover with Mars and Venus before a ruin and Time in flight above, circa 1750, 8cm. wide.
(Christie's) $4,066

A pair of Doccia figures of Harlequin and Columbine from the Commedia dell'Arte, in black masks and iron-red and yellow checkered theatrical costumes, circa 1770, 12.5cm. high.
(Christie's) $13,150

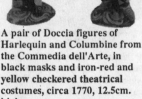

One of a set of three Doccia coffee cans and saucers, cylindrical with scroll handles, painted in an Oriental palette, late 18th century.
(Christie's) $1,318

A Doccia white group of the Virgin and Child, modeled after Giovanni Battista Foggini, the mother suckling her infant, last quarter of the 18th century, 42cm. high. (Christie's London) $17,200

A Doccia baluster coffee-pot and cover painted with scattered sprays of flowers, the reeded dragon's head spout and scroll handle enriched in yellow, blue and puce, circa 1760, 20cm. high.
(Christie's) $1,280

DOUCAI

Doucai, or Tou t'sai, means literally 'contrasting color' and refers to a decorative technique consisting of a pattern outlined in a thin, penciled, underglaze blue, infilled with translucent, enameled overglaze colors, principally red, yellow and green.

Examples exist from the early Ming Dynasty, and the technique seems to have been perfected in the Cheng-hua period.

Imitations and new-style wares were made under Yung Cheng and Ch'ien Lung and the 18th century saw the period of greatest output in this style.

Two of a set of twelve Doucai saucer dishes, painted and enameled on the interior with a stylized splayed leaf pattern, 21cm. diameter.
(Christie's)
(Twelve) $9,741

A fine large Doucai jardiniere, Qianlong seal mark, finely painted to the side with five medallions filled with lotus flowers and feathery foliate, 13in. diameter.
(Christie's) $232,000

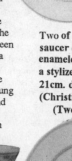

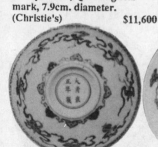

A Doucai Zhadou, the globular body painted with a lotus scroll, the flower-heads alternating with peaches, Qianlong seal mark, 7.9cm. diameter.
(Christie's) $11,600

A pair of small Doucai 'Birthday' saucer dishes, enameled to the center with five bats round a peach branch, Yongzheng character marks and of the period, 11.7cm. diameter.
(Christie's) $10,626

A fine Doucai and famille rose moonflask, Qianlong seal mark, elaborately painted to each circular face with the 'three abundances', pomegranate, peach and finger citrus, 12¼in. high. $440,000

A fine Doucai bowl, encircled Yongzheng six-character mark, painted delicately around the sides with hongbao, the eight Daoist emblems, between a band of linked ruyi-heads, 5¼in. diameter.
(Christie's) $25,548

A pair of Doucai 'Dragon' saucer-dishes, the interior with a five-clawed dragon chasing a flaming pearl amidst cloud scrolls below four stylized clouds, 5¾in. diameter.
(Christie's) $6,400

A Doucai bowl, finely painted to the exterior with six iron-red lotus blossoms framed within elaborate scrollwork, all between a double line below the rim, 5¾in. diameter.
(Christie's) $5,600

DOULTON

The Doulton story began in 1815, when Henry's father John, known as the 'best thrower of pint pots in London' set up a pottery business in partnership with a widow called Jones and a journeyman called Watts. The Watts Doulton part of the association continued until the former's retiral in 1853, by which time the premises had moved to Lambeth High Street, where earthenware bottles, chimney pots, garden ornaments and tiles were produced.

'Old Salt' D.6110, a Doulton wall pocket, printed and painted marks, 7¼in. high.
(Christie's) $719

Royal Doulton pottery jardinière, 'The Gallant Fishers', 9in. high.
(G. A. Key) $352

In 1835 John's second son Henry joined the company. He responded to the calls to improve urban sanitation by commencing the manufacture of sewage and water pipes, and at one time the Doulton works were producing these at the rate of 10 miles a week and exporting them all over the world.

With a solid financial base established, Henry decided he could afford to branch out and indulge some of his other interests. In the late 1850's his father had already been approached by John Sparkes, head of the newly established Lambeth School of Arts, who had requested that some of his students should try potting. It was Henry who finally responded to this request. He set up a pottery studio in a corner of the works, and it is worth noting that George Tinworth and the Barlows, Arthur, Florence and Hannah, were among the first intake.

Henry had the wisdom to show the results at the various international exhibitions which were taking place in that period,

Doulton, 'Blue Children' seriesware jardinière, decorated with a lady and child within garden overlooking lake, 8in. diameter.
(Peter Wilson) $575

The 'Lily Maid', a Royal Doulton polychrome glazed stoneware fountain figure, designed by Gilbert Bayes, 61.5cm. high. (Christie's) $16,000

Royal Doulton 'Aubrey' patterned slop pail and top with bound cane handle, English, early 20th century.
(G. A. Key) $294

Royal Doulton plate 'Nothing venture nothing win', 'Count your chickens before they are hatched'.
(Lyle) $320

DOULTON

and they were so enthusiastically received that by 1880 the number employed by the studio had risen to 200. Within the next twenty years it was to double again.

By this time Henry had also acquired an earthenware factory in Burslem, which he renamed Doulton and Co. Here, he began to make bone china in 1885, again creating a studio for artists and potters on the premises.

Experimentation and constant development were the keynotes for both establishments and they attracted terrific resources of talent. Charles J Noke, for example, joined the company in 1889 and finally became Artistic Director at Burslem. He experimented with Copenhagen and Sèvres type wares and in recreating oriental techniques. The results of the latter were the renowned Flambé, Sung, Chinese jade and Chang pottery. Under Noke, too, the company embarked on one of its most successful lines of all, figure models, the first of which were exhibited at Chicago in 1893.

A continuing supply of such talent ensured the survival of the Lambeth studio until 1956, while at Burslem activity continues unabated to this day.

A fine Royal Doulton Crombie series ware bowl, circa 1925, 24cm. diameter.
(Sotheby's) $1,650

Royal Doulton 'Nelson' commemorative loving cup, number 245 of an edition of 600, signed by *H Fenton*, 10in. tall.
(G. A. Key) $608

A pair of large Royal Doulton ceramic baluster vases, early 20th century, painted in shades of brown, green and amber with pastoral landscapes, 22in. high.
(Christie's) $2,429

A Doulton Lambeth Holbein ware charger, by Charles Noke, the center painted with a bust portrait of a medieval gentleman, 39cm. diameter.
(Christie's) $480

'The Pied Piper', a limited edition Doulton loving cup, painted in colors, printed factory marks, 10¼in. high.
(Christie's) $786

A Royal Doulton 'Chang' vase, with inverted rim, covered in a thick crackled mottled white, black, red, ocher glaze running over mottled shades of ocher, red, blue and black, 11cm. high.
(Christie's) $788

DOULTON

Doulton Lambeth earthenware jug, two tone brown, mask top and plated lip, 7in. high.
(G. A. Key) $67

Royal Doulton sampler water jug and teapot, pattern No. D3749, English, early 20th century.
(G. A. Key) $195

Royal Doulton 'Chang' baluster vase, the blue iridescent glazed lower body with off-white neck, 15in. high.
(Canterbury) $3,675

Royal Doulton slater patent jug, designed in the 'Black Jack' style and inscribed with Landlords Caution, 7in. high
(G. A. Key) $59

A Royal Doulton 'Reynard the Fox' coffee service, printed marks and pattern number H4927.
(Dreweatt Neate) $507

A Doulton Blue Children ware vase, on pedestal foot, the spherical body flanked by reeded loop handles, 23³/₄in. high.
(Christie's) $719

A Doulton Lambeth advertising jug, 1904, numbered *9073*, initialed *EB* and entitled *Colonel Bogey whiskey*, 7¹/₂in. high.
(Bonhams) $570

Pair of Doulton Lambeth Art pottery vases, circa 1900, in squat globular form with floral banded design, by Mark Marshall, 5³/₄in. high.
(Eldred's) $467

Doulton Lambeth silicon ware brown ground simulated leather tankard, incised *Here's Luck*, hallmarked silver band, London 1910, 6in.
(G. A. Key) $52

DOULTON CHARACTER JUGS

Charles Noke was the inspiration behind the immensely popular Doulton range of character jugs, the first of which, John Barleycorn Old Lad, was produced in the 1930s. A huge variety were made, featuring figures from folk lore and personalities past and present. Some continued in production for years. Others were quickly withdrawn, perhaps, as in the case of Churchill, because the subject didn't like them or, as in the case of Clark Gable, because it was claimed they infringed copyright. In consequence, these are now exceedingly rare, and are correspondingly valuable. Slight variations on a standard type also make an enormous difference to the value of a piece. A hatted version of Sir Francis Drake will fetch less than $150, whereas the hatless version is worth over ten times more.

Harry Fenton was one of the foremost designers of character jugs, and variations on his 'Arry and 'Arriet costermongers (when he has a blue collar and white buttons and she has a blue collar and maroon hat) will now command thousands of dollars. One useful factor for collectors is that each jug bears the back stamp of the company and is numbered according to Doulton's own system.

Touchstone D5613, designed by C Noke, issued 1936, withdrawn 1960. $230

Mae West D6688, designed by C Davidson, issued 1983, withdrawn 1985. $120

Churchill (Natural) D6170, Two handled Loving Cup, very rare, designed by C Noke, issued 1940, withdrawn 1941.
$20,000

Clown D6322, (White Haired), designed by H Fenton, issued 1951, withdrawn 1955.
$880

Pearly Boy (Blue), designed by H Fenton, issued 1947.
$3,600

Ugly Duchess D6599, designed by M Henk, issued 1965, withdrawn 1973. $475

DOULTON CHARACTER JUGS

Jockey D6625, designed by D Biggs, issued 1971, withdrawn 1975. $360

Punch and Judy Man D6590, designed by D Biggs, issued 1964, withdrawn 1969. $475

'Gladiator', D6550, designed by M. Henk, issued 1961, withdrawn 1967. $475

'The McCallum', a large Kingsware character jug made for D & J McCallum Whisky Distillers, circa 1930. $1,600

'Churchill' (White), D6170, designed by C. Noke, issued 1940, withdrawn 1941. $5,600

'The Fortune Teller' D6467, designed by G. Sharpe, introduced 1959, withdrawn 1967.
(Peter Wilson) $475

Dick Whittington D6375, designed by G Blower, issued 1953, withdrawn 1960. $360

A Royal Doulton character jug 'Captain Hook', numbered D6597, 18.5cm. high.
(Spencer's) $475

'Ard of 'Earing' D6588, a Royal Doulton character jug, printed factory marks, 19cm. high.
(Christie's) $1,000

DOULTON CHARACTER JUGS

'Mad Hatter', D6598, designed by M. Henk, issued 1965, withdrawn 1983. $135

A Royal Doulton pottery large character jug 'Old King Cole', with yellow crown, 14cm. high. (Spencer's) $2,400

A large Royal Doulton character jug, entitled, 'Regency Beau', withdrawn 1967. (Bearne's) $720

A Royal Doulton character jug, Granny, 6¹/₂in. high, toothless version. (Dee, Atkinson & Harrison) $720

'Drake' (hatless), a Royal Doulton character jug, large, D6115, designed by H. Fenton, introduced 1940, withdrawn 1941. (Louis Taylor) $2,400

Field Marshal the Rt. Hon. J. C. Smuts, no number, should be D6198, designed by H. Fenton, introduced 1946, withdrawn 1948. (Peter Wilson) $1,350

'Mephistopheles', D5757, designed by H. Fenton, issued 1937, withdrawn 1948. $1,200

Lord Nelson D6336, designed by G Blower, issued 1952, withdrawn 1969. $320

'Clown' (Red Haired), D5610, designed by H. Fenton, issued 1937, withdrawn 1942. $2,000

163

DOULTON FIGURES

The first Doulton figures were made by George Tinworth, one of the original group of art potters who came to the company via the Lambeth School of Art. His output was small, however, and it was not until Charles Noke joined the firm in 1889 that figure making really became big business. Noke was inspired by the figures produced by Derby, Bow, Meissen and also, nearer home, by the Staffordshire figure making industry. Initially, the colors used tended to be rather dull, and the figures did not sell well, so their production was suspended until 1912, when a new range, including the famous 'Bedtime/Darling' by Charles Vyse, was introduced. (This was originally entitled Bedtime, but was rechristened after Queen Mary, seeing it while on a visit to the factory, exclaimed 'What a darling!')

The new figures benefited from brighter colors, and a talented team of modelers now set to work. These included Leslie Harradine, Harry Tittensor and later Peggy Harper.

More than 200 Doulton figures are still in production today, and even they can fetch surprisingly high prices.

Negligee, HN1228, designed by L. Harradine, issued 1927-1938, 5in. high.
$720

Sweet and Twenty (Style one) HN1298, designed by L Harradine, issued 1928, withdrawn 1969, 5¾in. high.
$360

Maytime HN 2113 designed by L. Harradine, issued 1953-1967, 7in. high.
$320

China Repairer HN 2943, designed by R. Tabenor, issued 1983-1988, 6¾in. high.
$260

Rhythm HN1903, designed by L Harradine, issued 1939, withdrawn 1949, 6¾in. high.
$1,275

Magic Dragon HN 2977 designed by A. Hughes, issued 1983-1986, 4¾in. high.
$240

DOULTON FIGURES

Sweet Anne HN1453, designed by L Harradine, issued 1931, withdrawn 1949, color variation, 7in. high. **$350**

Love Letter HN2149, designed by M Davies, issued 1958, withdrawn 1976, 5½in. high. **$440**

Moira, HN1347, designed by L. Harradine. issued 1929-1938, 6½in. high. **$1,360**

Bather (Style two) HN1227, designed by L Harradine, issued 1927, withdrawn 1938, color variation, 7½in. high. **$1,000**

In The Stocks HN 1475, designed by L. Harradine, issued 1931-1938, 5¼in. high. **$1,280**

Mam'selle, HN724, designed by L. Harradine, issued 1925-1938, 7in. high. **$960**

Fairy, (Style One) HN1324, designed by L Harradine, issued 1929, withdrawn 1938, 6½in. high. **$560**

Reverie HN 2306, designed by P. Davies, issued 1964-1982, 6½in. high. **$360**

Sunshine Girl HN1344, designed by L Harradine, issued 1929, withdrawn 1938, 5in. high. **$1,920**

DOULTON FIGURES

'Patricia' H.N.1462, a Royal Doulton bone china figure, printed and painted marks. (Christie's) $480

Europa and The Bull, HN2828, designed by R. Jefferson, issued 1985, 10½in. high. limited edition of 300. $1,520

Young Love, HN2735, designed by D.V. Tootle, issued 1975-1990, 10in. high. $480

Boatman, HN 2417, designed by M. Nicholl, issued 1971-1987, 6½in. high. $264

Isadora, HN2938, designed by P. Gee, issued 1986, 8in. high. $264

Royal Doulton figure 'Lady Charmian' HN1949. (Peter Wilson) $320

A Royal Doulton group entitled, 'The Wardrobe Mistress', H.N.2145, withdrawn 1967. (Bearne's) $390

A Royal Doulton group entitled 'The Perfect Pair', H.N.581, withdrawn 1938. $720

Huntsman, HN 2492, designed by M. Nicholl, issued 1974-1978, 7½in. high. $264

DOULTON FIGURES

Master HN2325, designed by P. Davies, issued 1967-1992, 6¼in. high. **$216**

Dick Turpin, HN3272, designed by G. Tongue, issued 1989 in a limited edition of 5000, 12in. high. **$720**

'Calumet' H.N.1689, printed and painted marks, 6½in. high. (Christie's) **$640**

A Royal Doulton figure entitled 'Prudence', H.N.1883, withdrawn 1949. **$480**

Rustic Swain HN1746, designed by L. Harradine, issued 1935-1949, 5¼in. high. **$1,200**

Eve HN2466, designed by P. Davies, issued 1984 in a limited edition of 750, 9¼in. high.

$720

Captain Cook HN2889, designed by W.K. Harper, issued 1980-1984, 8in. high. **$390**

'The Flower Seller's Children', a bone china group, printed and painted marks, 7¾in. high. (Christie's) **$480**

Owd Willum HN2042, designed by H. Tittensor, issued 1949-1973, 6¾in. high. **$312**

DOULTON FLAMBÉ

ROYAL DOULTON FLAMBE

The name describes the streaky, flame like effect of the deep blood red glaze which was produced by mixing copper oxide and other minerals and allowing certain amounts of oxygen to be admitted to the kiln during firing. The technique was first discovered by Bernard Moore, a chemist and innovator who worked in conjunction with Doulton at the turn of the century. After two years' experimentation the first examples of Flambé were shown at the St Louis Exhibition of 1904 and it had a huge appeal. Although it is expensive to make, Flambé is still being produced.

Monkeys embracing, Model 486, 5½in. high. $225

Mallard, Model 654, 4in. high, designed by Noke, introduced 1920, withdrawn 1961.
$312

Elephant, trunk down, 12in. high, circa 1930.
$1,200

Penguin, double, Model 103, HN133, 6in. high, circa 1929.
$320

The Sung glaze was developed by Charles Noke, and it is remarkable for the mottled and veined effect produced by high temperature firing. The first examples were exhibited at the British Industry Fair at the Crystal Palace in 1920 and were animal and figure models. All Sung pieces are signed by Charles Noke.

Fox, sitting, head up, Model 102, 9½in. high, designed by Noke, introduced 1962, withdrawn 1965. $360

Flambe vase with view of Kendal, signed Fred Moore, 11in. high, circa 1940.
$720

DOULTON STONEWARE

Stoneware was the first material produced by John Doulton in 1815, and the company concentrated at first on mass produced items such as bottles and jugs.

When Henry Doulton joined the firm he diversified into architectural stoneware and set his protegés from the Lambeth School of Art to work. They included such famous names as the Barlows, George Tinworth and Eliza Simmance. At first their designs were fairly simple, but they subsequently embarked on pâte-sur-pâte work, whereby a raised outline was built up by delicate brush work. This led to more sophisticated designs and particularly the stylized carved foliage which presaged the Art Nouveau style.

DOULTON & SLATERS PATENT

After 1914 production was limited, and it ceased entirely when the factory closed in 1956.

Salt glazed stoneware jug depicting Lord Nelson by Doulton and Watts, Lambeth, circa 1830. $480

Doulton Lambeth stoneware jardinière, ovoid and embossed with classical profile heads and flowers within geometric borders, 8in. high.
(Hobbs & Chambers) $240

Salt glazed stoneware vase designed by Mary Ann Thompson and Jessie Bowditch, circa 1880, 9in. high. $1,120

'Play Goers' by George Tinworth, the group glazed pale brown with a blue and brown shaped base, 1886, 5¼in. high. $2,000

A Doulton Lambeth stoneware jug commemorating Victoria's Diamond Jubilee, inscribed *'She brought her people lasting good'*, 24cm.
(Phillips) $360

'Hunting', a frog and mouse group with the frogs riding mice over a water jump, circa 1884, 4½in. high. $1,750

DOULTON STONEWARE

Doulton Lambeth stoneware pilgrim vase, England, circa 1885, serpent handles, impressed marks and *Frank A. Butler* signature, 12³/₄in. high. (Skinner Inc.) $1,210

A pair of Doulton stoneware bottle vases with everted rims, decorated by Eliza Simmance, 25cm. high. (Bearne's) $715

A Doulton Lambeth stoneware mug of waisted form, applied with molded white figures of a bowler, 5³/₄in. high. (Bonhams) $462

A pair of Doulton Lambeth art stoneware candlesticks, with stiff leaf molded circular drip pans issuing from gilt whorl decorated incised stems, 17cr.. high. (Spencer's) $251

A Royal Doulton stoneware tyg, the body applied and molded with flowerheads, leaves and foliate rosettes, in mottled green, brown and blue glazes, 18cm. high. (Spencer's) $152

A pair of Doulton Lambeth stoneware vases, circa 1890, decorated by Florence Barlow, in raised slip with panels of birds within a tube-lined stylized floral border, 13¹/₂in. high. (Sotheby's) $1,705

A Doulton Lambeth art stoneware ink pot, cover and liner, with incised stiff leaf border over a column molded body and bead stamped base, dated *1877*, 12cm. high. (Spencer's) $220

A pair of Doulton Lambeth vases by George Tinworth, with incised and applied decoration of a central band of scrolling foliage set with floral medallions, dated *1875*, 25cm. high. (Christie's) $750

A large and good Doulton Lambeth biscuit barrel by Hannah Barlow, incised with a band of horses, impressed mark and dated *1883*, 7¹/₄in. high. (John Nicholson) $802

DOULTON STONEWARE

Doulton stoneware ornament, a suffragette figured ink well, 3in. high.
(G. A. Key) $491

A good pair of Doulton Lambeth vases and covers by Hannah Barlow, incised with a band of lions, 13in. high.
(John Nicholson) $2,332

Doulton Lambeth Hannah B. Barlow pitcher, England, circa 1895, with incised hounds and pâte-sur-pâte quail on a stippled background, 9in. high.
(Skinner Inc.) $2,090

Doulton Lambeth Hannah B. Barlow jardinière, England, dated 1883, with an incised frieze of a coach being pulled by a team of horses towards grazing sheep and cattle, 7¾in. diameter.
(Skinner Inc.) $1,870

Three Doulton Lambeth graduated jugs, molded in relief with portrait medallions of Queen Victoria between bands of flowers and foliage, largest 23cm. high.
(Christie's) $800

Doulton Lambeth three handled mug, the silver rim inscribed To Joseph McWilliams, and dated 1880, the three handles molded with geometric designs, by Hannah Barlow, incised marks 1876, 5½in.
(G. A. Key) $675

Four Doulton Lambeth stoneware decanters in original wicker basket, the shoulder molded in relief with fruiting vine, 21cm. high.
(Christie's) $809

A fine pair of Doulton stoneware candlesticks, each baluster stem and domed foot applied with beads and incised with leaves, 18.8cm. high.
(Bearne's) $387

A good and large Doulton Lambeth stoneware clock case, the whole incised with flowers and molded with husks, dated 1882.
(Spencer's) $997

DOULTON TOBY JUGS

Whilst jugs have been made in human form since time immemorial, the toby jug was almost certainly the creation of an anonymous Staffordshire potter in the 18th century. It was designed to amuse, and quickly became one of the most popular jugs ever made in human likeness, its fame spreading to North America and other countries also. Just how it got its name is more obscure, though there are some obvious possibilities. The similarity to the word 'toper' is one. then again, its association with conviviality reminds one irresistibly with the character of Sir Tony Belch in Shakespeare's Twelfth Night, or even My Uncle Toby from Sterne's Tristram Shandy. Among the most prolific manufacturers of toby jugs were Ralph Whieldon and the Woods, and they were made well into the 19th century by a host of potters both in England and the US.

At Doulton, toby jugs had been produced since the establishment of the company in 1815. Early examples were in the brown saltglaze style which had characterized them for centuries, however, and it was not until the 1930s that Charles Noke decided not only to revive the earlier toby jug tradition, but also to adopt a completely new approach to traditional face jugs. It was out of this idea that the Doulton character jug was born, which was to be such a runaway success. The Doulton toby revival was more modest in scale, but a range of tobies, painted in colors and modeled by Charles Noke and Harry Fenton are still in production today.

Doultonville Toby Mr Tonsil, D6713 designed by W. Harper, issued 1984-1991, 4in. high. $55

Cliff Cornell, issued 1956 in a limited edition of 500, 9¼in. high. $400

Charlie Chaplin, issued circa 1918, 11in. high. $3,200

Sherlock Holmes D6661, designed by R. Tabbenor, issued 1981-1991, 8¾in. high. $105

Falstaff D6063, designed by C. Noke, issued 1939-1991, 5¼in. high. $70

Happy John, D6031, designed by H. Fenton, issued 1939-1991, 8¾in. high. $105

DOULTON TOBY JUGS

Jolly Toby, D6109, designed by H. Fenton, issued 1939-1991, 6½in. high. **$70**

Winston Churchill, designed by H. Fenton, issued 1941-1991, 9in. high. **$120**

Huntsman, a Kingsware Toby jug by Royal Doulton, 7½in. high. **$560**

Sir Francis Drake, D6660, designed by M. Abberley, issued 1981-1991, 9in. high. **$105**

The Best is Not Too Good, D6107, designed by H. Fenton, issued 1939-60, 4½in. high. **$310**

Charringtons Toby jug made by Royal Doulton, 9¼in. high. **$760**

Old Charley, D6030, designed by H. Fenton, issued 1939-1960, 8¾in. high. **$230**

George Robey, issued circa 1925, 10½in. high. **$3,200**

Huntsman, D6320, designed by H. Fenton, issued 1950-1991, 7½in. high. **$105**

173

DRESDEN

There can be few people today who are not familiar with the term 'Dresden china', often used as a comparison when trying to convey an idea of delicacy and fragility. Try looking up 'Dresden' in any textbook, however, and it is mysteriously absent, for Dresden, in fact is simply an alternative for the more correct term of Meissen.

The misnomer dates from the 18th century itself, when 'Dresden' was enough to describe this first hard paste European factory, and when Derby was established in 1756, it became known as 'The New Dresden'.

Matters were further complicated by the fact that in the 19th century small workshops and decorators set up in the city of Dresden itself, making and decorating inferior copies of early Meissen. Often the marks were also copied.

Principal decorators in the mid-late 19th century working in Dresden were Donath, Hamann, Klemm, A Lamm and F Hirsch, all of whom decorated in the Meissen style. Many of their pieces are marked *Dresden*, with a crown or star.

A Dresden model of a crouching rabbit with white and gray-brown fur, its nose, mouth and inner ears painted in pink, circa 1880, 11¼in. long.
(Christie's) $3,281

A pair of 19th century Dresden porcelain figural candelabra, modeled as a German and his female companion
(Academy Auctioneers)
                               $1,543

A decorative Dresden dessert service with pierced trellis panels alternating with pierced flower sprays painted in colors, circa 1880.
(Phillips) $2,850

An impressive pair of Dresden Helena Wolfsohn porcelain large vases and covers, of ovoid form, painted in colors with courtiers and peasants seated in open landscapes, 50cm. high.
(Spencer's) $1,538

A pair of Dresden white-ground baluster vases and domed covers with conical finials, painted in a bright palette with large vignettes of birds perched on leafy branches, blue AR monograms, circa 1880, 24½in. high. (Christie's) $4,959

A pair of Dresden yellow ground porcelain vases, each painted to both sides with scenes of peasants in courtyards, 21½cm. high, late 19th century.
(Christie's) $1,200

A pair of Dresden claret-ground bottle-vases and flat covers, painted predominantly in shades of pink, yellow and gray with Watteauesque scenes, 20th century, 19¾in. high.
(Christie's) $1,159

DRESDEN

A Dresden porcelain figure group modeled as a courting couple, the gentleman embracing the lady from behind as a young man looks on, circa 1900, 12½in. high.
(Christie's) $2,274

A pair of Dresden bottle-coolers, the spirally-gadrooned bodies painted with pairs of birds on leafy branches, blue AR monograms, circa 1880, 6½in. high.
(Christie's) $391

A Dresden pink-ground globular jar and domed cover, painted with lovers in 18th century-style dress in idyllic gardens, late 19th century, 11¼in. high.
(Christie's) $1,005

A 'Dresden' porcelain two-handled pedestal vase with pierced cover, painted with alternate panels of figures in gardens and flowers, 30cm. high.
(Bearne's) $386

A pair of Dresden white groups of Marly horses after the models by Guillaume Coustou, the rearing stallions to left and right, each with a scantily draped attendant, circa 1880, 21¾in. high.
(Christie's) $7,539

A Dresden center-piece formed as a young man and a woman wearing striped and flowered 18th century-style rustic dress, playing hide-and-seek around a tree, circa 1880, 28½in. high.
(Christie's) $2,815

A Dresden figural clock-case, with a detachable top modeled after J. J. Pradier as Sappho wearing striped and flowered clothes and sandals, circa 1880, 22¾in. high.
(Christie's) $4,658

A pair of Dresden China table lamps, 19th century in the form of rose encrusted urns supported by three putti.
(Lots Road Galleries) $1,200

A Dresden porcelain clock-case, circa 1880, modeled as a broad scroll-molded column applied with garlands and a putto scantily clad in pink drapery, 23in. high.
(Christie's) $5,485

EUROPEAN

Just about every European country had its indigenous pottery and later porcelain industries, even if it consisted mainly of minor factories aping the production of the greats such as Meissen and Sèvres. Even where no confident attribution can be made 'Continental' pieces often have a vitality and quality which make them worthy of inclusion in thoroughly respectable ceramic collections. Flamboyance perhaps best characterises European china of the early part of this century. A host of very different talents flourished across the continent at this time, and none of them produced anything that could be classed as insipid or even terribly delicate! Some of the most avant-garde pieces were produced by the versatile Gallé and by Robj, also in France. Many whimsical, even impudent pieces were also made. Striking colors and arresting shapes were the keynote of this fascinating period.

Wall mask in Continental porcelain, 5in. high, 1930s. (Muir Hewitt) $150

Pincushion with half doll in Continental porcelain. (Muir Hewitt) $75

A Faenza blue and white crespina, the center with a circular medallion painted with a man shooting at duck on a pond within a border of buildings in mountainous wooded landscape vignettes, circa 1650, 30.5cm. diameter. (Christie's) $1,600

A Portuguese faience blue and white tile-picture in the form of a gallant painted in bright-blue wearing a peruke, and long frock-coat with wide buttoned cuffs, late 17th/early 18th century, 173.5cm. high. (Christie's) $15,200

An Austrian terracotta twin-handled vase in Egyptianesque style, flanked by dragon handles, gilded and cold-painted in colors, impressed *Wsss*, 10½in. high. (Christie's S. Ken) $48

'Manuelita', a Manna polychrome painted pottery figure, of a young woman wearing floral patterned dress and headscarf, 11in. high. (Christie's) $253

A Boch Frères pottery vase, molded in low relief with a band of stylized pelicans in flight, between borders of clouds, enameled in yellow, blue and turquoise, 13½in. high. (Christie's) $400

EUROPEAN

A Fornasetti earthenware tea caddy, printed in colors with an array of kitchen implements, 8½in. high. (Christie's S. Ken) $145

An Elton pottery twin-spouted teapot and cover, of globular shape, one spout having human mask end, 18.5cm. high. (Phillips) $520

'Allegro Pasto', a Manna polychrome painted ceramic group modeled as a young girl in gingham dress, 11¼in. high. (Christie's S. Ken) $520

An Aladin polychrome painted porcelain box and cover, modeled as an Egyptian seated with knees drawn up, in exotic pattern robes in yellow, rust and black, 8in. high. (Christie's) $175

Four Pesaro graduated albarelli boldly painted with yellow, orange, blue and manganese flowers and scrolling foliage, between concentric blue line rims, late 18th century, 12cm. to 17cm. high. (Christie's) $4,000

A Böttger miniature pagoda figure seated with his left knee raised, holding a teabowl and saucer, his head, hands and pantaloons gilded and his robe enriched with gilt flowerheads, circa 1715, 5.5cm. high. (Christie's) $6,800

A Katshutte Thuringia ceramic figure of a dancing girl, standing in profile with arms held aloft, printed factory mark (restored), 12¼in. high. (Christie's S. Ken) $560

A Brussels cabbage-tureen and cover, the naturally modeled overlapping leaves with waved everted edges and raised midribs, circa 1770, 30.5cm. wide. (Christie's) $4,800

An Elton pottery jug, with compressed base and tall cylindrical neck, sparrow beak spout and sinuous handle, 28.5cm. high. (Phillips) $520

A pair of Continental figures of Malabars, bearing blue crossed sword marks, on circular rocky bases, 14in. high.
(Christie's) $7,475

One of a pair of Nyon coffee cans and saucers painted in colors with sprays and garlands of flowers, fish marks.
(Phillips) $1,000

A large and colorful matched pair of portrait busts, probably representing King Leopold of Belgium and Princess Charlotte, 50cm. and 52cm. high.
(Bearne's) $11,026

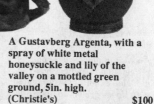

A Vi Bi polychrome pottery figural group, modeled as a naked young woman struggling in the tentacles of an octopus, 40cm. high.
(Christie's) $3,680

A pair of treacle glaze pottery tobacco jars and covers in the form of pug dogs, 22cm. high.
(Spencer's) $438

A Gustavberg Argenta, with a spray of white metal honeysuckle and lily of the valley on a mottled green ground, 5in. high.
(Christie's) $100

A pair of Continental majolica olive-green-ground jardiniéres and pedestals, the bulbous bodies modeled with large satyr's mask handles enriched in a dull gilding, circa 1900, 38in. high.
(Christie's) $2,418

A Soviet porcelain dish, 'The Commissar, Uritskii Square', with underglaze mark of the Imperial Porcelain Factory, period of Alexander III and later, dated *1921*, 12in. diameter.
(Christie's) $8,446

A matched pair of Ernst Wahliss porcelain vases, molded as squat globular buds opening to reveal long cylindrical trunks, 17³/4in. high, printed *Alexander Porcelain Works*.
(Bonhams) $1,200

EUROPEAN

A Continental chinoiserie black and gilt lacquered pottery garden seat, circa 1880, decorated with a wide band of female figures, 19in. high. (Christie's) **$8,625**

A mid 18th century Brussels faience boar's head tureen, cover and stand, the stand 40cm. long. **$8,800**

A wall pocket in the form of a mask of Pan, covered in a mottled turquoise glaze over a green ground, 24cm. high. (Christie's) **$303**

A Spanish faience blue and white baluster vase boldly painted with three panels, two with figures and one with a stylized monkey, late 17th century, perhaps Catalan, 17.5cm. high. (Christie's) **$1,016**

Goebel container formed as a portly monk, wearing a brown habit; together with two matching graduated jugs, printed and incised marks, 9$^{1}/_{2}$in., 6in. and 4in. (G. A. Key) **$166**

A Continental porcelain cup and saucer painted with a mermaid emerging from the sea to embrace her lover seated on the rocky shore, circa 1850, 5in. high. (Christie's) **$227**

A pair of Continental porcelain oviform vases each painted with a girl, one playing with a kitten, the other with a puppy on her lap, 19th century, 16in. high. (Christie's) **$2,298**

A Soviet porcelain propaganda plate, 'He who does not work does not eat', with underglaze mark of the Imperial Porcelain Factory, dated *1922*, 9$^{5}/_{8}$in. diameter. (Christie's) **$3,167**

Pair of large good quality 19th century Continental porcelain figures of a lady and gallant, on circular naturalistic bases each bearing a pseudo Meissen mark, 18in. high. **$1,080**

A Baltic faience rectangular tray painted in puce monochrome with ships at sail by a harbor with a town in the distance, circa 1790, the tray 89cm. by 61cm. (Christie's) $32,000

A Gustavsberg ceramic footed cylindrical vase, covered in a mottled green glaze and embossed in white metal with fish amongst bubbles, 5³/₄in. high. (Christie's S. Ken) $280

A Brunswick trompe l'oeil bowl of fruit and cover, circa 1760, the central bunch of grapes forming a small tureen 10³/₄in. diameter. (Christie's) $7,130

A Marieburg blue and white two-handled circular tureen and cover, circa 1760, painted with roses and other flowers within feuilles de choux borders, 9¼i. wide. (Christie's) $3,565

A Rouen two-handled wine cooler, circa 1740, with twisted handles spotted in blue and with formal lappets and garlands, 9½in. wide. (Christie's) $3,921

A Hannoversch-Münden reticulated punch bowl and cover, circa 1765, each piece with three molded rococo foliage and scroll cartouches, 11¼in. high. (Christie's) $17,805

A Hutschenreuther Hohenburg rectangular plaque painted by Wagner with the Duchess of Devonshire, late 19th century, plaque 7in. x 4³/₄in. (Christie's S. Ken) $1,050

Two Magdeburg reticulated rococo baluster vases and covers, circa 1770, painted in grand feu colors, 12¼in. high. (Christie's) $9,804

A Boch Frères pottery vase decorated by Catteau, molded in low relief with a band of deer between bands of stylized foliage, 12¹/₄in. high. (Christie's) $320

EUROPEAN

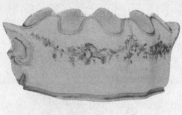

Stylized Continental wall mask, 8in. high, 1930s.
(Muir Hewitt) $427

A Buen Retiro two-handled seau crenelé painted with two continuous garlands of flowers hung from blue bows, the shell-shaped handles enriched with blue and gilt lines, circa 1765.
(Christie's) $6,000

Pottery figurine, 1930s, 8in. high.
(Muir Hewitt) $53

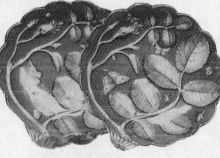

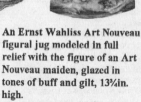

A rare early Faenza maiolica inkstand or holy water stoup, early 16th century, the shallow bowl surmounted by kneeling figures of the Virgin and Joseph and the Child, 23cm. high.
(Phillips) $15,960

A pair of Continental porcelain 'Blind Earl' pattern leaf-form dishes, each scalloped gilt dish molded with rosebuds, 8½in. long.
(Butterfield & Butterfield) $805

An Ernst Wahliss Art Nouveau figural jug modeled in full relief with the figure of an Art Nouveau maiden, glazed in tones of buff and gilt, 13¾in. high.
(Bonhams) $320

A group emblematic of Plenty in a pink robe holding a cornucopia, seated on a lion surrounded by putti on a rockwork base, circa 1890, 10in. high.
(Christie's) $1,468

A Flörsheim Enghalskrug, circa 1765, painted in grand feu colors with a large bouquet of garden flowers between initials P and M, 10½in. high.
(Christie's) $5,704

One of a pair of Czechoslovakian polychrome painted wall masks, each modeled as a young girl wearing a jester's cap, with an owl perched on the left shoulder, 6¾in. high.
(Christie's) $600

FAENZA

It was the Italian city of Faenza, situated between Bologna and Rimini, that was to give its name to the tin glazed earthenware which came to be known as faience. From the late 14th century it had been associated with maiolica manufacture and from the mid 15th century developed a very distinctive style. Apart from the usual drug pots, fine baluster vases decorated with heraldic devices, contemporary figures or gothic foliage, were produced.

Later some large pieces in full relief were attempted. By the 16th century several Faenza painters were engaged in painting in the style now associated with Urbino, and referred to as istoriato. Far Eastern influence was also beginning to filter through and about this time a style called bianchi di Faenza, with a minimum of decoration and a white tin glaze was developed.

In 1693 Count Annibale Ferniani bought a Faenza pottery where tiles and tablewares were made, which continued almost to this day.

Full signatures of painters or potters appear only rarely on 15th century Faenza ware, but in the 16th century these become more common.

A Faenza compendiario pierced tazza, the center painted in blue and pale manganese with Cupid leaning against a slender jar, circa 1600, 20.5cm. diameter. (Christie's) $1,016

A large albarello, Faenza, circa 1740, painted in ocher, green, manganese and blue on a cream ground with stylized peacock feathers, 8⅝in. high. (Christie's) $17,250

A maiolica group of the Virgin and Child seated holding the Christ Child on her knee, her features enriched in blue, wearing an ocher veil and ochre-trimmed blue cloak, most probably Faenza, circa 1540, 40cm. high. (Christie's) $27,000

A fluted crespina, Faenza, circa 1545, attributed to Virgiliotto Calamelli, molded with shells and painted a quartieri in blue, green, yellow and ocher heightened with white, the central medallion with a female martyr, 10⅛in. diameter. (Christie's) $13,800

A massive 'Talavera' faience vase, decorated in typical blues, greens and yellows with an oval panel depicting a bacchanalian scene, 61cm. high. (Spencer's) $723

A Milan faïence polychrome soup plate, Felice Clerici factory, circa 1770, painted in a Kakiemon palette with a bird perched on a branch of a flowering prunus tree, O mark in manganese, 9¹/₁₆in. diameter. (Sotheby's) $2,300

Large faienza oviform wine jar, 18th century, painted with a roundel of leaves and fruit enclosing a cherub's head with halo and blue and green wings below, 22¼in. high. (Butterfield) $1,650

FAMILLE ROSE

Famille rose is a style of decoration based on Chinese porcelain painting introduced during the Yongzheng period around 1730. A deep rose pink enamel derived from gold features strongly in the palette and by mixing this with white a variety of pinks and deep rose colors were now obtainable. It was much in demand for tableware produced for the nouveau riche of the Industrial Revolution.

A set of three famille rose figures of Star Gods, Qing dynasty, 19th century, each wearing brightly colored robes, tallest 45cm.
(Sotheby's) $4,264

A famille rose figure of a kylin, Qing dynasty, Jiaqing (1796–1820), the highly colored animal later mounted in ormolu, 26cm.
(Sotheby's) $2,398

A pair of Chinese famille rose porcelain pheasants, Qianlong period, proudly standing on tree trunk form pierced bases, 14¹/₈in. high.
(Christie's) $20,700

A pair of large Chinese famille rose jardinières, each enameled on one side with two cockerels amongst peony, 19th century, 24³/₄in. diameter.
(Christie's) $35,880

A pair of 19th century famille rose candlestick figures, standing in richly decorated robes and with peacock-feather mantelet, holding a lotus-petal vase, 11¹/₂in. high.
(Tennants) $4,800

Pair of 'Famille Rose' double vases, circa 1900, each two-sectioned vase of baluster form, with a four-character Qianlong mark in iron red to the base, 9³/₄in. high.
(Butterfield & Butterfield) $7,150

A Chinese porcelain famille rose warming-pot and cover, late 19th century, fitted with a removable inner dish, decorated on the sides with figures at leisure and in garden settings, 6¹/₂in. diam.
(Christie's) $690

A fine and rare pair of famille rose square pear-shaped vases, iron-red Qianlong seal marks, painted on the exterior in various shades of pastel enamels, 11¹/₂in. high.
(Christie's) $112,000

FAMILLE ROSE

A famille rose seated Buddha, Qianlong/Jiaqing, seated on a detachable double-lotus base, wearing a polychrome tiara 11¼in. high.
(Christie's) $8,400

One of a pair of brilliant famille rose lotus-flower teapots and covers, each molded with petals and applied with flowering stems, 4¾in. high, Qianlong.
(Tennants) $2,500

A large famille rose bottle vase, enameled with nine peaches issuing from gnarled, flowering branches, Qianlong seal mark, 19th century, 47cm. high.
(Christie's) $10,800

A rare famille rose long-necked oviform vase, iron-red Xianfeng six-character mark and of the period, enameled on the broad body with two clusters of flowering chrysanthemum, peony and magnolia, 12in. high.
(Christie's) $18,452

A pair of famille rose lotus-petal dishes, Qianlong seal marks and of the period, each enameled to the exterior to simulate a lotus blossom with three layered lotus petals over the yellow stigma, 6³/₄in. diameter.
(Christie's) $15,645

A famille rose 'figural' vase, Huairentang Zhi mark, 20th century, finely painted to the exterior with Shoulao and a young attendant offering a ripe peach to a dancing maiden beside a flower basket, 10⁷/₈in. high, box.
(Christie's) $8,121

A rare famille rose watch stand and cover, the body with a circular aperture surrounded by insects and butterflies amongst moulded scrolling floral sprays, 8¼in. high, Qianlong.
(Bonhams) $1,480

A fine famille rose rubyback eggshell deep plate, Yongzheng, the center with a multi-robed elegant seated lady with two playing children flanking her, 8¼in. diameter.
(Christie's) $17,600

A fine famille rose baluster vase, iron-red Daoguang seal mark and of the period, delicately enameled on the broad body with a procession of Chinese and European figures, 11¼in. high.
(Christie's) $56,774

FAMILLE ROSE

A fine Famille Rose bowl, Jiaqing seal mark and of the period, the rounded sides rising to a slightly flaring rim, painted with clusters of fruiting pomegranate vines entangled with bamboo, 4½in. diam. (Christie's) $5,973

An unusual relief-decorated famille rose teapot and cover of pear shape, brightly enameled on either side with a butterfly, 4½in. high, Yongzheng/early Qianlong. (Tennants) $920

A rare large famille rose kneeling boy pillow, Qianlong, the plump infant crouching on all fours with a smiling face raised to the left and his feet in the air, 15in. long. (Christie's) $39,000

A very fine famille rose charger, Yongzheng, brilliantly enameled in all the colors of the early Qing palette at the center with two black and white birds perched on a long curling branch of leafy blossoming tree peony, 20¾in. diameter. (Christie's) $17,600

A pair of famille rose blue-ground double-gourd vases, iron-red Qianlong seal marks, Daoguang, each raised on a flaring foot and surmounted by a tall neck with a floral rim, 8¾in. high. (Christie's) $7,111

A fine and rare famille rose yellow-ground bowl, blue enamel Qianlong four-character seal mark and of the period, densely enameled on the exterior with four large flower-heads amongst elaborate scrolling foliage, 5⅞in. diameter. (Christie's) $14,194

A fine and very rare famille rose celadon-ground molded lobed vase, underglaze-blue Qianlong seal mark and of the period, the slightly-flattened gourd-shaped vase with splayed foot and flaring neck, 14¼in. high. (Christie's) $384,028

One of a rare pair of 19th century Canton famille rose lotus-petal jardinières and stands, each piece molded on the exterior with overlapping petals detailed in bright enamels, 6¾in. high. (Tennants) (Two) $4,000

A famille rose baluster vase, iron-red Qianlong seal mark, the turquoise body enameled in white with scrolling lotus, applied round the shoulders and base with six Chinese boys, 12¼in. high. (Christie's) $4,400

FAMILLE ROSE

A Chinese famille rose porcelain monkey, Qianlong period, holding aloft in one hand a pink-tinged green peach, 8½in. high. (Christie's) $3,680

A pair of famille rose bowls, Qianlong seal marks and of the period, enameled on the exterior with butterflies, ripe citrus and bamboo, 4¼in. diameter. (Christie's) $35,000

A Chinese famille rose porcelain duck, Qianlong period, his long body with feather details picked out in brown enamel, 7in. high. (Christie's) $6,900

A pair of famille rose baluster jars and covers, the domed covers surmounted by seated gilt Buddhistic lion finials, the porcelain Yongzheng/early Qianlong, 61½in. high. (Christie's) $53,820

A pair of famille rose flattened double-gourd vases, blue enamel Le Xian Tang Zhi hall marks, 19th century, similarly painted to both faces with the wufu (five bats), in flight amidst clouds, 7in. high. (Christie's) $6,000

A pair of famille rose oviform vases, Hongxian Yuzhi marks, painted in mirror image with an elegant gentleman leaning against a green bamboo fence, 11in. high. (Christie's) $5,200

A Chinese famille rose jug, the neck with cartouches of landscapes in puce, having gilt dragon handle, Qianlong, 18th century, 9¾in. wide. (Woolley & Wallis) $880

Two famille rose globular teapots and two covers, each with buddhistic-lion handles and spouts, molded and enameled with flower-heads, Qianlong, 7in. wide. (Christie's) $1,332

A famille rose yellow-ground Tibetan-style vase, iron red Jiaqing seal mark, painted to the bulbous body with stylised lotus and scrolling foliage dividing the eight Buddhist emblems, 10⅞in. high. (Christie's) $17,600

FAMILLE VERTE

Famille verte is a style of Chinese painting with prominent use of bright green and shades of yellow and aubergine purple together with line drawings in black. It was introduced during the Kangxi period at the end of the 17th century.

A fine fluted famille verte dish. (Greenslade Hunt) $3,553

Chinese famille verte porcelain figure of Wenshu, 19th century, riding a lion, 15in. high. (Skinner Inc) $1,440

A pair of Chinese famille verte biscuit buddhistic lion joss-stick holders, Kangxi, each seated on a rectangular plinth with opposite forepaws raised, 8¼in. high. (Christie's) $699

A famille verte fish bowl, the exterior painted with a scene of warriors proceeding to battle, 25in. diam. $6,400

Pair of famille verte Fu lions, 19th century, each creature ferociously bearing its fangs, each supported on a separated fashioned rectangular pinth, 19in. high. (Butterfield & Butterfield) $6,050

A Worcester octagonal cup, painted in famille-verte palette with flowering plants and scattered insets, 6cm. (Phillips) $1,200

Pair of Chinese famille verte porcelain ormolu mounted parrots, Kangxi period, 18th century, perched on a pierced aubergine rockwork base, 9in. high overall. (William Doyle) $1,840

A famille verte oval incense basket and cover with high strap handle, Kangxi, 12.5cm. wide. $3,500

FAMILLE VERTE

A famille verte 'month' cup finely painted to one side with a flowering peach tree, inscribed to the reverse with a couplet, 2⁵/₈in. diameter.
(Christie's) $26,000

A famille verte cylindrical brushpot, Kangxi, well painted with insects flying above peony, 5in. high.
(Christie's) $4,025

A rare famille verte faceted jardinière, Kangxi, each of the four broad sides decorated with naturalistic vignette, 51.5cm. across.
(Christie's) $74,000

A famille verte 'month' cup, encircled Kangxi six-character mark and of the period, decorated to the exterior with blossoming tree peony issuing from a grassy patch among pierced rockwork, 2¹/₂in. diameter.
(Christie's) $17,600

A pair of Chinese famille verte ovoid bottles, late 17th century, each painted with lotus, prunus and peonies within petal shaped panels, carved wood covers, 18.2 and 20.4cm. overall.
(Sotheby's) $4,600

A famille verte 'month' cup, encircled Kangxi six-character mark and of the period, painted to one side with two clumps of flowering narcissus before rockwork and a single long stem with a red rose, 2⁵/₈in. diameter.
(Christie's) $7,200

A fine Chinese famille verte rouleau vase, late 17th century, painted with a warrior and attendants in a hilly landscape, 47.8cm. high.
(Sotheby's) $12,650

A pair of black-ground famille verte dishes, each painted to the rounded exterior with a composite floral scroll including lotus, clematis and peony blooms, 5⁷/₈in. diameter.
(Christie's) $22,400

A rare Chinese export famille verte puzzle jug, circa 1700, from an English delftware original, the body with green cell diaperwork ground, 21.2cm. high.
(Sotheby's) $3,000

FOLEY

The Foley pottery was established in Fenton, Staffordshire in the mid 19th century and was operated from 1903 by E Brain & Co. Its porcelain is noted for the simplicity of its design. That said, in the 1930's work was commissioned from leading contemporary artists such as Graham Sutherland and Laura Knight and is marked with the maker's name and the signature of the artist and decorator. The Foley marks include the brand name *Peacock Pottery*, with a peacock in a rectangle and Staffordshire knot.

A Foley Intarsio small oviform jardinière printed and painted in colors with band of carp amongst waves, 4¹/₂ in. high.
(Christie's S. Ken) $345

A Foley Intarsio vase, printed and painted in colors with panels of seagulls in fiords, above a band of entrelac foliate motifs, 8¹/₂ in. high.
(Christie's S. Ken) $353

A Foley Intarsio miniature grandfather clock printed and painted in colors with Father Time and bearing the inscription *Time and Tide wait for no man*, 10in. high.
(Christie's S. Ken) $780

A Foley Intarsio single-handled spherical vase, printed and painted in colors with a band of buttercups and flowerheads on the shoulders, 6in. high.
(Christie's S. Ken) $300

A Foley Intarsio three-handled vase and cover, printed and painted in typical colors with panels depicting the Queen of Hearts, 8in. high.
(Christie's S. Ken) $780

A Foley Intarsio baluster vase printed and painted in colors with kingfishers perched on branches above a band of carp, 9in. high.
(Christie's S. Ken) $450

A Foley Intarsio cylindrical biscuit barrel with electroplate mount and cover, printed and painted in colors with panels of drinking scenes and flowers, 7¹/₄ in. high.
(Christie's S. Ken) $1,147

A Foley Intarsio twin-handled baluster vase, printed and painted in colors with band of lavender and yellow flowers, 9¹/₄ in high.
(Christie's S. Ken) $150

FRANKENTHAL

When Louis XV, ever jealous for his Sèvres protegé, refused Paul Hannong a licence to continue making porcelain at Strasbourg in 1755, Hannong took his know-how across the Rhine to Frankenthal, where the Elector Carl Theodor allowed him to set up in some disused barrack buildings.

Hannong quickly set to work, and within a few months was producing pieces of a standard high enough to be used as court gifts. He subsequently returned to Strasbourg, leaving his elder son, Charles-François-Paul as director at Frankenthal. Charles died in 1757, however, whereupon his younger brother Joseph Adam took over, and in 1759 bought the factory from his father. In 1762, the Elector himself bought it out, and it continued in production until 1800. On its closure, many molds went to Grünstadt, Nymphenburg and elsewhere, where they were later used to make reproductions of early Frankenthal pieces.

As they had at Strasbourg, the Hannongs made pieces which were strongly rococo in style. Their tableware owes more to Sèvres than any other German factory. Leading painters were Winterstein, who painted scenes after Teniers, Osterspey (mythology) and Magnus, who specialised in battle scenes.

Figure-making featured largely in the Frankenthal output. Early examples were designed by J W Lanz, whose subjects are characterised by their small heads and theatrical poses.

The usual mark is *CT* for Carl Theodor, under an Electoral crown, though *PH* and *PHF* are to be found impressed on a few early pieces. More rare is *JAH* with a crowned lion rampant.

A Frankenthal group of a seated young man and two young women, modeled by K. G. Luck, dating from 1778, 23cm. wide. $4,800

A Frankenthal figure of a lady emblematic of Spring modeled by J.W. Lanz, stepping forward and holding her flower-laden apron before her, circa 1760, 14cm. high.
(Christie's) $2,250

A Frankenthal baluster ewer and cover probably painted by Jakob Osterspey with Bacchus and Venus reclining beside him scantily clad in brown and pink drapes, circa 1758, 23.5cm. high.
(Christie's) $14,500

A pair of Frankenthal figures of Oceanus and Thetis modeled by Konrad Linck, the sea god standing extending his arm towards his companion, circa 1765, 28.5cm. and 24cm. high.
(Christie's) $100,000

A Frankenthal group of chess players modeled by J. F. Luck, blue crowned Carl Theodor mark, circa 1765, 17cm. high.
(Christie's) $12,000

A Frankenthal figure of a trinket-seller modeled by Johann Friedrich Lück, holding up a shell-shaped snuff-box in her right hand, blue crowned CT mark above R, circa 1758, 18cm. high.
(Christie's) $7,742

FRANKFURT

The Frankfurt faience factory was established in 1666, making mainly imitations of Chinese porcelain. Late Ming styles were particularly popular for plates, with decoration of plants, trees, birds and Chinese figures. It is often hard to distinguish Frankfurt faience from delft, for, like delft, it has a clear lead glaze, or kwaart, applied over blue and white painting. Examples most commonly found are nine-lobed large plated vases and ewers with rope-like handles and long narrow necks. The most famous decorator at the factory was J.K. Ripp (see Bayreuth), but towards the end of the 17th century much of the decorating was done by Hausmaler.

The factory mark *F* is commonly found and pieces were also often signed by the painters. Ripp's own mark is *KR.*.

A large Frankfurt blue and white oviform jar, circa 1720, painted with four panels of Oriental figures in river landscapes, 16½in. high. (Christie's) $6,099

A German faience bottle vase, painted in blue with an Oriental style river landscape with Chinamen, 13½in., possibly Frankfurt. (Bonhams) $448

A Frankfurt Faience teapot and cover, painted in a bright blue with Chinese style figures, 13.5cm. high. (Phillips) $2,400

A good Frankfurt faience polychrome silver-mounted jug, 1670–90, the baluster-form body affixed with a scroll-tipped loop handle issuing from beneath a molded ridge below the rim, 10¹¹/₁₆in. high. (Sotheby's) $10,350

A Frankfurt, blue and white faience fluted circular dish with scenes of figures in a landscape, in the Chinese style, circa 1700, 34cm. diameter. (Christie's) $475

A Frankfurt blue and white paneled baluster vase and domed cover painted with fruiting flowering branches issuing from rockwork, circa 1700, 35cm. high. (Christie's) $2,957

A Frankfurt faience silver-shape dish painted in colors with chinoiserie scenes of figures in landscapes within molded fluted borders, circa 1700, 11³/₄in. diameter. (Christie's) $428

FRENCH

Early lead-glazed pottery was made in France from the 14th century onwards, The 16th century saw considerable refinements and the genre directly presages the peasant pottery made particularly in the north of France to this day.

French pottery production was always susceptible to outside influences. The 16th century maiolica production from Rouen, Nîmes, Lyons and Nevers is hard to distinguish from its Italian prototypes, although Nevers did develop a distinctive style in the 17th century with the use not only of maiolica colors but also of a deep blue polychrome.

A seminal blue-decorated faience was developed at Rouen in 1680, which influenced many other factories, such as Paris and St. Cloud, over a long period. In the 18th century Rouen again set a trend with Chinese and rococo style polychrome wares.

In the late 17th century Moustiers was influential in creating a fashion for finely painted pictorial panels, first in blue and later in yellow, green and manganese. In the mid 18th century Paul Hannong's Strasbourg factory copied the porcelain style of enamel painting for faience, and this practice was in turn copied by, among others, Niderviller, Rouen and Moustiers.

The first French porcelain was of the soft-paste type and was made at Rouen in 1673. Similar wares were subsequently produced also at Chantilly, Mennecy, St Cloud and finally Vincennes-Sèvres.

Vincennes Sèvres held the monopoly for porcelain production from about 1750-1770, after which other factories again tried to make hard-paste porcelain, and in the 19th century production became largely concentrated in the kaolin district of Limoges.

Pair of French 19th century vases decorated with hunting trophies and dead game, gilt highlighted borders and ring handles, 9¹/₂in. high. (Ewbank) $480

French flower decorated pot pourri jar with pierced cover, the supports in the form of three dolphins, gilt pierced cover, 8¹/₂in. high. (Ewbank) $350

Pair of French flower encrusted figures of a boy and a girl carrying baskets, on round bases, 10¹/₂in. high. (Ewbank) $260

A Lallemant pottery vase, painted with a scene of Chopin playing at the piano before two devoted lady admirers, 28cm. high. (Christie's) $620

A pair of French pink-ground baluster vases, painted with continuous friezes of mythological figures in wooded landscapes, circa 1860, 20¹/₂in. high. (Christie's) $3,980

A French oval porcelain plaque painted with a young girl wearing 18th century-style dress, late 19th century, plaque 6in. long. (Christie's S. Ken) $520

FRENCH

An attractive Guerhard & Dihl (Duc d'Angoulême's factory) teapot and cover, probably painted by Salembier with a scene of a young woman spinning cotton, 13.5cm. (Phillips) $1,522

A pair of French polychrome biscuit figures of a lady and her gallant on square plinths, circa 1845, 47.5cm. high. (Duran, Madrid) $3,479

An early French harvest flask of Palissy-type, the body molded in relief with a crowned head and one side molded with a crowned coat of arms incorporating three fleur-de-lys, 20cm. (Phillips) $406

A pair of French two-handled vases, mid-19th century, the mouth extending into side handles in the form of a Sèvres vase oreilles, 12in. high. (Christie's) $2,429

Alphonse Mucha portrait plaque, colorful handpainted woman in the Art Nouveau manner after the 1899 color lithograph 'La Primevere Polyanthus', 16¹/₂in. diameter. (Skinner Inc.) $1,210

A pair of French porcelain vases, decorated in Naples, the handles in the form of female terms, painted with Neapolitan views, 42.2cm. high, circa 1830. (Finarte) $7,462

'Reverie', a bisque and gilt-bronze bust of a lady cast from a model by Théophile François Somme, French, late 19th century, 10¹/₄in. high. (Christie's East) $750

A large pair of Turn porcelain figures of young women, each wearing a long dress, gathered at the waist, slight chipping, 62cm. high. (Bearne's) $2,055

A Continental pottery green-glaze flower-holder modeled as a seated pig, the back pierced with three lines of apertures, 19th century, 8in. long. (Christie's) $95

FRENCH

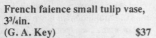

French faience small tulip vase, 3³/₄in.
(G. A. Key) $37

A pair of French Art Deco pottery book ends modeled as Pierrot and Columbine, painted in colors, 19cm. high.
(Christie's) $635

One of a pair of massive Continental pink-ground vases, late 19th century, of tapering ovoid shape, 33¹/₂in. high.
(Christie's)
(Two) $5,750

A French porcelain cabinet-plate painted by Wagner with a head-and-shoulders portrait of Napoleon I in half-profile to the left within a ciselé gilt cartouche, circa 1880, 9³/₄in. diameter.
(Christie's) $1,315

A pair of French majolica squat baluster vases, circa 1865, each applied with green buds encircled by three leaves, 3³/₄in. high.
(Christie's) $805

Round faience bowl, depicting execution via guillotine, *'Van Second de la Republique Francaise Execution de Louis Capet 21 Janvier 1793'*, decorator's initials *NV* on reverse.
(Schrager) $40

Sarreguemines majolica centerpiece, France, circa 1875, the bowl with pierced ringlets to the sides and supported by a center stem flanked by sea nymphs, 14³/₄in. high.
(Skinner Inc.) $880

Two French faience blue and white tobacco jars with lion's mask handles, painted with oval panels inscribed *Tabac de Robillard* and *Tabac de St Omer 2me qualite*, later metal covers, circa 1780, the jars 10¹/₈in. high.
(Christie's) $1,517

A René Buthaud earthenware vase, decorated with floral reserves and bands in turquoise, black and brown, 1920s, 19.8cm. high.
(Christie's) $1,180

FRENCH

A Boch Frères vase, by Charles Catteau, incised with stylized deer between borders of abstract roundels, 40.5cm. high. (Christie's) $850

A Pont Au Choux model of a pug, circa 1760, recumbent on a shaped base applied with leaves and flowers, 7³/₈in. high. (Christie's) $2,530

A French faience pot pourri vase and 'crown' cover, the ovoid body molded with mask handles, 12¹/₄in. high, circa 1800. (Bonhams) $224

A French biscuit porcelain figure of a musician modeled as a young man in 17th century dress, standing, one hand by his ear, the other on his purse, 56cm. high, circa 1870.(Christie's) $1,373

A pair of French green-ground cache pots, 19th century, each of rectangular form, with pierced gilt rim, raised on four lion paw feet, 6¹/₈in. high. (Christie's) $1,776

Continental porcelain figural vase, 19th century, tree-trunk form vase with encrusted base, birds and hound figures, 14¹/₂in. high. (Skinner) $230

An unusual Continental porcelain wall plate, the image based on a design by Alphonse Mucha for Sarah Bernhardt as La Samaritaine, 50cm. diam. (Phillips London) $825

A pair of French gilt-metal-mounted white-ground inverted pear-shaped vases and covers, the bodies painted in the style of Wouvermans with figures beside encampments, circa 1910, 33in. high. (Christie's) $8,217

French barbotine portrait vase, circa 1880, decorated by François H. A. Lafond, Limoges style glaze, with portrait of a dog in shades of white with brown, 14³/₈in. high. (Skinner) $1,380

A French Art Deco porcelain night light, from a model by M. Béver, in the form of a young girl, dressed in pink, rust and blue harlequin costume, 9¹/₄in. high.
(Christie's) $354

A pair of large French Empire Revival cachepots, probably Paris, circa 1880, the bronze tapering bodies applied on each side with a gilt-bronze lion, 44cm. high.
(Sotheby's) $7,517

A lifesize French biscuit bust of Apollo, after the Antique, from a model by Gills Jeune, truncated at the shoulders, 28in. high.
(Christie's) $1,610

A pair of massive French colored biscuit busts, signed *Paul Duboy*, of two blonde ladies with roses in their hair, 59cm. high.
(Phillips) $3,400

A gilt metal mounted French white biscuit porcelain group modeled as a man seated at a piano, another standing by a cello, playing a guitar and two ladies, standing, 42cm. wide, late 19th/early 20th century.
(Christies) $1,373

A pair of porcelain centerpieces, French, late 19th century, in Meissen style, each modeled as a pair of lovers before a pierced and flower encrusted urn, 43cm. high.
(Sotheby's) $1,954

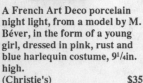

A French faience jardinière or ice pail, possibly Sceaux, finely painted in colors with exotic birds, 7in. high.
(Bonhams) $80

A pair of Sèvres-style turquoise ground oviform vases with rams head and grape handles, painted in colors with maidens in landscape, circa 1860, 14¹/₂in. high.
(Christie's) $1,273

J. Martel for Edition Lehmonn, stylized water carrier, 1920s, in cream crackle glazed earthenware heightened with metallic silver glaze, marked *J. Martel*, 28.5cm.
(Sotheby's) $2,049

FULPER

The Fulper pottery was originally established in 1805 in Flemington New Jersey, to produce drain tiles from local clay. From 1860 onwards it also turned out a range of domestic wares but it was not until 1910 that it turned to art pottery. Early pieces showed much Chinese influence and used colors from the famille rose palette. Lamps with pierced pottery shades were also produced and vases which were characterized by their angular shape. The pottery used a number of glazes including a brownish black intended to resemble dark oak. In 1926 Fulper bought out a pottery in Trenton, NJ, and the operation moved there in 1929, though a showroom was retained in Flemington.

Exceptional Fulper vase, shape #604, covered with a rich, even silvery mirrored black glaze, raised oval mark 8½in. high. (Skinner) $575

Fulper pottery copper dust vase with two handles, Flemington, New Jersey, circa 1915, 6in. diam. (Skinner) $200

Rare and important Fulper Pottery and leaded glass mushroom table lamp, matt gunmetal glaze over matt olive green glazed and reticulated dome shade, 17in. high. (Skinner) $26, 450

Fulper Pottery urn, Flemington, New Jersey, circa 1915, cucumber green crystalline glaze, vertical ink mark, 13in. high. (Skinner Inc.) $1,700

Fulper Pottery vase, Flemington, New Jersey, semi-matt glazed in shades of green at rim and ring handles with rose on lower body, 12½in. high. (Skinner) $320

Fulper Pottery vase, no. 61, Flemington, New Jersey, matt glazed in blue streak over amethyst drip on rose, 5½in. high. (Skinner) $201

Fulper pottery three-handle vase, green crystalline glaze over blue, black vertical ink stamp, 6¾in. high. (Skinner) $172

197

FULPER

Fulper Pottery center bowl, Flemington, New Jersey, gloss flambe glaze in shades of blue, 3½in. high.
(Skinner) $144

Fulper pottery buttress vase, with glossy streaked glaze in muted green and metallic brown flambé, 8in. high.
(Skinner Inc.) $400

Fulper Pottery center bowl, no. 559, Flemington, New Jersey, gloss interior in pale yellow with caramel and light blue, 3¾in. high.
(Skinner) $173

Fulper Pottery vase with mottled brown-green glaze flowing over a brown and white speckled body, black vertical ink stamp, 5in. high.
(Skinner) $173

Rare Fulper Pottery leaded glass mushroom lamp, shade with matte gunmetal crystal trailings and brown highlighting, 16in. high.
(Skinner) $11,500

Fulper pottery double handled vase, Flemington, New Jersey, circa 1915–25, no. 575, glossy green and eggplant glaze, impressed vertical mark, 6¾in. high.
(Skinner Inc.) $225

Fulper Pottery vase, circular ribbed tapering body, crystalline blue-green glaze, impressed *Fulper, 4061*, 10in. high.
(Skinner) $575

A Fulper Pottery centerpiece on pedestal base, hammered olive-green on paler green glaze, circa 1915, 10½in. high.
(Skinner) $1,400

Early 20th century Fulper pottery candle lantern, 10½in. high.
(Skinner) $600

FÜRSTENBERG

For an operation which is still going strong today, the Fürstenberg porcelain factory got off to a distinctly unpromising start. In 1747, one Johann Christoph Glaser approached Duke Carl I of Bavaria, claiming to know all there was to know about making fine porcelain, and offering his services. The Duke was delighted, put a castle at Glaser's disposal, and the Duchess was so excited that she threw out all her porcelain, believing it could be ground down and formed afresh!

Glaser was a charlatan, but he managed to get a small operation going to make faience until 1753 when Johann Benckgraff was persuaded to come to Fürstenberg from Höchst. Though he brought with him the modeler Simon Feilner and the painter Johann Zeschinger, Benckgraff promptly died before he could reveal much about porcelain manufacture!

It has been claimed that the high relief and extravagant ornamentation on early Fürstenberg was used to conceal the many imperfections in the clay. However, by 1760 quality had improved sufficiently to allow the safe manufacture of simple forms which relied on enamel and gilt chinoiserie decoration, and in the 1770s some very fine figures were made by a number of modelers,

In 1795 L V Gerverot was in charge of the factory. He had worked previously at Sèvres and Wedgwood and followed neo-Classical fashions to produce black basalts and biscuit porcelain busts. In 1859 the factory was in private hands and still manufactures today.

Fürstenberg is marked with various forms of a cursive *F* in underglaze blue. Biscuit busts bear the impressed mark of a running horse.

A Furstenberg globular teapot and cover, blue script F and figure 3 to base, circa 1765, 19cm. wide. **$3,200**

A large Furstenburg figure of a warrior, standing on a rocky base, wearing elaborate armor decorated in gray and gold, 33cm., *F* mark in blue. (Phillips) **$775**

Pair of Furstenberg porcelain figures of a young man and woman, circa 1770, each on a low shaped oval base mottled in green, 7¼in. high. (Butterfield & Butterfield) **$9,900**

A Fürstenberg circular sugar-bowl and cover, painted in green camaieu with wooded landscapes above gilt and puce scroll and scale demi-cartouches, circa 1775, 4¼ in. diam. (Christie's) **$796**

A Furstenberg group of Perseus, modeled by Desoches, blue script F mark, circa 1780, 26.5cm. high. **$640**

A Furstenberg figure of a stonemason standing, blue script F mark, circa 1775, 11cm. high. (Christie's) **$680**

GALLÉ

While Emile Gallé (1846–1904) is best known as an artist in glass, he also worked in other media as diverse as furniture and ceramics. He established a small workshop in 1874 at Nancy (Meurthe et Moselle) and there produced earthenware, which was first exhibited in 1890. Later, he also experimented with stoneware and porcelain.

His forms were for the most part simple, sometimes even a little clumsy, though some of his shapes were borrowed by the Rookwood pottery in the USA, who acknowledged their debt to him.

His decorative motifs included heraldic themes and scenes which were reminiscent of delft. Perhaps inevitably, too, he used standard Art Nouveau motifs such as plant designs of orchids, chrysanthemums, orchids etc, and his glazes were flowing and opaque, sometimes mingling two or more colors.

Apart from his own distinctive style, he was much influenced by Japanese styles, as reflected in some of the 'Origami' pieces he produced, the angular shapes of which presage Art Deco themes . Amongst the most charming of his pieces are his cats, which sit, regarding the onlooker with their glass eyes and an expression on their faces which is variously described as 'sweet faced' or a 'silly smile'.

All his pieces were marked, either with the impressed initials *EG*, *Em Galle Faiencerie de Nancy*, or with various versions of his signature.

Emile Gallé, crouched nodding cat, circa 1880, pale pink-colored tin glazed earthenware decorated with flowered jacket and a medallion, 15.5cm. (Sotheby's) $10,750

A Gallé faience model of a rabbit, depicted standing by a hollow tree trunk on grassy oval base, signed, 35.2cm. high. (Phillips) $4,000

A pair of Gallé faience 'Origami' models each as an abstract folded creature painted with yellow and blue bands, 8cm. high. (Phillips) $640

A Gallé tin glazed faience cat, the white and blue ground polychrome painted and gilded with flowers and a locket and chain, 33.3cm. high. (Christie's) $8,039

Emile Gallé, seated cat, circa 1880, yellow tin glazed earthenware body decorated with abstract blue designs, with glass eyes, 13in. (Sotheby's) $3,634

A Galle faience bowl of squat dimpled bulbous shape, 1890's, 14cm. $240

GARDNER

The success of the Imperial Porcelain factory in the mid 18th century and the demand for its products led private individuals to set up their own porcelain making enterprises in Russia. Among them was Francis Yakovlevich Gardner, an Aberdonian by birth, who arrived in Russia in 1746 and made his fortune in a Moscow banking office. He received an Imperial permit in 1766 and started work the following year. While early Gardner pieces cannot rival the porcelain of Meissen, he was successful in making products of a lovely off-white hue, which soon attracted royal patronage. Many commissions followed for grand services for use on ceremonial occasions in the Winter Palace, adorned with badges and ribbons of chivalric orders. Gardner also turned out a series of delightful little biscuit 'dolls', producing 800 of these in 1770 alone.

While Gardner's products showed some neo-classical influence as the century wore on, they remained resolutely Russian in spirit. The factory was made a company in 1857, and was taken over by the firm of Kuznetsov in 1892.

The marks include a *G*, either in Cyrillic or Roman, while crossed swords or a star are found towards the end of the 18th century. After the early 19th century *Gardner* appears in Cyrillic with the Arms of Moscow. From 1855–1881 the Russian two headed eagle appears above the arms encircled with a band on which is inscribed *Fabrik Gardner v Moskve*.

A porcelain biscuit figure of a peasant, seated on a bench, by the Gardner Factory (impressed mark), circa 1885, 14cm. high.
(Christie's) **$1,160**

A Gardner biscuit group of two peasant children cracking Easter eggs, both in tunics and breeches, on a rectangular base, 16cm.
(Phillips) **$731**

A porcelain biscuit group of a child seated on a trestle (hands repaired) and another playing a horn, by the Gardner Factory, circa 1885, 4¾in. high.
(Christie's) **$640**

A biscuit group of three tipsy men standing on an oval base, by Gardner, printed and impressed marks, 23.5cm. high. **$1,200**

A porcelain biscuit group of Gogol's Dead Souls, portraying Chichikov haggling with two men, by the Gardner Factory, circa 1885, 5½in. high.
(Christie's) **$1,600**

A Gardner biscuit figure of a peasant, reputedly Tolstoy, seated on logs and wearing a pink tunic, pale blue breeches and boots, 17cm.
(Phillips) **$528**

GERMAN

Medieval German pottery consists mainly of jugs and cups, most of which are undecorated. Cologne and the Rhineland were particularly prominent pottery areas at this time.

From the 16th century very fine salt glazed stoneware was made in the four centers of Cologne, Siegburg, Raeren and Westerwald, the last with incised decoration, while in the 15-17th centuries the Hafner, or local stove makers, were responsible for the production of earthenware with fine green and colored glazes.

The German faience industry dates from the 17th century and aimed mainly at reproducing Chinese style blue and white. It centered round Hanau and Frankfurt, and Hanau is also notable for having pioneered the work of the Hausmaler, or outside decorators, whose work was to have such importance both for faience and later for porcelain. Faience was also produced at Nuremberg (where most of the Hausmaler worked) and Bayreuth; this was notably baroque in style and used high temperature colors. A clutch of factories in Thuringia also made blue and white and high temperature polychrome faience.

Germany took the lead in true porcelain manufacture, when Böttger discovered its secret for Augustus the Strong in 1708-9. No other German factory succeeded in copying it for almost fifty years, but from the middle of the century numerous other princes endeavoured to set up their own manufactories. Interest was at its height between 1750-75, and this was when much of the finest work was done.

Pair of 19th century German porcelain cherub candle holders, 7in. high.
(G. A. Key) $550

An Erhardt & Söhne biscuit barrel, of cylindrical form, wood inlaid in brass with floral cartouches, 23.5cm. high.
(Christie's) $319

A pair of Villeroy & Boch stoneware vases with entwined handles, each molded with four oval panels with portrait busts of figures emblematic of the Continents, late 19th century, 16¹/₄in. high.
(Christie's) $639

German porcelain portrait plate, late 19th/early 20th century, depicting Countess of Harrington, titled on the reverse, the central enameled portrait signed *Wagner*, 9³/₈in. diameter.
(Skinner) $488

Pair of German porcelain figures of a couple from the Malabar Coast, after a Meissen model by F.E. Meyer, circa 1900, 12in. tall.
(Butterfield & Butterfield) $935

A Kreussen pewter-mounted stoneware Apostle Humpen, dated *1671*, applied with figures of the twelve apostles, their names inscribed above, 6¹/₈in. high.
(Sotheby's) $2,300

GERMAN

Continental porcelain group of 'Blind Mans Buff', a couple together with a child, probably German, 19th century, 8¹/₂in. high.
(G. A. Key) $162

A German porcelain architectural cabinet cup, cover and saucer, of square section molded with Corinthian columns, 4³/₄in.
(Bonhams) $640

Continental porcelain group of two lovers, he wearing a puce tunic and she holding a dove on her arm, late 19th century, 9in. high.
(G. A. Key) $447

A German porcelain oval-section snuff box painted with scenes of figures in 18th century dress, with gilt-metal mount to the rim and with fitted gilt-metal four-legged stand, the porcelain mid 18th century, Meissen or Fürstenberg.
(Christie's) $1,096

German porcelain monkey band, late 19th century, consisting of eight musicians in 18th century costumes, conductor 7in. high.
(Skinner Inc.) $2,420

A blue painted gray stoneware cylindrical jug, decorated in relief with berries and leaves in diamond shapes, with metal cover, German, Höhr-Frenzhausen, circa 1910, 34cm. high.
(Kunsthaus am Museum)
    $558

A large Bellarmine stoneware jar of rotund form, a bearded face on the neck, a medallion below, covered in a mottled brown glaze, 34cm. high.
(Bearne's) $507

A rare pair of bisque busts of children, the boy cradling a dog, the girl with a cat, 11in. high, probably early Heubach.
(Christie's S. Ken) $3,200

A German porcelain oval plaque, finely painted with two young women, 22 x 16.5cm., set in a carved and gilded wood frame.
(Bearne's) $2,533

GERMAN

A mid 18th century Fulda faience frog, 8cm. long. $5,200

A pair of German porcelain figures of a youth and companion, wearing floral rustic costume, 17½in. high. (Christie's S. Ken) $600

A German faience lobed dish painted in blue with birds in an extensive stylized landscape 35cm. (Phillips) $280

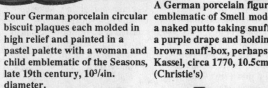
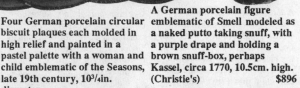

A Hanau pewter-mounted Enghalskrug painted in blue and yellow and outlined in manganese with an Oriental seated among flowering shrubs, circa 1700, 27.5cm. high. (Christie's) $3,326

Four German porcelain circular biscuit plaques each molded in high relief and painted in a pastel palette with a woman and child emblematic of the Seasons, late 19th century, 10³/₄in. diameter. (Christie's) $1,948

A German porcelain figure emblematic of Smell modeled as a naked putto taking snuff, with a purple drape and holding a brown snuff-box, perhaps Kassel, circa 1770, 10.5cm. high. (Christie's) $896

A pair of J. Uffrecht & Co. painted earthenware figures of Lohengrin and Elsa, painted predominantly in gray, apricot and shades of cream, late 19th century, 20½in. (Christie's) $2,125

A German porcelain plaque depicting Amor and Psyche, each scantily clad, flying above the clouds, 25.3cm. x 17.8cm., in a gilt Florentine frame. (Bearne's) $1,848

A pair of R. M. Krause majolica figural candlesticks, modeled as a man, standing wearing a Romanesque tunic, his female companion wearing a head dress, 54cm. and 52.5cm. high. (Spencer's) $809

GERMAN

A German topographical circular plaque painted with a view of Dresden from the banks of the Elbe, circa 1810, 16.5cm. diameter.
(Christie's) $4,435

A pair of German porcelain birds, 19th century, mounted as lamps, the male and female birds perched atop a tree stump over rockage, 34in. high.
(Butterfield & Butterfield) $3,162

A Flörsheim fluted bough-pot with flared rim, painted in grand feu colors with flowering plants, manganese F monogram mark, circa 1775, 15.5cm. wide.
(Christie's) $801

A brown salt glazed bellarmine, pear shaped with inscription band flanked by portrait medallions, Cologne, 16th century.
(Kunsthaus am Museum) $933

Pair of 19th century Continental porcelain cabinet plates, the central circular panels painted with bust length portraits of a young boy and girl in 16th century attire, 30cm. diameter.
(Spencer's) $1,078

A Nuremberg fayence (Kordenbusch Workshop) Walzenkrug of cylindrical shape, painted in blue with St. Francis receiving the stigmata, 18.6cm. high.
(Phillips) $2,233

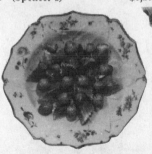

Pair of German gilt-bronze-mounted porcelain covered urns, mid 19th century, painted on the front and back with scenes of eighteenth century lovers and musicians in a garden setting, 27^1/$_8$in. high.
(Butterfield & Butterfield) $5,500

A German shaped circular trompe l'oeil plate molded with leaves and applied with wild strawberries naturalistically colored, circa 1765, 23cm. diam. (Christie's London) $3,200

A pair of late 19th century Continental porcelain comports, the pillars surmounted frolicking cherubs and climbing roses on rococo base, 14^1/$_2$in. high.
(Dee, Atkinson & Harrison) $765

GERMAN

Fine porcelain double master salt with surmounting figure of Cupid, bears the mark of the Royal Porcelain Manufactory, Berlin, circa 1820, 5in. high. (Eldred's) $363

A J. von Schwarz earthenware and nickle-plated brass tray, the base with impressed and polychrome glazed decoration of a maiden's profile, 46cm. long. (Christie's) $974

A Continental figural incense burner, fashioned as a seated clown, in yellow and black costume, 20.5cm. high, marked *Edition Kaza*. (Phillips) $225

Art Nouveau ceramic ewer, attributed to Johan Marsch, Germany, circa 1900, high relief decoration, 17³/₄in. high. (Skinner) $690

A pair of German seated pug dogs, with blue ribbon-tied collars hung with yellow bells, possibly Braunschweig, circa 1750, 14.5cm. and 15.5cm. high. (Christie's) $5,600

A Durlach blue and white fluted oval two-handled tureen, cover and stand molded with flutes and on four scroll feet, circa 1750, the stand 40.5cm. wide. (Christie's) $12,834

A North German dated blue and white rectangular tea caddy, the base inscribed *Fuls Spu Huls 1740* pewter mount and cover, 18cm. high. (Christie's London) $760

A Merkelbach stoneware bowl and cover, designed by Paul Wynand, of globular form on three feet, decorated with an all over design of scale like stippling, 28cm. high. (Phillips London) $280

A Künersberg rectangular plaque, the center painted en camaieu rose with the Penitent Magdalene before the Cross, circa 1750, 16.5 x 13.5cm. (Christie's) $23,173

GOLDSCHEIDER

It was in 1886 that Friedrich Goldscheider founded his factory in Vienna. After his death in 1897, production continued there under the direction of his widow and brother Alois, until, in 1920, the business was taken over by his two sons Marcel and Walter. In 1927, however, Marcel broke away to form the Vereinigte Ateliers für Kunst und Keramik.

While such things as vases were produced, the factory is best known for the figures and wall masks which epitomised the Art Nouveau and perhaps even more, the Art Deco styles.

A Goldscheider polychrome painted pottery figure, from a model by Dakon, of a young girl, emerging from a blue hat box, 16cm. high.
(Christie's) $1,683

A Goldscheider polychrome painted pottery figure of a young female dancer, wearing blue dress painted with bubbles and vines, 15¼in. high.
(Christie's) $1,300

A Goldscheider terracotta wall hanging, modeled as a female bather standing amongst rushes, with towel draped over right forearm, 15in. long.
(Christie's S. Ken) $1,012

A large Goldscheider terracotta group of three boys, each seated, two wearing caps and all with jackets and trousers, circa 1890, 22½in. high.
(Neales) $3,225

A Goldscheider pottery bust of a young woman in the Art Deco style, signed F. Donatello, 23½in. high.
(Outhwaite & Litherland) $720

A Goldscheider polychrome painted pottery group from a model by Bouret, of two children walking arm in arm, 9in. high.
(Christie's) $876

Lorenzl for Goldscheider, Butterfly Girl, 1920s, polychrome earthenware, modeled as a young girl in a butterfly dress, 47.5cm.
(Sotheby's) $3,089

A Goldscheider polychrome painted pottery figure, from a model by Lorenzl, of a dancer, in high stepping pose with shawl draped behind, 37cm. high.
(Christie's) $1,094

GOLDSCHEIDER

Goldscheider ceramic figural, Austria, designed by Dakon, decorated in rose and black on white ground, 8^{7}/$_{8}$in. high. (Skinner) $488

A Goldscheider pottery double face wall plaque, the two females in profile, 12in. high. $640

A Goldscheider Art Nouveau pottery figure of a naked maiden supporting a circular mirror on her thigh, 30in. high. (Christie's S. Ken) $1,680

A Goldscheider terracotta wallmask modeled as an exotic woman partially concealed behind a mask, 14in. long. (Christie's S. Ken) $420

A pair of Goldscheider pottery figures of negro children, each in a long dress carrying a broad brimmed hat, late 19th century, 25cm. high. (Bearne's) $640

A Goldscheider terracotta wallmask, modeled as a young woman with green coiled hair and orange features, 25cm. high. (Christie's) $500

Parisienne, a Goldscheider polychrome ceramic figure modeled by H. Liedhoff, printed factory marks, 13¾in. high. (Christie's) $680

A Goldscheider pottery figure of a dancer, in a floral lilac dress with bonnet, 12in. high, circa 1930. $560

A Goldscheider polychrome-painted pottery figure of a dancer, modeled by Dakon, wearing blue spotted bodice and floral divided skirt, 10½in. high. (Christie's S. Ken) $810

GOLDSCHEIDER

A Goldscheider pottery figure of a dancing girl, designed by Lorenzl, 16in. high.
$1,120

An unusual Goldscheider pottery wallmask modeled as Shirley Temple, painted in colors, 10in. long. (Christie's S. Ken)
$712

A china Art Deco figure of a woman by Goldscheider, Vienna, 12½in. high. (Skinner)
$560

A Goldscheider terracotta wallmask, modeled as the stylized head of a woman with pierced eyes, orange hair and lips, 12in. long. (Christie's S. Ken)
$682

A pair of Goldscheider pottery bookends, in the style of Wiener Werkstätte, each modeled as a kneeling girl with head turned to the side, 8in. high. (Christie's)
$2,531

A goldsheider terracotta wall mask of a female profile painted with turquoise ringlets, orange-banded black hat and yellow scarf, 10in. long. (Christie's S. Ken)
$450

A Goldscheider pottery figure of a woman wearing a beaded costume, on a black oval base, 18in. high. (Christie's)
$3,000

Goldscheider porcelain figure by Lorenzl, 14in. high. (Muir Hewitt)
$1,230

A Goldscheider figure of a woman in a long dress and hat, enameled in shades of mauve, blue and black, 31.3cm. high. (Christie's London)
$1,080

GOLDSCHEIDER

A Goldscheider painted plaster bust of a young boy wearing a straw hat, and a scarf tied around his neck, 46cm. high. (Phillips) $669

A Goldscheider earthenware wall mask, 1920's, 17cm. high. $440

Goldscheider painted terracotta bust of a girl wearing a headscarf and shawl, signed, impressed and with seal mark, 16in. high. (Lawrences) $684

A Goldscheider pottery figure modeled by Dakon, of a young woman wearing a sailor's hat, swimsuit and pink trousers, 39cm. high (Christie's) $2,207

A Goldscheider figure of a girl, by Dakon, modeled wearing a green gingham dress and reading a book, 25cm. high. (Phillips) $720

A Goldscheider pottery figure, modeled as a sailor holding a girl, 30cm. high. $600

A Goldscheider pottery mask of a girl looking down, Made in Austria, circa 1925, 23cm. high. $600

A Goldscheider polychrome painted pottery figure of a young girl, wearing pleated sleeveless dress with butterfly patterned split skirt, 23cm. high. (Christie's) $1,170

A Goldscheider terracotta wall mask modeled as the head of young girl holding a fan across her neck, 11in. high. (Christie's) $560

GOLDSCHEIDER

A Goldscheider terracotta wallmask, in the form of a young woman holding an apple to her throat, impressed *6774*, 19cm. long.
(Christie's) $508

A fine Goldsheider terracotta figure of a Blackamoor holding a tray, on a shaped square base, 23½in. high. $3,200

A Goldscheider polychrome terracotta bust of a young turbanned Arab, signed, late 19th century, 78cm. high.
(Finarte) $3,755

A Goldscheider polychrome painted pottery figure of a young woman, stepping forward and grasping the hems of her skirt, 34cm. high.
(Christie's) $269

A Goldscheider pottery group by Lorenzl, modeled as a naked girl standing in a relaxed pose with her borzoi behind her, 36.5cm. high.
(Phillips) $800

A Goldscheider ware group of a mother and child seated and standing on a rock peering into a rock pool, 24in. high, impressed marks and numbers *3581-141*, signed *Petri*.
(Anderson & Garland)

$270

Hosteas for Goldscheider, dancer with turban, 1920s, modeled as a scantily clad female dancer in mid-step, 44.75cm.
(Sotheby's) $2,907

A Goldscheider terracotta head, of a young woman with pale green combed and curled hair, tin glazed in shades of white, orange and green, 29cm. high.
(Christie's) $2,340

A Goldscheider ceramic figure of a negro dandy, dressed in three piece suit, wing collar and tie, with a glass monocle, 20¹/₂in. high.
(Christie's) $4,440

GOSS

The Goss factory was established in 1858 by William Henry Goss, who had learned his trade at the Copeland Works, where he rose to become chief artist and designer. When he set up on his own, he continued to produce the parian busts and figures which he had worked on at Copelands, and also brought out a small amount of terracotta ware. Another early line was jeweled scent bottles and vases, made from pierced and fretted parian and inset with cut glass jewels. No more of these were made after 1885.

The advent of his son Adolphus into the company revolutionised production. Adolphus realised that a huge market existed among the new Victorian day-trippers for souvenirs of the places they had visited, and he hit on the idea of producing small china ornaments bearing the towns' coats of arms. William Henry did not appreciate this inspiration at first, but his son finally persuaded him and soon the factory's bust and figure output had been completely replaced by the new heraldic ware.

It was Adolphus too who arranged the marketing and distribution of his idea, and he became the firm's principal salesman. One agent per town was appointed as sole distributor, and they could only sell pieces bearing their own town's coat of arms, though after 1883 they were allowed to select from a wider range of shapes. Despite Adolphus' success, relations with his father were very strained, and when William Henry died in 1906 he was excluded from a share in the business. It fell finally to a fourth son, Huntley, in 1913, who was no business man. He tried to survive and capitalise on the Great War by introducing a range of

Shepherd boy holding a horn. (Goss & Crested China Ltd.) **$1,125**

Haddon Hall Norman Fort. (Goss & Crested China Ltd) **$98**

Goss teapot stand with 'Old Scarlett' decoration. (Crested China Co.) **$115**

A very rare W. H. Goss porcelain figure of the Trusty Servant, 20cm. high. **$2,400**

W. H. Goss model of Shakespeare's house, printed marks, 3½in. high. (G. A. Key) **$92**

Goss Parian plate *Eat thy bread with Thankfulness*, 345mm. diameter. (Crested China Co.) **$440**

GOSS

battleship and military designs, but eventually failed and sold the firm in 1929. The new owners continued to make heraldic ware for four more years, during which time all pieces were marked *Goss*, *Goss England* or *Made in England*. Harold Taylor Robinson tried to revive the company in 1931 as W H Goss Ltd, but failed and went bankrupt in 1932.

After this, throughout the 30s a colorful range to match the Art Deco mood of the times was produced. Cottage ware was a particularly successful line, and commemorative mugs and beakers were produced for coronations and jubilees. Production ended in 1940 and the Goss site is now owned by Portmeirion Potteries.

A number of marks were used during the production period, some of which have already been mentioned. A Goshawk with outstretched wings was in continuous use from 1862, and indeed, the factory was known locally as the Falcon Works.

Goss trinket tray decorated with multiple crests. (Crested China Co.) $184

Goss toby jug. (Crested China Co.) $280

Little girl Goss doll with real hair, porcelain arms, head and legs. $720

Arcadian figure of Red Riding Hood as a sugar caster. (Crested China Co.) $192

Lincoln leather jack with City Ringers decoration. (Goss & Crested China Ltd.) $1,200

Sulgrave Manor, Northamptonshire. (Goss & Crested China Ltd.) $1,650

Goss oval wall pocket with acanthus leaf decoration. (Crested China Co.) $323

Goss cruet set and stand.
(Crested China Co.) $130

Goss hand painted drake.
(Crested China Co.) $312

Goss Chester Roman vase, with
Chester Arms.
(Goss & Crested China Ltd)
    $30

Goss third size Aberdeen bronze
pot with arms of Owen
Glyndwr.
(Crested China Co.) $60

Goss Stratford sanctuary
knocker cup.
(Goss & Crested China Ltd)
    $300

Goss Caernarvon ewer.
(Goss & Crested China Ltd)
    $15

William Wordsworth's Home,
Dove Cottage, Grasmere, 100mm.
long. (Goss & Crested China Ltd)
    $800

Goss Norwegian horse-shaped
beer bowl.
(Goss & Crested China Ltd)
    $50

Goss Fruit basket with coral
handle, first period, 200mm.
long.
(Goss & Crested China Ltd)
    $360

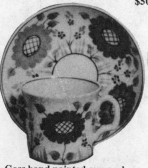

Goss Stirling pint measure.
(Goss & Crested China Ltd)
    $20

Goss hand painted cup and
saucer.
(Crested China Co.) $136

Goss worded jug *Seek out the
good in every man.*
(Crested China Co.) $70

GOSS

W.H. Goss miniature teaset, Forget-me-nots. (Crested China Co.) **$330**

Goss swan. (Crested China Co.) **$192**

W.H. Goss toast rack. (Crested China Co.) **$100**

German yacht in full sail. (Goss & Crested China Ltd) **$15**

Goss fruit dish. (Crested China Co.) **$104**

Preserve jar and lid with grapefruit decoration, 110mm. (Goss & Crested China Ltd.) **$100**

A Goss Agent's Change Tray, 140mm. diam. (Goss & Crested China Ltd) **$480**

Goss Isaac Walton's cottage, Shallowford. (Goss & Crested China Ltd) **$640**

Goss teapot stand, with a William MacCall verse. (Goss & Crested China Ltd) **$60**

Goss parian bust of Queen Victoria in mob cap. (Crested China Co.) **$192**

Goss Bagware teapot with crest of sailing ship and *God speed Greenock*. (The Crested China Co.) **$105**

Goss Kirk Braddan cross. (Goss & Crested China Ltd) **$160**

GRAYS POTTERY

Edward Gray (1871-1959) began his career as a salesman for the pottery wholesaler H.G. Stephenson of Manchester. Believing he could improve on the products he had to sell, he went into the business himself, setting up in 1907 first simply as a wholesaler, but expanding to become a pottery decorating concern. In 1912 the company moved to larger premises in Mayer Street, Hanley.

Throughout his career, Gray remained dedicated to improving standards of quality and design. This led to an enlightened approach to his apprentices, who were encouraged not only to pursue their studies at evening classes, but were also offered an early form of day release. In this, he cooperated closely with Gordon Forsyth, Head of the Burslem School of Art, and Forsyth, who was himself a brilliant ceramic artist, supplied Grays with designs for their highly successful luster ware.

Susie Cooper is, of course, the most famous name to be associated with Grays. She joined them in 1922 and remained for seven years, in which time she was promoted to Art Director. She designed a number of floral banded and geometric patterns, many of which can be identified by her name or initials incorporated into the backstamp. Cooper-designed Gloria luster vases now attract a sizeable premium. In 1933 the firm moved again to larger premises in Stoke. Edward Gray retired in 1947 and died in 1959, when the factory was sold to Portmeirion Potteries, though the name continued in use until 1962.

A Gray's Pottery plate, the well painted with stylized flowers in shades of pink, purple and green, 27cm. diameter.
(Christie's) $194

'Moon and Mountain', a Gray's Pottery Paris jug and twin-handled dish, painted in shades of red, blue, green and black, dish 28cm. wide.
(Christie's) $448

A Gray's Pottery coffee set for six painted in ruby luster and orange with fruiting vine frieze, coffeepot 19cm. high.
(Christie's) $345

A Gray's Pottery vase of ovoid form with everted rim, painted with flowers and foliage on a powder blue ground, 21cm. high.
(Christie's) $259

'Cubist', a Gray's Pottery coffee set for six, comprising coffeepot and cover, milk jug and sugar basin, six cans and saucers, height of pot 21cm.
(Christie's) $4,400

A Gray's Pottery bowl designed by Susie Cooper, the well painted with alternating bunches of grapes and vine leaves, 25cm. diameter.
(Christie's) $232

GRAYS POTTERY

A Gray's pottery Susie Cooper spherical lampbase, painted with golfers and a caddie, 15cm. high.
(Christie's) $806

A Gray's pottery tea for two, painted with floral sprays in blue, green, yellow and orange on a black ground, height of teapot 4½in.
(Christie's S. Ken) $645

A Gray's Pottery coffeepot and cover, designed by Susie Cooper, painted with pink bellflowers, 20cm. high.
(Christie's) $194

GREATBATCH

William Greatbatch (1735-1813) was a Staffordshire modeler and potter who worked at Fenton. For a time he served under Thomas Whieldon, but in 1759 set up on his own to make earthenware. He produced items in fruit and vegetable shapes, such as pear and apple teapots and cauliflower dishes, which he then supplied to Wedgwood for glazing. He also modeled designs of figures and landscapes for use on saltglaze and green-glazed earthenware.

A Staffordshire tortoiseshell tea canister, possibly by Greatbatch, of upright rectangular shape with green glazed canted corners, circa 1770, 11cm.
(Phillips) $480

A Greatbatch creamware cylindrical teapot and cover, circa 1780, printed and enameled with The Prodigal Son in Excess and The Prodigal Son in Misery, 5³/₈in. high.
(Christie's) $2,300

A Greatbatch creamware cylindrical teapot and cover, circa 1775, enameled with four Chinamen within arched panels, 5³/₄in. high.
(Christie's) $633

A Greatbatch creamware cylindrical teapot and cover, printed with scenes from the Prodigal Son, circa 1775, 13cm. high.
(Christie's) $3,680

A documentary Greatbatch creamware cylindrical teapot and cover dated 1778, printed and painted with The Fortune Teller and with The XII Houses of Heaven, 5in. high.
(Christie's) $6,325

GRIMWADE

The company started life as Grimwade Bros. in 1886 at the Winton Potteries in Hanley and the Elgin Potteries in Stoke, becoming Grimwades in 1900. They incorporated the Rubicon Art Pottery in 1913 and later the Atlas Tile Co.

A circular trademark was used on their Royal Winton floral range, with various variations of *Royal Winton, Grimwades England* and *Royal Winton Ivory England*. After 1950, however, the circular mark was phased out, and the same words were used horizontally.

Grimwade pottery plate with decorative edging 'Where did that one go to?' $80

Grimwade vase 'Well Alfred, 'ow are the cakes'. $95

Grimwade shaving mug with transfers of 'Old Bill' and Arms of Margate. $72

Grimwade vase depicting 'Old Bill', 'At present we are staying at a farm'.
    $95

A Grimwades Cube luster tea-pot, printed and painted with fairies, cobwebs and toadstools, printed factory mark, 4in. high. (Christie's S. Ken) $195

Grimwade pottery plate 'Well if you know of a better 'ole go to it'. $65

Grimwade mug 'Well if you know of a better 'ole go to it'. $65

Grimwade pottery plate 'With a loaf of bread beneath the bough'. $65

GRUEBY

The Grueby Faience Co was formed in 1897 by William H Grueby in East Boston, MA, initially manufacturing tiles, Della-Robbia style plaques and vases. From 1898 matt glazes of opaque enamel were used in shades of blue, brown, yellow and sometimes red. The most characteristic of these, however is dark green with a veined effect. Vases were hand thrown, some plain, others decorated with geometrical patterns or plant forms in low relief. From 1904 glazed paperweights were made in scarab form.

Grueby Pottery Eros tile, red clay square decorated by raised cupid with bow against matt black background, 6 x 6in.
(Skinner) $165

Exceptional Grueby vase, decorated with molded crisp leaves, stems and tooled flowers, 4½in. high.
(Skinner) $23,000

Rare and important Grueby pottery vase, Boston, circa 1900, designed by George P. Kendrick, modeled by Wilhelmina Post, matt green glaze on high-relief decorated form, 12½in. high.
(Skinner) $34,500

Grueby pottery two-color lamp base, Boston, circa 1905, bronze foot signed Gorham Co., 18in. high.
(Skinner) $16,000

Rare and important Grueby Pottery vase, molded by Miss Lillian Newman, cucumber green matt body decorated with three hand molded blossoms arising from spiked leaf clusters, 12¾in. high.
(Skinner) $12,000

Grueby Pottery vase, bulbous base, alternating leaves and buds under a matt green glaze with white highlights, 7¼in. high.
(Skinner) $2,070

Grueby Pottery vase, Boston, matt green glaze, on high relief wide leaf blade alternating with bud on stem decoration, 4¼in. high.
(Skinner) $1,725

Grueby Pottery vase, Boston, circa 1910, designed by George P. Kendrik, matt yellow glaze on high relief decorated form, 10¾in. high.
(Skinner) $23,000

GRUEBY

Grueby pottery vase, Boston, Gertrude Stanwood, matt navy blue glaze with incised alternating floral and leaf decoration, 5⁷/₈in. high. (Skinner)   **$990**

Grueby Pottery wide-mouth vase, Boston, circa 1905, with moulded leaf decoration, matte oatmeal glaze exterior, 3¹/₂in. high. (Skinner Inc.)   **$375**

Grueby pottery lotus bulb vase, heavy walled sphere with seven broad green leaf forms around central light blue matt bottle-top, 8¹/₂in. high. (Skinner)   **$3,190**

A Grueby pottery experimental drip glaze vase, Boston, Massachusetts, circa 1905, with wide rolled rim and short neck, 11¼in. high. (Skinner)   **$3,443**

Late 19th century Grueby Faience Co. bust of 'Laughing Boy', based on a statue by Donatello, 11in. high. (Skinner)   **$1,485**

Grueby Faience Co. vase, Boston, Massachusetts, circa 1902, with bulbous vase molded design, matte green glaze, 7in. high. (Skinner Inc.)   **$650**

Grueby Pottery vase, matt green glaze, overlapping tooled leaves, impressed marks, 6in. high. (Skinner)   **$860**

Grueby Pottery vase, Boston, matt green drip glaze, impressed mark, 5¾in. high. (Skinner)   **$1,035**

Grueby pottery vase, Boston, circa 1905, partial paper label and artists monogram *JE* (minor nicks), 12in. high. (Skinner Inc.)   **$2,300**

GRUEBY

Grueby faience pumpkin vase, squat melon-ribbed organic body with autumn harvest yellow matt glaze, 9in. high.
(Skinner) $2,310

Grueby Pottery vase, circular form bulbous base tapering in toward top, broad and narrow alternating leaf pattern, 4¾in. high
(Skinner) $4,025

Rare Grueby Pottery lidded jar, Boston, curdled matt blue glaze with dark blue speckling, 6¾in. high.
(Skinner) $2,530

Grueby pottery monumental floor vase, Boston, Massachusetts, circa 1905, the body with repeating broad thumb molded and ribbed decoration, 21in. high.
(Skinner) $4,000

Grueby pottery two tile scenic frieze, Boston, circa 1902, depicting four cows in various states of grazing and repose.
(Skinner) $5,850

Grueby Pottery two-color vase, leaf-carved jardinière form with textured butterscotch yellow matt glaze decorated by eight white matt enamel flower buds, 7in. high.
(Skinner) $4,400

Grueby pottery vase, Boston, circa 1904, modeled by Marie Seaman, matt-ocher glaze on repeating high-relief foliate decoration, impressed mark, 10½in. high.
(Skinner) $1,725

Navy blue Grueby pottery vase, Boston, circa 1910, impressed and artist initialed (glaze imperfection and bubble bursts), 5½in. high.
(Skinner Inc.) $1,900

Impressive Grueby Pottery vase, attributed to Wilhelmina Post, crisp leaves under a mottled green glaze, 11¼in. high.
(Skinner) $4,600

GRUEBY

Grueby pottery vase, Boston, matt green glaze, impressed mark, 12¹/₂in. high.
(Skinner) $1,760

Grueby Pottery bowl, Boston matt green glazed exterior and interior rim, 4in. high.
(Skinner) $1,035

Grueby pottery vase, Boston, matt dark green glaze, impressed mark, 13in. high.
(Skinner) $605

Rare Grueby vase, double gourd form, three recessed panels creating a raised stylized flower and leaf pattern, 7³/₄in. high.
(Skinner) $2,300

A Tiffany leaded glass lamp shade on Grueby pottery base, early 20th century, with dome shaped shade in acorn pattern, artist initialed *A.L.* for Annie Lingley, 17¾in. high.
(Skinner) $20,000

Grueby pottery vase, Boston, circa 1902, designed by George P. Kendrick, modeled by Wilhelmina Post, matt cucumber-green glaze on low-relief foliate decoration, 16¹/₂in. high.
(Skinner) $20,700

Important Grueby pottery vase, Boston, attributed to Wilhelmina Post, matt green glaze, 11¹/₄in. high.
(Skinner) $7,150

Grueby pottery bowl, Boston, Wilhemina Post, bisque form with carved and incised overlapping leaves, 8¹/₂in. diameter.
(Skinner) $825

Grueby pottery vase, Ruth Erickson, circa 1905, impressed mark and incised artist's cipher, 16³/₈in. high.
(Skinner) $29,900

HADLEY, JAMES

James Hadley (1837–1903) was an English ceramic modeller who worked at the Worcester factory between 1870–5. He took his inspiration from the Japanese style, producing pieces with reticulated decoration and others in the Shibayama style.

From 1875 he worked independently, supplying models to the Royal Worcester factory until 1896. He also made a series of table figures after Kate Greenaway, carrying baskets and enriched with gilding. His own porcelain, mainly in the form of vases with molded relief decoration in tinted clay, was marketed as Hadley ware. He was succeeded by his sons, until the firm was sold to the Worcester factory in 1905. His marks include the printed or impressed monogram *JH & S* or *Hadley's Worcester*, later also with a ribbon label.

James Hadley, a majolica ware model of an elephant carrying a howdah on its back, 22cm.
(Phillips London) $760

A pair of Royal Worcester figures, date *1884*, modeled by James Hadley, as a boy and girl in Kate Greenaway style, 16.5cm. high.
(Phillips) $1,200

A good pair of Royal Worcester 'Queen Anne' sweetmeat dishes, dated 1888, modeled by James Hadley, the 'Kate Greenaway' boy and girl both seated on a tree bough, 17.5cm. wide.
(Phillips) $1,440

A good pair of Royal Worcester figures from the 'Countries of the World' series, dated *1887*, modeled by James Hadley, comprising Ireland and a seated Scotsman, 15.5 and 17cm.
(Phillips) $800

A pair of Royal Worcester figures of a satyr and a bacchante, modeled by James Hadley, he attired in a goatskin, date code for 1891, 74.5cm. high overall.
(Bonhams) $4,680

James Hadley, set of five figures of the Down and Out Menu Men, fully colored, and standing on gray brick bases, approx. 15cm.
(Phillips) $2,000

A pair of Royal Worcester figural lamp bases, modeled by James Hadley, in the form of classical maidens carrying amphora, year code for 1896, 80cm. high overall.
(Bonhams) $6,240

HAMADA

Shoji Hamada (circa 1894–1978) was a Japanese potter whose early work was influenced by the Korean ceramics of the Yi dynasty. He worked mainly in stoneware, producing vases, bowls etc. in simple sturdy shapes colored usually in brown, olive, gray and black. In 1920 he came to England with Bernard Leach, and worked with him at St Ives for the next three years. Here, he became fascinated with English medieval pottery and also participated in experiments with lead-glazed slipware. On his return to Japan, he took many ideas with him, and helped found the Japanese Craft Movement in 1929. He became a strong influence in modern Japanese ceramics, and his later pieces, made during the 50s and 60s are characterised by their use of slablike, angular forms.

A stoneware teapot by Shoji Hamada, with floral decoration, orange, buff and brown, circa 1942, 7in. wide.
(Bonhams) $514

A stoneware teabowl by Shoji Hamada, browns and orange, circa 1940, 5in. diameter.
(Bonhams) $768

An outstanding circular dish by Shoji Hamada, reddish brown with black specks, with a wax resist cream foliate motif, circa 1960, 29cm. diameter.
(Bonhams) $3,000

A fine stoneware bottle vase by Shoji Hamada, covered in a brown glaze beneath bands of matt pale sage-green, khaki green and tenmoku, 22.5cm. high.
(Christie's) $3,828

An important stoneware cut sided bottle by Shoji Hamada, tenmoku glaze over red body, circa 1951, 11in. high.
(Bonhams) $5,995

A stoneware square dish by Shoji Hamada, khaki, the upper surface with resist stepped cross pattern, 10½in. square.
(Bonhams) $2,840

A hexagonal stoneware vase by Shoji Hamada, khaki glaze with three floral motifs, circa 1965, 7¾in. high.
(Bonhams) $2,840

HAMADA

A tenmoku stoneware teabowl by Shoji Hamada, with central ridge, decorated with rust colored splashes, 4¼in. high.
(Bonhams) $3,000

A fine stoneware bottle vase by Shoji Hamada, tenmoku with wax resist floral decoration, in a fitted wooden box with Japanese characters, 8in. high.
(Bonhams) $8,000

A stoneware press-molded bottle vase by Shoji Hamada, rectangular with square section tapering neck, covered in a mottled metallic brown glaze, 19.5cm. high.
(Christie's) $3,350

A two handled white pot by Shoji Hamada, with a brown rim, 5¾in. high.
(Bonhams) $960

A stoneware press-molded bottle vase by Shoji Hamada, covered in a speckled pale khaki glaze, the neck, shoulder and two side panels with brushed olive-green, 19.8cm. high.
(Christie's) $3,200

A stoneware teabowl by Shoji Hamada, with brushed pale gray hakeme band below rim over sage green, 4in. high.
(Bonhams) $960

A stoneware wax resist decorated dish by Shoji Hamada, with a floral motif, rust, buff rim and motif, 11in. diameter.
(Bonhams) $2,800

An outstanding curved stoneware vase by Shoji Hamada, speckled gray with white vertical lines and brown foliate decoration, in fitted wooden box with Japanese characters, 10in. high.
(Bonhams) $12,000

A stoneware plate by Shoji Hamada, covered in speckled ocher glaze, with iron-brown brushwork to the well, 18.8cm. high.
(Christie's) $640

HAMPSHIRE

The Hampshire pottery was set up in Keene, New Hampshire, in 1871 to produce domestic earthenware. Another production line comprised souvenirs for tourists, while some majolica was also made. Transfer printing in black was a favored style of decoration.

Marks consist of *Hampshire Pottery* and the signature of the proprietor *J.S. Taft.*

Hampshire Pottery lamp base, matt green base with eight-panel slag glass shade, impressed mark, 15in. high.
(Skinner) $862

Hampshire Pottery vase, Keene, New Hampshire, designed by Cadmon Robertson, matt mottled green glaze with brown swirling drip, 6¾in. high.
(Skinner) $374

Hampshire vase, heavily embossed leaves with vine handles under a green matt glaze, impressed mark, circled *M*, 8¼in. high.
(Skinner) $575

Hampshire Pottery cobalt blue vase, decorated with embossed stylized leaf decoration under iridescent glaze, impressed *Hampshire Pottery/118/MO.*, 5in. high.
(Skinner) $862

Hampshire pottery vase, Keene, New Hampshire, circa 1900, with repeating molded tulip and running stem decoration, 9in. high.
(Skinner) $480

An early 20th century Handel lamp on Hampshire pottery base, with Mosserine shade, 20in. high.
(Skinner) $1,200

Hampshire Pottery double handle vase, Keene, New Hampshire, designed by Cadmon Robertson, decorated form with split branch handles, 5½in. high.
(Skinner) $230

Hampshire Pottery chamberstick, Keene, New Hampshire, designed by Cadmon Robertson, matt green glaze, 5½in. high.
(Skinner) $201

HAN

The pottery of the Han period (206BC–220AD) is the earliest really attractive Chinese ware, for it was about this time that the ornamental qualities of the medium were realised. Also, at this time there was a certain amount of contact with the near East and even the West, which led to the general introduction of glazes, which had been in use in Egypt from ancient times.

Han pottery is usually either red or slaty gray, depending on the provenance of the clay, and varies in texture from soft earthenware to something approaching stoneware. The bulk of it is glazed, the typical glaze being a translucent greenish yellow, though this is subject to many variations. One of the characteristic features of pottery of this period is the frequent appearance of 'spur marks', usually three in number, around the mouth or base of a piece, which were made by the supports used when the ware was placed in the kiln.

Han pottery is decorated in various ways: either by pressing in molds with incuse designs, giving a low relief effect, or by the use of stamps or dies, or by applied strips of ornament, all of which would be covered by the glaze.

It was the fortunate custom to bury the dead together with many of the objects which surrounded them in life, and it is to tomb excavations that we owe most of the Han pottery in existence today.

A fine green-glazed stoneware jar, incised with a continuous band of birds and fish, Han Dynasty, 30cm. high.
(Christie's) $6,118

A large Han period horse's head of burnt gray tone, and wooden socle, 22.5cm. high.
(Galerie Koller) $2,816

A pottery figure of a caparisoned Mongolian pony, with saddle cloth and high ridged saddle, Han Dynasty, 15¾in. long.
(Christie's) $3,896

A green-glazed red pottery model of a farm, the courtyard containing an archer, a miller, ducks and two dogs, Han Dynasty, 12 x 13½in.
(Christie's) $4,959

A painted gray pottery cocoon-shaped jar, some earth encrustation, Han Dynasty, 26.5cm. wide.
(Christie's) $1,360

A Han Dynasty funerary sculpture of a seated dog, 23cm. high.
(Stockholms Auktionsverk) $823

HISPANO MORESQUE

In 711 the Moorish armies of the Caliph of Damascus invaded Spain, where they were to remain until their final expulsion by Ferdinand and Isabella in 1492. Thus for almost 800 years Spain formed the point of convergence of Eastern and Western civilizations, and nowhere is this dual influence seen more clearly than in its pottery.

Islamic potters had learned the art of tin-glazing with the addition of copper and silver oxides from their Mesopotamian counterparts. They brought this knowledge with them, and there are reports of a thriving export trade of lusterware from the Malaga region of Spain dating from as early as the mid 12th century.

Some of the forms of the early wares would be difficult to reproduce even today.

In the 14th century many Muslim potters from Malaga and Murcia moved to the Valencia area, and Manises became the renowned center of 'golden' pottery. Here it became subject to gothic influence, and the representation of a wide range of birds and animals became popular.

Towards the end of the 15th century came a demand for lighter tablewares, resulting in the introduction of a new range of shapes and more precise techniques similar to those used by Staffordshire potters, such as, for example, the greater use of molds.

In the early 17th century animal forms take on more stylized forms, and the fine draughtsmanship of earlier pieces is lacking. From the 19th century many reproductions were made. It is worth remembering that no regular marks ever appear on genuine Hispano Moresque ware.

An Hispano-Moresque tapering waisted albarello decorated in blue and copper-luster with two bands of stylized bunches of grapes, late 15th century, 18cm. high. (Christie's) $4,400

An Hispano-Moresque lusterware charger, 16th century, the central flower form boss with an armorial shield, 15¼in. diameter. (Sotheby's) $3,500

An Hispano-Moresque lusterware charger, 16th century, the raised well surrounded by alternating bands of zigzag patterns and leaves, 16¼in. diameter. (Sotheby's) $3,500

An Hispano-Moresque copper-luster oviform jar, the short cylindrical neck with four grooved loop handles divided by waisted panels of flowers and loop-pattern, 17th century, 22cm. high. $6,400

A Cantagalli 'Hispano-Moresque' ewer, the compressed globular body below tall neck applied with strap handle, early 20th century, 36.5cm. high. (Christie's) $480

An Hispano-Moresque blue and copper-luster large dish with a raised central boss with a quatrefoil surrounded by a band of radiating fronds, 16th century, 41cm. diameter. (Christie's) $4,000

HÖCHST

Hard paste porcelain was first produced at Höchst-am-Mein in 1750 by Johann Benckgraff and Josef Jakob Ringler, who had both come from Vienna. The operation was never on a sound financial or administrative footing and the Elector had to make several reorganisations before his successor took over completely in 1778. The factory closed in 1796.

Early wares were characterised by a rather coarse body and a milky glaze, but quality soon improved and there was a large output of figures as well as of tableware. Especially important are the figures from the Commedia dell' Arte, set on high square pedestals. These are similar to those subsequently produced at Fürstenberg (the modeler Feilner may have been responsible for both) but the Höchst models are livelier and less fussy.

Höchst was among the earliest factories to make pastoral groups and arbor scenes. These were mainly by J.F. Lück. Laurentiis Russinger made rather larger groups in the manner of Boucher. He was succeeded in 1767 by Johann Peter Melchior, whose delightful groups of children gave way in the early 1770s to groups of classical sentimentality.

When the factory closed the molds passed on to works in Damm and Bonn, both of which made falsely marked reproductions. In the early years of this century further fakes were made at Passau.

From 1750–60 the mark is usually that of a wheel with between four and eleven spokes. Six is the most common, and eight often denotes a fake. These were either incised or impressed. A similar mark in underglaze blue was used between 1760–96; and an Electoral Hat 1760–64.

One of a pair of Höchst teacups and saucers painted with pastoral scenes after engravings by J.E. Nilson, circa 1765. (Christie's) $6,000

A Höchst cream jug, the slightly swollen body on a narrow foot ring, with green branch handle, circa 1765-70, 7.5cm. high.
(Lempertz) $827

A Höchst tea and coffee service comprising pear-shaped coffee and small pot, sugar basin, teapot, teacaddy, slop basin and six cups and saucers, painted with scattered flowers, fruit and butterflies, circa 1750-55, height of coffee pot 23cm.
(Lempertz) $14,698

One of a pair of Hochst pot-pourri vases painted in the manner of Andreas Phillipp Oettner, circa 1765, 25cm. high.
(Christie's) $22,000

A Höchst rectangular lobed tea caddy and cover, circa 1750, molded in relief and painted in colors with trailing flowering branches, 13cm.
(Christie's) $12,477

A Höchst pug dog naturally modeled and seated on his haunches to the right and scratching his chin, circa 1755, 10cm. high. (Christie's) $4,435

A Hoechst group of Die erlegte Taube, perhaps modelled by J. P. Melchior as a scantily draped youth, with a distressed maiden kneeling at his feet, circa 1770, 17.5cm. high. (Christie's London) $1,360

A German porcelain model of a putto riding a dolphin, with red tail and fins, scantily draped in a flowered gilt-edge cloth, circa 1770, perhaps Höchst, 10.5cm. wide. (Christie's) $880

A Höchst figure emblematic of Winter modeled by J.P. Melchior, as a putto wrapped in an ermine-lined cape with a muff seated on a grassy hummock, circa 1760, 16.5cm. high. (Christie's) $1,000

A Hochst group of Wandering Musicians, modeled by J. P. Melchior, underglaze blue wheel mark to base. circa 1770, 23cm. high. $7,200

A Höchst cylindrical tea-caddy and cover, the sides painted with two gilt scroll cartouches with a couple of peasants on a bridge in a landscape, circa 1765, 11.5cm. high. (Christie's) $2,402

A Höchst group of the fortune-teller modeled by Simon Feilner, as a gallant standing beside his seated companion while a bearded fortune-teller examines her hand, iron-red wheel mark, circa 1755, 17cm. high. (Christie's) $8,797

A Hoechst milking group, modeled by J. P. Melchior, she milking a brown marked cow drinking from a pail, her companion holding it by a tether, circa 1770, 18.5cm. wide. (Christie's) $2,800

A Höchst group 'Der Chinesische Kaiser', circa 1765, formed as a majestic figure in gilt and turquoise crown, a figure in pink-striped grey dress and pink trousers making obeisance, 14in. high. (Christie's) $36,800

IMARI

The name Imari derives from the port through which the porcelain of 17th century feudal Japan was exported. It has been adopted to describe the palette of underglaze blue and overglaze iron red and gilt of the Arita export wares. Most 17th century Japanese porcelain was blue and white and, due to fluxing of the cobalt with the glaze, the blue decoration characteristically bleeds into the surrounding area. It was to overcome this fault that early workmen painted iron red and gold onto the glaze to conceal the blurred edges.

A pair of Imari baluster jars and covers, Imari, early 18th century, each decorated with shaped panels of blossoming prunus, peony and bamboo sprigs, 56cm. high. (Sotheby's) $7,725

An Imari charger, the central roundel with peony and plum blossoms in a vase on a terrace, late 17th century, 53.4cm. diameter. (Christie's) $7,360

A Samson Imari vase, with two shaped panels depicting bijin beneath plum surrounded by peonies and scrolling foliage, late 19th century, 41cm high. (Christie's) $3,871

A pair of Imari jars of square section, each facet painted with a jardinière of chrysanthemums, 24.5cm. (Bearne's) $1,760

An Imari jar and cover, the upper part decorated in underglaze blue with pine and plum tree beneath a band of shippo pattern, late 17th century, 21.5cm. high. (Christie's) $8,832

A large Imari fluted dish decorated with a central medallion of three gambolling karashishi among scrolling peony flowers, 19th century, 64.3cm diam. (Christie's) $1,760

A pair of rare and unusual Imari bijin, the partially clad figures decorated in iron-red, green, aubergine and black enamels and gilt, Genroku period, 31.5cm. high. (Christie's) $22,000

Imari style charger, early 20th century, painted in gilt, underglaze blue and red enamels with a flower basket at the well, 17½in. diameter. (Butterfield & Butterfield) $489

IMARI

A pair of Imari jars and covers decorated in iron-red, green, yellow, black and aubergine enamels and gilt on underglaze blue, late 17th century, 40.5cm. high.
(Christie's) $8,000

An Imari model of an actor, his kimono decorated with chrysanthemum and cherry blossom flowers and foliage amongst brocaded ribbons, circa 1700, 39cm. high.
(Christie's) $4,800

A pair of Imari baluster vases and covers with vertical 'S' scroll designs and roundels depicting wave pattern, all interspersed with flower sprigs, circa 1700, 61.6cm. high.
(Christie's) $13,600

An Imari jar decorated with three shaped panels depicting two bijin walking under a parasol in a garden, the panels divided by vivid floral designs, late 17th/early 18th century, 41cm. high.
(Christie's) $10,000

An Imari circular tureen, cover and stand decorated in iron-red, green and aubergine enamels and gilt on underglaze blue, lappet handles, kiku mon, circa 1700, dish 27.7cm. diameter, tureen 19.8cm. high.
(Christie's) $17,336

An Imari charger decorated in typical colored enamels and gilt on underglaze blue, circa 1700, mounted as a Victorian giltwood and composition occasional table on column supports, 58.5cm. diameter. $11,600

An Imari charger, the central roundel depicting a bijin walking up stairs leading to a porch behind which stands a blossoming cherry tree, circa 1700, 54.3cm. diameter.
(Christie's) $5,450

A pair of fine Imari octagonal vases and covers decorated with various shaped panels of landscapes and foliage, late 17th/early 18th century, 51cm. high.(Christie's) $13,167

A fine Imari charger decorated with three lobed panels containing a ho-o bird hovering above waves beside various flowers and foliage amongst rockwork, late 17th/early 18th century, 54.7cm. diameter.
(Christie's) $6,772

IMARI

A pair of hexagonal Imari vases and covers, the body with four lappet panels containing alternate pinks and ho-o among clouds, circa 1700, 52.0cm. high. (Christie's) $21,000

An Imari pierced box decorated in iron-red, black, yellow, green and aubergine enamels and gilt on underglaze blue, late 17th/ early 18th century, 9cm. high, approx. 14.6cm. square. (Christie's) $3,200

A pair of octagonal Imari vases and covers decorated with shaped panels of birds among flowers and foliage, late 17th/ early 18th century, 63.5cm. high. (Christie's) $12,227

An octagonal Imari vase and cover, the body with alternate vases of chrysanthemums and cherry blossom, the shoulder with four lappet-shaped panels, circa 1700, 65cm. high. (Christie's) $11,600

A pair of Meissen Imari tureens and covers, each freely painted in the typical palette enriched with gilding, with two exotic cockerels among flowering peony and chrysanthemum, circa 1735, 34cm. high. (Christie's) $56,000

An Imari octagonal tureen and cover decorated with panels of karashishi and cranes (cover and bowl with extended crack and chips), late 17th/early 18th century, 41cm. high. (Christie's) $4,514

An Imari charger decorated with lush peonies and bamboo, bordered above and below by panels of geometric design, late 17th/early 18th century, 53.5cm. diameter. (Christie's) $9,000

A pair of Imari models of actors, the robes with roundels containing the character ju among sprays of flowers, foliage and blossom, late 17th century, 31.8cm. high. (Christie's) $8,700

An Imari shallow dish decorated in iron-red and gilt on underglaze blue, the central roundel with a cockerel and a hen and their young standing beside buildings, circa 1700, 27.6cm. diameter. (Christie's) $3,200

IMARI

Imari charger decorated in the typical manner in colors, with central panel of jardinière and flowers etc., early 20th century, 23in. diameter.
(G. A. Key) $525

A pair of large ormolu-mounted Japanese Imari dishes, each decorated in four colors, the center with flowers within a landscape border, the mounts 19th century, 20½in. diameter.
(Christie's) $11,178

A Japanese Imari barber's bowl painted in underglazed blue and iron-red with a central vase of flowers, late 17th/early 18th century, 10½in. diameter.
(Christie's) $1,452

A fine Imari tankard decorated in iron-red enamel and gilt on underglaze blue, the ovoid body with three shaped panels, the loop handle pierced for a mount, Genroku period, 22.5cm. high.
(Christie's) $6,800

A pair of Imari decorated Japanese plates of lobed circular form, 19th century, 64.5cm. diameter.
(Stockholms Auktionsverk) $4,307

An Imari model of a potter standing at his wheel making a large vase decorated with mythical birds in flight among foliage, 19th century, 20cm high.
(Christie's) $791

A large Japanese Imari charger, late 19th century, decorated with two roundels, one containing a bird in a flowering cherry tree, the other a dragon, 25in. diameter.
(Christie's) $3,146

Two Imari square bottles and covers decorated in various colored enamels and gilt on underglaze blue, late 17th century, 26.7 and 25.6cm. high.
(Christie's) $6,217

An Imari dish decorated in various colored enamels and gilt on underglaze blue, on a ground of scrolling foliage and chrysanthemum heads, 19th century, 40cm diam.
(Christie's) $2,375

IMARI

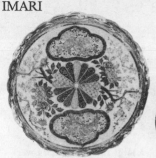

An Imari foliate rimmed bowl decorated in iron-red and green enamel and gilt on underglaze blue, late 19th century, 32.1cm. diameter.
(Christie's) $2,011

A large pair of 19th century Japanese Imari bottle vases, each decorated with leaf shaped panels of pine branches and prunus blossom, 66cm. high.
(Spencer's) $5,236

Large 19th century Imari salver, traditional blue, rust and green palette, scalloped border, 17in. wide.
(G. A. Key) $457

An Imari coffee urn on three shaped feet, with a molded dragon head spout above the base, decorated with shaped panels of floral sprays, circa 1850, 30.2cm. high. (Christie's London) $5,000

A pair of Imari plates, each molded in relief with a sumo wrestler standing on a dohyo, 19th century, 34cm. diameter.
(Christie's) $5,152

Louis XV style gilt-bronze-mounted Imari porcelain centerbowl, the porcelain Meiji Period, the ovoid bowl painted with shaped panels.
(Butterfield & Butterfield) $5,750

An Imari barber's bowl decorated in underglaze blue, iron-red and gilt with a central jardinière of peonies and plums, 18th century, 27.2cm diam.
(Christie's) $2,463

Pair of Japanese Imari large baluster vases with ribbed borders, decorated in the typical manner in traditional colors, 19th century, 12in.
(G. A. Key) $544

A 19th century Imari porcelain charger with decoration of scroll paintings on a floral ground, 17¾in. diameter.
(Eldreds) $1,100

IMARI

A large and massive Imari vase and cover, decorated with a continuous panel of bijin beside flower carts, late 17th/early 18th century, 103cm. high.
(Christie's) $16,929

An Imari koro and cover modeled as a seated karashishi decorated in iron-red, green, black enamels and gilt, late 17th/early 18th century.
(Christie's) $10,000

A large Imari vase and cover decorated with panels of chrysanthemum sprays among informal gardens, beaneath a band of irises and other foliage, late 17th century, 71cm. high.
(Christie's) $10,722

A pair of Imari bottle vases decorated in iron-red enamel and gilt on underglaze blue, the globular body with plants set in roundels and birds on a ground of cloud pattern, late 17th century, 25cm. high.
(Christie's) $4,160

An ormolu-mounted Imari coffee urn and cover, the fluted sides with a continuous design of ho-o birds among flowering and fruiting boughs, the cover similarly decorated, late 17th century, overall height 30.5cm.
(Christie's) $21,000

A pair of Imari baluster vases and covers decorated in iron-red enamel and gilt on underglaze blue, the domed covers surmounted by karashishi finials, late 17th/early 18th century, 47.0cm. high.
(Christie's) $9,900

A massive Imari vase, 19th century, of baluster form, the exterior decorated with two large panels each depicting a garden landscape with flowering hibiscus, 48¼in. high.
$9,200

An Imari tureen and cover decorated with stylized chrysanthemum flowerheads with geometric and floral patterns surrounded by flowers and scrolling foliage, late 17th century, 38cm. high.
(Christie's) $6,070

Late 17th century Imari vase, richly decorated in iron red, blue and gold with flowering bushes on a terrace, Genroku period, 63cm. high.
(Christie's) $24,000

ITALIAN

The word maiolica came into use about the middle of the 15th century to describe firstly lustered Spanish pottery and then all kinds of tin glazed earthenware. The principal centers for the production of the latter were Orvieto, Tuscany and Faenza. Deruta joined them not long afterwards and featured, from 1501, a golden and a ruby luster.

Decorative styles and themes were to some extent common, which can make identification difficult, though some characteristic features, such as the blue stained enamel of Faenza and the gray and blue of Castel Durante, did emerge. The istoriato pictorial style was perfected by Pellipario, first at Castel Durante and later at Urbino. Urbino was also the source of a new style of grotesque decoration after Raphael from the mid 16th century.

The 17th and 18th centuries saw imitations of Dutch delft emerging from Savona and elsewhere, while Florence has the distinction of producing the only porcellanous ceramic material to be made in Renaissance Europe. This 'Medici' porcelain is of an artificial soft-paste type.

As far as true porcelain is concerned, the Vezzi factory at Venice was started in 1719 with the help of a Meissen renegade, while Doccia, from 1737, drew its styles from Vienna. French-style soft-paste porcelain was made at Capodimonte from 1742, and production was resumed in Naples in 1770.

Italian porcelain is characterised by its gray color, and this is common to the products of Nove, Treviso, Doccia and Venice.

NOVE.

A pair of Faenza berettino-ground albarelli, each with the initials *SM* beneath a yellow star surrounded by alla porcellana and strapwork beneath a robianna, circa 1520, about 16.5cm. high.
(Christie's) $26,000

An Italian rectangular casket and cover with a detachable surmount formed as a youth and maiden embracing, holding a goblet and bunch of grapes, attended by a putto, circa 1880, 12½in. high.
(Christie's) $3,044

A Cantagalli charger, possibly by Farini, the central roundel depicting two putti rowing a galleon across choppy waters, 51cm. diameter.
(Phillips) $1,360

Two Faenza waisted albarelli decorated in the workshop of Virgiliotto Calamelli and named 1525, 27cm. high.
(Christie's) $35,000

A pair of Faenza small waisted albarelli named in blue gothic script for *Pill aure* and *Pill eolie* on blue ribbons beneath portrait medallions flanked by foliage, circa 1560, 13cm. high.
(Christie's) $9,750

A Ferniani coffee pot and cover, painted in blue, red, yellow, olive green, brown and manganese, with a Japanese Imari style garden landscape with giant flowers, 34cm. high.
(Phillips) $782

ITALIAN

An 18th century South Italian maiolica dish painted with the Sacrifice of Isaac in turquoise, yellow, ocher, green and manganese, 46.5cm. diameter. (Finarte) $3,731

An early 20th century Italian figure, modeled as a young girl, decorated in bright polychrome enamels, monogram and painted blue N & Crown marks to base, 5in. high. (Peter Wilson) $201

An Italian maiolica tazza painted in the martyrdom of St. Barbara kneeling in the center and her executioner, 24.5cm., possibly Paduan. (Phillips) $800

An armorial sgraffito storage jar, Tuscan (probably Florentine), lae 15th/early 16th century, the ovoid body with two side handles, painted with a coat-of-arms within a robbiana, 9⅝in. high. (Christie's) $9,200

A North Italian cruet painted with birds perched among scrolling red and yellow flowers with blue berries beneath blue scroll borders, probably Turin, circa 1750. (Christie's) $2,000

A fiasca, circa 1530, the bottle vase of 'Orsini-Colonna' type, painted in blues, yellows, green and ocher on a cream ground with Apollo reserved within an acanthus scroll, labeled for *aq plantagine*, 15⅝in. high. (Christie's) $68,500

A maiolica wet drug jar named for *Oi Violat*, circa 1700, probably Le Nove, 8¼in. high; and an Italian maiolica albarello, circa 1700, probably Le Nove, 6¾in. high. (Christie's) $927

A Cantagalli globular jar twin-handled, painted with peacocks on a ground of peacock feathers beneath a flared neck, 11in. high, circa 1900. (Christie's) $1,173

A South Italian armorial waisted albarello painted in blue, ocher and manganese with the Arms of the Dominicans, first quarter 18th century, 18.5cm. high. (Christie's) $935

ITALIAN

An Italian trefoil rim jug, the globular body inscribed in Greek within a scroll cartouche, circa 1780, 9in. high. (Christie's) **$548**

A pair of Viterbo circular dishes painted in green, ocher, yellow and brown with a portrait of a girl and a warrior, 17th century, 28.5cm. diameter. (Christie's) **$4,635**

An 18th century Italian albarello, with griffin handles and blue and yellow decoration of foliage and painted figures, 36cm. high. (Arnold) **$3,118**

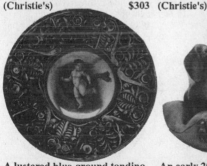

An Italian maiolica small armorial albarello of waisted form, named for *Troc:Di:Reobarbaro* on a yellow and blue banner, circa 1720, probably South Italian, 4¼in. high. (Christie's) **$303**

A pair of large Italian maiolica chargers, the centers painted with figures, the borders with playful cherubs holding leafy sprigs of flowers, within an ocher rim, late 19th century, 23½in. diameter. (Christie's) **$1,417**

An albarello, early 16th century, probably Cafaggiolo, labeled for *D:Cassia* below a winged angel head and above the pharmacy cipher of a long-necked bird, 8⅝in. high. (Christie's) **$4,025**

A lustered blue-ground tondino, Gubbio, circa 1527, workshop of Maestro Giorgio Andreoli, of cardinal's hat form, the deep well with a winged putto suspended against a gold luster ground, 9¼in. diameter. (Christie's) **$34,500**

An early 20th century Italian figure group modeled as a child seated with a dachshund, decorated in polychrome enamels, monogram mark and blue painted N & Crown to base, 4in. high. (Peter Wilson) **$286**

An armorial istoriato charger, Cafaggiolo, circa 1520, painted in green, yellow, red, ocher, blue and white, the center with Orpheus Charming the Animals within a border of grotteschi, 16⅞in. diameter. (Christie's) **$123,500**

239

ITALIAN

A Faenza waisted portrait albarello named in blue gothic script for *Eu. Forbio* with a portrait of a young woman in profile to the left, circa 1550, 27cm. high $16,000

A Lodi shaped oval tray painted in a vibrant palette with Moses striking the rock surrounded by other figures and animals beneath a blue and yellow sky, circa 1720, 48cm. wide. (Christie's) $9,680

A Faenza waisted portrait albarello named in blue gothic script for *Sangue. drag°* with a portrait of a Turk in profile to the left flanked by the initials *MS*, circa 1550, 27cm. high. (Christie's) $16,000

One of a pair of Albissola sponged-manganese-ground plates painted in manganese and lightly enriched in ocher and green with figures walking and on horseback among buildings and trees, circa 1740, about 24cm. diameter. (Christie's) $2,560

A famiglia gotica slender waisted albarello named in blue gothic script on an ocher and blue-lined manganese scroll flanked by scrolling foliage and peacock feather, perhaps Faenza or Naples, late 15th century, 31cm. high. $19,600

A Castelli armorial small dish painted in the Grue workshop and lightly enriched in gilding, the center with Venus scantily draped and combing Cupid's hair, late 17th/early 18th century, 24.5cm. diameter. (Christie's) $8,963

An Urbania tazza painted in a vibrant palette in the manner of Ippolito Rambaldotti with Christ meeting His Mother on the way to Calvary, mid 17th century, 28.5cm. (Christie's) $8,000

A finely painted Venetian large oviform jar painted with the forefront of a galloping horse, amongst military and musical trophies, 32.5cm., mid-16th century. $40,000

A Faenza berettino-ground armorial tondino of cardinal's hat form and Casa Pirota type, the central arms suspended from a winged cherub's head, circa 1530, 18.5cm. diameter. (Christie's) $52,500

ITALIAN

A Tuscan wet-drug jar with short waisted neck, the oviform body decorated in blue and ocher with the sacred *YHS* monogram, circa 1460, 25cm. high. (Christie's) $6,800

An Angarano majolica circular plate, early 18th century, painted in colors with peasants walking amongst monumental ruins, 10¼in. diameter. (Bonhams) $8,000

A Deruta waisted albarello named in blue for *DIA. ANISV* on a rectangular label within a green and yellow foliage wreath and flanked by blue grotteschi on a yellow and orange ground, circa 1510, 21.5cm. high. (Christie's) $30,000

An Urbino istoriato tazza painted with Marcus Curtius leaping into the abyss on a white stallion surrounded by soldiers before a tree, circa 1545, 25.5cm. diameter. (Christie's) $13,871

A waisted albarello painted in dark-blue and ocher with blue-edged ocher diamond-ornament within rectangular panels edged with scrolling grasses, perhaps Faenza or Naples, late 15th century, 21cm. high. (Christie's) $9,750

A circular maiolica plate by Giacinto Rossetti, Turin, 1737, painted with a satyr, urn and flowers within a foliate border, signed *Fabrica Reale di Torino GR 1737* on base, 40cm. diameter. (Finarte) $9,157

A Castel Durante Armorial saucer dish with a coat of arms above a hilly landscape, within a wide blue border, 22.5cm., circa 1570. (Phillips) $9,562

A vaso a palla indistinctly named in gothic script for *rotag¹* on an oval yellow cartouche held by mermaids, the reverse with three circular portrait medallions, circa 1560, 33cm. high. (Christie's) $26,000

An Albissola sponged-manganese-ground dish, with figures walking among trees and buildings within bright-yellow quatrefoil cartouches, manganese beacon mark, circa 1740, 26cm. diameter. (Christie's) $1,200

241

JAPANESE

While clay and earthenware were produced in Japan from earliest times, it was the Korean settlers of the 5th century who brought important new pottery techniques into the country. Chinese influence was strong too in the Nara period (646-794) and led to the development of colored glazes.

Porcelain first appeared in the 17th century, but the continuing demand for sturdy, robust pottery meant that it did not reach preeminence until the Edo period, and Kyoto replaced Seto as the main center of the industry at the beginning of the 19th century.

In the west of the country the most popular types at this time were Karatzu and Satsuma wares, the latter of course, also finding immense popularity in the West as trade with Japan opened up.

An unusual Japanese pierced porcelain bowl, late 17th/early 18th century, with French Napoléon III gilt-bronze figures, circa 1870, 27cm. high. (Sotheby's) $5,072

A broad pear-shaped tripod koro and pierced cover, painted and gilt with a coiled dragon among Buddhist priests in a rocky landscape, 4in. high. (Christie's) $230

Large Fukagawa hexagonal platter, Meiji/Tashio Period, decorated with a large blossoming peony radiating wavy brocade patterned bands, 20³/₄in. diameter. (Butterfield & Butterfield) $3,738

Ki-Seto model of a koma-inu, 19th century, the mythical beast seated on its rear haunches and with its straight forelegs resting to the front of the oval base, 11⁷/₈in. high. (Butterfield & Butterfield) $1,320

A Japanese yellow-glazed model of a fruit, of globular form, tapering at the top with five rounded nodes encircling a central aperture, 8in. high. (Christie's) $2,300

A pair of late 19th century Japanese porcelain chargers, the borders with diaper, floret and triangular patterning, 18¹/₄in. diameter, circa 1890. (Tennants) $972

A large seifu vase decorated in underglaze colored enamels on a pink ground with a dove in the branches of a Ginko tree, late 19th century, 44cm high. (Christie's) $1,408

A Hirado blue and white temple bell decorated with Raijin and ho-o birds among clouds, late 19th century, 24.5cm. high.
(Christie's) $4,138

A small flattened kettle and cover, with cane handle, painted and gilt with panels of seated ladies and children within foliate borders, 3¹/₂in. long.
(Christie's) $315

A Yabu Meizan koro and cover decorated with a continuous procession of courtiers and samurai, signed *Yabu Meizan*, late 19th century, 10.5cm. high.
(Christie's) $7,148

An inlaid stoneware oviform vase by Tatsuzo Shimaoka, the exterior inlaid in white slip with a cell pattern against a celadon ground, 19.5cm. high.
(Christie's) $574

A pair of Kiyomizu hexagonal sake bottles decorated in green and blue enamels and gilt with trailing prunus branches, 19th century, 17cm and 17.5cm high.
(Christie's) $4,223

A fine shigaraki tsubo, the bluff slightly waisted cylindrical body splashed with a pale green glaze on one side, early Edo period, 30cm high.
(Christie's) $5,279

A fluted dish, painted and heavily gilt with a coiled dragon entwined among Kannon and Buddhist priests, the underside with mon and foliage, 10¹/₂in. diameter.
(Christie's) $563

An early 20th century Japanese earthenware vase, decorated in gilt and colored enamels with seated grim faced immortals, with pagodas and mountains beyond, 31cm. high.
(Spencer's) $1,318

A 19th century fine Japanese porcelain saucer-shaped charger, decorated with the traditional Imari pattern, within a scalloped border, 23in. diameter.
(Riddetts) $673

An Imari charger painted and gilt with bijin below pine, in a border of dragon and phoenix panels, 18¼in. diameter.
(Christie's) $1,120

A Japanese celadon glazed tripod squat ovoid koro and pierced domed cover in the form of a kiku head, 5in. high.
(Christie's) $960

One of a set of four Arita blue and white foliate rimmed dishes painted with fish amidst aquatic plants, 7¾in. diameter.
(Christie's) (Four) $640

One of a set of five Arita blue and white circular dishes painted with central roundels of pomegranates, 18th century, Chenghua marks, 21cm. diameter.
(Christie's) (Five) $1,200

A Japanese blue and white tapering ovoid vase painted with a long-tailed bird perched on a prunus branch, 12¼in. high.
(Christie's) $640

An Imari charger decorated in colored enamels and gilt with a ho-o among clouds and dragon amid foaming waves, 43.5cm. diameter.
(Christie's) $1,100

A Japanese studio vase of baluster form, painted with a striding oni on a graduating pink ground, signed Kozan, 31cm. high.
(Christie's) $960

A set of five Nabeshima style leaf shaped dishes, painted and molded with mandarin ducks among wooden walkways, running Fuku marks, 11.5cm. long.
(Christie's) $1,920

A large Japanese studio baluster vase molded and painted in colored enamels with peony sprays on a yellow ground, signed Kozan, 47.6cm.
(Christie's) $4,000

JONES, GEORGE

George Jones (d. 1893) was a Staffordshire potter working at the Minton factory. In 1863 he established the Trent pottery, where he manufactured white and transfer printed earthenware for the domestic market as well as majolica. From 1872, by which time he was trading as George Jones & Sons, he was producing ornamental wares with pâte-sur-pâte decoration, such as wall pockets and vases. Porcelain was introduced in 1876 in the form of basket shaped flower holders etc and around 1880 vases with colored earthenware body and painted decoration were also being made. The factory was renamed Crescent Pottery in 1907.

A George Jones majolica fruit tray, the lobes molded with palm fronds within leafy vine branches, the central handle as a Bacchic putto, circa 1865, 35.5cm. wide.
(Phillips) $5,210

One of a set of six George Jones & Sons claret ground plates painted by W. Birbeck with loose sprays of flowers within roundels, date codes for 1925, 22.6cm. diameter.
(Phillips) $521

A George Jones majolica cheese dish and cover, modeled as a cylindrical tower, the brickwork molded with ivy and ferns, 1873, 32.5cm. high.
(Phillips) $2,431

A George Jones majolica strawberry dish, of quatrefoil form and naturalistically molded with strawberry blossom, mark for 1873, 29.5cm. wide.
(Christie's) $656

A George Jones & Sons pâte sur pâte dish by Frederick Schenk, with water nymphs by a pool, signed, late 19th century, 30.5cm. diameter.
(Christie's) $2,480

A George Jones majolica trefoil shallow basket, the pinched rims molded to simulate gathered material, circa 1870, 22cm. wide.
(Christie's) $729

A George Jones majolica jardiniere and stand of tapering square section, molded with Canterbury bells, 19.5 cm. high, circa 1870.
(Christie's) $2,100

JONES, GEORGE

A good Victorian majolica game dish in the style of George Jones, basket molded and of oval section.
(David Lay) $560

A George Jones majolica chamber-stick with a branch-molded loop handle and blossoming terminals, circa 1870, 6¼in. diameter.
(Christie's) $622

A George Jones jardiniere, cobalt blue with turquoise interior and naturalistic colouring, 33cm. high.
(Christie's) $1,200

A George Jones majolica cheese-dish and domed cover, the turquoise cover molded in relief with leafy blossoming twigs issuing from a double branch- molded handle, circa 1870, 10¼in. high.
(Christie's) $1,239

A George Jones majolica sweetmeat-dish with two faun vintner supporters, both with wreaths of fruiting vine adorning their hair, one standing wearing a lion-pelt around his thighs, the other kneeling holding a bunch of grapes, circa 1870, 9¼in. high.
(Christie's) $1,727

A George Jones majolica cheese-dish and cylindrical cover molded to simulate a barrel with yellow bands entwined with blossoming bramble leaves, circa 1873, 11¼in. high.
(Christie's) $1,122

A George Jones majolica punch-bowl modelled as Mr. Punch lying on his back, being crushed beneath the weight of a large bowl, the surface moulded and coloured to simulate orange-rind, circa 1874.
(Christie's) $4,750

A massive George Jones earthenware vase of plain ovoid shape decorated with colourful chrysanthemums on a ground of black stripes, 48cm. high.
(Phillips) $542

A George Jones majolica game-tureen and cover of tapering oval form, the cover with a crouching fox, the turquoise base molded in relief with game and hunting trophies, circa 1870, 10½in. wide.
(Christie's) $4,250

JONES, GEORGE

A majolica glazed Stilton cheese dish and cover, probably by George Jones & Sons, late 19th century.
(G. A. Key) $280

Three George Jones majolica baluster lotus jugs in graduated sizes, the sides molded in relief with clumps of bulrushes dividing large stylized green leaves, circa 1865, 6¹/₄, 7¹/₄ and 8¹/₄in. high.
(Christie's) $2,418

A George Jones 'majolica' circular cheese dish and cover, circa 1880, 28cm. diam.
(Christie's) $640

A George Jones majolica sweetmeat-dish formed as a young faun kneeling on a mound before a hollow cluster of fern leaves, supporting a turquoise and pink nautilus shell swathed in white drapery on his knee, circa 1865, 9in. high.
(Christie's) $1,295

Pair of George Jones majolica garden seats of cylindrical form, circa 1874, 18.1/8in. high. $10,400

A George Jones model of a camel, partially glazed on a dark-brown parian body, supported on a cluster of green leaves with two turquoise saddle-bags bound with gilt and black cord suspended from its back, circa 1868, 8¹/₂in. high.
(Christie's) $2,100

A Victorian George Jones majolica game tureen, the cover with a boar's head, twin boar's head handles, set with twin panels of a boar brought to ground by hounds.
(Academy Auctioneers) $1,911

A George Jones majolica dark-blue-ground drum cabaret, the globular forms bound with molded brown buckled straps and with yellow rope secured with white staples, the interiors glazed in turquoise, registration marks for 1877, tray 15¹/₂in. wide.
(Christie's) $8,289

A George Jones (and Sons Ltd) strawberry dish, painted with a butterfly beside raised flowering leafy tendrils, circa 1874-90, 25.5cm. long.
(Phillips) $651

KAKIEMON

There is a charming tradition that Sakaida Kizai-emon, an Arita potter, made an ornament in the form of twin persimmons (kaki) for his feudal overlord, who was so pleased with it that he conferred on him the honorary name of Kaki-emon. Sakaida adopted this as his family name and it was thus that the porcelain got its name. Sakaida worked for a merchant named Toshima Tokuyemon, who had learned the secret of enameling in colors, and together they mastered the art to commence one of the most important ceramic productions.

At first, white glazed pieces were brought to the Kakiemon workshops for coloring, though they later acquired their own kiln. Their vibrant designs and colors made such an impact on the European market that within a few years every European factory was trying to produce direct imitations. Early pieces, dating from 1640–70, use thick bright turquoise and iron red in imitation of the orange–red of ripe persimmons. Additional colors are azure blue, soft orange, primrose yellow, lavender blue and grass green.

Early pieces were for the use of the patron, and were strictly in the Japanese taste. However, in time decoration became more refined, and instead of covering large areas of the piece, became sparser, showing the water-color quality of the enameling. Marks rarely appear before the 18th century, and the most common are the *fuku* (happiness) and *kin* (gold) marks. Pieces were made in a wide variety of shapes, from baluster jars to human and animal figures. From the 18th century many designs show a strong European influence.

A kakiemon blue and white shallow dish with a pair of quail pecking amongst autumn grasses, late 17th century, 15cm. diameter.
(Christie's) $10,800

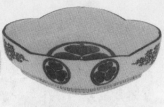

A kakiemon blue and white four-lobed dish, the central decoration a large Tokugawa mon, the exterior with smaller versions of the same, circa 1700, 15.2cm. long.
(Christie's) $9,750

A rare and important kakiemon model of an Indian elephant, late 17th century, standing with its trunk curled and vividly decorated in yellow, green, iron-red, blue and black enamels, 33½cm. high.
(Christie's) $1,236,675

A Meissen shallow dodecagonal Kakiemon bowl painted with The Hob in the Well pattern, tall bamboo and flying birds within a border of chrysanthemum and blue foliage alternating with peony and branches of leaves, circa 1730, 25cm. wide.
(Christie's) $44,000

A kakiemon blue and white foliate-rimmed dish decorated with a goose among reeds on a riverbank, another hovering above, circa 1700, 25cm. wide.
(Christie's) $4,400

A Kakiemon hexagonal teapot and cover decorated in iron-red, blue, green and black enamels, the pinched sides with panels of mixed flowers and foliage, late 17th century, 15.2cm. long.
(Christie's) $3,600

KAKIEMON

A kakiemon rectangular sake bottle decorated with children playing and flying a kite among plum blossom, bamboo, birds and rockwork, late 17th century, 15cm. high.
(Christie's) $6,750

A pair of kakiemon beakers, late 17th century, each decorated in iron red, green, yellow, blue and black enamels with a cockerel among flowers and foliage, 9¼cm. diameter.
(Christie's) $6,199

A kakiemon style celadon kendi decorated in iron-red, blue, green and black enamels, late 17th century, 19.6cm. high.
(Christie's) $3,000

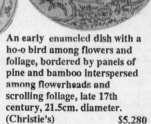

A kakiemon blue and white shallow dish with a central roundel containing a pavilion in a lakeside landscape perched on a rocky precipice, fuku mark, seven spur marks, late 17th century, 25.8cm. diameter.
(Christie's) $6,750

A set of five kakiemon blue and white dishes, late 17th/early 18th century, decorated in underglaze blue with scattered maple leaves and grass, 18¼cm. high.
(Christie's) $4,782

An early enameled dish with a ho-o bird among flowers and foliage, bordered by panels of pine and bamboo interspersed among flowerheads and scrolling foliage, late 17th century, 21.5cm. diameter.
(Christie's) $5,280

A kakiemon blue and white shallow dish decorated with gourd vine tendrils and leaves, fuku mark, late 17th-early 18th century, 21.4cm diameter.
(Christie's) $3,600

A pair of Kakiemon vases and covers, the hexagonal jars with domed covers surmounted with a knob finial, late 17th century, approx. 38cm. high.
(Christie's) $880,000

A Kakiemon octagonal deep bowl, the interior with chrysanthemums, peonies and prunus issuing from rockwork within a border of scrolling foliage, late 17th century, 19.5cm. diameter.
(Christie's) $20,000

KAKIEMON

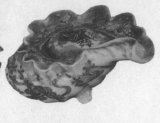

Late 17th century Kakiemon teabowl with later ormolu mounts, the bowl 6.75cm. diam., fitted box.
(Christie's) $1,920

An ormolu mounted Kakiemon porcelain vase of bombe shape, the porcelain late 18th century, 5in. wide.
(Christie's) $1,600

A Kakiemon style blue and white conch shaped tureen, with scattered flowerheads among stylized clouds and a stream, late 17th century, 21.5cm. long.
(Christie's) $9,200

An important oviform Kakiemon vase decorated with three panels each containing figures standing beneath a parasol holding an uchiwa, circa 1680, 39cm. high.
(Christie's) $385,000

Pair of Kakiemon cockerels standing on rockwork bases, circa 1680, 28cm. high.
(Christie's) $40,000

A fine rare and unusual Kakiemon ewer decorated in iron-red, yellow, blue, green and black enamels, late 17th century, 16cm. high.
(Christie's) $9,200

A kakiemon octagonal dish, the center with two quali among millet and chrysanthemums, the everted rim with a band of lappets, late 17th century, 24cm wide.
(Christie's) $25,000

One of a pair of Kakiemon oviform jars and covers, circa 1680, 29.5cm. high.
(Christie's) $24,000

A rare Kakiemon foliate rimmed dish decorated in vivid iron-red, green, blue and black enamels and gilt, late 17th century, 19cm. diam.
(Christie's) $12,350

KAKIEMON

An early enameled Kakiemon vase decorated in iron-red, blue, green and yellow enamels with a pair of stylized pheasants, late 17th century, 26cm. high. (Christie's) $98,580

A Kakiemon teapot and cover, the lobed sides with panels of various flowers and foliage, the cover with ho-o birds, circa 1680, 16.5cm. long. (Christie's) $6,400

A Kakiemon incense-burner, decorated with flowers below a flared lip with half-circles, late 17th century, 13.5cm. high. (Christie's) $5,152

A Kakiemon compressed globular kendi or gorgelet with short bulbous spout, decorated in iron-red, blue and green enamels, late 17th century, 20.2cm. high. (Christie's) $8,000

A pair of Kakiemon cockerels standing on rock work bases displaying their plumage, late 17th century, 23cm. and 24.5cm. high. (Christie's) $89,835

A multi-faceted Kakiemon type vase decorated with sprays of peony, chrysanthemum and other flowers and foliage, late 17th century, 19.5cm. high. (Christie's) $11,600

A Kakiemon dish, decorated in iron-red, blue, green and black enamels and gilt on underglaze blue with quail, late 17th/early 18th century, 21.6cm. diameter. (Christie's) $18,400

A Kakiemon oviform vase and cover, decorated in various colored enamels on underglaze blue with peonies and other flowers, late 17th century, 31cm. high. (Christie's) $11,000

A Kakiemon type shallow dish decorated with a central roundel containing a village in a lakeside landscape, late 17th century, 25cm. diam. (Christie's) $6,800

A Kakiemon blue and white shallow dish, the interior decorated with three feathers and a ho-o bird on a background of wild flowers and brushwood sheaves, late 17th century, 21.6cm. diameter. (Christie's) $5,760

An early enameled Kakiemon style teapot decorated in iron-red, blue, green, yellow and black enamels, with two shaped panels depicting ho-o birds, late 17th century, 15cm. long. (Christie's) $35,000

A foliate-rimmed Kakiemon dish decorated with a continuous design of entwined vine to the edge, chocolate rim, late 17th/early 18th century, 26.1cm. diameter. (Christie's) $14,500

A Kakiemon vase and cover, the shoulder with geometric and foliate designs including hanabishi, the domed cover with flattened knop finial, late 17th century, 32.5cm. high. (Christie's) $64,750

A pair of Kakiemon cockerels, vividly decorated in iron-red, green, blue, yellow and black enamels, late 17th/early 18th century, mounted on wood stands, 28cm. high. (Christie's) $99,693

A rare Kakiemon oviform ewer of Islamic form, decorated in iron-red, green, aubergine, yellow and black enamels and molded in low relief, late 17th/early 18th century, 30cm. high. (Christie's) $15,180

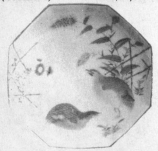

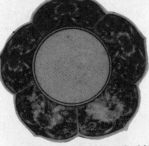

A Kakiemon-style octagonal dish with two quails beside overhanging flowers and foliage on a trellis, the underside with sprays of scrolling foliage, late 17th/early 18th century, 14.4cm. diameter. $12,000

An early enameled Kakiemon vase with boats in a lakeside landscape, beneath willows and other trees among rocks, late 17th century, 19cm. high. (Christie's) $38,000

A kakiemon style blue and white six-lobed dish, the plain central roundel bordered by six panels, each containing a flower blossom, late 17th/early 18th century, 13.1cm. diameter. (Christie's) $1,600

KANGXI

The Kangxi period in Chinese porcelain follows directly on the so-called Transitional period (1620–82) when there was great unrest and the Dutch, forbidden to continue their activities, turned their attention to Japan.

In 1682, however, the emperor Kangxi appointed Ts'ang Ting-hsuan as director of the Imperial factory, and following this appointment Chinese porcelain was to reach an unprecedented perfection of quality. During Kangxi's reign (1662–1722) porcelain decorated in underglaze blue was produced in ever increasing quantities for the European market. These are usually far superior to late Ming export material.

During the reign of Kangxi many wares for the home market were produced with monochrome glazes including a lustrous mirror black and fine translucent greens and yellows. It was probably during the later years of the reign, too, that the rose crimson enamel derived from gold was first introduced from Europe, and it was this that was to form the basis of the famille rose palette.

A pair of aubergine-glazed bowls, the rounded sides rising to a straight rim, encircled Kangxi six-character marks and of the period, 12.4cm. diameter. (Christie's) $6,500

A Chinese porcelain vase decorated in underglaze blue and overglaze polychrome enamel colors, 6¾in. high. Kangxi 1675–1690. (Tennants) $1,004

A pair of Louis XV ormolu-mounted turquoise-glazed models of parrots on aubergine rockwork bases, the porcelain Kangxi, 9¾in. high. (Christie's) $25,000

A fine blue and white cup, encircled Kangxi six-character mark finely penciled to the exterior with a continuous mountainous landscape and huts obscured behind willow, 3in. high. (Christie's) $43,750

A large Chinese blue-glazed vase, Kangxi, early 18th century, of baluster form, with trumpet neck, 80cm. high. (Sotheby's) $6,996

A pair of famille verte dishes, each enameled with magnolia and peony issuing from rockwork, with panels of chrysanthemum and prunus around the well, Kangxi, 35cm. diameter. $5,000

A fine blue and white beaker vase, Jaijing mark, Kangxi, finely painted to the flaring neck with a high official on horseback 17¾in. high. (Christie's) $11,000

KANGXI

An aubergine and green-glazed incised circular 'dragon' bowl, encircled Kangxi six-character mark, spiritedly carved on the exterior with two five-clawed dragons above breaking waves, 11.2cm. diameter.
(Phillips) $4,800

A pair of Kangxi Buddhistic lion joss stick holders, 20.5cm. high. $480

A peachbloom-glazed beehive waterpot, taibo zun, Kangxi six-character mark, the well-potted domed sides rising to a narrow waisted neck, 5in. diameter.
(Christie's) $35,000

A fine 'green dragon' dish, Kangxi six-character mark, painted to the center of the interior with a circular panel of a scaly dragon reaching for a flaming pearl, 7³/₄ in. diameter.
(Christie's) $11,500

A pair of Chinese famille verte biscuit officials, Kangxi, each seated on a semi-circular chair, wearing long loose green-glazed robes splashed with aubergine, 7in. high.
(Christie's) $1,049

A large green-glazed 'Blue and Yellow Dragon' saucer-dish painted at the center with a striding dragon chasing a flaming pearl, Kangxi period, 32.2cm. diam, fitted box.
(Christie's) $41,000

A Kangxi porcelain vase, of inverted baluster form, painted in underglaze blue with a continuous rocky mountainous river landscape, 27.5cm. high.
(Henry Spencer) $240

An iron red decorated brushpot, Kangxi, the sides painted in red and black with a gathering of literati, 17.2cm. diameter.
(Christie's) $5,175

A famille verte pear-shaped vase, Kangxi, brightly enameled in iron-red, green, turquoise, aubergine and gilt, 9in. high.
(Christie's) $4,000

A blue and white and under-glaze copper red fish bowl, Kangxi, 40cm. diam.
$4,400

A pair of famille verte figures of The Laughing Twins, Hehe Erxian, Kangxi, 27cm. high.
$1,280

A Kangxi blue and white baluster jar, 10.8cm. high.
(Christie's) $1,200

A rare large foliated blue and white charger painted in the Yuan style with a central design of a quatrefoil enclosing floral sprays around a floral roundel on a fretted ground, Kangxi, 21.9cm. diameter.
(Christie's) $4,800

A pair of 'egg and spinach' bowls, covered in a lustrous green, yellow, brown and white splashed glaze, 4³/₄in. diameter, Chenghau nianzhi mark, Kangxi.
(Bonhams) $1,200

An aubergine and green yellow-ground incised 'dragon' dish, encircled Kangxi six-character mark, the center of the interior with an aubergine and a green incised five-clawed dragon, 5¹/₂in. diameter.
(Christie's) $1,500

A rare glazed biscuit erotic group brushwasher, Kangxi, well modeled with a man making amorous advances to a woman, spied on by an attendant, 4½in. high.
(Christie's) $5,750

A pair of blue and white baluster jars, Kangxi, each painted with scenes of birds flying around trees, 26cm. high.
(Christie's) $4,600

A blue and white jar and cover, Kangxi, the ovoid body decorated with a mountainous landscape panel on one side, 25.1cm. high.
(Christie's) $2,185

A blue and white 'hibiscus' dish, painted to the centre of the interior with four stylized hibiscus blossoms issuing from leafy stalks within a circular panel, 8¹/₈in. diameter. (Christie's)　　　**$3,800**

A peachbloom beehive waterpot, taibo zun, Kangxi six-character mark and of the period, the exterior incised with three archaistic dragon roundels, 5in. diameter. (Christie's)　　　**$9,600**

An iron-red 'dragon' dish, encircled Kangxi six-character mark, painted at the center with a five clawed dragon chasing a flaming pearl amidst fire scrolls, 8½in. diameter. (Christie's)　　　**$3,200**

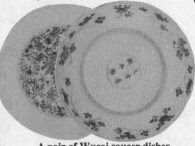

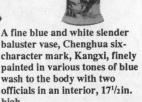

A fine small Kangxi famille verte rouleau vase, delicately enameled with seven exotic butterflies in flight amongst scattered flower-sprays and small insects, 7¹/₂in. high. (Christie's)　　　**$5,000**

A pair of ormolu-mounted Chinese blue porcelain peacocks, each with tail feathers up and seated on a naturalistic base, the porcelain Kangxi, 9¹/₂in. wide. (Christie's)　　　**$11,000**

A fine blue and white slender baluster vase, Chenghua six-character mark, Kangxi, finely painted in various tones of blue wash to the body with two officials in an interior, 17¹/₂in. high. (Christie's)　　　**$11,200**

A blue and white brushpot, Chenghua four-character mark, early Kangxi, finely painted with the scene of a scholar on a donkey followed by an attendant, departing from a lady on a cart with a male and female attendant in front of a city gate, 5¹/₈in. high.　　　**$1,200**

A pair of Wucai saucer dishes, encircled Kangxi six-character marks and of the period, with a floral roundel of dense torn-off sprays of daisy, magnolia, lotus, prunus, camellia and peony, the underside with five torn-off sprays, 6¹/₂in. diameter. (Christie's)　　　**$30,000**

A fine blue and white cylindrical brushpot, Bitong, Chenghua six character mark, early Kangxi, painted around the exterior with a continuous scene illustrating scholarly pursuits, three observers watching two scholars playing go, 6¹/₂in. diameter. (Christie's)　　　**$6,800**

KANGXI

A blue and white jardinière, Kangxi, painted to the exterior with The Three Friends, pine, prunus and bamboo below a band of key pattern, 17in. diameter.
(Christie's) $1,200

A blue and white brush-pot of cylindrical form painted with groups of scholars and attendants on a terrace, Kangxi, 18.5cm. diam.
(Christie's London) $4,000

A blue and red square brushpot, Kangxi six-character mark, painted in underglaze-blue and copper-red on the waisted body, 6¹/₂in. square.
(Christie's) $3,600

A famille verte 'magpie and prunus' rouleau vase, Kangxi, decorated to the cylindrical body with two magpies perched on a blossoming prunus tree amongst bamboo, 17³/₄in. high.
(Christie's) $9,600

Three gilt-decorated powder blue ground rouleau vases, Kangxi, variously decorated in gilding, 45.4, 44.8 and 47.6cm. high.
(Christie's) $10,350

A Chinese egg and spinach-glazed reticulated garden seat, Kangxi, pierced at the center with a wide band of cash, divided by a pair of molded lions' masks, 14¹/₂in. high.
(Christie's) $4,600

A blue and white silver mounted jar and cover, painted with panels of Long Eliza and prunus blossom below a band of cloud scrolls, 5¹/₄in., Kangxi.
(Bonhams) $400

A pair of Wucai and Doucai 'dragon' saucer-dishes, encircled Kangxi six-character marks and of the period, each interior painted with a blue five-clawed dragon striding in pursuit of another green-bodied dragon, 5³/₄in. diameter.
(Christie's) $27,500

A blue and white ginger jar of ovoid form, painted with cartouches enclosing precious objects, wood stand and cover, 10in. high, Kangxi.
(Bonhams) $520

KINKOZAN

Kinkozan was the name of an artist potter, and subsequently his studio, producing Satsuma wares in the late 19th and early 20th centuries. These vary enormously in quality, from the most basic mass produced types to extremely fine studio and experimental examples. Pieces were very often signed by the particular artist who produced them, and such a signature can make quite a difference to the value of the item.

A Satsuma circular box and cover, signed *Kinkozan*, Meiji period, decorated in enamels and gilding with a design of samurai and ladies at leisure, 5.75cm. diameter.
(Phillips) $951

Small Kinkozan caddy with inner lid and outer cover, the body with fine panels of figures or birds.
(Graves, Son & Pilcher)
                                       $2,200

A Kinkozan vase decorated with numerous revelers, the shoulder with a band of brocade designs, signed and sealed *Kinkozan sei* and *Masayasu*, 17.4cm. high.
(Christie's) $3,950

Four Kinkozan plates, decorated in various colored enamels and gilt each depicting a season, signed *Kinkozan zo*, late 19th century, 22.3cm. diameter.
(Christie's) $4,023

Late 19th century Kinkozan baluster vase, signed Dai Nihon Teikoku Kinkozan zo Kyoto Awata-yaki Shozan hitsu, 31cm. high.
(Christie's) $6,400

Fine Kinkozan Satsuma vase, 19th century, signed *Dai Nihon*, tapering globular form, reserves of eight immortals and samurai, 15in. high.
(Skinner Inc.) $9,500

A Kinkozan koro and cover, decorated in various colored enamels and gilt with two panels, signed, late 19th century, 20cm. high.
(Christie's) $2,760

A box and cover modeled as a hokkai box, painted and heavily gilt with panels of warriors in landscapes, 4^1/$_2$in. high, signed *Kinkozan*.
(Christie's) $955

KINKOZAN

A Kinkozan vase decorated with detailed figurative scenes, divided by scattered brocade designs, stamped *Kinkozan zo*, late 19th century, 27cm. high.
(Christie's) $4,514

A Satsuma-style part tea set, signed *Kinkozan*, Meiji period, consisting of four tea cups and four saucers, each cup with a different samurai.
(Phillips) $805

A Kinkozan vase and cover, decorated in various colored enamels and gilt on a dark blue ground, signed, late 19th century, 25.5cm. high.
(Christie's) $4,232

A Satsuma square section tea caddy and cover, signed *Kinkozan*, Meiji period, resting on four low feet, 9.5cm. high.
(Phillips) $1,554

A fine pair of Kinkozan vases, painted with figures of women, children, warriors and room interiors, 18.2cms.
(Bearne's) $12,800

A blue ground Kinkozan oviform vase decorated in various colored enamels and gilt with two panels, signed *Kinkozan zo*, late 19th century, 38cm. high.
(Christie's) $11,885

A Satsuma globular vase decorated with two panels of ladies and children at leisure before a pavilion in a mountainous river landscape, signed and with impressed mark *Kinkozan zo*, 19th century, 24.4cm high.
(Christie's) $4,927

A set of five dishes, painted with shaped panels of exotic birds among prunus, irises, daisies and other flowers, 7in. diameter, signed and sealed *Kinkozan*.
(Christie's) $2,640

A miniature cylindrical box and cover painted and gilt with bands of boys at play on a ground of dense chrysanthemum flowerheads, 2in. high, signed *Kinkozan, Kyoto*.
(Christie's) $728

KLOSTER VEILSDORF

Of all the many small factories which flourished in the Thuringian forests in the 18th century, the best known is probably that of Kloster Veilsdorf.

It was established in 1760 by Prince Friedrich Wilhelm von Hildburghausen and employed many specialists from other factories, such as Abraham Ripp, a kiln worker, Nikolaus Paul, the arcanist, Caspar Schumann, a painter, and most famous of all, Wenzel Neu, the modeler. With such a collection of talent, it was not surprising that they produced practical wares of excellent quality, skilfully decorated by such painters as Schumann and Döll.

Wenzel Neu is probably responsible for most of the figure output between 1760–65. The quality is not particularly high, but the style is very typical of Thuringian ware in general. Many groups were made using the same models in various guises. In about 1780 allegorical figures of the four Continents were produced, which was a completely new departure. These were probably modeled by Franz Kotta, who subsequently worked at the Volkstedt factory. He also produced a fine bust of Prince Friedrich, the factory's founder.

The factory was purchased in 1797 by the sons of Gotthelf Greiner, who then used the clover leaf mark from their Limbach factory. The earlier mark consists of *CV*, sometimes in monogram, sometimes with a shield of arms between the two letters, and sometimes drawn to look like Meissen crossed swords.

A Kloster Veilsdorf figure salt modeled by L.D. Heyd, with a figure of a seated lady, flanked by two white basket salts, 11.5cm.
(Phillips) $581

A Kloster Veilsdorf figure of Harlequin, modeled by Wenzel Neu, in black mask and skull cap, circa 1770, 5¾in. high.
(Christie's) $13,950

A Kloster Veilsdorf figure of a crouching leopard, probably modeled by Pfranger snr., circa 1775, 12cm. long. $800

A Kloster Veilsdorf figure of Cadi-Leskier, modeled by Pfranger, circa 1770, 14cm. high. $5,600

A Kloster Veilsdorf group of Summer, modeled as a young man and companion, standing and seated before sheaves of corn, circa 1775, incised *P*, 12.5cm. high.
(Christie's) $2,325

A Kloster Veilsdorf figure of Pantalone modeled by Wenzel Neu, 1764-65, 14.5cm. high. $3,600

KUTANI

Kutani wares, in contrast to Kakiemon, were directly derived from late Ming colored pieces. They are the most highly prized of all Japanese porcelains and are very difficult to date, as no records of the old factories survive. Broadly speaking, the early pieces are referred to as Ko- (old) kutani, as opposed to the Ao- (new) Kutani revivalist stonewares of the 19th century.

Ko-kutani pieces usually have a whitish gray body with a milky white glaze. The colors are rich and harmonious and include vivid green, egg yellow, aubergine, Prussian blue and iron red. Decoration is mainly representative of birds and insects among flowering trees and shrubs, and rarely features animals, while figures are Chinese in conception. They were probably made during the latter part of the 17th century for the use of the overlord and his court.

As the 18th century wore on the power of the Shogunate, the main patrons of such kilns, began to wane, and the Kutani kiln, which had been under the protection of the daimyo Maeda, collapsed in the last years of the century, following his fall from favor. In 1816 Yoshidaya Denyemon revived the kiln, and production continued until the 1860s. These Ao-kutani pieces lack the vitality and originality of the earlier products. They are often heavily enameled, with green or yellow grounds, and the decoration is outlined in black. They also bear a small two character mark which was lacking on the earlier pieces.

The Arita kilns, which fared much better during the early 19th century, continued to produce pieces in the Ko-kutani style.

A late Kutani (Kaga ware) box and cover formed as a chest attended by three karako, signed *Takayama ga,* late 19th century, 25cm. high. (Christie's London) $5,200

A late Kutani minature tsuitate, the centre with a panel depicting birds in flight above flowering grasses, 19th century, 30.5cm high. (Christie's) $1,760

An important Ko-Kutani dish decorated with chrysanthemum flowerheads and foliage scattered among stylized waves, late 17th century, 21cm. diameter. (Christie's) $52,000

A Kutani koro and cover of typical form, painted all over in iron-red and gilt with Shishi and cash symbols, $11^{3}/_{4}$ in., Meiji period. (Bonhams) $880

A 19th century Japanese Kutani porcelain punch bowl on teakwood stand, $14^{3}/_{4}$in. diam. (Skinner) $1,600

An important Ao-Kutani deep dish, with two fans interspersed on a ground of chrysanthemum flowerheads, late 17th century, 28cm. diam. $64,000

KUTANI

A Kutani koro amusingly modeled in the form of a Shishi, the rounded body raised on four legs, the tail forming the handle, Meiji period, 7³/₄in. high. (Bonhams) $360

A pair of 19th century Kutani-style shaped vases, with Oriental figure decoration to complete body in burnt orange and charcoal gray color, 14in. (Giles Haywood) $2,100

A Kutani elephant with tasselled saddling decorated with ho-o bird, carrying on its back an elaborate cage resting on an ornately fenced base, 19th century, 50cm. high. (Christie's $11,600

A rare Kutani double gourd shaped bottle, the wide lower section with sprays of chrysanthemum amongst rockwork, circa 1670, 19.5cm. high. (Christie's) $10,800

A garniture of three Kutani vases, the central covered jar with Buddist lion knop, each painted on one side with a woman and children in a garden, 30cm. (Bearne's) $1,150

One of a pair of Kutani vases, painted in iron-red and gilt with cockerels amongst peony between ho-o, 14in. high, Meiji period. (Bonhams) $1,050

A ko-Kutani dish decorated in various colored enamels, the central roundel containing two overlapping panels, one depicting a bird perched on bamboo, late 17th century, 21.5cm. diameter. (Christie's) $7,200

A pair of hexagonal late Kutani (Kaga ware) vases decorated with six oval panels, surrounded by various designs including ho-o birds and clouds, late 19th century, 37cm. high. (Christie's London) $3,700

A fine Ko-Kutani deep dish with slightly inverted rim and ring foot, enameled in green, blue, yellow and black, the center with a rocky landscape bordered by six medallions, Fuku mark, late 17th century, 28cm. diameter. (Christie's) $97,000

KYOTO

Kyoto was both the seat of the Japanese Imperial court and an important area of ceramic production in the Edo period (1615–1868). In the 17th century, the potter Ninsei had developed an enameled and gilt pottery, which continued to be manufactured in the 18th century onwards, principally by Kenzan and his successors. Individual potters thrived all over the city, making not only faience, but porcelain in blue-and-white, kinrande and three-color Ming styles. Notable among them were Y Seifu in the Meiji period and later K Kawai and M Ishiguro.

Late 19th century Kyoto chrysanthemum-shaped deep bowl decorated in colors and gilt, signed Kizan kore o tsukuru, 29.8cm. diam.
$2,520

A 19th century large Kyoto-Satsuma oviform vase, signed Nihon Kyoto Kinkozan zo, 83cm. high.
(Christie's) $4,000

Pair of fine Kyoto School studio ware vases, Meiji period, signed *Hozan*, each with wide trumpet necks and high rounded shoulder tapering gradually inward toward the base, 30in.
(Butterfield & Butterfield)
$2,875

Pair of late 19th century almost life-sized stoneware models of a courtier and a courtesan, probably Kyoto ware, 149cm. high.
$11,600

A pair of Kyoto carthenware vases decorated in enamels and gilding, 7¾in. high. $720

A Kyoto tapering rectangular vase painted with panels of a daimyo and his retainers, signed Nihon Yozan, Meiji period, 12.7cm. $1,350

A fine Kyoto pottery canted square dish, painted and richly gilded with a group of musicians, 16.2cm., six character seal mark, circa 1900.
(Tennants) $1,071

A Kyoto trumpet-shaped beaker vase decorated in colored enamels and gilt, signed Kinkozan, Meiji period, 17.8cm. high.
$1,750

BERNARD LEACH

Born in 1887, Bernard Leach was brought up in Japan, and Japanese influence predominates in his work. After studying under Frank Brangwyn in the UK, he returned to Japan in 1909 and began to develop influences which led to the Japanese folk art movement. In 1920 he settled in St Ives in Cornwall where, initially with the help of Shoji Hamada, he made stoneware and raku, using local materials. Throughout his life he returned frequently to the East, and he is noted not only for his own output but also as a teacher and a writer. His pottery is remarkable for the carefully planned relationship of body and glaze and by the variety of decorating techniques which he employed. He died in 1979.

A St. Ives stoneware bottle vase, by Bernard Leach, covered in a mottled brown and olive green glaze, with incised decoration of a weeping willow, circa 1955, 19.6cm. high.
(Christie's) $1,453

A large stoneware charger by Bernard Leach, with decoration of a bird in flight, wax resist, covered with tenmoku rust glaze, circa 1970, 13¹/₂in. diameter.
(Bonhams) $5,872

A St. Ives stoneware vase, by Bernard Leach, incised decoration of two pairs of leaping salmon and birds in flight, circa 1960, 22cm. high.
(Christie's) $1,635

A superb stoneware 'pilgrim' bottle by Bernard Leach, tenmoku with orange markings, impressed BL and St. Ives seals, 14in. high.
(Bonhams) $6,400

An outstanding stoneware dish, 'The Pilgrim', by Bernard Leach, with stencils of a pilgrim against mountains and sky, circa 1965, 12¹/₂in. diameter.
(Bonhams) $6,423

A superb stoneware vase by Bernard Leach, with incised mountain design, glazed brown above gray, 9½in. high.
(Bonhams) $10,093

A large stoneware bowl by Bernard Leach, the interior a celadon glaze with foliate painted decoration, circa 1960, 12¹/₄in. diam.
(Bonhams) $1,750

LEACH

A Yingqing porcelain bowl by Bernard Leach, the exterior covered in a pale greenish white glaze, circa 1970, 17.5cm. diam. (Christie's) $760

A St. Ives stoneware vase by Bernard Leach, with flange rim, incised linear motifs, covered in a speckled oatmeal glaze beneath brushed white with rust red and blue brushwork floral decoration, 15cm. high. (Christie's) $1,378

A rare stoneware plate by Bernard Leach, decorated with a painted mountain goat, impressed BL and St. Ives seals, circa 1955, 9³/₄ in. diameter. (Bonhams) $2,560

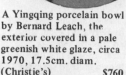

A St. Ives stoneware jar and cover by Bernard Leach, with domed cover, covered in a pale mushroom colored glaze, two sides with blue panels and iron-brown brushwork, circa 1970, 16.5cm. high. (Christie's) $1,531

A large and two smaller St. Ives stoneware bowls, attributed to Bernard Leach, each covered in a pale mushroom colored glaze with painted 'Z'-shaped iron-brown brushwork, circa 1945, 24cm. wide and 13.7cm. wide. (Christie's) $365

An outstanding stoneware vase by Bernard Leach, glazed in tenmoku, this 'bottle form' would have been thrown on the wheel then beaten and shaved to a square section, impressed BL and St. Ives seals, circa 1963, 14in. high. (Bonhams) $6,400

A large stoneware vase by Bernard Leach, covered in a speckled pale buff-colored glaze beneath white, stopping short of the foot, circa 1955, 32.6cm. high. (Christie's) $3,828

A fine stoneware charger by Bernard Leach, the cream glazed ground with wax-resist decoration of a bird in flight, the rim with diagonal bands, 36.5cm. diameter. (Christie's) $16,434

A porcelain preserve pot and cover decorated by Bernard Leach, covered in a mushroom glaze decorated with gray blue band with iron brown scrolling brushwork, 12cm. high. (Christie's London) $560

A tall stoneware fish vase by Bernard Leach, covered with a rust wax resist glaze revealing four vertical bands of aquatic forms, circa 1970, 16in. high.
(Bonhams) $1,652

A stoneware jar and cover by Bernard Leach, with domed cover, the dark ground covered in a translucent celadon glaze, impressed BL with St. Ives Pottery seal, 15.5cm. high.
(Bonhams) $1,760

A St. Ives stoneware hexagonal vase by Bernard Leach, with everted rim and circular aperture, covered in a blue and iron brown mottled speckled glaze, 20.4cm. high.
(Christie's) $1,181

A blue and white porcelain circular box and cover by Bernard Leach, the domed cover with cobalt blue bands and red enameled birds, 7cm. high.
(Christie's) $2,250

An outstanding tall stoneware vase by Bernard Leach, white with combed decoration and vertical indents, impressed *BL* and *St. Ives* seals, circa 1965, 16³/₄in. high.
(Bonhams) $13,860

A fine porcelain dish by Bernard Leach, pale celadon, with an embossed deer surrounded by two circles, impressed BL and St. Ives seals, circa 1967, 7¹/₂in. diameter.
(Bonhams) $2,100

An impressive stoneware vase by Bernard Leach, tenmoku with incised tooling around the shoulder, impressed *BL* and *St. Ives* seals, circa 1960, 14¹/₂in. high.
(Bonhams) $2,310

A magnificent stoneware Pilgrim dish by Bernard Leach, with the figure of a pilgrim, rust, khaki and black tenmoku, impressed BL and St. Ives seals, circa 1970, 13in. diameter.
(Bonhams) $8,500

A St. Ives stoneware vase by Bernard Leach, with incised decoration, covered in a thick matt pale yellow green glaze running and pooling at the foot, circa 1960, 34.2cm. high.
(Christie's) $2,871

LEEDS CREAMWARE

Very fine Leeds creamware was made under the proprietorship of Hartley Green & Co between 1780–1800. A perforated ware was typical of the output, each opening being made with a separate punch, and not, as was later the case at Wedgwoods, by a multiple tool.

Marks are *Hartley Green & Co* and *Leeds Pottery*, either alone or repeated in a cross. The old molds were reused at Slee's pottery in Leeds from 1888 and were marked like the originals.

A Leeds creamware plate, the center painted with the portraits of the Prince and Princess William V of Orange, 24.7cm.
(Bearne's) $320

A creamware fluted sucrier and cover, circa 1780, perhaps Leeds, enameled in puce with feathered edges, 3¼in. high.
(Christie's) $1,150

A Leeds creamware teapot and cover with 'beaded' edges, brightly painted with Chinese figures in a garden, 17cm., late 18th century.
(Bearne's) $400

An English creamware veilleuse, probably Leeds, circa 1785, the cylindrical body applied on the front and reverse with a lady's mask surrounded by patterned piercing, 10¹¹/₁₆in. high.
(Sotheby's) $2,070

A creamware punch-kettle and cover, painted in a famille rose palette with Orientals among furniture, vases and shrubs, probably Leeds, circa 1775, 21cm. high.
(Christie's) $1,120

A documentary dated creamware snuff box, probably Leeds, of circular shape with a screw top, the lid inscribed *John Claytons Tobackah Box, Huddersfield, 1776*, 7.8cm. diameter.
(Phillips) $2,584

A Leeds creamware baluster coffee-pot and domed cover, the green striped body with entwined strap handle, circa 1775, 22.5cm. high.
(Christie's) $4,800

A Leeds saltglaze two-handled cup, circa 1760, with scrolling foliate handles enameled in iron-red, pink, green, blue and yellow with loose bouquets of flowers, 5¼in. high.
(Christie's) $633

LENCI

The Lenci pottery was active in Turin during the 1930's, and produced three distinctive types of wares. The first, consisting of wall plaques in the form of female heads in scarves, as if going to Mass and figures of the Madonna and Child, were aimed at the domestic market. In stark contrast was the second group, made up of female figures, either nude or clad in contemporary costumes.

The third, and less well-known type, consists of vases and dishes decorated with Cubist-style painted scenes.

A Lenci pottery wall mask modeled as a young girl wearing a head scarf, 11½in. wide. **$338**

A Lenci centerpiece, modeled as a young naked girl, 46cm. high. (Christie's) **$1,350**

A Lenci Art Deco ceramic figure with box and cover, molded as the head, shoulders and torso of a young woman, 21.4cm. high. (Phillips) **$1,725**

A Lenci pottery vase, by Beppe Ferinando, painted in shades of orange, yellow, brown and black with geometric pastoral village scene, dated *1933*, 25.5cm. high. (Christie's) **$1,000**

A Lenci polychrome ceramic figure of a mermaid and her baby astride a giant turtle, painted in shades of green and brown, 12¾in. high. (Christie's S. Ken) **$1,920**

A Lenci Art Deco ceramic figure, modeled as a girl wearing an orange hat, black jacket and black, white and gray checkered skirt, 37.5cm. high. (Phillips) **$3,300**

L Cacio Selle Colombe, a Lenci pottery figure modeled as a girl sitting with her floral and striped skirts spread out around her, 24.5cm. high. (Phillips) **$900**

A Lenci ceramic head of stylized form, the hair and eye sockets painted in shades of blue and green, 14in. high. (Christie's) **$1,500**

LENCI

A large figure of a native girl, marked 'Lenci Torino Made in Italy', 1930's, 55.5cm. high. $690

A Lenci pottery box and cover, painted in shades of green with a gingham pattern, 12.5cm. long. (Christie's) $390

A Lenci ceramic figure, the young girl in geometric patterned dress, 9½in. high, painted marks. (Christie's) $720

A Lenci pottery model of a young naked girl wearing a black and white checkered tammie, holding a book, and with a dog on top of a globe, 19¼in. high. (Christie's) $8,270

A Lenci ceramic group, modeled as a seated figure of a girl wearing a black dress, a colored and patterned cape and a purple scarf, 34.8cm. high. (Phillips) $1,500

A Lenci polychrome painted pottery figure of a young woman wearing a short black dress, relaxing with her feet up in a floral patterned armchair, 25cm. high. (Christie's) $2,356

A Lenci polychrome pottery wallmask, modeled as a young woman wearing a gray top hat, factory marks, 35cm. high. (Christie's) $2,495

A Lenci figure of a rooster, painted marks Lenci 1936 S.P., 29cm. high. (Christie's) $3,000

A good Lenci ceramic group modeled as a mer-child holding a fish aloft, she kneels on the back of two open-mouthed fish, 51cm. high. (Phillips) $4,725

LENCI

A Lenci pottery model of a naked female, dancing with arms outstretched, on a black mound base, 11¹/₂in. high. (Christie's) $1,811

A Lenci earthenware box and cover, cover molded with a dozing elf, dated *4.2.32*, 21cm. $517

A large Lenci polychrome painted pottery dish, modeled in the form of an otter trying to catch a salmon in a pond, dated *1938*, 54cm. diameter. (Christie's) $1,009

A Lenci polychrome pottery figure of a young girl standing with shoulders sloping, wearing a black and white polka dot dress, 39.5cm. (Christie's) $8,556

A pair of Lenci book ends each modeled as a naked young girl with short blond hair, kneeling between a book and a small dog, 23.5cm. high. (Christie's) $1,431

A Lenci polychrome pottery figure of a young woman wearing a blue and black tweed dress, holding her hat, 37cm. high (Christie's) $6,773

A Lenci polychrome pottery figure modeled as a young woman wearing a yellow jacket and green floral trousers, 44.5cm. (Christie's) $3,208

'Amore Paterno', a Lenci pottery group, modeled by Sandro Vachetti, of a man clasping a young baby to his lips, painted in colors, dated *1931*, 17cm. high. (Christie's) $1,240

A Lenci figure group, of a bare-breasted native woman wearing an abstract patterned wrap-around skirt in yellow, green and black, 44cm. high. (Phillips) $1,417

LIBERTY

Arthur Lazenby Liberty was the archetypical Victorian entrepreneur. Starting life as an assistant in a London emporium, he rose to be the manager of a firm called Farmer and Rogers which sold Oriental imports to the rapidly increasing clientele of customers in search of beautiful things for their homes. Recognising the magnitude of the new market, Liberty took a chance and opened his own shop in Regent Street in 1875. Within five years it had proved to be a huge success.

Two Liberty & Co. terracotta jardinières, designed by Mrs. F. G. Watts, after Archibald Knox. (Bonhams) **$1,495**

A pair of Liberty jardinières on pedestals, each with shallow hemispherical bowl decorated with entrelac border in relief. 80cm. high. **$3,150**

LIMBACH

The Limbach factory was established in the mid 18th century by Gotthelf Greiner, who had previously been a glass maker. It turned out simple, cheap tablewares, which had the unique distinction of being almost over marked, some bearing the marks of the painter, workshop, factory, and date!

Figures were also made in the style of Meissen and though the quality is inferior, they do have a pleasing simplicity. Again, as if to underline their relation to that factory, they often bear the marks of crossed hayforks!

Four Limbach figures emblematic of the Seasons, each modeled as a gallant, two with puce and one with sepia crossed L marks, circa 1775, 15.5–17cm. high. (Christie's) **$6,774**

A Limbach group emblematic of Winter, he wearing a puce and blue hat, she with a puce and black hat, circa 1780, 16cm. high. (Christie's) **$1,200**

LIMEHOUSE

Limehouse is a shadowy factory, of which few concrete facts are known. Sometime between 1745 and early 1748 Joseph Wilson and Co. made blue and white teapots, sauceboats and pickle dishes at Duke Shore in Limehouse, East London. They experimented with a new secret formula which included soaprock, a Cornish-mined steatite. The wares were crude, with poor translucence, and the factory quickly failed.

An important Limehouse model of a cat, modeled and seated upright with its whiskers and paws picked out in underglaze blue and with a solid wash of blue between the paws, 16.3cm. (Phillips) **$8,160**

A very rare Limehouse dish of canted rectangular shape, painted in blue with two Oriental figures at a table, 17cm. x 22cm. (Phillips) **$6,175**

LIMOGES

The first hard paste porcelain factory to open in this area did so in 1771, and came under the protection of the Comte d'Artois. It used kaolin from nearby Saint-Yrieux. In 1784 it came under the royal patronage of Louis XVI, and began to produce wares for decoration at Sèvres.

While this factory closed in 1796 others established themselves thereafter in the area, producing creamy colored tableware, often decorated with sprigs of flowers.

Pair of Limoges Art Nouveau enamel vases decorated with the image of a woman, floral highlights, circa 1900, 6in. high.
(Du Mouchelles) $1,700

A Limoges Art Nouveau porcelain box and cover, of squat baluster form, the cover painted with the profile of a young woman, 20cm. wide.
(Christie's) $542

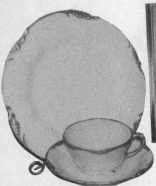

Jean Pouyat Limoges porcelain dessert service, circa 1900, 36 pieces, with fired gold edges.
(Du Mouchelles) $350

Set of four Limoges enamel plaques, each with a figure of a woman or harlequin standing in a landscape, circa 1900, each 12 x 7½in.
(Butterfield & Butterfield) $5,175

A stoneware wine jug, relief decorated in ocher, white, green and gold enamels with leafy branches and flowers, Charles Haviland, Limoges, circa 1900, 23cm. high.
(Lempertz) $805

Limoges handpainted plate with still life of hanging game, signed *DeNerval*, early 20th century, 18in. diameter.
(Eldred's) $275

A pair of Limoges Art Deco porcelain vases painted in colors and gilt on a yellow ground with stylized palmettes and foliage, 29.5cm. high.
(Christie's) $712

Limoges handpainted plate with still life of fish, gilt edge, signed *DeNerval*, early 20th century, 16in. diameter.
(Eldred's) $242

LINTHORPE

The Linthorpe Pottery was established in 1879, near Middlesborough, with Henry Tooth as manager, and, until 1882, Christopher Dresser as art director and designer. Their early wares were designed on simple, flowing lines with equally flowing glazes in two or more rich colors, while later sgraffito or pâte-sur-pâte decoration was introduced. It ceased production in 1890. Pieces are marked with *Linthorpe*, sometimes over the outline of a squat vase. Some are signed by Dresser, and or initialed with Tooth's monogram.

A Linthorpe teapot, the design attributed to Dr. C. Dresser, 21.3cm. high. (Christie's) $400

A Linthorpe pottery vase, designed by Christopher Dresser, decorated with stylized linear patterns, 21cm. high.
(Phillips) $1,300

A Linthorpe vase, designed by Dr. Christopher Dresser, the streaky glaze in tones of green and brown, with incised decoration of a single fern encircling the gourd, 19cm. high. (Christie's) $1,750

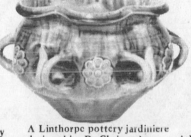

A Linthorpe pottery jardiniere designed by Dr Christopher Dresser, the swollen dimpled form with foliate rim, decorated with double loop handles and alternating rosettes, 13.8cm. high. (Christie's) $640

A Linthorpe earthenware jug designed by Dr Christopher Dresser, covered in a thick predominantly green and brown glaze, (slight restoration to lip rim) 16.7cm. high.
(Christie's) $400

A Linthorpe vase, designed by Dr Christopher Dresser, decorated with four grotesque heads, each forming a handle, covered in a streaky green glaze, 22.5cm. high.
(Christie's) $1,600

A Linthorpe pottery jug, designed by Dr. Christopher Dresser, with everted rim continuing to form an angled handle, terminating in a rippled design, covered in a streaky caramel, green and crimson glaze, 21cm. high.
(Christie's) $3,200

A large Linthorpe Pottery vase designed by Christopher Dresser, of almost egg shape, covered with a brown, milky green, milky blue and amber glaze, 43.5cm. high.
(Phillips) $2,250

LINTHORPE

A Linthorpe goat's-head vase, designed by Dr. Christopher Dresser, double gourd shape, decorated with four goats' heads, 28cm. high.
(Christie's) $5,200

A Linthorpe vase, designed by Dr. Christopher Dresser, formed as a cluster of five pointed gourd shapes encircling a central funnel-shaped neck, 11cm. high.
(Christie's) $2,400

A Linthorpe vase, designed by Dr. Christopher Dresser, with frilled lug handles and incised decoration of a bearded face on one side, 22cm. high.
(Christie's) $4,800

A Linthorpe vase, designed by Dr. Christopher Dresser, the gourd-shaped body with double angular spout and curved carrying-bar, streaked glaze of green and brown.
(Christie's) $1,900

A Linthorpe earthenware vase molded on each side with grotesque fish faces, 17.9cm. high.
(Christie's) $800

A Linthorpe face vase, designed by Dr. Christopher Dresser, domed cylindrical shape with double angular spout, decorated with a stylized face on one side, 15.5cm. high.
(Christie's) $1,120

A Linthorpe vase, designed by Dr. Christopher Dresser, glazed in streaky pale and dark green, with molded maze patterns and linear designs, 22.5cm. high.
(Christie's) $880

A Linthorpe twin-handled pottery vase designed by Christopher Dresser, the vessel of flattened oviform with bulbous neck, 20.8cm. high.
(Phillips) $320

A Linthorpe jug, designed by Dr. Christopher Dresser, humped shape with vertical spout and carved handle, incised geometric pattern, 18cm. high.
(Christie's) $1,040

LIVERPOOL

There were seven porcelain factories in Liverpool in the 18th century, of which three, Chaffers, Christians and Penningtons are generally regarded as forming the mainstream tradition from 1754–99.

The Chaffers' factory (1754–65) made a bone ash and a soapstone porcelain which are often difficult to tell apart as most of the standard shapes were identically produced in both.

Blue and white made up the bulk of production and showed a strong Worcester influence in terms of both shape and decoration, being painted in a free and pleasant style. Distinctive characteristics are the upturned lips of jugs and the fact that cream and sauceboats are often molded.

The decoration of the polychrome pieces was also of a high quality, often featuring Chinese figure and floral subjects.

The Christian factory (1765–76) produced examples which were well potted but on which the decoration was competent rather than outstanding. Blue and white teawares are very common but flatware is rare, while the polychrome output was again decorated with floral or Chinese mandarin subjects. Christian's specialised in garniture sets of vases, decorated with floral reserves on a gros bleu ground.

The output of the Pennington factory (1769–99) consisted largely of imitations of Christian's wares but was generally of inferior quality as regards both potting and painting. Again, blue and white predominates, and among the finest examples are ship's bowls, which were sometimes named and dated.

A Liverpool coffee cup, with a plain loop handle, painted in colors with flower sprays, 2³/₈in. high.
(Bonhams) $210

Liverpool transfer printed creamware pitcher, circa 1800, with Independence, the reverse with Washington and Justice, Liberty, and Victory, 8in. high.
(Skinner) $1,650

Liverpool transfer decorated and handpainted creamware pitcher, England, early 19th century, handpainted in polychrome with Caleb Bate's ship, "Venilia", 10¹/₂in. high.
(Skinner Inc.) $39,600

A Liverpool porcelain 'Chelsea ewer' cream-jug, probably Seth Pennington's factory, spirally fluted and molded with a band of leaves, 3in. high, circa 1780-90.
(Christie's) $340

A very rare Liverpool tin-glazed stoneware coffee cup, painted in blue with a curious ruined arch or folly in an otherwise Chinese style landscape, 6.2cm.
(Phillips) $2,945

Liverpool transfer-printed creamware masonic large jug, probably Herculaneum, early 19th century, 13in. high.
(Butterfield & Butterfield) $1,500

275

LIVERPOOL

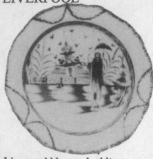

Liverpool blue and white pottery plate, Oriental figure and pagoda pattern to center, 9½in., English, 19th century. (G. A. Key) **$119**

A Liverpool tin-glazed stoneware blue and white oviform teapot and cover painted with bamboo and foliage beside fences, circa 1750, 12.5cm. high. (Christie's) **$2,080**

A Liverpool plate, circa 1760, decorated in colors with orange and yellow flowering branch issuing from blue rockwork beside a fence, 8⅞in. diameter. (Christie's) **$935**

Liverpool handpainted and transfer printed creamware jug, England, early 19th century, handpainted scene entitled *Washington in His Glory*, 10.5in. high. (Skinner) **$10,350**

A Pennington Liverpool ship bowl painted in blue with a ship in full sail, inscribed *Success to the Perseus, Capt. Gibson, 1790*, 25cm. (Phillips London) **$5,600**

Liverpool creamware transfer-printed and enameled large jug, 1795–1800, the barrel-shaped body printed in black on one side with a full-rigged ship, 11¼in. high. (Sotheby's) **$18,400**

Liverpool transfer printed creamware pitcher, circa 1790, with L'Enfant's *Plan of the City of Washington*, the reverse with *Peace, Plenty and Independence*, 9⅛in. high. (Skinner) **$2,860**

One of a pair of Liverpool teabowls and saucers transfer-printed in black with The Rock Garden or Rural Conversations, Philip Christian's factory, circa 1766. (Christie's) (Two) **$541**

A Liverpool creamware transfer-printed jug, circa 1799, printed darkly in black on one side with a scene of cows, 9in. high. (Sotheby's) **$1,150**

LONGTON HALL

Longton Hall was one of the first porcelain factories in the entire United Kingdom, and production commenced around 1750. Unsurprisingly, in these circumstances, initial output was somewhat primitive in quality, but the standard of both potting and decoration rapidly improved. Early pieces consisted mainly of the so-called 'Snowman' figures and mugs, plates, dishes etc. decorated in 'Littler's' blue. The underglaze was often runny and uneven, but has a brightness which was no doubt in imitation of Vincennes. The reserves were often left unfilled, giving the pieces a somewhat unfinished appearance.

William Littler had joined the venture in 1751 and by 1753–4 there was an improvement in the standard of potting, though decoration was still quite primitive. At this time the scarce Longton Hall powder blue vases, teapots and bottles were made. Between 1754–7 some really beautiful pieces were produced, including a range of leaf-molded wares in the Meissen style. A large proportion of the output of that time was in fact molded in remarkable shapes with leaf, fruit and vegetable motifs.

Decoration was carried out by, among others, the 'Castle' painter who specialised in European scenes, and the 'Trembly rose' painter whose floral motifs bear a resemblance to Red Anchor Chelsea. Bird painting was often really superb.

The polychrome wares produced between 1758–60 are also finely decorated, and the products transfer printed in black by Sadler were made at this time.

From 1754 blue and white was also made, but examples of this are now fairly rare.

One of a pair of Longton Hall teabowls and saucers, painted in an attractive palette of green, pink, yellow, turquoise and brown.
(Phillips) (Two) $1,085

A Longton Hall two-handled oviform vase painted with loose bouquets, flower-sprays and scattered foliage, circa 1755, 23cm. high.
(Christie's) $1,276

A pair of Longton Hall pigeon-tureens and covers, the naturally modeled birds to left and right with purple feather markings, circa 1755, 22cm. long.
(Christie's) $10,800

A Longton Hall figure of a flower seller, seated on a tall scroll molded base, wearing a yellow coat with fan collar, 4⅝in. high, circa 1755.
(Tennants) $1,120

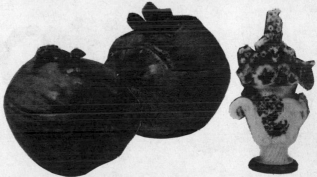

A rare pair of English porcelain apple boxes and covers, 3in. high, probably Longton Hall, circa 1755.
(Tennants) $2,430

A Longton Hall rococo scroll molded vase and flower-encrusted cover, the vase with two oval panels, 23cm. high.
(Spencer's) $450

LONGTON HALL

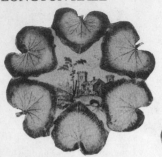

A good Longton Hall leaf dish, the border molded with six brightly colored hollyhock leaves, 21.5cm.
(Phillips) $1,860

A Longton Hall figure of a seated flower seller on a rococo scroll base, 4⁷/₈in. high.
(Bonhams) $375

A Longton Hall strawberry leaf dish, the border molded with leaves and fruit picked out in bright colors, 23.5cm.
(Phillips) $853

A rare Longton Hall mug, the angular handle with a leaf-molded thumbrest, painted with a root, chrysanthemums and bamboo by a fence, 9cm. high, circa 1755.
(Phillips) $1,347

A rare Longton Hall pierced leaf basket of deep circular shape, the overlapping leaves with light puce ribs, 25.5cm. wide.
(Phillips) $6,000

A Longton Hall coffee cup, with rare clip handle and leaf-molded thumbrest, painted in characteristic colors with a fantastic bird on a towering rock, 6.5cm.
(Phillips) $496

A Longton Hall paeony dish, modeled as a pale purple flower between two green leaves, 7in. wide.
(Bonhams) $1,200

A Longton Hall cream jug molded with vine leaves, the twisted stems as a handle, 7.7cm. high, late 18th century.
(Bearne's) $2,025

A Longton Hall circular melon tureen and cover, puce W mark, circa 1755, 11.5cm. high.
                       $17,500

LOWESTOFT

Lowestoft did not really set out to become a top-class manufacturer of porcelain, and the proprietors' diffident approach can be seen in their original description of themselves as 'China Manufacturers and Herring Curers'! The factory was established by four partners in 1757, with the humble purpose of producing useful wares for the local inhabitants, and it leapt to spurious fame when some 19th century ceramic writers wrongly ascribed to it a hard paste Chinese porcelain being made expressly for the European and American market.

The earliest Lowestoft pieces were decorated only in a soft underglaze blue in the style of Nanking and no colored enamels were introduced before 1770. The blue and white ware was often relief molded and often, too, associated with the modeler James Hughes.

The 1770s saw the introduction of enameled pieces in Imari type designs, but as the porcelain remains of the soft-paste European variety they are quite distinctive. It is mostly tea wares which received this sort of treatment. There followed a more sophisticated type of decoration in the European style, with bold flowers and no distracting borders, and some Chinese type designs were also adopted.

From about 1790 a sparse and simple sprig motif became popular, often in enamel colors but sometimes only in gold. The factory at this time also made some of the earliest seaside souvenir porcelain in the form of mugs and inkwells bearing inscriptions such as *A Trifle from Lowestoft*, for by now the town was a fashionable watering place.

A rare Lowestoft custard cup painted in colors with a 'Redgrave' pattern beneath an egg and flower border, 6cm.
(Phillips) $545

A very finely painted Lowestoft covered jug, painted in blue with two Chinese figures discussing a small vase, 26cm. high.
(Phillips) $2,400

A good pair of Lowestoft models of pugs, with curled tails, decorated with sponged underglaze manganese, 8.5cm.
(Phillips) $5,805

A Lowestoft blue and white eye-bath of boat shape painted with flower-sprays within molded floral cartouches, circa 1765, 5.5cm. high.
(Christie's) $4,991

A Lowestoft miniature teapot and cover of globular shape, printed in blue with a version of the 'Three Flowers' pattern, 8.5cm.
(Phillips) $800

A Lowestoft blue and white molded globular jug cylindrical neck and loop handle, painted with Orientals at discussion, circa 1765, 26cm. high.
(Christie's) $3,200

LOWESTOFT

A Lowestoft blue and white rectangular octagonal tea caddy, circa 1765, 13cm. high. **$1,950**

A Lowestoft oviform punch-pot and cover painted in a famille rose palette with Oriental figures at various pursuits, circa 1780, 22cm. high. (Christie's) **$4,400**

A Lowestoft cylindrical mug, the scroll handle with thumb rest, 15cm. high. (Phillips) **$3,200**

A Lowestoft blue and white fluted baluster coffee pot and cover transfer printed with loose bouquets, circa 1780, 26.5cm. high. (Christie's London) **$1,600**

A Lowestoft blue and white leaf-shaped pickle dish with molded stalk handle and veins, circa 1765, 6in. wide. (Christie's) **$800**

Lowestoft jug, blue and white chinoiserie pattern of landscapes and figures, approx. 7in. (G. A. Key) **$320**

An unrecorded Lowestoft ship bowl inscribed *Success To The Cruizer Cutter/Henry Major Master*, 27cm. (Phillips London) **$3,850**

A Lowestoft globular teapot and cover painted with a Curtis type pattern of loose sprays of flowers below diaper panels suspending swags, 15cm. high, circa 1785. (Christie's) **$951**

A rare Lowestoft saucer dish, the border printed in blue, the center inscribed *A Trifle from Lowestoft*, 19.5cm., circa 1790. (Phillips) **$2,736**

LUDWIGSBURG

In 1758 Johann Jakob Ringler established a porcelain factory for Duke Carl Eugen of Württemberg. Ringler had arrived there via Vienna, Höchst and various other centers, but it was at Ludwigsburg that he remained until his death in 1802.

The factory produced a distinctive smoky brown body, which, if the exquisite detail on some of the figures is anything to go by, was nevertheless excellent for modeling. Tablewares and vases really show little originality, but some fine modelers were employed on figure production. Among the earliest were groups of dancers, reflecting the Duke's interest in ballet, probably by Jean Louis, who also is credited with having designed the tiny Venetian Fairs series. Both of these were subsequently the subjects of many inferior reproductions. Other modelers include J C W Beyer, who composed 'lean and hungry' figures, and Johann Göz.

The Duke was generous with money for the factory, but after his death in 1793 it rapidly declined, and closed in 1824.

The most common mark is two interlaced back to back Cs below a ducal crown. After the accession of Duke Ludwig in 1793 the Cs were replaced by an L and from 1796–1816 and FR monogram for King Frederick. In 1816 Frederick was succeeded by William, and the mark became WR. Three stag's horns in a shield were sometimes used around 1800.

 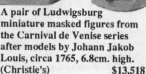 

A pair of Ludwigsburg miniature masked figures from the Carnival de Venise series after models by Johann Jakob Louis, circa 1765, 6.8cm. high. (Christie's) $13,518

A Ludwigsburg figure of Arion, blue interlaced L mark and impressed I.L.F. 53. and with iron-red painter's mark of Sausenhofer, circa 1765, 15cm. high. $480

 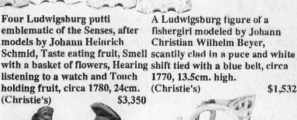

Four Ludwigsburg putti emblematic of the Senses, after models by Johann Heinrich Schmid, Taste eating fruit, Smell with a basket of flowers, Hearing listening to a watch and Touch holding fruit, circa 1780, 24cm. (Christie's) $3,350

A Ludwigsburg figure of a fishergirl modeled by Johann Christian Wilhelm Beyer, scantily clad in a puce and white shift tied with a blue belt, circa 1770, 13.5cm. high. (Christie's) $1,532

A pair of Ludwigsburg figures of a gallant and companion modeled by Franz Anton Bustelli, circa 1760, 13cm. high. (Christie's) $5,710

A Ludwigsburg group emblematic of the Seasons perhaps modeled by Pierre François Lejeune, the four figures about an arbor, circa 1770, 19cm. high. (Christie's) $12,478

LUDWIGSBURG

A Ludwigsburg chinoiserie group, modeled by J. Weinmuller, incised Geer mark, circa 1770, 34cm. high. **$3,000**

Porcelain group of two canaries, flanking a birds nest, possibly Frankenthal or Ludwigsburg, late 19th century, 4in. high. (G. A. Key) **$293**

A small Ludwigsburg group of a girl and boy with a goat, on oval scrolled base, decorated in pale colors, 9.5cm., blue mark. (Phillips) **$558**

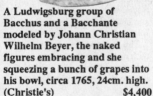

A Ludwigsburg figure of a lady with a musical score, modeled by P. F. Lejeune, scantily clothed in a white blouse, circa 1770, 13.5cm. high. (Christie's) **$1,200**

A pair of rare Ludwigsburg tureens and covers, painted with sprays of flowers in colors, surmounted by finials of cabbage, onion and garlic, 25cm. wide. (Phillips) **$3,740**

A Ludwigsburg group of Bacchus and a Bacchante modeled by Johann Christian Wilhelm Beyer, the naked figures embracing and she squeezing a bunch of grapes into his bowl, circa 1765, 24cm. high. (Christie's) **$4,400**

A Ludwigsburg group of a bacchanalian scene, 19th century, 20cm. high. (Arnold Frankfurt) **$485**

A Ludwigsburg group of dancers modeled by Franz Anton Bustelli, blue crowned crossed-C mark and incised UM 3 to base, circa 1760, 16cm. high. **$20,000**

A Ludwigsburg group of two putti, blue interlaced C's and impressed IO marks, circa 1765, 17cm. high. **$640**

LUSTER

Luster decoration consists of a thin deposit of metal applied to the surface of pottery. This often has an iridescent effect achieved by painting glazed pottery with a metallic oxide and then firing it in a reducing atmosphere using a muffle kiln. A film of metal, gold, copper or platinum, is thus left on a piece.

The first luster items of English origin were produced in the early 19th century, and much of the output was exported to America.

English lusterware pitcher, decorated with a pink molded deer in a pink and green landscape, 5¹/₄in. high. (Eldred's) $88

A creamware pink luster jug printed in black with a scene of Peterloo and a bust of Henry Hunt, 15cm. (Phillips) $613

An English yellow-glazed earthenware jug for the American market, circa 1815, the baluster-form body transfer-printed in black, 6⁵/₈in. high. (Sotheby's) $1,035

A De Morgan luster vase, decorated in ruby luster with fish swimming against pale amber waves, 15.6cm. high, 1888-97. $577

A Staffordshire copper luster canary-yellow-ground commemorative jug, 1825–35, portrait of La Fayette, 7¹/₈in. high. (Sotheby's) $575

A William De Morgan luster dish painted by Charles Passenger, with a crane with blue silver, mauve and pale ruby amid silver and ruby luster bulrushes, 28cm. diam. (Phillips London) $5,600

A Staffordshire pink luster Royal Wedding Commemorative jug, molded with named bust portraits of Princess Charlotte and Prince Leopold, 6⁵/₈in. high, circa 1816. (Tennants) $446

A William de Morgan ruby luster circular dish, painted with a pair of griffin-like creatures prowling in alternate directions, 36cm. diam. (Phillips) $4,400

MAJOLICA

Majolica is a glazed or enameled earthenware often decorated in relief, and it was 16th century Italian mastery of this medium which provided the inspiration for its revival some three centuries later. In this country, Minton in particular made a wide range of objects in majolica, from garden ornaments to small figures, from 1850 onwards, under the guidance of Leon Arnoux. Some of his work was shown at the Great Exhibition in 1851.

A Minton's majolica model of a recumbent sporting hound on a rectangular base, poured with colored glazes, circa 1910, 7in. long.
(Christie's) $313

A rare Minton 'majolica' Chinaman teapot and cover, he holds a grotesque aubergine mask from which the green spout emerges, 13.5cm., impressed *Mintons*.
(Phillips) $1,613

A Minton majolica bottle-cooler of campana shape with a scroll and acanthus-leaf-molded rim and two goat's mask handles, impressed date code for 1859, 9¾in. high.
(Christie's) $1,554

A pair of Minton majolica cornucopia vases, circa 1872, modeled as putti astride cornucopiae issuing from dolphins, 27in. high.
(Christie's East) $4,800

A Minton style majolica jardinière and stand, the rims molded with petal-like designs, painted in typical green, brown and cream enamels, total height 25cm.
(Bearne's) $520

A Minton majolica ware Christmas dish made for the Crystal Palace Art Union, molded in relief in the center with a white rose within a garland of mistletoe, 39cm., date code for 1859.
(Phillips) $1,928

An English majolica tobacco-jar and cover in the form of a pug dog, glazed in shades of brown and with a pink interior, circa 1860's, 8in. high.
(Christie's S. Ken) $520

A Minton majolica triform vase modeled as three bulbous radishes, their white skins shading to pink at the shoulders and with a ring of everted green leaves forming the necks, date code for 1866, 4in. high.
(Christie's) $1,727

MALING

The Maling Pottery was founded in North Hylton, near Sunderland, in 1762 by the Maling family, in whose possession it remained until the mid 19th century. They produced plain and decorated earthenware.

In 1853 the name was changed to C.T. Maling and the company was bought by the Ford Co. in 1854.

In the early part of the 20th century they produced attractive cream-colored domestic occasional wares, decorated with bold flower patterns and with a slight luster effect.

Maling teapot, 1930s, with grapevine decoration.
(Muir Hewitt) $60

Maling plate with floral decoration, 10in. diameter.
(Muir Hewitt) $300

Maling decorated bowl with pink ground enhanced with blue pansies, 9½in. diameter., 1930's.
(Lyle) $225

Maling green ground jug decorated with a floral band of colored rosettes, 10in. high 1930's.
(Muir Hewitt) $140

Maling plate with stylized Oriental decoration, 10in. diameter.
(Muir Hewitt) $300

Maling decorative circular dish with small handles and a white ground with colored rosettes, 7in. wide, 1930's.
(Lyle) $65

Maling hand painted bowl, 10in. diameter, 1930s.
(Muir Hewitt) $195

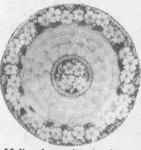

Maling decorative circular dish, the rim with luster decoration of colored rosettes, pattern no.6450T, 10½in. diameter
(G.A. Key) $93

285

MARBLEHEAD

The Marblehead pottery was established in 1905 with the view of providing occupational therapy for patients in a local Massachusetts sanatorium. After a short while, however, it was operating as a separate commercial venture. The pottery produced earthenware vases and bowls, in simple, often straight-sided shapes, and covered in muted matt glazes. Characteristic decoration includes animal and flower motifs and also features of the Massachusetts coast such as seaweed, fish, ships etc. Its produce was sold from 1908 onwards. The Marblehead mark consists of an impressed *M* and the emblem of a sailing ship, with the potter's initials incised.

A decorated Marblehead pottery four-color vase, Mass., circa 1910, 6in. high.
$1,980

Marblehead Pottery decorated vase, Massachusetts, early 20th century, with repeating design of parrots on branches, 7in. high. (Skinner) $1,275

Pair of Marblehead Pottery sailing ship bookends, Massachusetts, matt glaze decorated in blue, dark blue, light blue, red, black and mustard, 5½in. high. (Skinner) $460

Marblehead Pottery decorated vase, Marblehead, Massachusetts, early 20th century, with incised and painted repeating design of flowers, 3³/₄in. high. (Skinner Inc.) $2,000

Marblehead pottery experimental landscape vase, executed by Arthur E. Baggs, circa 1925, 7¼in. high. (Skinner Inc.) $3,200

Important Marblehead Pottery vase, matt blue ground glaze, incised decoration at shoulder consisting of five panels, each with a stalking panther, 7¹/₂in. high. (Skinner) $11,500

Marblehead Pottery decorated vase, Massachusetts, early 20th century, with design of alternating elongated trees, 6³/₈in. high. (Skinner Inc.) $1,200

286

MARSEILLES

Marseilles faience was made by a number of factories in the 18th century, but the name most often associated with it is that of Pierrette Caudelot, la Veuve Perrin.

After the death of her husband in 1748, she ran the factory until her own death in 1793. Until 1764, when he set up his own concern, she was in partnership with Honoré Savy who claimed to have invented the style of decoration where a translucent green enamel is applied over black painting. Other popular forms of decoration include chinoiserie scenes in the style of Pillement and scenes after the artist Teniers, while Mediterranean fish were often used to decorate large soup tureens.

Another of her former employees who set up on his own was Joseph Robert. He was responsible in no small degree for the high quality of the decoration at the Perrin factory and he set up his own factory in 1766 to produce porcelain. His products have a highly distinctive style, and the decoration is quite different from the mainstream of French production of the time. It often features individual flower painting and landscape scenes strongly reminiscent of the Meissen style of the late 1730s. The factory did not survive the Revolution and closed in 1793. While Perrin and Savy may also have manufactured porcelain, no confident ascriptions of their pieces can be made.

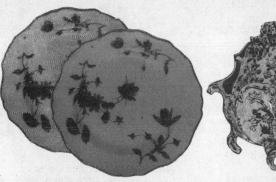

A pair of Marseilles (Veuve Perrin) shaped circular plates painted en camaieu verte with bouquets of flowers, circa 1765, 25cm. diameter. $1,600

One of a pair of Marseilles bouquetiers and covers, circa 1760-70, 28½in. high. $2,400

A Marseilles faience pear-shaped ewer and two-handled oval basin, 14¾in. wide, circa 1765. $720

A French faience holy water stoup, painted in colors with St Louis kneeling before an altar in a landscape vignette, third quarter of the 18th century, probably Marseilles 44cm. high. $1,760

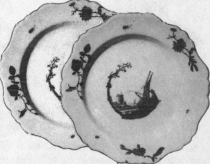

A Marseilles faience casket in the form of an armoire, late 18th century, 14½in. high. $1,450

A pair of Marseilles circular dishes painted en camaieu verte, Savy's factory, circa 1770, 28½cm. diameter. $3,200

287

MARTINWARE

The Martin Brothers cooperative, which set up in 1873, consisted of Robert Wallace Martin, who had worked for the Fulham pottery, and his brothers Walter and Edwin, who had previously been employed by Doulton. Walter was thrower, and Edwin decorator, while a further brother, Charles, became the business manager and ran a shop in Brownlow Street, London.

Martinware comes in a wide variety of shapes. The decoration is mainly incised, with the colors reminiscent of Doulton stoneware. The most common motifs are plants, birds, animals and grotesques, of which perhaps the most notable are R W Martins 'wally birds'. These are often found as tobacco jars, with the heads forming the lids, and generally have a somewhat menacing air. Some of the later production tended more towards the abstract, relating it to later studio pottery. The works closed in 1914.

A Martin Brothers 'monk' bird and cover, circa 1894, with broad smile and balding head, 7¹/₂in. high.
(Sotheby's) $5,456

A Martin Bros. stoneware grotesque, double face jug with strap handle, 1897, 22.8cm. high.
(Christie's) $2,400

A rare Martin Brothers triple bird group of 'Two's company, three's none', circa 1906, modeled as a central, complacently smirking male bird with his wings about two females, 7¹/₂in. high.
(Sotheby's) $14,492

A large Martin Brothers jardinière, the swollen form with everted pie-crust rim, on short ridged foot, incised decoration of scrolling plants and foliage, 1888, 50cm. high.
(Christie's) $4,000

A Martin Brothers stoneware vase, painted with grotesque fish, eels, a starfish and aquatic foliage in browns, white, black and blue, 21.5cm. high.
(Phillips London) $1,040

An amusing Martin Brothers stoneware model of a baby owl, 27.50cm. high, signed *Martin Bros. London & Southall* and dated *10–1895.*
(Phillips) $5,200

A Martin Ware two handled vase of baluster form, decorated with fish and seaweed, signed and dated *1888,* 9in. high.
(Russell, Baldwin & Bright) $1,320

MARTINWARE

A Martin Brothers grotesque jug, the salt-glazed stoneware body modeled in relief with two humorous faces, dated *7/1898,* 19cm. high.
(Christie's) $1,600

An R.W. Martin and Brothers stoneware jug in the form of a grotesque animal squatting on four feet with scaled body, 21cm. high.
(Bearne's) $5,104

A Martin Brothers stoneware single-handled ewer incised with medieval fishermen by a lakeside, amongst stylized foliage, 23cm. high.
(Christie's) $640

A small Martin Brothers grotesque bird, mounted on oval ebonised wooden base, the head incised *R.W. Martin Bros, London & Southall, 19.8.1913,* 16.5cm. high.
(Christie's) $1,181

A pair of Martin Brothers vases, the slab contructed stoneware bodies of baluster form and rectangular section, dated *11/1899,* 30.5cm. high.
(Christie's) $1,200

A Martin Brothers stoneware vase, each side incised with ferocious dragons, covered with mottled green glaze, 26cm. high.
(Christie's) $400

A Martin Borthers stoneware vase incised with ferocious dragons, painted in shades of green and blue on a black ground, 20cm. high.
(Christie's) $800

A Martin Brothers grotesque jug of spherical form with angled handle, incised signature, dated *8/1898,* 22cm. high.
(Christie's) $2,000

A Martin Brothers vase, with incised floral decoration, covered in a matt brown glaze with painted brown, green, white and blue, dated *1887,* 20.1cm. high.
(Christie's) $985

MARTINWARE

A Martin Bros. stoneware jug, the bulbous body suggesting a sea-creature, 21.8cm. high. $720

A Martin Bros stoneware spherical vase, London Southall, 1892, 9in. high. (Christie's) $640

A stoneware Martin Bros. grotesque double-face jug, dated 1903, 19cm. high.

$1,800

A Martin Brothers John Barleycorn jug, the ovoid body modeled with grinning face, 18cm. high, incised mark and 6-1911. (Lawrence Fine Arts)

$1,200

A pair of Martin Brothers stoneware candlesticks, incised with panels of water birds, 8in. high. (Christie's) $391

A Martin Brothers stoneware vase, decorated with magnolia blooms and insects nearby, against a textured ground glazed in brown and white, 23.60cm. high. (Phillips) $600

An unusual ceramic and pewter inkwell, cast in the style of a Martin Brothers bird with the head forming the hinged cover, 4¼in. high. (Christie's S. Ken) $338

A Martin Brothers vase, the body glazed in dark green with an incised cellular pattern, incised *Martin Bros., London & Southall*, 18.5cm. high. (Christie's) $760

A Martin Brothers vase, the writhen globular body with four handles modeled as snakes biting the rim of the vase, 1899, 27.5cm. high. (Christie's) $3,675

MASON

Miles Mason was a dealer in Chinese porcelain who in around 1800 set up his own manufactory at Lane Delph, to replace stock which he could no longer obtain from the East. There, he produced both bone china and 'hybrid' hard paste porcelain, mostly decorated with underglaze blue printing in simple Chinese patterns. Their teaware and dessert ware shapes were mostly unique of their type and so are readily recognisable. Later, however, the factory moved on to produce ironstone pottery, with such success that Mason's Ironstone is a leading name to this day.

Mason's Ironstone toilet set, with oriental pattern of pagodas, foliage etc., 19th century.
(G.A.Key) $418

A Miles Mason pale apricot-ground D-shaped bough pot and pierced dome cover, circa 1805, 25cm. high.
(Christie's) $2,400

Pair of Miles Mason urn vases, each painted with two landscape panels on blue ground, 6½in. high.
(Russell, Baldwin & Bright)
                    $2,149

One of a pair of Mason's ironstone baluster vases with fluted trumpet necks, circa 1820, 14½in. high.
                    $1,200

Fine Mason's Ironstone ice pail of oval form, the sides applied with two scrolled handles, molded as frogs heads, 19th century, 15in.
(G. A. Key) $1,650

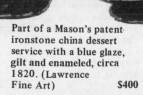

Part of a Mason's patent ironstone china dessert service with a blue glaze, gilt and enameled, circa 1820. (Lawrence Fine Art) $400

A massive Mason's ironstone ewer of vase shape with double scroll handle, circa 1820, 67cm. high.
(Christie's) $1,200

MEISSEN

At the beginning of the 18th century the race was on in Europe to find the secret of the manufacture of Chinese-type porcelain. The winner was Augustus the Strong, Elector of Saxony, thanks to his sequestration of a young alchemist, J F Böttger, whom he originally employed to turn base metal to gold. When Böttger failed at this, Frederick set him the alternative task of porcelain manufacture under the eye of Ehrenfried Walther von Tschirnhaus, a Saxon physicist who was also fascinated by this challenge. Success finally came in 1710, and a new red and white porcelain manufactory was set up in the Albrechtsburg at Meissen.

Production problems persisted, however, and it was not until 1713 that the first pieces were offered for sale, the decoration of which was largely influenced by the court silversmith Johann Irminger, and featured molded and applied vine leaf and foliage reliefs and modeled and applied rose sprays.

The king wanted color, but Böttger was never really successful in finding enamels which would withstand the firing temperatures required to fuse them into the glaze, and much of his output remained white.

Poor Böttger never enjoyed his triumph. He was still under guard until 1714, and at the mercy of a capricious ruler who refused to entertain his plans for improved kilns etc. In 1719 the factory's arcanist, Stölzel, smuggled its secrets out to Vienna enabling a rival establishment to be set up there, and when Böttger died in March of that year, at the early age of 37, the factory was in disarray.

Immediately however a turn-round occurred. The king made instant management reforms.

A Meissen kakiemon bullet-shaped teapot and cover with bird's head molded spout and wishbone handle, Pressnummer 3, circa 1740, 9.5cm. high.
(Christie's) $4,805

An oval sugar-box and cover, painted with a continuous estuary scene and wooded landscape, the cover with two scenes flanking the finial, circa 1730, 13cm. high.
(Christie's) $15,708

A Meissen Purpurmalerei écuelle, a cover and a stand, painted with estuary and landscape scenes, buildings, figures and ships, circa 1740, the stand 23.5cm. diameter.
(Christie's) $8,400

A large Meissen baluster vase and domed cover, the front and back painted with scenes after Watteau with quatrefoil cartouches, the sides with smaller panels painted with Venetian scenes after Melchior Küsel, circa 1740, 39cm. high.
(Christie's) $63,360

A Meissen olive-green-ground chinoiserie square sander painted in the manner of Johann Ehrenfried Städler with Orientals holding fans by shrubs, circa 1730, 5.5cm. square.
(Christie's) $4,066

A Meissen group of two maidens and Cupid, one standing wearing a flowered turquoise robe, the other seated on clouds, circa 1880, 8in. high.
(Christie's S. Ken) $2,250

MEISSEN

installed the new kilns he had denied Böttger, and underglaze blue was achieved. From Vienna too came the repentant Stölzel, bringing with him the enamel painter Gregorius Höroldt, who quickly perfected a superb range of overglaze enamels and used them to create fine copies of oriental wares as well as his own chinoiserie inventions. Through Höroldt, Meissen finally came to fame and fortune, and the first marks were introduced. For 15 years painted decoration remained paramount, and was only superseded by J J Kaendler's relief molding and figurines in the late 1730s.

From 1740 Kaendler's output was phenomenal. In addition to a constant supply of naturalistic figures, he designed new relief patterns for tablewares, and it is to him more than anyone that Meissen owes its long triumph, which started to wane only after the peace of 1763, when the victorious Frederick the Great of Prussia was successful in luring several fine modelers (though not Kaendler) to his new factory in Berlin.

The rococo Meissen style came to look increasingly out of date in the new Neo Classical age. Throughout the late 18th and early 19th century the factory struggled for survival in the face of disappearing markets (as imports were forbidden by several countries to protect their domestic products), and the new dominance of English creamware. Though the Napoleonic Wars temporarily cut off the supply of English goods, other German potters had learned to imitate Wedgwood cream and Jasperware, and finally Meissen too came to manufacture imitations, both of this, and their own earlier pieces.

A Meissen circular tureen and cover with crisply molded fish handles and finial enriched in purple and iron-red and with gilt supports, circa 1728, 29.8cm. wide.
(Christie's) $55,440

A Meissen royal presentation gold-mounted armorial snuff-box of oval bombé form, painted by J.G. Herold with a portrait of Augustus the Strong, circa 1730, 7cm. wide.
(Christie's) $379,000

A Meissen (Augustus Rex) yellow-ground coffee-cup painted with a moustached chinoiserie figure bending forwards and beckoning with his hand and standing on a terrace before a fence, circa 1730, 7cm. high. (Christie's) $23,000

A Meissen salt modeled as a centaur and Cupid supporting a scallop shell, the beast recumbent to the left, smiling and holding one end of the shell on his upraised right arm, circa 1880, 10¼in. high.
(Christie's) $1,461

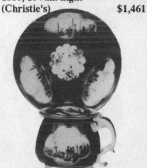

A Meissen group of three cherubs allegorical of Architecture, after the original model by M.V. Acier, the figures scantily clad and modeled constructing a Corinthian capital, circa 1880, 9in. high.
(Christie's) $2,374

A Meissen powdered-purple-ground cream-pot, cover and stand of squat baluster form, painted in the manner of J.G. Höroldt with harbor scenes. circa 1730, the stand 17.5cm.
(Christie's) $19,500

MEISSEN

A 19th century Meissen porcelain Bacchanalian group, comprising two male figures, one riding an ass, a seated female, and a putto, 8¹/₂in. high. (Andrew Hartley) $1,335

Pair of 18th century Meissen porcelain figures, of cockatoos standing on floral decorated tree trunks as a mouse observes, 14¹/₂in. high. (Eldred's) $1,155

A Meissen group of Europa and the Bull, the nymph modeled astride the bull, holding his horns, blue crossed swords marks, 8¹/₂in. high, 19th century. (Christie's) $1,353

A large Meissen Imari dish, circa 1730, K mark for Kretzscmar, the center painted in bright colors with chrysanthemum and other flowers, 16in. diameter. (Christie's) $6,900

A pair of Meissen dark-blue-ground 'Limoges enamel' vases of amphora shape, the handles with anthemion terminals, the bodies painted in white, shaded in dark blue, with mythological scenes, circa 1865, 15³/₄in. high. (Christie's) $15,521

A Meissen chinoiserie large dish, the centre painted in the manner of C. F. Herold with Orientals at various pursuits, blue crossed swords mark, circa 1735, 30.5cm. diameter. (Christie's) $35,650

A Meissen baluster coffee-pot and cover with S-scroll handle and richly gilt spout, painted with extensive harbor scenes, circa 1735, 21.5cm. high. (Christie's) $28,838

A pair of large and decorative Meissen groups of 'The Decisive Choice' and 'The Noble Decision', after models by Acier, 32cm., crossed swords marks, incised 149 and 160, circa 1850. (Phillips) $3,648

A late Meissen group of Summer and Autumn modeled as a girl with baskets of flowers and apples, and a boy with a bottle and glass standing before a barrel, 16cm. high. (Phillips) $884

MEISSEN

Meissen porcelain figural group, 19th century, depicting three putti with scientific instruments, factory marks, 7in. high.
(Skinner) $2,875

Two unusual late Meissen models of Bolognese hounds, their faces, ears and patches of their coats picked out in brown, 26cm.
(Phillips) $3,451

A Meissen group of lovers dancing, she in a striped and flowered dress and he wearing a tricorn hat, pale-green coat, circa 1890, 5³/₄in. high.
(Christie's) $2,227

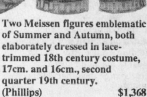

A pair of Meissen figures of a gardener and companion wearing flowered 18th century dress and holding baskets of flowers, with Pressnummer 74, blue crossed swords marks, circa 1880, 19³/₄in. high.
(Christie's) $3,799

A pair of Meissen articulated figures of pagodas, the grinning male and female figures with 'nodding' heads, tongues and hands, circa 1880, 12¹/₄in. and 12³/₄in. high.
(Christie's) $14,904

Two Meissen figures emblematic of Summer and Autumn, both elaborately dressed in lace-trimmed 18th century costume, 17cm. and 16cm., second quarter 19th century.
(Phillips) $1,368

A Meissen (K.P.M.) chinoiserie teapot and cover of pear shape, painted in the manner of J. G. Höroldt, one side with a couple at a table, circa 1723, 13.5cm. high.
(Christie's) $9,804

A Meissen spade-shaped scent flaçon and cover, circa 1742, the sides painted with gentlefolk in an Italianate harbor landscape and with English and Turkish merchants on a foreshore, 6¹/₄in. high.
(Christie's) $25,300

A rare Meissen wine bottle stand of flattened section intended to hold a moon-shaped glass bottle, pierced with strongly molded white trellis, 22.5cm. wide, crossed swords mark and impressed 26, circa 1740. (Phillips) $426

MEISSEN

A baluster coffee-pot and domed cover with gilt spout and molded S-scroll handle, blue crossed swords mark, gilder's 67., Dreher's X, circa 1730, 21cm. high.
(Christie's) $24,024

Meissen porcelain snuff box, the sides and lid decorated with hunting scenes on a turquoise ground, with gilded interior, 7cm. wide, circa 1740.
(Finarte) $9,497

A Meissen purple and gold-ground armorial teabowl and saucer, one side of the teabowl and the saucer with the quartered Arms of Benada, circa 1738.
(Christie's) $5,544

A Meissen figure of a cook seated on a small brick wall, holding a dark brown leg of meat in one hand and a saucepan in the other, 18cm.
(Phillips) $2,240

A Meissen chinoiserie table-bell and stand painted by Christian Friedrich Herold and Bonaventura Gottlieb Häuer with Orientals in harbor scenes, circa 1730, the bell 12cm. high.
(Christie's) $129,360

A Meissen figure of a lady, modeled by P. Reinicke after Huet, standing and wearing a white overdress with pale yellow frilled underskirt, 13cm.
(Phillips) $3,040

A Meissen group of a goat and four putti, the figures lightly clad in loose flowered and spotted robes holding bunches of grapes, circa 1880, 6¹/₂in. high.
(Christie's) $2,191

A Meissen blue and white plate, the center painted with birds perched and in flight among flowering shrubs issuing from rockwork, circa 1727, 24cm. diameter.
(Christie's) $8,870

A Meissen group of three musicians modeled as a young woman playing the harp, a young man seated opposite her holding an open score wearing a pink-lined blue coat, circa 1880, 7¹/₂in. high.
(Christie's) $2,922

MEISSEN

A Meissen écuelle, cover and stand, painted with figures in a harbor scene and in a wooded estuary, circa 1728, the stand 18cm. diameter.
(Christie's) $48,048

A Meissen box and cover modeled as a tortoise probably by Georg Fritzsche, with a yellow head and tail with black and iron-red markings and four yellow feet with black claws, circa 1725, 19.5cm. long.
(Christie's) $38,000

A Meissen Bergleute milk-jug and cover, painted in the manner of Bonaventura Gottlieb Häuer with two vignettes of miners by huts, circa 1740, 11.5cm. high.
(Christie's) $6,653

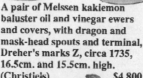

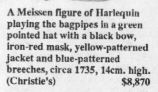

A Meissen group of Venus, Cupid and a nymph, after the original model by Schoenheit, on a rocky oval base molded with a band of yellow and gilt lozenges, circa 1880, 8¼in. high.
(Christie's) $2,739

A pair of Meissen kakiemon baluster oil and vinegar ewers and covers, with dragon and mask-head spouts and terminal, Dreher's marks Z, circa 1735, 16.5cm. and 15.5cm. high.
(Christie's) $4,800

A Meissen figure of Harlequin playing the bagpipes in a green pointed hat with a black bow, iron-red mask, yellow-patterned jacket and blue-patterned breeches, circa 1735, 14cm. high.
(Christie's) $8,870

A Meissen armorial dish from the Sulkowsky Service, the center with the double Arms flanked by gilt lions standing on a stepped plinth, circa 1735, 29.5cm. diameter.
(Christie's) $12,936

A Meissen figure of a lady beside a spinning-wheel wearing a lace-trimmed spotted white bonnet tied with blue ribbon, a yellow-lined flowered pink jacket, and blue shoes, circa 1880, 6¾in. high.
(Christie's) $2,008

A Meissen molded plate, the center painted in iron-red and gilt with a bird in flight between three flowering branches, blue crossed swords mark, Dreher's//, circa 1735, 23cm. diameter.
(Christie's) $17,556

MEISSEN, J.J. KAENDLER

A Meissen group of shepherd lovers modeled by J.J. Kändler, she with a sheep on her lap and he with a dog at his side, circa 1740, 15cm. high. (Christie's) $6,239

A pair of Meissen teapots and covers naturally modeled by J. J. Kändler as a cockerel and a hen with chicks, circa 1740, the cockerel 20.5cm. long. (Christie's) $14,260

A Meissen group in the manner of J. J. Kändler, with a young boy removing eggs from bird's nest, with his mother seated by the base, 8¼in. high. (Christie's) $4,349

A pair of Meissen figure candlesticks, emblematic of Summer and Winter, modeled by J. J. Kaendler, the elaborate rococo scroll supports heightened in gold, 29.5cm. (Phillips) $2,015

A pair of late Meissen busts, after the models by Kaendler, of Prince Louis Charles de Bourbon and the Princess Marie Zephirine de Bourbon, 23cm. (Phillips) $1,836

A pair of ormolu-mounted Meissen figure groups emblematic of Autumn, circa 1774, from models by J. J. Kändler and Peter Reinecke, the mounts later, 16½in. high. (Christie's) $13,800

A fine Meissen crinoline figure, modeled by Kändler, standing and holding a pug dog under her left arm and with another at her feet, 28cm., crossed swords mark, circa 1745. (Phillips) $4,560

Two Meissen figures of cockatoos, after the original models by J. J. Kändler, with white plumage, painted faces and iron-red feathers around their necks, circa 1890, 14¼in. high. (Christie's) $5,888

A Meissen model of 'pigs hunt', dated 1910, blue crossed swords and commemorative date mark, after a model by J. J. Kändler, 9in. high. (Christie's) $1,495

298

MEISSEN, J.J. KAENDLER

A Meissen figure of Harlequin teasing a dog modeled by J.J. Kändler, in yellow-edged green hat with a red rosette, circa 1740, the figure 16.5cm. high. (Christie's) $10,695

A pair of Meissen models of doves modeled by J. J. Kaendler, the naturalistically modelled and colored birds sitting on shaped round bases, circa 1745, both about 16cm. wide. (Christie's) $9,600

A Meissen figure of a fruit-vendor after the model by J. J. Kändler as an old woman in gray scarf, turquoise and black bodice, circa 1745, 17.5cm. high. (Christie's) $2,033

A Meissen group of the Spanish lovers, Beltrame and Columbine modeled by J. J. Kändler, she in yellow-plumed hat, black and purple bodice and white crinoline with green underskirt, circa 1745, 19.5cm. high. (Christie's) $7,392

Two Meissen figures of dancing Chinese boys, circa 1748, modeled by J.J. Kändler, with leaf hats, both with puce-edged pink robes, the bases with applied flowers in colors, 83/4in. high. (Christie's) $5,520

A Meissen white bust of the Mater Dolorosa after the model by J.J. Kändler, ordered by Cardinal Albani, the strongly modeled countenance looking upwards to her right beneath her flowing veil, circa 1743, 35cm. high. (Christie's) $40,000

A Meissen model of a mallard probably after a model by Johann Joachim Kändler, on a circular green-washed base, circa 1750, 28cm. high. (Christie's) $28,028

A pair of Meissen models of a pug-dog and a bitch modeled by J. J. Kändler, with pale-brown coats, black muzzles and tails, wearing iron-red and puce collars, circa 1750, 15cm. high. (Christie's) $6,686

A Meissen ewer in the form of a monkey with her young, after the model by Johann Joachim Kändler, circa 1740, 18.5cm. high. (Christie's) $7,608

One of two Meissen hunting groups, probably modeled by J.J. Kändler, each of a doe being dragged to the ground by three hounds, circa 1750, 5¼in. wide.
(Christie's) $2,852

A pair of Meissen models of cockatoos, modeled by J.J. Kändler, perched astride conical tree stumps, circa 1740, 8½in. high.
(Christie's) $55,180

A Meissen group of two Bolognese terriers and a pug dog, modeled by J.J. Kändler, one terrier scratching his chin, circa 1755, 5¾in high.
(Christie's) $12,447

A Meissen white bust of Carolus VII from the series of busts of Holy Roman Emperors (Kaiserbusten), made for the House of Habsburg and modeled by J.J. Kändler and P. Reinicke, 1743–46, 38cm. high.
(Christie's) $23,232

A pair of Meissen miniature pug dogs, modeled by J.J. Kändler to left and right, seated on their haunches scratching one ear, circa 1740, 2¼in. high.
(Christie's) $12,477

A Meissen figure of a lady of the Mopsorden modeled by J.J. Kändler, in a puce dress with a crinoline skirt enriched with gilding and a turquoise flowered underskirt, circa 1745, 28.5cm. high.
(Christie's) $10,138

A Meissen figure of a drunken peasant modeled by J.J. Kändler, vigorously dancing with his arm raised to his black hat, circa 1740, 6¾in. high.
(Christie's) $6,417

A pair of Meissen models of quail by J.J. Kändler, on circular mound bases applied with corn and water weeds, circa 1745, 14cm. high.
(Christie's) $10,800

A Meissen swordsmith from the series of Craftsmen, modeled by J.J. Kändler and P. Reinicke, holding a hammer and a dagger, circa 1750, 9in. high.
(Christie's) $3,921

MEISSEN, KAENDLER

A Meissen group of the Eavesdropper at the Fountain after the original model of J.J. Kändler, on a shaped-oval grassy base molded with white and gilt scrolls, circa 1880, 8³/₄in. high.
(Christie's) $3,100

A Meissen Fläschenhalter from the Swan service modeled by J.J. Kändler and J.F. Eberlein for Count Brühl, of compressed oval shape with a gilt undulating rim, 1737–41, 24cm. wide.
(Christie's) $21,000

A Meissen group of the house-keeper modeled by J J Kandler, wearing a white cap, yellow-flowered jacket over a turquoise skirt, sitting at a table with cabriole legs and writing her books, circa 1755, 15.5cm. high. (Christie's) $4,800

A Meissen group of the hand kiss modeled by J.J. Kändler, the gallant wearing a gilt flower and black foliage gray waistcoat over black breeches and yellow shoes with red rosettes, circa 1740, 18cm. high. $6,800

A Meissen armorial circular dish from the Swan Service modeled by J.J. Kändler and J.F. Eberlein for Count Brühl, the shell-patterned surface molded with swans among bulrushes, herons, fish and shells, 1737–41, 42cm. diameter. (Christie's) $63,360

A Meissen equestrian group emblematic of Europe from the series of the Continents modeled by J.J. Kändler, the female figure, sitting on a rearing white horse, wearing a gilt crown, circa 1745, 19cm. high.
(Christie's) $3,200

A Meissen figure of a seated harlequin with a bird-cage after the model by J.J. Kändler and J.F. Eberlein, in a pink hat, and playing-card jacket over yellow trousers, circa 1745, 13.5cm. high. (Christie's) $19,008

A Meissen armorial sugar-box and cover from the Swan Service modeled by Johann Joachim Kändler, of crisply molded oval shell form, circa 1738, 13.2cm. wide.
(Christie's) $81,312

A Meissen group of Harlequin and Columbine after the model by J.J. Kändler, Harlequin wearing a mask and a tunic half checkered and half with playing cards, circa 1740, 15.5cm. high.
(Christie's) $9,750

MENNECY

The Mennecy factory was set up in 1734 in Paris by Louis François de Neufville, Duc de Villeroy under the directorship of François Barbin. For the first year it produced faience, but then turned to porcelain and in 1748 moved to Mennecy.

For its early products it drew heavily on the shapes manufactured at Rouen, and on St Cloud (blue lambrequins) and Chantilly (Kakiemon) for its decorations. Mennecy soon developed its own style however. Its paste was characterised by its lovely dark ivory color and its glaze by its wet-looking brilliance. The factory did not have a wide range of shapes, but those it did produce were admirably simple in form, tall, globular teapots with gently curving spouts, and cups and saucers which were either straight sided, tapering down or pear shaped. Among its most characteristic pieces were spirally fluted custard cups and sugar bowls with lids surmounted by a rosebud.

Painted decoration was very beautiful, dominated by cool blues and pinks and often depicting naturalistic flower or bird designs and delicate polychrome landscapes where brown and green predominate. Mennecy also excelled at figure modeling, especially under the sculptor Gouron, who came to the factory in 1753.

Mennecy continued producing rococo style, mainly useful wares into the 1770s, after which quality declined. It continued in production until 1800, by which time porcelain had been abandoned in favor of faience and cream colored earthenware. Mennecy porcelain is marked *DV* for the Duc de Villeroy. After the factory moved to Bourg la Reine in 1773 the mark *BR*, often incised, was used.

A soft paste porcelain tulip vase, decorated with polychrome flowers on a turquoise base, possibly Mennecy, circa 1770, 10cm. high.
(Finarte) $498

A Mennecy silver-mounted snuff-box modeled as a seated Buddha patting his tummy in a puce-flowered open-necked robe with a fur collar, décharge for Éloy Brichard, Paris 1756–1762, circa 1755, 5.5cm. high.
(Christie's) $2,830

A pair of Mennecy figures of pug dogs, circa 1750, 14cm. long. $8,000

A pair of Mennecy figures of a young man and woman, circa 1740, 17.5cm. high. $3,200

A Mennecy silver gilt mounted oval snuff box, circa 1750, the mount with Paris décharge for 1750-55, modeled as a sportswoman in blue jacket, 2¾in. (Christie's) $786

A Mennecy biscuit porcelain two handled baluster vase, the neck pierced with flowerheads, on short stem and circular foot, mid 18th century, 18cm. high. (Christie's) $450

MERRIMAC

The Merrimac Pottery was established at Newburyport, Massachusetts in the last years of the 19th century. Their wares, consisting largely of occasional pieces, such as vases and jardinières, are generally thickly potted and characterised by matt, often green glazes.

METTLACH

The original Mettlach factory was established in 1809 at the Abbey of Mettlach in the Rhineland. In 1836 it merged with the factories of Villeroy and J F Boch and together this group produced earthenwares. Stoneware was also made from 1842 onwards, with a high proportion of the output being exported to America.

Art Pottery, decorated with inlaid clays in contrasting colors (Mettlach ware) was also introduced, and among the top artists working there was J Scharvogel. In the later part of the 19th century terracotta and mosaic tiles were added to the range. Marks include Mettlach castle with the monogram of *VB*, and a circular mark with Mercury looking over *Villeroy & Boch* and *Mettlach*.

Merrimac Pottery vase, Newburyport, Massachusetts, circa 1904, matt black drip glaze over mottled matt moss green glaze, 4¼in. high.
(Skinner) $920

Merrimac pottery jardiniere, collar rim over bulbous base, matte and glossy green glaze, unmarked, 7½in. high.
(Skinner) $201

Mettlach pottery covered punch bowl with undertray, late 19th century, with grapevine and gnome decoration, 17½in. high.
(Eldred's) $632

A Mettlach pottery ewer, the cylindrical body with short neck, incised with green and brown foliage, having a metal collar and lid, 38.5cm. high.
(Phillips) $263

A Mettlach plaque of a spring landscape, signed H. Cradl?, stamped Villeroy & Boch, 17½in. diam., Germany, 1910.
                          $1,200

A Mettlach tankard of tapered cylindrical form with pewter cover, Germany, 1898, 7in. high. $480

MING

When Chu Yuang Chang founded the Ming dynasty at Nanking in 1368, the art of producing high fired porcelain had already been mastered and was being used to make not only small pieces but also huge storage jars. The glaze on these is often cracked, so that it is possible to see clearly how the base, lower body, shoulders and neck were made separately and then stuck together with a watered down porcelain clay before drying and decorating.

Underglaze painting too had already been discovered during the previous Yuan period, and Ming decorators exploited the possibilities of both iron red, and the favored Burmese cobalt blue to the full.

Ming pieces can often be dated by appearance. Fourteenth century pieces, often painted with brilliant precision in loosely composed designs, were made from a finely mixed white clay with a thin grayish glaze, whereas on those dating from the 15th century, the glaze is often thick and clear and has allowed the blue to bleed into it during the firing, giving an effect of enhanced depth and richness.

Celadons had been produced during Sung times, and their use was continued during the Ming period, but they were used for heavily potted wares, storage jars, lanterns etc which were carved or applied with a premolded design and covered with a thick celadon glaze. These proved extremely popular in the near East, Burma and India, perhaps because it was believed that poison would boil if it touched a celadon surface!

The enamel painting of porcelain was first successfully introduced at the

A very fine Ming-style blue and white moon flask, Qianlong seal mark and of the period, painted to each side in rich cobalt-blue with eight petals, 19¼in. high. (Christie's) $192,519

A fine Ming-style yellow and green-glazed blue and white dish, encircled Yongzheng six-character mark and of the period, 10⅝in. diameter. (Christie's) $99,355

A fine Ming blue and yellow saucer-dish, encircled Zhengde four-character mark and of the period, painted in underglaze-blue with a central hibiscus branch of two flowers and one bud among leaves, 7¾in. diameter. (Christie's) $70,968

A rare early Ming blue and white jar, encircled Xuande six-character mark and of the period, painted around the body with two long-tailed phoenixes in flight amidst leafy vines, 5¼in. high. (Christie's) $94,779

A dated late Ming blue and white cylindrical censer with molded lion masks around the base, painted with dragons among fire-scrolls, 25.5cm. diameter. (Christie's) $3,600

A fine small late Ming Wucai bowl, encircled Wanli six-character mark and of the period, painted and enameled on the exterior with three figures and a caparisoned deer in a landscape, 4⅜in. diameter. (Christie's) $22,710

MING

end of the fifteenth century. This was done by applying the colors to clear glazed pieces and then refiring them in a low temperature 'muffle kiln'.

The late Ming period saw the opening up of an export trade extending far beyond the traditional markets of the near East and Southeast Asia. In 1595 the Dutch established a trading post at Canton, and it was the Dutch East India Company who first brought back the Kraak porselyns which were to provide the inspiration for European porcelain manufacture.

It is worth remembering that the marks on Ming pieces should not be taken as gospel. If a potter were successful in reproducing an earlier style to the same standard as the original, he would apply the mark of the emperor of the period of the original. This was done for honorific reasons, and not, then at least, from any desire to deceive.

A Ming-style yellow-ground blue and white dish, Qianlong seal mark and of the period, 21.2cm. diameter.
(Christie's) $6,892

An early Ming blue and white small Jar painted with a band of four blooming lotus flowers on a continuous leafy vine below closed flower buds, 13cm. high.
(Christie's) $44,000

A rare pair of celadon-glazed candlesticks, early Ming Dynasty, formed probably in three parts with small petal-molded sconces, 9¹/₄ in. high.
(Christie's) $14,500

A fine early Ming blue and white 'Dice' bowl, Xuande six-character mark below the rim and of the period, the heavily-potted rounded sides painted to the exterior, 11³/₈in. diameter.
(Christie's) $241,290

A Sancai tilemaker's figure of a Lokopala standing with his legs apart and his arms clenched at his waist, wearing elaborate ribbons, armor and waist sash Ming Dynasty, 49cm. high.
(Christie's) $12,799

A Ming imperial yellow dish potted with well-rounded sides rising to an everted rim, all under an even egg-yolk yellow glaze, Zhengde six-character mark and of the period, 20.3cm. diameter.
(Christie's) $10,000

A fine Ming-style yellow-ground green-glazed blue and white dish, decorated in the center with a bouquet of ribbon-tied lotus and water weeds, Qianlong seal mark and of the period, 21.2cm. diameter.
(Christie's) $53,163

MING

A fine late Ming blue and white small jar painted in bright blue tones with three peacocks, 5¼in. high.
(Christie's) $19,000

A rare early Ming large blue and white bowl, finely painted in characteristic grayish-blue tones with areas of 'heaping and piling', Hongwu, 42.5cm.
(Christie's) $31,464

Chinese amber glazed biscuit roof tile, Ming Dynasty, 17th century, depicting a celestial deity mounted astride a phoenix, 13¾in. high.
(William Doyle) $690

A very rare early Ming under-glaze-blue yellow-ground saucer-dish, painted in strong cobalt tones with a spray of flowering pomegranate, Xuande period, 29.4cm. diam.
(Christie's) $352,000

A large Ming blue and white 'Hundred boys' jar, painted to the exterior with a continuous scene of boys at play, with a group acting out the scene of a high official flanked by advisers in audience and a kneeling subject, 15¾in. diameter.
(Christie's) $45,000

Late 17th/early 18th century shield-shaped Arita dish, the base with three spur marks and a Ming Chenghua mark, 12.4cm.
$1,120

An early 16th century large Ming blue and white baluster jar, Guan (minor restoration), 36.5cm. high.
(Christie's) $7,200

A Ming blue and white square box and cover, the sides painted in bright blue tones with a lotus scroll, Longqing period, 11cm. square. (Christie's) $20,000

A late Ming Wucai barrel-shaped jar and cover, the base with Wanli six-character mark and of the period, 15cm. diam., fitted box.
$56,000

MINTON

Thomas Minton was born in 1765 and apprenticed at the Caughley Works where he was trained in the art of engraving copper plates for underglaze-blue painted designs. In 1793 he established his own works at Stoke on Trent, where it traded as Minton & Co from 1845 and Mintons Ltd from 1873. It was noted from the first for the high quality and diversity of its output, which at first consisted mainly of blue printed earthenware, though porcelain was added to the range in 1797, The original pattern book of that period survives today.

From 1847 large quantities of parian ware were produced, and figures were made by a number of eminent modelers. Various partners took responsibility for various branches of the firm, and by 1868 these separated. Minton, Collins & Co specialised in tile manufacturing, while C H Campbell became responsible for earthenware.

Minton had a strong presence at the Great Exhibition of 1851 where they displayed Sèvres style porcelain vases, terracotta and majolica garden ornaments, parian figures and tiles, all of which attracted much favorable comment. Pâte-sur-pâte decoration was introduced by the Sèvres-trained decorator and modeler Marc Louis or Miles Solon, who worked for Minton between 1870 and 1904. Dinner services were commonly painted or printed in the Japanese taste with flowers, chickens or butterflies.

Art Nouveau vases, again decorated by Solon, were popular around the turn of the century, and were usually decorated with colored glazes contained by raised lines of trailed slip.

A pair of Minton majolica ware figure sweetmeat dishes, with seated figures of a girl and boy, 17.5cm., date code for 1869. (Phillips) $1,705

Minton majolica jardiniere, predominantly blue, green, brown and amber glazing, English, mid 19th century. (G.A. Key) $630

An important pair of 19th century Minton majolica jardinières on stands, the planters with green wreath rim, the bases fluted 26½in. high. (Dee, Atkinson & Harrison) $11,400

A Minton stoneware encaustic bread plate, designed by A. W. N. Pugin, the rim with the text *Waste Not, Want Not*, circa 1849, 33cm. diameter. (Christie's) $1,544

A pair of Minton figures of the Coachee and Easy Johnny with nodding heads, circa 1860, 7½in. high. (Christie's) $1,223

A Minton majolica ware tavern jug, with two figures of topers on one side, green handle, 25.5cm., date code for 1864. (Phillips) $899

MINTON

An impressive Minton majolica cistern, circa 1849–1850, designed by Baron Carlo Maraschetti, the oval body supported on claw feet, with scrolling foliate Italian Renaissance design and double snake handles, 4ft. wide.
(Sotheby's) $18,755

A Minton majolica oyster-stand modeled with four tapering circular tiers of oyster shells with white-glazed interiors and brown exteriors, date code for 1862, 11in. high.
(Christie's) $3,600

A Minton majolica oval seafood dish, the cover modeled as a large crab resting on a bed of green seaweed, the fronds curling up its back to form a loop handle, date code for 1859, 15³/₄in. wide.
(Christie's) $6,600

A Minton royal-blue-ground porcelain and parian flower-basket center-dish from a dessert service modeled as four parian figures emblematic of the Seasons, circa 1851, 24¹/₄in. high.
(Christie's) $5,250

A pair of majolica wall-brackets each modeled as three loosely draped children flanked by eagles on columns, possibly Minton, circa 1865, 14in.
(Christie's) $1,250

A Minton majolica ewer in the form of a heron, after a model by Hugues Protât, the handle spout modeled as the body and gaping mouth of a pike caught in the beak of the bird, date code for 1878, 21¹/₄in. high.
(Christie's) $2,500

A Minton majolica dark-blue-ground jardinière and stand with two bamboo-molded handles extending to encircle the rim and foot, date code for 1870, 9in. high.
(Christie's) $2,190

A Minton pottery wall plaque, Kensington Gore Period, circa 1871, of Japanesque inspiration, decorated with two exotic birds perched amongst branches of flowering prunus blossom, 17in. diameter.
(Sotheby's) $1,961

A Minton dark-blue-ground japanesque jardinière and stand, with two cranes perched on a sinuous gnarled tree-trunk with clouds of foliage on meandering boughs, 1874, 12¹/₄in. high.
(Christie's) $1,159

MINTON

A Minton majolica ewer and stand after a model by Hughes Protût, the tapering dark-brown body with a knopped shoulder molded with bands of gadroons and applied with the seated figures of a putto riding a dolphin, impressed date code for 1859, 24¹/₂in. high.
(Christie's) $2,800

A Minton majolica monkey teapot and cover, the smiling creature's head forming the detachable cover and its curling tail forming the handle, date code for 1874, 6in. high.
(Christie's) $2,000

A large Minton majolica flower vase in the form of a fawn after a model by Paul Comolera, the young animal with a matt gray-brown body and white spotted markings, circa 1875, 32³/₄in. high. (Christie's) $13,695

A pair of Minton 'cloisonné' vases, circa 1878, decorated in the manner of Christopher Dresser, with Chinese flowers, furniture and objects within circular panels, 5³/₄in. high.
(Sotheby's) $3,751

Two Minton majolica models of boys steering rowing-boats each figure seated at the stern of the twin-sectioned vessel and holding the tiller, date code for 1866, 6³/₄in. long.
(Christie's) $968

A pair of Minton four-light candelabra after a model by A. Carrier de Belleuse, the stems modeled with figures emblematic of Night and Day, date code for 1866, 25¹/₄in. high. (Christie's) $3,500

A Minton majolica lamp base modeled as a boy and girl putto scantily clad in manganese drapes tied in ocher, date code for 1872, 13³/₄in. high.
(Christie's) $1,990

A Minton pottery wall plaque, circa 1873, finely painted with a kingfisher perched on branches of flowers and foliage, reserved on a terracotta ground, 18¹/₂in. diam. (Sotheby's) $1,364

A Minton majolica bacchanalian group of three putti with a ram, the ram drinking from a goblet proffered by one putto, another putto seated on its back holding reins, date code for 1862, 15in. high. (Christie's) $2,400

MINTON

A Minton majolica green and treacle glazed teapot and cover with shell finial, modeled as a tortoise, circa 1878 impressed *Minton*, 8¼in. long.
(Christie's) $4,112

A pair of Minton candle-snuffers modeled as ladies wearing brightly-colored and gilt eighteenth century dress, circa 1830, 9.5cm. high.
(Christie's) $1,500

An unusual Minton pottery figure of a cat, seated upon a maroon and orange decorated base, striped fur in light and dark gray, 13in. high.
(Spencer's) $2,464

A Minton majolica-ware 'Baroque vase', molded with four grotesque bacchanalian satyr masks linked by rope festoons, 32cm. high, 1873.
(Phillips) $1,020

A Minton majolica ware 'Shell Carrier' with two Bacchic children swathed in wheat and vines and supporting a central shell, 27cm. high, date code for 1867; and another similar, 27.5cm.
(Phillips) $3,100

A Minton olive-brown ground pâte-sur pâte large vase, designed by Louis Solon, signed and dated *1884*, impressed date mark for 1883, 25⅝in. high.
(Christie's) $25,300

Mintons blue and white jardinière on stand of circular form, the flared neck with keyhole border, impressed date cipher for 1879, 11½in. diameter.
(G. A. Key) $408

A fine pair of Minton porcelain pedestal jars and covers in the Sèvres manner, 41cm., circa 1860.
(Bearne's) $5,600

A Minton majolica 'Lazy Susan', the flat circular tray with 'encaustic' decoration, the central white flowerhead enclosed within a purple-ground disk including quatrefoils, circa 1873, 18¼in. diameter.
(Christie's) $1,187

MINTON

A Minton Majolica cheese stand and cover molded with lilies, and having flower finial.
(Russell, Baldwin & Bright)
$476

A. W. N. Pugin, pair of garden seats, 1868, manufactured by Minton & Co., in polychrome glazed earthenware of hexafoil section, 48cm. high.
(Sotheby's)
$1,863

A Minton majolica group of a young man pushing a wheelbarrow, modeled by J.B. Klagmann, date code for 1873, 12$\frac{1}{2}$in. high.
(Christie's)
$2,194

A Minton majolica ware stemmed bowl and cover, in Renaissance style, the bowl with incised green panels below satyr masks and pendant swags, 26cm.
(Phillips)
$1,240

A pair of Minton vases modeled as putti, scantily clad in manganese drapes, each straining to support a fluted vase formed as a rhyton with a goat's head, date codes for 1868, 14$\frac{3}{4}$in. high.
(Christie's)
$4,145

A Minton majolica lavender-ground garden seat, molded in relief with stylized honeysuckle alternating with passion flowers, date code for 1869, 18$\frac{1}{2}$in. high.
(Christie's S. Ken)
$1,500

A majolica turquoise-ground jardinière and circular stand, with entwined branch-molded handles issuing oak leaves and acorns, circa 1875, possibly Minton, 13in. high overall.
(Christie's)
$1,186

A pair of Minton twin-handled 'cloisonné' vases, designed by Dr. Christopher Dresser, gilt and polychrome enamel decoration of floral reserves on a turquoise ground, numbered 1592, circa 1871, 28cm. high.
(Christie's)
$6,359

A Mintons majolica fluted jardinière, the dimpled dark-brown ground molded in relief with leafy sprays of pink and white foxgloves and overlapping fern-leaves, date code for 1873, 13in. high.
(Christie's)
$2,985

MINTON

A Minton majolica group of a putto riding a hippocamp after a model by A. Carrier de Belleuse, incised ermine mark, date code for 1859, 15½in. high.
(Christie's) $1,040

A pair of extremely large Minton 'Dresden vases' and nosegay covers painted with exotic birds in woodland clearings, 61cm.
(Phillips) $7,360

A Minton's Art Pottery moon flask, the sage green body painted in colors, 21.5cm. high.
(Christie's) $217

A Minton majolica centerpiece modeled as a Bacchanalian putto standing supporting a circular basket, impressed ermine mark and date code for 1860, 20¼in. high.
(Christie's) $1,572

A pair of Minton majolica figures of the Hogarth match boy and girl wearing 18th century-style rustic dress, date codes for 1865, 7¾in. high.
(Christie's) $795

A massive Minton majolica group of two frogs courting under a bunch of leaves, their faces turned towards each other with fond devotion and their hands entwined around the stem of the leaves, date code for 1876, 48in. high.
(Christie's) $31,042

A Minton majolica teapot and cover in the form of a seated Chinaman, holding a grotesque mask, his detachable head forming the cover, circa 1874, 7in. high.
(Christie's) $1,600

A pair of Minton pâte-sur-pâte vases, circa 1872–1894, decorated by L. Birks, with birds perched on bullrushes reserved on a blue ground, 10in. high.
(Sotheby's) $3,069

A Minton majolica center-dish in the form of a putto dragging a cart behind him, clad only in a wreath of vine and a blue drape tucked into an orange sash, date code for 1873, 15in. high.
(Christie's) $1,360

MINTON

A fine Minton majolica ewer and stand, circa 1862, designed by Emile Jeannest and painted by Thomas Kirkby, signed, 32in. high.
(Sotheby's) $10,230

A Minton majolica tureen and cover, circa 1861, molded with basket-weave and supported by three fan-tailed pigeons perched on oak branches, 12in. wide.
(Sotheby's) $7,161

A Minton majolica figure of a begging white spaniel seated on its haunches, wearing a yellow collar, date code for 1868, 6¼in. high.
(Christie's) $994

A Minton majolica jug, the mottled manganese and blue body molded in high relief with two pairs of peasants drinking and dancing flanking a seated figure, code for 1873, 10½in. high.
(Christie's) $1,200

A Minton majolica circular 'Christmas' plate for the Crystal Palace Art Union, the brown-glazed well molded in relief with a flower within a wreath of mistletoe, date code for 1859, 15½in. diameter.
(Christie's) $994

A Minton majolica jardinière in the form of a nautilus shell resting on coral and rocks, the shell with a whitish glaze on the exterior splashed with manganese beads, date code for 1873, 26in. high.
(Christie's) $6,600

A Minton majolica ware Palissy vase, with barrel shaped body, four Bacchic putti disporting themselves below the helmet shaped spout, 37cm., impressed mark and date code for 1870.
(Phillips) $1,705

A Minton majolica dark-blue-ground jardinière, each corner with a single bulrush among leaves molded in relief below a yellow-line rim, date code for 1864, 7in. high.
(Christie's) $662

A Minton Kensington Gore Studios moonflask, circa 1871, possibly painted by John Eyre and after a Coleman design, signed, painted with three dancing cherubs, 17in. high.
(Sotheby's) $1,620

MOCHAWARE

Mochaware was produced from about 1780 until 1914 and was named from mocha quartz. It is characterised by its decoration , by which tree, moss and fernlike effects were introduced by means of a diffusing medium, which was described as 'a saturated infusion of tobacco in stale urine and turpentine'! It was inexpensive to make, and was first made of creamware and subsequently of pearlware and cane ware. It was designed mainly for domestic use, for public house serving jugs and mugs for measures used to serve shrimps, nuts etc.

Mochaware chamber pot, England, 19th century, 8⅞in. diameter.
(Skinner) $316

Mochaware pitcher, England, 19th century, decorated with undulating lines in cream slip, (rim chips) 6¾in. high.
(Skinner) $720

Mochaware pitcher, England, 19th century, with incised green bands enclosing central bands of butternut, brown and white with twig, wave and cat's eye decoration, 8in. high.
(Skinner) $2,750

Mochaware mug, England, 19th century, wormed decoration on blue ground, 3.5in. high.
(Skinner) $690

Mochaware pitcher, England, 19th century, decorated with bands of "worming" on ecru and siena grounds, 8in. high.
(Skinner) $1,280

Mochaware pitcher, England, 19th century, blue decorated with light blue and white worming, 7in. high.
(Skinner) $720

Mochaware mustard pot, England, 19th century, brown seaweed decoration on pumpkin ground, 4in. high.
(Skinner) $690

Mochaware pitcher, England, early 19th century, with four large brown, rust and white tobacco leaves, 9½in. high.
(Skinner) $6,000

MONTELUPO

In the 17th and 18th centuries a coarse, heavy earthenware was produced at Montelupo, near Florence. It was characterised by the somewhat rough and ready painting of caricature figures of soldiers and men dressed in curious contemporary Italian costumes and bristling with weapons, striding across the plates.

In the mid 17th century, marks are found referring to Rafaello Girolamo and Jacinto or Diacinto Monti of Montelupo.

A Montelupo wet-drug jar, with strap handle painted a foglie in blue, ocher and yellow, third quarter of the 16th century, 24.5cm.high. $1,950

A Montelupo à Quatieri crespina painted in blue, ocher, yellow and green with a putto in a landscape, 27cm.
(Phillips) $1,450

A Tuscan armorial baluster jug, painted in ocher and blue with a coat-of-arms flanked by scrolling tendrils within an ocher, blue and yellow cartouche, early 16th century, probably Cafaggiolo or Montelupo, 25cm. high.
(Christie's) $1,571

Two Montelupo circular dishes, painted in ocher, green, blue and manganese with equestrian figures in landscapes, mid-17th century, 31.5cm. diameter.
(Christie's) $10,552

A Montelupo two-handled oviform wet-drug jar and a cover, with dolphin handles, painted with a shield with the initials D.F. below a Maltese cross, mid 16th century, 46cm. high overall.
(Christie's) $4,635

A Montelupo crespina, the center with the bust portrait of a girl draped in a green shawl and inscribed VESTRO within a border of radiating panels, early 17th century, 23.5cm. diameter.
(Christie's) $2,900

A Montelupo maiolica oviform wet drug jar with twin serpent handles, named for AP.DILATVGA within scrolled cartouche, circa 1580, 38cm. high.
(Christie's) $1,136

A massive Montelupo dish boldly painted with the interior of a bakery with figures kneading dough and removing bread and cakes from the oven, late 16th century, 50.5cm. diameter.
(Christie's) $19,690

MOORCROFT

The son of the noted designer
and china painter Thomas
Moorcroft, William
Moorcroft (1872-1945)
studied at Burslem School of
Art and the National Art
Training School. He
qualified as an art teacher,
but in 1896 went to work as a
designer for James Macintyre
of Burslem. When
Macintyre's Art Pottery
department closed in 1913,
Moorcroft built his own kiln
and workshops at Cobridge,
where he specialised in floral
and landscape designs on
deep blue and green grounds,
as well as magnificent plain
luster glazes.

Although on the whole his
style remained wedded to
naturalistic decoration
throughout, an Art Deco
influence did appear in the
late 1920s in bands of
geometric motifs and a
certain stylisation of his plant
forms. He was hugely
successful and his products
sold worldwide; he was
appointed potter to HM
Queen Mary in 1928.
Moorcroft struggled to keep
his factory going during the
war, dying in 1945 just as his
son, Walter, arrived back
from the forces to take over.

A twin-handled square biscuit
barrel and cover decorated in
the 'Hazledene' pattern, in shades
of green and blue, 6½in. high.
(Christie's) $800

A twin-handled vase, decorated
in Florian Ware cartouches of
pink roses and green foliage on
a blue ground, 8in. high.
(Christie's) $5,000

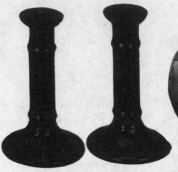

A pair of cylindrical
candlesticks decorated in the
'Pomegranate' pattern, in
shades of pink, ocher and green
on a mottled green and blue
ground, 8in. high.
(Christie's) $1,765

A spherical vase decorated
with stylised fish among
waterweeds, in shades of
red and ocher on a speckled
salmon pink ground, the
interior blue, 6in. high.
(Christie's) $2,000

A Florian Ware twin-handled
vase, decorated with scrolling
cartouches of peacock feathers
and flowerheads, in shades of
pale and dark blue, 8in. high.
(Christie's) $1,500

A twin-handled square biscuit
barrel and cover, decorated in
the 'Pomegranate' pattern, in
shades of pink and blue on a
sage green ground, 6¼in. high.
(Christie's) $760

A large twin-handled vase,
decorated with a band of plums
and foliage, in shades of pink,
mauve and green on a dark blue
ground, 12½in. high.
(Christie's) $2,549

Moorcroft Flambé vase, 10in. high, 1930s.
(Muir Hewitt) $540

An ovoid vase with everted rim decorated with a band of frilled orchids, in pastel tones on a cream ground, 8½in. high.
(Christie's) $480

A baluster vase decorated in the 'Eventide' pattern, in shades of ocher, pink, green and blue, 13in. high.
(Christie's) $1,216

A tapering cylindrical vase decorated with a bland of orchids, in shades of yellow, pink and purple on a graduated blue ground, 5in. high.
(Christie's) $480

A pair of Florian Ware baluster vases, decorated with scrolling cartouches of poppies and foliage, in shades of pale and dark blue, 12in. high.
(Christie's) $1,600

An oviform vase decorated with a band of vine leaves and berries, in shades of yellow, pink and green on a deep blue ground, 12in. high.
(Christie's) $686

A Flamminian vase made for Liberty, embossed on the shoulder with three foliate roundels, covered in a rose pink glaze, 6½in. high.
(Christie's) $320

A twin-handled tapering cylindrical jardiniere, made for Liberty, decorated in the 'Hazledene' pattern, in shades of blue and green, 8¼in. high.
(Christie's) $960

A Moorcroft 'Pansy' pattern vase, white ground with decoration of yellow and purple pansies amid green foliage, circa 1916, 23cm. high.
(Christie's) $1,378

MOORCROFT

A miniature William Moorcroft vase, tube-lined with pommels of forget-me-nots on a powder-blue ground, 3³/₈in. high.
(Bonhams) $329

Moorcroft pottery bowl, green/blue ground, decorated with aquilegia, impressed and monogrammed mark, 8in. diameter.
(G. A. Key) $123

A William Moorcroft Liberty & Co. pewter mounted 'Claremont' jar and cover, 8¹/₄in. high.
(Bonhams) $1,495

Moorcroft potpourri and cover, England, circa 1905, pomegranate and pansy design in green, blue, red, yellow and blue, 5in. high.
(Skinner Inc.) $880

A pair of Moorcroft Florian ware vases, tube-lined with iris and leafy flowers, in shades of blue, 20.2cm. high.
(Bonhams) $969

Moorcroft Florian ware squat oviform three handled vase, decorated in the 'Daisy' pattern in applied raised slipware in shades of yellow, green and blue, 5in. high.
(Peter Wilson) $675

Florian Ware Moorcroft Art pottery vase, white floral form on cobalt blue ground, 8in. high.
(Skinner) $920

A Moorcroft pottery fruit bowl of circular form, painted with fish, seaweed and sea anemones in shades of red, blue, yellow and green, 24.5cm. diameter.
(Spencer's) $840

A Moorcroft 'Willow Tree' vase, footed ovoid, tube-lined with weeping willows in pink and green, 16cm. high.
(Bonhams) $1,292

MOORCROFT

A small Moorcroft covered jar, 4in. high.
(Dee, Atkinson & Harrison)
$106

A Moorcroft jug, tube-lined with fish amongst weeds, in gray/blue and brown on a matt cream ground, 13.1cm. high.
(Bonhams)
$678

A good William Moorcroft Liberty & Co. 'Poppies' flambé cookie barrel and pewter cover, 6¹/₂in. high.
(Bonhams)
$1,495

A Moorcroft 'Liberty & Co.' Florian ware vase, tube-lined with poppies in blue and green, on a yellow ground, 12.4cm. high.
(Bonhams)
$807

A Moorcroft pair of ovoid vases, the blue/ivory ground divided by green leaves and pink buds, green signature mark, 20.8cm.
(Bristol)
$1,094

A William Moorcroft 'Pomegranate' tobacco jar and cover, tube-lined with a band of large fruits, berries and foliage, 7¹/₂in. high.
(Bonhams)
$568

A Moorcroft shouldered oviform vase, with a band of leaf and berry design in shades of pink and green on a deep blue ground, 27cm. high.
(Christie's)
$702

A Moorcroft Hazeldene pattern bowl with incurved rim, decorated in the center with a large central tree and smaller trees at the side, 24cm. diam.
(Phillips London)
$640

An attractive Moorcroft Florian ware vase, slip trailed in white and decorated in shades of blue with a flower pattern.
(Spencer's)
$380

319

MOORCROFT

A Macintyre Florian 'Poppy' pattern preserve jar on saucer, with domed cover, white ground with raised slip decoration of blue poppies, with brown printed Macintyre stamp, circa 1904, 14cm. diameter.
(Christie's) $591

An octagonal bowl with everted rim, the interior decorated with alternate panels of peacock feathers and tulips, 10in. wide.
(Christie's) $560

An oviform powder bowl and cover decorated with pansies, in shades of mauve and green on a deep blue ground, 3½in. high.
(Christie's) $480

A Liberty vase, of tapering waisted cylindrical form, decorated in the 'Hazledene' pattern, in shades of blue and green, printed factory marks, signed in green, 9in. high.
(Christie's) $1,333

A Macintyre 'Claremont' pattern bowl, streaked blue and green ground with decoration of pink, green and blue mushrooms, circa 1903, 12cm. high.
(Christie's) $1,477

A dimpled oval section vase of finely ribbed form, decorated with a fish amongst waterweeds, in shades of red, yellow, green and blue under a light flambé glaze, impressed factory and facsimile signature, signed in blue, 11½in. high.
(Christie's) $824

A Moorcroft 'Pomegranate' pattern two-handled vase, mottled dark blue ground with decoration of pomegranate amid foliage, in pink, amber, purple and green, 27cm. high.
(Christie's) $1,575

A pierced oval soap dish decorated in the 'Moonlit Blue' pattern, in shades of blue and green, 7¾in. long.
(Christie's) $560

A Moorcroft 'Chrysanthemum' pattern two-handled vase, blue-green raised slip decoration of chrysanthemums in amber, yellow, green and purple, 31cm. high.
(Christie's) $3,544

A Moorcroft Florian-Ware vase of squat form with tall neck, decorated in relief with blue forget-me-nots and yellow cornflowers, 13cm. high. (Phillips) $845

A William Moorcroft 'Pansy' vase, tube-lined with purple, yellow, mauve and pink open flowerheads, 5in. high. (Bonhams) $478

A Moorcroft pottery shouldered and waisted vase with pansy decoration on pale cream ground, 10½in. wide. (Andrew Hartley) $794

Moorcroft glazed earthenware moonlit blue landscape design vase, second quarter 20th century, painted and slipped with a scene of trees and mountains, 12½in. high. (Butterfield & Butterfield) $1,610

A Moorcroft brown chrysanthemum vase, the twin-handled vessel decorated with red flora against a blue green ground, 9.5cm. high, signed and dated 1913. (Phillips) $750

A Moorcroft Chrysanthemum pattern urn shaped vase, the white piped decoration of chrysanthemums amongst scrolling foliage, covered in a puce, green and amber glaze, 1913, 21.6cm. high. (Christie's London) $2,800

A Moorcroft Eventide Landscape pattern dish, with green piped decoration of trees in hilly landscape, covered in amber, crimson, green and blue glaze, circa 1925, 27.5cm. diam. (Christie's) $2,000

A William Moorcroft Liberty & Co. 'Pomegranate' pewter mounted trumpet vase, tube-lined with a band of large fruits amongst berries, 6³/₈in. high. (Bonhams) $508

A Moorcroft baluster vase, the green piped decoration of poppies in scrolling leaf cartouches, covered in pale green and blue glaze, circa 1935, 20.9cm. high. (Christie's London) $800

MOORCROFT

A Moorcroft 'Moonlit blue' plate, the obverse tube-lined with trees in a landscape, 21.9cm. diameter. (Bonhams) $614

A Moorcroft large two-handled vase with design of pomegranate, grapes, etc., 14in., green signature. (Russell, Baldwin & Bright) $1,444

A Moorcroft pottery bowl in the 'Pomegranate' pattern, centered with a band of large red fruit with leaves and purple berries, 21cm. diameter. (Phillips) $400

A Moorcroft Cornflower pattern three handled cylindrical vase, with white piped decoration of cornflowers, covered in a yellow, blue and green glaze against a cream ground, 19cm. high. (Christie's London) $2,400

A pair of Moorcroft pottery spill vases with pomegranate pattern on deep blue ground, 12½in. high. (Andrew Hartley) $942

A Moorcroft tall cup shaped vase, incised with horizontal bands, the green piped decoration of scrolling leaves, covered in a blue and white glaze, 26.4cm. high. $1,120

A Moorcroft pottery vase, the ovoid body painted with the anemone pattern on a red ground, 16.5cm. (Bearne's) $400

A Moorcroft pottery 'Claremont' pattern jardinière decorated with mushrooms and colored in streaked red, blue and yellow glaze against a green ground, 12.5cm. high. (Phillips) $840

A Moorcroft 'Claremont' pattern vase designed by William Moorcroft, blue and green mottled ground with yellow, pink, green and blue mushrooms, circa 1920, 17cm. high. (Christie's) $574

MOORCROFT MACINTYRE

William Moorcroft (1872–1945) was a Staffordshire potter who trained as an art teacher, but became designer for Jas. Macintyre & Co at Burslem. He designed vases, bowls etc. decorated with plant forms and scale patterned borders and panels mainly in blue, red and gold (Aurelian ware). His Florian ware (1898–1904) was decorated with violets, poppies and cornflowers in underglaze colors. His flowers were often stylized and depicted in darker shades of the base color.

A Macintyre plate decorated with three swirling sprays of irises, in shades of green and blue, 8in. diameter.
(Christie's) $1,120

An early 20th century Macintyre Moorcroft Florian ware poppy pattern jug, with simulated bamboo molded handle, 22cm. high.
(Spencer's) $533

A fine pair of Macintyre Moorcroft circular tapered two-handled vases, with raised and painted floral and foliage decoration, 8½in. high.
(Anderson & Garland)
                    $1,271

A Moorcroft Macintyre Florian ware vase, tube-lined with poppies, in blue and green on a cream ground, 10cm. high.
(Bonhams) $307

A pair of Macintyre Green and Gold Florian Ware vases, decorated in shades of green and gilt with cartouches of poppies and curvilinear foliage, 10¼in. high.
(Christie's) $960

A Macintyre Florian 'Poppy' pattern vase designed by William Moorcroft, white ground with raised slip decoration of blue poppies, with brown printed Macintyre stamp, circa 1904, 31cm. high.
(Christie's) $2,560

An attractive pair of early 20th century James Macintyre & Co., Moorcroft Florian ware cornflower pattern vases, 16cm. high.
(Spencer's) $1,254

A Macintyre Green and Gold Florian Ware twin-handled coupe, with cartouches of curvilinear poppies and tulips, in shades of blue, green and gilt, 7½in. high.
(Christie's) $880

323

MOORE

Bernard Moore (1853–1935) was a Staffordshire artist potter who, with his brother Samuel, succeeded to his father's porcelain factory at St Mary's Works, Longton in 1870. Trading as Moore Bros. they made high quality tableware, which was sometimes highly ornamental, together with lamps, baskets etc. They used a clear turquoise glaze and metallic colors and favored decorative motifs were modeled cupids, animals, especially dogs, and plant forms. Chinese cloisonné imitations were also produced and pilgrim bottles with pale pâte-sur-pâte decoration and gilding.

The Moore Bros. factory was sold in 1905. Thereafter, at Wolfe St, Stoke, in conjunction with C Bailey of Doulton, Moore tried out flambé glazes.

MORAVIAN

The Moravian Pottery and Tile Works was established at the turn of the century in Doylestown, Pennsylvania. Their aim was to produce pottery with a homespun, hand-crafted appearance. To this end they used numerous colored glazes and incised decoration, often borrowing motifs of medieval or Pennsylvania Dutch inspiration. Their tiles have relief patterns, for example, of knights, lions or dragons.

MORRIS WARE

Morris ware was produced from the 1890s into the early 20th century by the firm of S Hancock and Sons, an earthenware company in Stoke on Trent. The pieces were decorated by George Cartlidge (b. 1868) in plant forms outlined in trailed slip in the style of William Moorcroft, and usually also signed by him.

A Bernard Moore flambe baluster vase, decorated in gilt with a Japanese lady sitting at a table, 18cm. high. (Phillips) $360

A large Bernard Moore luster pottery jardiniere, 11½in. high. $1,200

A Moravian brown-glazed fish flask, Salem or Bethabara, North Carolina, early to mid-19th century, the full-bodied holloware form molded in the shape of a fish, 4¾in. long. (Christie's) $4,830

A Moravian green-glazed ring flask, Salem or Bethabara, North California, early 19th century, the circular holloware form with double-reeded ring decoration, 5¾in. high. (Christie's) $3,220

A large S. Hancock & Sons Morrisware baluster vase, decorated with mauve and inky blue thistles on a greeny yellow ground, 32.9cm. high. (Christie's) $1,500

A Morrisware pottery vase, decorated with peonies in mauve, crimson and olive-green against a sea-green ground, 16.5cm. high. (Phillips) $450

MOUSTIERS

The Moustiers factory was established in around 1670 in a remarkably remote corner of France, about 60 miles north east of Marseilles. Early wares were in the blue and white made popular by Rouen, and many fine dishes with pictorial scenes were made. Pierre Clerissy took over in 1679 and started a business that under his grandson Pierre II, was to flourish until 1757.

In about 1710 designs were adopted based on the engravings of Jean Berain, who as designer to the King in the Department of Occasional Expenses had been responsible for the backgrounds for court galas and entertainments at Versailles.

Polychrome wares were also designed at Moustiers by Jean-Baptiste Laugier and Joseph Olerys, which often depicted mythological or biblical scenes surrounded by elaborate festoon borders. They also designed some with fantastic human and animal figures, sometimes indulging in less than decorous pursuits. Their monogram *LO* is common and often faked. Genuine Moustiers is very light, finely potted and has a smooth, milky white glaze.

MYOTT

The factory which came to be known as Myotts had operated at Crane Street, Hanley since the beginning of the 19th century and in 1897 it was inherited by Ashley Myott, who became chairman at the tender age of 19, and his elder brother Sydney. Up to 1930, the company had some 21 backstamps. The one most often found on Art Deco pieces dates from the mid-1930s and comprises a gold crown above *Myott, Son & Co.* with *England* below.

A very large Moustier dish, first half of 18th century, 21½in. diameter.
(Dreweatt Neate) $1,170

A Moustiers faience 'Seau a Rafraichir' with double plumed mask handles, attributed to Olerys and Laugier, circa 1740, 21cm. diam. $1,450

A French blue and white faience cream-jug, probably Moustières, painted with a coat-of-arms within stylized pendant and scroll borders, 2¾in. high, circa 1740.
(Christie's) $505

A Moustiers shaped circular plate, manganese GOL and cross mark of Olerys and Laugier, circa 1740, 25cm. diam. $1,300

Myott flower vase complete with liner, 9in. wide on stepped base.
(Muir Hewitt) $110

Myott flower jug with hand painted decoration, 7in. high, 1930s.
(Muir Hewitt) $75

NANTGARW

The history of the Nantgarw pottery began in 1814 when William Billingsley and his son-in-law Samuel Walker arrived there. Billingsley had been a painter at Derby and had also experimented with porcelain bodies in the hope of modifying the Derby paste to resemble that of Sèvres.

At Nantgarw, a useful site both for the proximity of coal supplies and a link with the Bristol Channel in the form of the newly opened Glamorgan canal, they succeeded in making a soft paste porcelain which was of amazing quality and translucence. To do so however had cost them all their capital, and they were lent further funds by a local surveyor, W W Young. Also, the President of the Royal Society sent the proprietor of the Swansea works, L W Dillwyn, to have a look. Dillwyn was greatly excited by what he saw at Nantgarw and arranged for Billingsley and Walker to move to Swansea. There, Billingsley oversaw the painting, while Walker experimented with a more reliable body than that which had been produced at Nantgarw.

In 1819, both returned there and the second Nantgarw period began.

Due to financial problems, Billingsley and Walker left Nantgarw again in 1820, and Young was left with the pottery. He employed Thomas Pardoe, a Derby-trained potter who had worked at Swansea, to decorate the remaining stock. Pardoe's free, slightly naive style was in stark contrast to London decorated Nantgarw. He painted birds, landscapes and figure subjects, using often broader strokes and heavier color than other painters. The pieces were sold at two auctions in 1821 and 22.

A Nantgarw (London-decorated) ornithological soup-plate, the center painted with Black Grouse, named on the reverse, circa 1820, 24cm. diameter. (Christie's) $3,200

A Nantgarw porcelain tea cup and matching saucer, the cup interior painted in gold with a band of foliage around a central bouquet of flowers, pattern No. 822. (Bearne's) $324

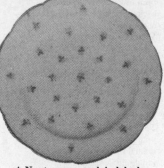

A Nantgarw London-decorated gold-ground circular two-handled sauce tureen and stand, the body and stand painted with garden flowers on a gilt band, circa 1820, the stand 18.5cm. diam. $4,800

A Nantgarw porcelain lobed Bourbon Sprig pattern plate, the molded rim with chocolate lining, 9in. diameter. (Peter Francis) $400

A Nantgarw plate, the center painted by James Plant with a yokel and companion with cattle, circa 1820, 23.5cm. diam. (Christie's) $3,600

A Nantgarw armorial cabinet-cup and saucer, the central arms within a garter with the motto *Deus et Patria*, circa 1820. (Christie's) $3,600

NAPLES

The Royal Factory of Naples was established in 1771 by Ferdinand IV, son of Charles III, and employed many of the ex-workers of the latter's Capodimonte factory.

Domenico Venuti was made Director in 1779. He engaged skilled modelers etc from other factories and the first really successful pieces produced at Naples were huge services, used as Royal gifts, and often featuring a biscuit figure centerpiece.

The decoration often drew heavily on themes from the new discoveries at Herculaneum and Naples and books were published explaining the various classical allusions. Commoner today are tablewares decorated with a central medallion showing peasants in traditional garb, with borders of wreaths or Pompeian fret.

With regard to body, early pieces tend to be rather yellow, but a fine white or creamy body was developed during the 1780s. Early painting shows a marked resemblance to Capodimonte of the later rococo period.

Some figures were produced, usually off white, either glazed or in biscuit. Some, of individuals strolling along alone or in pairs, are interesting for having no base, but are balanced on their own feet. Naples, of course, first employed the much copied crowned *N* mark. Unless the piece is soft paste porcelain however the mark is fraudulent. *FRF* is also used in blue black or red enamel, under a crown.

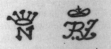

A Ferdinand IV Naples porcelain plate painted with a philosopher in a landscape, circa 1785, 24cm. diameter. (Finarte) $2,207

A Naples 'Fabbrica Reale Ferdinandea' cup and saucer, painted with classical scenes. (Bearne's) $4,437

A pair of Naples armorial waisted albarelli, the central quartered Arms in ocher, yellow and blue within a beaded cartouche, mid-16th century, 23cm. high. $12,800

A Naples (Real Fabbrica Ferdinandea) group of a gallant and companion, he in a black top hat, she in a black shawl over a purple patterned skirt and yellow shoes, circa 1790, 18.5cm. high. $14,500

A Naples two-handled ecuelle, cover and stand painted with vignettes of five dated nocturnal eruptions of Vesuvius, circa 1794, stand 23.5cm. diam. (Christie's) $21,600

A Naples (Real Fabbrica Ferdinandea) Royal portrait medallion with the heads of King Ferdinando IV and Queen Maria Caroline, circa 1790, 6.5cm. (Christie's) $3,200

NEVERS

When the Duke Luigi Gonzaga of Mantua became Duke of Nevers in 1565, he brought with him from Italy some leading faienciers, notably Domenico Conrado and his brothers from the Savona area. The Conrados prospered and were to hold a virtual monopoly of faience manufacture in Nevers until around 1630. Through the influence of Guilio Gambini, an Italian potter from Lyon, who was in partnership for some time with Augustino Conrado, much early production was in the late Urbino pictorial style, with designs of biblical and mythological scenes. Some large figures were also made at Nevers and were probably made by Daniel Lefebvre, who worked there between 1629-49.

Given the brothers' origin it is unsurprising that much Nevers faience was decorated in the Savona style though both the clay and glaze were harder than those used there. Because the firing was done at unusually high temperatures, the colors sometimes have a faded look, and the final protective covering of a glassy lead glaze normally found on Italian maiolica was also omitted.

The Conrados also introduced a new painting technique, whereby cobalt was added to the basic tin glaze to make blue, and designs were painted on this base in a thick white enamel paste. It is called the 'Persian' style, but probably owes more to Limoges enamels. Pseudo oriental designs in time superseded those of Italian inspiration as the potters copied Chinese inspired Dutch faience.

Early marks often include the decorator's name with *A Nevers* or *DF* and a date incised for Lefebvre's work.

A Nevers (Conrade) armorial blue and white tondino, the center painted with a huntsman blowing a horn accompanied by his hound, circa 1680, 30cm. diam. (Christie's) $1,750

A pair of faience bucket-shaped jardinières, the sides painted in yellow, green, iron-red and underglaze blue with an Oriental by shrubs in a garden, probably Nevers, circa 1680, 13.5cm. high. (Christie's) $5,450

Late 17th century Nevers bleu persan shallow bowl with everted rim, 23.5cm. diam. (Christie's)
          $720

A handled basket, the deep rectangular body on a slightly flared foot, with blue and manganese decoration, possibly Nevers, 18th century, 27cm. long. (Lempertz) $1,537

A French istoriato tazza painted with Diana and Acteon, the alarmed Diana and her attendants covering her with drapes, probably Nevers, last quarter of the 16th century, 28cm. diam. (Christie's London) $2,500

A massive Nevers bleu persan bucket-shaped jardinière, the strapwork and foliage handles with bearded mask terminals, circa 1680, 47cm. high. (Christie's) $3,700

NEWCOMB POTTERY

This American pottery was set up in 1895 at Newcomb College, New Orleans, a women's section of Tulane University, Louisiana. Essentially, the work of professional potters was bought in to be decorated by the students and the emphasis was on local materials and decorative motifs, such as indigenous trees like magnolia or palms. The products were mainly low fired earthenware painted in underglaze colors, predominantly blue, green and yellow.

Newcomb College Pottery bowl, New Orleans, possibly Sadie Irvine, circa 1920, matt glaze decorated pale blue/green leaves with pale rose berries in low relief, 3in. high.
(Skinner) $863

Newcomb College Pottery low bowl, New Orleans, Henrietta Bailey, circa 1915, matt glazed and decorated at shoulder with low relief stylised bearded irises, 2½in. high.
(Skinner) $489

Newcomb pottery vase, New Orleans, circa 1915, Henrietta D. Bailey, matt glazed pale-pink, blue and green on low-relief pine cones and needles, 6⅞in. high.
(Skinner) $1,495

A Newcomb College pottery high glaze mug, New Orleans, signed by Ada W. Lonnegan, circa 1901, 4¼in. high.
                           $1,440

Newcomb College Pottery scenic vase, New Orleans, Anna Frances Simpson, circa 1915, matt glazed decoration with green/blue mossy trees in low relief, 7¼in. high.
(Skinner) $2,185

Early 20th century Newcomb College pottery vase, Louisiana, stamped and initialed KS, 5in. high. $720

Newcomb College covered jar, glossy glaze, decorated with blue and green flowers and leaves on white ground, 5½in. wide.
(Skinner) $1,600

A Newcomb pottery floral vase, New Orleans, circa 1928, initialed by Henrietta Bailey, 5¼in. high.
(Skinner) $800

NEWHALL

The Newhall or New Hall factory at Shelton, Stoke on Trent, made hard paste porcelain from 1782-1812 and bone china thereafter. Their product however was quite different from the true porcelain of China and Germany; in reality it was somewhere between a hard and soft paste, and the term 'hybrid paste' has been coined to try and describe it.

Newhall produced exclusively useful wares, and specialized in tea services. Although the overall output was huge, catering for the middle rather than the upper classes, early pieces are still quite rare.

Newhall three piece tea service, printed with landscape views, comprising teapot, sugar and cream jug. **$720**

Newhall porcelain tea pot, oval panel shape with sprig flower decoration, complete with cover. (G. A. Key) **$200**

A rare New Hall coffee pot and cover, circa 1785, painted in enamel colours with a Chinese boy giving a flower to a lady, 27cm. high.
(Phillips) **$248**

A rare New Hall tea and coffee service of spirally shanked, oval form, gilded with a band of scrolling, hung with colored cornflower sprigs, 28 pieces.
(Phillips) **$480**

A New Hall coffee pot and rare matching stand of plain pear shape with pierced baluster knop, decorated in the so-called Knitting pattern, no. 195, 25cm.
(Phillips) **$320**

A rare New Hall teapot and cover and a bowl, circa 1785, the teapot with clip handle and vase shaped finial, both pattern no. 20, 15.5 and 11.5cm.
(Phillips) **$325**

A New Hall helmet-shaped jug and a saucer painted with pattern 20, and a New Hall type bowl painted with flowers, circa 1785.
(Christie's) **$240**

An unusual teapot and cover in New Hall style, circa 1800, painted with simple flower sprays and border in colors , 15cm.
(Phillips) **$279**

NEWPORT POTTERY

The Newport pottery was a subsidiary of A J Wilkinson Ltd operating in the 1930s, and is distinguished by having among its designers the legendary Clarice Cliff.

An amusing Newport pottery model of an owl wearing a suit, signed *M. Epworth*, 18.5cm. (Bearne's) $180

A Bizarre single-handled 'lotus' vase, 29.3cm. high. Newport, late 1930's. $540

An 'Original Bizarre' candlestick of tapering square form, painted with diamonds and triangles in green, stamped *Hand Painted by Clarice Cliff Newport Pottery England*, 7¾in. high. (Christie's) $320

An 'Original Bizarre' Athens jug, painted with diamonds and triangles in blue, red and green, stamp *Hand Painted Bizarre by Clarice Cliff Newport Pottery England*, 8½in. diameter. (Christie's) $480

A large Delecia Lydiat pattern Yo-yo vase, shape no. 379, stamped *Delecia Hand Painted Bizarre by Clarice Cliff Newport Pottery England*, 18in. high. (Christie's) $6,400

A Newport pottery Bizarre charger, 1930s, stylized foliate design in blue, orange and green with blue border, 33.5cm. diam. $300

A Forest Glen pattern vase of footed trumpet form, marked *Clarice Cliff Newport Pottery England*, 9in. high. (Christie's) $640

An 'Original Bizarre' plate, painted with a central radiating star, printed mark *Hand Painted Newport Pottery England*, 8½in. diameter. (Christie's) $480

NIDERVILLER

The manufacture of hard paste porcelain began at Niderviller in 1765 and continues today. The factory was originally opened in 1754 by Baron Jean Louis de Bayerlé to make faience. In 1770 it was purchased by the Comte de Custine and passed on his death to Claude Francois Lanfrey.

For its styles, it drew heavily on the wares of Strasbourg, turning out vases, clocks and large tablewares in the high rococo taste, Forms and decoration were almost identical for both its faience and porcelain output, the latter comprising mainly oriental or European flowers, sprigs or landscapes.

Figures were produced, the majority being left unglazed. Many were modeled by Charles Sauvage, known as Lemire. When Paul Louis Cyfflé's Lunéville factory was sold in 1780 many of his molds also passed to Niderviller.

Marks are *BN* in monogram, *CN* in monogram, two interlaced *C*s or *N Nider* or *Niderviller.*

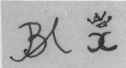

A Niderviller faience shaped hexafoil dish, circa 1775, 25cm. diam. $9,200

One of a pair of Niderviller covered vases and covers, 15¼in. high, circa 1780. $2,500

A pair of Niderviller white biscuit groups of children after models by Jacques Louis Cyfflé, circa 1800, 24 and 22cm. high.
(Christie's) $1,280

A biscuit porcelain figure group of Louis XVI and Benjamin Franklin, Niderviller factory, France, circa 1785, on a draped red and white marbleised base, 12⁷/₈in. high.
(Christie's) $50,600

A Niderviller figure of 'La Jardiniere', on a circular base, 20.5cm. high. $440

A Niderviller jardinière, the oval form on four curled feet, decorated with flowers and rocaille work, 1760-1770, 33cm. long.
(Lempertz) $1,517

A Niderviller miniature group of Venus scantily clad in a puce cloth leaning against billowing cloud scrolls, circa 1780, 8.5cm. high. (Christie's Geneva) $520

NOVE

In 1728 Giovanni Batista Antonibon established an earthenware and hard paste porcelain factory at Nove near Bassano. He was succeeded there by his son and grandson, and it continued in the family until the late nineteenth century.

It is noted for its tureens in the form of fish, and for practical rococo tablewares painted in high temperature colors. The mark of a star with a tail is common on 19th century pieces.

Good quality cream colored earthenware was also made at Nove from about 1780 by Giovanni Maria Baccin and others such as Baroni, Bernardi, Viero and Cacchetto.

A Le Nove maiolica oval silver shape footed bowl, painted to the interior and exterior with bright sprays of flowers within meandering bands, late 19th century, 36cm. wide. (Christie's) $556

A Le Nove coffee can and saucer, circa 1780, painted with stylized flowers and foliage emanating from rockwork, 6cm. (Phillips) $263

A Le Nove white group of a dancing gallant and companion, circa 1780, 16cm. high. (Christie's) $720

A Nove blue and white faience fluted dish, the silver shape dish painted to the center with a spray of flowers, circa 1770, 39.5cm. diameter. (Christie's) $821

Two Nove pistol-shaped handles painted with fruit and flowers, fitted with a steel four-pronged fork and a blade, 19th century, 7.5cm. and 8cm. long. (Christie's) $320

A Le Nove miniature figure of Pulchinella, in conical hat and suit edged in iron-red, circa 1780, 2½in. high. (Christie's) $2,139

A Le Nove two handled ecuelle cover and stand, painted in colors with scattered sprays of flowers, iron red star marks, circa 1770, the stand 22cm. diam. (Christie's London) $3,200

A Nove maiolica clock in the rococo style, surmounted by putto and bird, the circular dial with arabic numerals, 40cm. high. (Christie's) $695

NYMPHENBURG

Following the establishment of the porcelain factory at Meissen, the rulers of the other German states were anxious to set up their own ventures. One of the most successful was at Nymphenburg in Bavaria, where production began in 1753 and continues to the present.

The original factory was situated at Neudeck, under the patronage of the Bavarian Elector, who had married a granddaughter of Augustus the Strong, and it was transferred to Nymphenburg itself in 1761.

Throughout its early history a galaxy of talent was employed there, but financially things ran far from smoothly and a succession of managers were engaged to try to make it profitable. The fame of the Nymphenburg factory, however, rests essentially on the work of one man, the modeler Franz Anton Bustelli, who is to rococo what Kaendler was to baroque.

Nymphenburg porcelain is of the true hard paste variety, fairly white in color and covered with a fine and brilliant glaze. Early pieces were delicately colored and many left in the white. Flat washes of red-blue, black, pink and gold were used for coloring dresses. Small pieces, such as snuff boxes, and tablewares were also produced in profusion during this period.

Early Neudeck-Nymphenburg pieces often bear the diamond paned shield from the arms of Bavaria, and from 1765 a hexagram mark was additionally used. A lively 'seconds' market existed from the beginning, and defective pieces were sold in the white with the factory mark canceled by an engraved stroke.

A rare Nymphenburg model of a dog, modeled by Frans Anton Bustelli, seated on his haunches, looking over his shoulder, circa 1760, 4³/₁₀in.
(Woolley & Wallis) $9,457

A Nymphenburg silver-mounted cylindrical tankard, impressed Bavarian shield mark above o, silver marks, circa 1780, 6in. high overall.
(Christie's) $6,730

A Nymphenburg white figure of a beggar modeled by Franz Anton Bustelli, wearing tattered clothes, in a contra-posto pose holding out an empty tattered hat in his right hand, circa 1760, 17cm. high.
(Christie's) $39,380

A Nymphenburg baluster coffee pot and domed cover painted in colors to both sides with birds roosting in trees and perching on terraces, indistinct incised mark, circa 1760, 23cm. high. (Christie's London) $3,700

A Nymphenburg oil and vinegar stand with two bottles and hinged covers, circa 1765, the bottles 18cm. high.
          $14,500

A Nymphenburg two-handled tapering oval pail and domed cover in the Frankenthal style, with a striped multiple leaf finial, circa 1860, 20³/₄in. high. (Christie's) $7,771

OHR

George Ohr (1857–1918) was an American artist potter who was based in Missouri. His work was characterised by being of very thin porcelain, which was then distorted by being squeezed or folded into weird forms with handles then applied. His glazes were notable for their flowing colors, such as green and plum.

Most of his pieces are marked with *G E Ohr, Biloxi, Miss.*

A 20th century molded pottery 'steamboat' pitcher, cast after the original by George E. Ohr, 9in. high. $400

An unglazed earthenware Jug, stamped, *Geo. E. Ohr/Biloxi Miss*, circa 1890–1900, 10½in. high.
(Christie's) $161

George Ohr Pottery vase, bulbous base with two curving handles, blue and dark blue mottled glaze incised *G.E. Ohr, Biloxi, Miss.*, 7in. high.
(Skinner) $2,500

George Ohr Pottery vase, Biloxi, Mississippi, circa 1901, gloss translucent caramel glaze with green and charcoal streaking, 6in. high.
(Skinner) $1,495

Fine George Ohr vase with mottled brown and green glaze with hints of iridescent black on an ocher ground, stamped *G. E. Ohr, Biloxi, Miss.*, 6in. high.
(Skinner) $1,840

George E. Ohr Pottery vase, Biloxi, Mississippi, circa 1898, mottled olive green iridescent glaze, 4in. high.
(Skinner) $400

George E. Ohr Pottery vase, Biloxi, Mississippi, circa 1904, fluted top on cylindrical form, midnight blue over cobalt glossy glaze, 5in. high.
(Skinner) $675

George Ohr Pottery vase, cone-shaped over bulbous base with flaring foot, spaghetti handles and twisted neck, 9in. high.
(Skinner) $3,740

PALERMO

The maiolica manufactured at Palermo in the 16th and 17th centuries has much in common with the style of Castel Durante. Blue and yellow grounds predominate with profuse decoration. The forms are common to those being produced elsewhere at the time, i.e. albarelli, drug jars etc.

Marks are rare. One of the few which has been found, on an albarello of good quality is Fatto in Palermo 1606.

Fatto in Palermo

A Palermo wet drug jar with pointed ovoid body painted with flowerheads and leaves in yellow and green, on a blue ground, 20cm., 17th century.
(Phillips) $1,120

Early 17th century Palermo oviform vase, 27.5cm. high.
(Christie's) $1,600

A maiolica albarello, Palermo, dated *1612*, painted with a medallion with the profile of a soldier, 24cm. high.
(Finarte)   £7,221 $11,193

A pair of Palermo vaso a palla painted in colors with male portrait busts within stylized scroll cartouches, circa 1680, 32cm. and 33cm. high.
(Christie's London)
                         $7,200

An unusual dated albarello of waisted form with sloping shoulders, painted with a winged cupid, 25cm., Faenza or Palermo.
(Phillips) $19,200

PARAGON

The Paragon China Co. was established in Longton, Staffordshire, in 1920, for the manufacture of porcelain. It held a royal warrant and produced much commemorative ware. A variety of marks were used, including *Royal Arms* and *Paragon.*
Paragon is now part of Allied English Potteries Ltd.

Paragon china two handled loving cup, commemorating the Silver Jubilee of Her Majesty Queen Elizabeth II.
(G. A. Key) $284

Paragon Coronation plate, the molded border decorated between gilt lines with King George VI and Queen Elizabeth, dated *1937*, 10¹/₂in. diameter.
(G. A. Key) $138

PARIAN

In the early 19th century, Staffordshire potters were experimenting with formulae for unglazed white porcelain which could be modeled into statuary in imitation of the finest Greek marble sculptures found on the island of Paros. The firms of Copeland and Garrett and Minton were front-runners in the race, and it was Copeland who in 1842 released the first piece of 'parian' statuary, entitled Apollo as the Shepherd Boy of Admetus. Their success was due to the high quantity of feldspar in the formula and a firing process which permitted a large amount of air in the kiln. The result was a lustrous transparency and delicacy of molding.

Minton, who were the first to use the name Parian, contested Copeland's claim of a 'first', and the jury at the Great Exhibition produced a soothing statement which declared in effect a draw.

Copeland commissioned figures from many of the finest sculptors of the day, while Minton's principal modelers were John Bell and Albert Carrier Belleuse.

Wedgwood, Worcester and Coalport all produced parian ware, including some impressive tableware, where glazed and decorated bone china was successfully combined with lightly gilt statuary.

Standard parian was found to be excellent for relief molded fancy ware, with smear glazing. Colored backgrounds were achieved by tinted slip brush-applied to the appropriate parts of the mold, and the main colors were blue, sage and brown. Standard parian was criticised because the fine granular surface was easily soiled, though this was to some degree overcome from 1860 by the use of a thin coating of lead glaze.

Two Minton parian groups of putti riding on sea horses, with wings and curling fish tails, 34cm., impressed date symbols possibly for 1851 or 1855. (Phillips)   **$1,080**

Parian bust of Shakespeare, England, circa 1875, mounted on a raised circular base, Robinson and Leadbeater mark, 12³/₄in. high. (Skinner Inc.)   **$715**

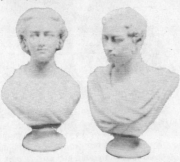

A pair of Copeland Crystal Palace Art Union parian ware busts, 'The Prince of Wales' and 'Princess Alexandra' by Marshall Wood and F. M. Miller. (Greenslades) $480

An English glazed Parian copy of the Portland vase, the figures in white relief on an apricot ground, circa 1880, 9¹/₂in. high. (Christie's) $658

A pair of glazed Parian figure brackets, allegorical figures in rock-like niches, 9¹/₂in. high.   **$426**

A large Parian group entitled 'Detected', signed R.J. Morris, 41cm. high. (Dee & Atkinson)   **$320**

337

PARIAN

Copeland bust of Comte d'Orsay. (Lots Road Galleries) $160

A bust of Daphne, the nude figure of a young girl with leaves in her hair, 23in. high, circa 1870. (Christie's) $1,600

A Copeland Parian bust of a young woman with flowing hair, 23in. high. $880

A Minton Parian figure of Ariadne and the Panther after a model by John Bell, the naked maiden with her hair en chignon adorned with a wreath of acanthus, date code for 1862, 14½in. high. (Christie's) $1,045

A colored parian group modeled as a young girl on rockwork, entitled 'You can't read', 12¼in. high, possibly by Robinson & Leadbetter. (Christie's) $400

Fine Parian figure group, depicting a woman and Cupid with doves, this once stood in the living room of Jabez Gorham, founder of the Gorham Silver Co., 15in. high. (Eldred's) $1,540

A Copeland bust of Juno, possibly after W Theed, in a coronet and with short ringlets, impressed mark, 20½in. high. (Christie's S. Ken) $1,600

A Parian figural group of sleeping children 'Le Nid', circa 1875, signed 'Croisy', 15in. high. (Skinner Inc.) $800

A parian ware bust after Paul Duboy of a young girl with floral garland in her hair, 21in. high. (GA Property Services) $2,000

PARIS

During the Neo-Classical period many small porcelain factories were scattered in and around Paris, most of which were under some form of noble patronage. Mainly they produced tableware and there was very little figure production.

Despite their numbers however, the porcelain they produced was surprisingly uniform in both shape and decoration, and it is often very difficult to tell the output of one from another unless they are marked. The severer neo-Classical style did not, of course, lend itself to the wilder flights of imagination in the same way as did Baroque and Rococo. Plates were usually plain and unmolded, coffee and teapots cylindrical or vase shaped, cups cylindrical and bowls often raised on feet.

One new form which did emerge at this time however was the semicircular bulb or flower pot, the fronts of which were divided into three panels with pilasters, and decorated with neo-Classical motifs.

Decoration of the period was not generally elaborate in content, consisting mainly of formal motifs, but its technical brilliance was truly amazing. There was much use of gilding and chased decoration which, together with colored grounds and borders, often matt, gave a remarkably rich effect.

Napoleon's expedition to Egypt and his elevation to Emperor saw the beginning of the Empire period, during which the Paris factories continued to thrive. In many aspects the Empire style is merely an extension of neo-Classicism, but wares now began to show a greater variety of form, with greater use of modeling for the handles and spouts of teapots etc. Egyptian motifs were understandably common.

A pair of Paris biscuit busts of a bacchante and satyr, after Clodion, modeled leering over opposing shoulders, both wearing vine wreaths heavy with grapes, 9½in. high. (Christie's) $805

A pair of Paris urn-shaped vases in the neo-classical manner, each with two upturned scroll handles with anthemion terminals, the lower bodies gilt with flutes, on later black stone plinths, circa 1830, 9in. high. (Christie's) $1,455

A pair of fine Paris 19th century male and female figures, he holding two white doves, she holding a damaged urn, 27in. high. (Anderson & Garland) $1,469

A Paris blue and green-ground parcel biscuit centerpiece, first quarter of the 19th century, modeled in the Empire style with two addorsed griffins, 18³/₈in. high. (Christie's) $10,925

A Paris gold-ground baluster coffee-pot and cover painted at Naples each side with figures watching a puppet-show and spaghetti vendors, circa 1800, 18.5cm. high. (Christie's) $3,200

A French cachepot, Paris, circa 1880, based on a model by Thomire, the brown glazed ceramic body with green interior, flanked by silvered metal putti, 43cm. high. (Sotheby's) $3,341

PARIS

A Paris porcelain cabinet cup
painted with a female gardener
with a watering can, 19th
century.
(Christie's) $246

Pair of Paris porcelain vases
with floral panels, 40cm. high,
circa 1825.
(Christie's) $4,947

A Paris porcelain inkstand,
painted with bouquets of flowers
and applied with a seated model
of a hound, blue mark for Jacob
Petit, 19th century.
(Christie's) $665

A pair of Paris porcelain twin-
handled vases, each painted
with a parrot, exotic and
native birds by lakes in the
garden of a château within
chased gilt oval panels,
38.8cm. high, 19th century.
(Christie's) $4,806

A pair of Paris gold-ground
chinoiserie vases of faceted
campana shape, the swelling
lower bodies molded in high
relief with oval bosses painted
and gilt to imitate jewels on a
broad black band, circa 1840,
14¹/₂in. high.
(Christie's) $9,424

A pair of late 19th century
French Paris porcelain and
ormolu mounted ornamental
ewers, the bleu celeste grounds
painted with landscape vignettes
and heightened in gilt, 9¹/₄in.
high.
(Christie's) $1,752

Two Paris porcelain
Napoleonic portrait coffee cans
and two saucers with a
quarter-length profile of the
Emperor, early 19th century.
(Christie's) $1,364

A pair of Paris porcelain
Schneeballen vases and covers
the flower-encrusted ground
applied with birds in flight
among blossoming branches,
19th century, 22¹/₂in. high.
(Christie's) $2,785

A Paris gold-ground plate
painted with a saint seated
holding a book, and with IC XC
above, late 19th century, 12¹/₂in.
diameter.
(Christie's) $401

PARIS

A Paris (Stone, Coquerel et le Gros) plate transfer-printed in sepia with a view of Chateau de Houghton, Comté de Norfolk, circa 1820, 23.5cm. diameter. (Christie's) $800

A pair of unusual French flambé porcelain vases, Paris, circa 1880, in 18th century manner, 68.5cm. high. (Sotheby's) $27,984

A Paris biscuit roundel of Napoleon, the head of the Emperor molded with a laurel wreath, pierced for hanging, circa 1810, 15.5cm. diameter. (Christie's) $720

A pair of French porcelain mounted vases and covers, Napoléon III, Paris, circa 1855, in Louis XVI manner, the blue ovoid bodies with mermaid handles in gilt-bronze, 44cm. high. (Sotheby's) $5,011

Pair of Paris porcelain fruit coolers, early 19th century, each gilt-highlighted ovoid urn with two handles in the form of cloaked terms on brackets, height 15¼in. (Butterfield & Butterfield) $1,610

A pair of French flambé porcelain vases and covers, Paris, circa 1890, each with a graded green to blue glaze and satyr's head handles, 50cm. high. (Sotheby's) $5,345

A Paris claret-ground cornucopia vase, painted with flowers and gilt scrolls, issuing from a scroll supported on a centaur, circa 1840, 13³/₄in. high. (Christie's) $3,646

A pair of porcelain urns, probably Paris, first quarter 19th century, depicting a portrait of George and Martha Washington, 9½in. high. (Christie's) $2,760

A Paris apricot-ground cornucopia vase, the fluted trumpet-shaped vase painted with a wreath of flowers below a scroll and shell-molded rim, circa 1840, 9in. high. (Christie's) $911

PAUL REVERE

The Paul Revere pottery was established in the early years of the 20th century in Boston, for the purpose of training girls from poor immigrant backgrounds, the profits to be used for their education in other subjects. It produced earthenware nursery and breakfast bowls and dishes etc. decorated with stylized floral motifs, mottoes etc, with the decoration often confined to the borders. Pieces were marked with initials or with *SEG* for Saturday Evening Girls (q.v.)

Paul Revere Pottery Saturday Evening Girl tile, incised Boston street scene, colored pink, blue, brown, white and gray with black outlines, 3¾x3¾in. (Skinner) $385

Paul Revere Pottery decorated tea tile, Boston, Massachusetts, early 20th century, with central decoration of a cottage, 5³/₄in. diameter. (Skinner Inc.) $375

Paul Revere Pottery Saturday Evening Girls decorated pitcher with an incised and painted band of stylised sailing boats, Mass., 1911, 9¾in. high. (Skinner) $1,280

Paul Revere Pottery vase, Boston, 1926, semi-matt glaze decorated with bands of tulips in yellow and green, 4¼in. high. (Skinner) $488

Paul Revere Pottery Saturday Evening Girls motto mug, Boston, 1918, with motto *In The Forest Must Always Be A Nightingale And In The Soul A Faith So Faithful That It Comes Back Even After It Has Been Slain,* 4in. high. (Skinner) $800

Paul Revere Pottery decorated vase, Boston, Massachusetts, early 20th century, with incised and painted band of tree design, 8¹/₂in. high. (Skinner) $3,200

Paul Revere Pottery Saturday Evening Girl planter of rectangular form with a decorated frieze of applied flowers, Boston, Mass., 9½in. long. $800

Paul Revere Pottery decorated vase, Boston, with incised and painted band of trees, hills and sky, 8¹/₂in. high. (Skinner Inc.) $800

PEARLWARE

Pearlware was the name given in 1780 by Josiah Wedgwood to a whitened version of his celebrated creamware which he had just developed successfully.

This was made by adding a touch of blue coloring to the body. It could be just as thin as porcelain, and formed an excellent background for blue printing, enabling it to compete favorably with Chinese wares. It was quickly adopted by many other potteries, and became extremely popular in the late 18th/19th centuries.

A pair of Staffordshire pearlware figures, circa 1790, one a gardener in black hat, his companion as a fish monger, in yellow smock, 6⅝in. high.
(Christie's) $460

A pearlware group of the 'Flight into Egypt', typically modeled with Joseph leading a donkey, before a flowering bocage, 7in. high, circa 1820.
(Christie's) $797

An early 19th century Documentary pearlware blue and white 'Grazing Rabbit' pattern large jug, overpainted in brown *William and Jane Baldwin, 1815*, 24cm. high.
(Spencer's) $832

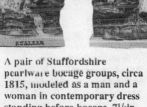

A pair of Staffordshire pearlware bocage groups, circa 1815, modeled as a man and a woman in contemporary dress standing before bocage, 7½in. high.
(Christie's) $1,725

A rare transfer printed early 19th century pearlware jug made to commemorate the Battle of Trafalgar, of baluster form with scroll handle, 18cm. high.
(Spencer's) $400

A pearlware model of Obadiah Sherratt type of The Flight into Egypt, the Virgin Mary modeled seated on a donkey, circa 1820, 7¾in. high.
(Christie's) $626

A pair of Sherratt-type pearlware portrait busts of William IV and Queen Charlotte, modeled wearing formal dress, 8in. high, circa 1817.
(Christie's) $4,428

A pearlware group of the 'Sacrifice of Isaac', of Sherratt-type, with Abraham raising a dagger above his son, 10¾in. high, circa 1820.
(Christie's) $886

PEARLWARE

A pearlware model of a cockerel modeled standing in an erect pose with its head turned slightly to its left, 9¾in. high. circa 1800.
(Christie's) $1,402

A Staffordshire pearlware model of a roaring lion with brown mane and black muzzle, circa 1790, 33cm. long. (Christie's London)
                                 $2,800

A pearlware figure group of a woman scything corn, a child gathering the sheaves at her side, possibly Yorkshire, circa 1810.
(Christie's) $500

A commemorative blue and white pearlware tankard, applied with a medallion, flanked by full length portrait of Lord Rodney and Lord Hood, 4⁵⁄₈in. high, late 18th/19th century.
(Christie's) $283

A pearlware shallow bowl on a small foot, the interior printed in blue with a double portrait busts of George III and Charlotte inscribed 'A King Rever'd, A Queen Belovd, Long May They Live', 19cm. (Phillips) $680

A Lakin & Poole pearlware group of the assassination of Marat, Charlotte Cordé standing holding a metal knife in her right hand, her bonnet embellished with a green bow, impressed mark, circa 1794, 35cm. high.
(Christie's) $3,350

A pearlware toby-jug holding a frothing jug of ale, in blue, yellow and manganese jacket, circa 1790, 10in. high.
(Christie's S. Ken) $1,950

A pearlware globular teapot and cover, printed with two circular panels of female archers, circa 1800, 7½in. wide.
(Christie's S. Ken) $320

A Staffordshire pearlware model of two lovers seated beneath a tree beside a stream, painted in light colors, circa 1790, 11in. high.
(Christie's) $643

PEARLWARE

A pearlware oviform propaganda jug, to the front a brown transfer-printed portrait of Queen Caroline, 12.5cm. high.
(Christie's) $692

A pearlware 'Bull Baiting' group, the tethered bull bearing down over a crouching terrier, 12½in. wide, early 19th century.
(Christie's) $2,834

A pearlware portrait bust of a male child, his head turned to the right, mounted on a gray marbelised socle, circa 1830, 10in. high.
(Christie's) $268

Late 18th century Staffordshire pearlware mask cup, modeled with three faces of Bacchus bordered with fruiting vines, 9cm. high.
(Peter Wilson) $142

A Staffordshire pearlware coffee-pot and cover modeled as a muzzled bear seated on his haunches, the spout formed by a dog held between his forepaws, impressed *J. Morris Store*, circa 1820, 12½in. high.
(Christie's) $12,512

A Staffordshire pearlware shaped rectangular plaque, molded in relief with a bust portrait of Queen Victoria, circa 1845, 8¾in. high.
(Christie's S. Ken) $320

English blue and white pearlware jug, decorated with chinoiserie panels, mask spout, 7¼in., English, 19th century.
(G. A. Key) $225

A 19th century pearlware slops jar and cover, of baluster form with grotesque animal mask handles, 11in. high.
(Spencer's) $1,450

A Staffordshire pearl-ware jug, in the form of a seated night watchman holding a lantern on his knee, 20.7cm. high.
(Bearne's) $168

A pearlware group of a tiger and hind, the tiger dragging the hind by the neck in its jaws, 14½in. wide, early 19th century. (Christie's) $14,168

A Staffordshire pearlware satyr mask mug, circa 1830, the bearded mask cup and handle issuing a vessel of phallic form bearing the slogan 'No sport' till I come', 11¾in. long. (Christie's) $5,750

A pearlware model of a cow with orange and brown markings with a seated milkmaid at its side, circa 1800, 7¼in. long. (Christie's) $790

A Staffordshire pearlware mug, circa 1790, molded as the head of a leering satyr and decorated in blue and white, 3⅞in. high. (Christie's) $161

Two pearlware figures emblematic of Hope and Charity modeled as women, circa 1820 8in. high. (Christie's) $500

A dated Staffordshire pearlware globular jug, inscribed 'Samuell Piggott 1799' and flanked by the farmer's arms, 7¼in. high. (Christie's S. Ken) $215

A rare Staffordshire pearlware ale bench group with figures of a lady and gentleman seated in yellow chairs and drinking, 21cm. high. (Phillips) $3,520

A Staffordshire pearlware cow creamer and stopper with a pink lustered border, a milkmaid seated to one side, 14cm. (Phillips) $898

A pearlware group of 'The Raising of Lazarus', of Sherratt-type, modeled with Christ standing between Lazarus, and Mary, 8in. wide, circa 1820. (Christie's) $4,959

PEARLWARE

A pearlware figure of a hound seated erect with a dead bird at its feet, on a shaped base, Staffordshire or Yorkshire, circa 1785, 10.5cm. wide.
(Christie's) $840

A pearlware figure of Jeremiah, of Sherratt-type, modeled standing, an arm raised, wearing long robes, 11in. high, circa 1820.
(Christie's) $744

A pearlware model of a lion, his paw resting on a ball, his tail curled, 6¹/₂in. high, circa 1800–20.
(Christie's) $1,771

A pearlware puzzle-jug with mask-molded spout printed and painted to one side with Masonic emblems, the spout molded as a satyr's head above the inscription W"Wood 1821, circa 1821, 7in.
(Christie's) $472

A pearlware figure of a fishwife wearing a white hat, with fish cradled in her apron, 6³/₄in. high, and similar figure.
(Christie's) $286

An English pearlware baluster-form large jug, 1815–25, painted in an Imari palette of cobalt-blue and iron-red, 9³/₄in. high.
(Sotheby's) $1,725

A Walton pearlware group of the 'Return From Egypt', typically modeled with Joseph leading a donkey ridden by the Virgin, 6³/₄in. high, circa 1820.
(Christie's) $1,594

A John Meir blue and white pearlware plate, the center printed with a portrait of Queen Caroline wearing a coat and feathered hat, 21.5cm.
(Bearne's) $600

A Hall pearlware group of a ewe and lamb, their coats splashed in iron-red, the ewe standing before a flowering bocage, circa 1820, 15.5cm. high.
(Christie's) $680

PESARO

Pesaro was another of the towns in the Duchy of Urbino with a strong potting tradition, and maiolica was made there during the late 15th and 16th centuries.

In 1462 mention was made of a loan of a large sum of money for the enlargement of a manufactory of vessels, and it is to this date that the commencement of maiolica manufacture is generally ascribed.

In 1546, Jean Sforza passed an edict in favor of Pesaro, forbidding the introduction from other factories of any but common vessels for oil and water and a similar edict was passed in 1552, naming the potters Bernardino Gagliardino, Girolamo Lanfranchi and Mo. Rinaldo as engaging to supply the town and country with vases and pieces painted with historical subjects. Girolamo Lanfranchi was succeeded by his son Giacomo, who in 1562 invented the application of gold to maiolica, fixed by fire.

A notable patron of the pottery was Guido Ubaldo II, who became Duke of Urbino in 1538, but on his death in 1572 the pottery began to decline and by 1718 there was only one potter still there who made ordinary vessels.

The manufacture of pottery was revived in the middle of the century, when Antonio Casali and Filippo Caligari from Lodi set up again to make practical wares such as drug jars, lamps and cups. These were decorated in the later French, imitation Sèvres style, with low fired enamel colors, probably by Pietro Lei, who came to the factory from Sassuolo in 1763. Favorite motifs were gold arabesques, medallions of flowers, and landscapes.

Imitation Urbino ware was made by Magrini & Co of Pesaro from 1870.

A Pesaro istoriato tazza painted in colors by Sforza di Marcantonio with Anchises and Aeneas arriving at Pallanteum, circa 1550, 27cm. diam. (Christie's) $5,200

A small Pesaro albarello of dumb-bell form, painted with the drug name *SEM. DI IVSQVI* (Seeds of Henbane) between bands of birds, 12.5cm. (Phillips) $386

An 18th century maiolica jug, the handle with serpentiform attachment, decorated with a two headed eagle in black, green, yellow and turquoise, Pesaro, 22cm. high. (Finarte) $1,017

A Pesaro dated istoriato dish painted in the Sforza workshop with a scene from the Punic wars, the coronation by Scipio of the two Roman soldiers, 1546, 43cm. diameter. (Christie's) $18,722

A Pesaro istoriato tondo painted in colors after Sforza Marcantonio with the legend of Perseus and Andromeda, circa 1570, 25.5cm. diam. (Christie's London) $40,000

An Italian late 17th century 7³/₄in. globular jug with crimped spout, painted panels of flowers and foliage in blue and yellow, marked *D.S.*, possibly Pesaro. (Anderson & Garland) $435

PETIT

Jacob and Mardochée Petit purchased their factory at Fontainebleu in 1830 and it remained in the family until well into the second half of the century. It was Petit perhaps more than any other who recaptured the spirit of the true rococo during its 19th century revival, and the clocks, lavish inkstands, vases and tea warmers which he modeled in the form of personages or figures are among the most popular of his works.

Many French factories of the time made products in styles attributed to Petit.

A Jacob Petit garniture of a clock and a pair of candlesticks all molded with rococo scrolls, shells and leaf motifs, 39.5cm. (Phillips) $1,683

A Paris (Jacob Petit) two-handled cup, cover and trembleuse-stand, blue JP marks, circa 1840, the stand 16.5cm. diam. (Christie's) $640

A pair of figurines of a Turk and his lady in polychrome enameled porcelain, attributed to Jacob Petit.
(Hôtel de Ventes Horta) $2,982

A pair of Paris (Jacob Petit) vases modeled as figures of a boy and a girl, circa 1850, about 22cm. high.
(Christie's) $720

A pair of Jacob Petit oviform ewers, painted with panels of figures and flowers, the handles molded with flowers, blue JP mark circa 1850, 14in. high.
(Christie's) $1,077

An attractive pair of early 19th century Jacob Petit porcelain taper holders, modeled as a Turkish sultan and his sultana, 16.5cm. high.
(Henry Spencer) $2,500

A pair of Jacob Petit vases of ogee shape with flared rims, painted in colors with bouquets on both sides, 18cm.
(Phillips) $720

A pair of Jacob Petit figural spill vases, modeled as a young man and girl, standing, wearing simple rustic dress, 21,4cm. high, circa 1840.
(Christie's) $549

PEWABIC

Mary Chase Perry (1868-1961) was an American porcelain painter and artist potter working out of Detroit, where in 1903 she established the Pewabic Pottery. This was named after a river in Michigan, the name of which in Chippewa means 'clay in copper color'. Her early work has relief decoration of stylized plant forms covered in matt glazes, whereas her later output is characterized by vases in simple shapes with rich glazes, the colors often combined or layered.

Pewabic pottery vase, late 1920's, globular form with upright neck, and flared lip, blue iridescent glaze, 8in. high. (Du Mouchelles) $1,500

Pewabic Pottery vase, Detroit, warty iridescent glaze in bronze and red, cream glazed interior, 15½in. high. (Skinner) $4,025

Pewabic Pottery vase, circa 1920, baluster form with tapered neck and round foot, yellow glaze, with Pewabic Detroit paper label, 10¼in. high. (Du Mouchelles) $640

A pair of Pewabic Pottery candlesticks, circa 1920, tapered shaft with ring under nozzle, wide round foot, iridescent gray to green glaze, 15in. high. (Du Mouchelles) $3,675

Pewabic Pottery vase, circa 1920, baluster form with iridescent blue, green, lavender and brown glazes, stamped *Pewabic Detroit* in a circle, 11¾in. high. (Du Mouchelles) $700

Pewabic Pottery vase, circa 1920, ovoid form with blue to green to brown glazes, rib about the neck, stamped *Pewabic Detroit* in a circle, 7¾ high. (Du Mouchelles) $700

Pewabic pottery vase, iridescent rose to blue to green glaze, sloped shoulder above steeply tapered sides terminating in a foot, mid 20th century, 6in. high. (Du Mouchelles) $800

Pewabic Pottery vase, sloped base with flared neck to rounded lip, blue to green glazes, stamped *Pewabic Detroit* in a circle, 10¼in. high. (Du Mouchelles) $1,700

PILKINGTON

Pilkington's Tile and Pottery Co. was set up in 1892 at Clifton Junction Lancashire, to manufacture tiles, but from 1897 the production range was extended to include buttons, vases etc. Shortly afterwards the decoration of bought-in biscuit vases also began.

Opalescent glaze effects were discovered in 1903 and from then on the production of glazed earthenware known as Lancastrian pottery began. These wares, which consisted of vases, bowls, trays etc. were usually simple in shape, but decorated in a wide palette of colors often with a crystalline or opalescent effect.

The company was run by two brothers, William and Joseph Burton, who were both ceramic chemists and who were instrumental in developing the luster decorated pottery which formed the bulk of the factory's 20th century production. Modeled, molded or incised decoration appears on these pieces, while the decorator R Joyce modeled animals and birds. Lapis ware was introduced in 1928, and tile production continued throughout.

The factory ceased production in 1937, midway between the deaths of the two brothers, though it started up again in a limited way ten years later, when potters were encouraged to produce individual pieces which were then decorated and signed with the artist's monogram.

Until 1904 the mark *P* was sometimes used, followed until 1913 by *P* and *L* and two bees. The Tudor rose was a later mark, and *Royal Lancastrian* is another variation.

A Pilkington luster pottery charger, by W. S. Mycock, with concentrically ribbed interior, with foliate border, dated 1918, 33cm. diam.
(Bonhams) $320

A Pilkington Lancastrian luster vase and cover decorated by Richard Joyce with a frieze of antelopes and stylized trees, 15.5cm. high.
(Christie's) $900

A Pilkington's Royal Lancastrian twin-handled vase decorated by Gordon Forsyth, 1908, 30.2cm. high.
                    $300

A Pilkington's Royal Lancastrian luster vase decorated by Gordon Forsyth, painted in red and gold luster with bands of tudor roses, 1915, 8½ in. high.
(Christie's) $540

A Pilkington Royal Lancastrian luster charger decorated by William S. Mycock, decorated with a flamboyant armorial crest, dated 1924, 30.6cm. diam.
(Christie's) $540

A Pilkington Royal Lancastrian luster vase and cover decorated by Gordon Forsyth, with two central reserves each surrounded by laurel leaves and flanked by two lions, 29cm. high.
(Christie's) $4,980

A Pilkington's Royal Lancastrian luster solifleur decorated by William S Mycock, painted monogram and dated 1923, 6in. high. (Christie's S. Ken) $930

A Pilkington's Lancastrian luster moonflask by Walter Crane and Richard Joyce, decorated with the coat of arms of the City of Manchester, 27cm. high. (Spencer's) $2,750

A Pilkington's Royal Lancastrian bottle vase decorated by Richard Joyce, the body with a continuous frieze of deer amongst foliage, 1915, 7¹/₂in. high. (Christie's S. Ken) $1,143

A large and important Pilkington Lancastrian luster vase, painted by Gordon Forsyth to commemorate the Brussels International Exhibition of 1910 where the British and Belgian sections burned, 51cm. high. (Phillips) $18,825

A Pilkington Lancastrian deep bowl designed by Walter Crane and decorated by Wm. S. Mycock, date code for 1913, 21.6cm. high. $1,320

A Pilkington's Lancastrian molded ovoid luster vase decorated by Richard Joyce, the body embossed with wild animals amongst grassland, 1915. (Christie's S. Ken) $1,170

A Pilkington Lancastrian pottery vase by Richard Joyce, impressed Bee mark and date code for 1909, 11¾in. high. (Christie's) $1,040

A Pilkington luster vase decorated by Gordon M. Forsyth, with gold luster rampant lion with a cartouche, code for 1908, 28cm. high. (Christie's) $680

A Pilkington 'Royal Lancastrian' luster vase by Richard Joyce, painted in golden luster with two mounted knights in armor 26.5cm. high. (Phillips) $1,600

CHINA

PINXTON

William Billingsley, in partnership with John Coke, established the Pinxton factory in Derbyshire in 1796. They produced a porcelain using a soft paste containing bone ash which was very similar to that of Derby.

Decoration tended to be simple, consisting of floral border patterns or landscapes, some of which were designed by Billingsley himself. Billingsley left the factory in 1799, after which poorer quality, near-opaque porcelain was produced.

A Pinxton teacup, coffee can and saucer, each painted with rural views and inscribed *'In Dove-dale'*, *'Matlock Cascade'* and *'Brookhill Hall, Derbyshire'*, circa 1800.
(Phillips) $1,064

A rare Pinxton bough pot with scroll molded foot painted with an oval panel of a basket of flowers, by William Billingsley, 12.5cm.
(Phillips) $1,209

A rare and important Pinxton vase and pierced cover, of goblet shape, painted with four panels of roses, tulips, an iris and a honeysuckle, by William Billingsley, 19½cm. high.
(Phillips) $5,270

A rare garniture of three Pinxton vases and pierced covers of flared form with slightly spreading base and twin scrolled handles, by William Billingsley, 16 and 15cm. high.
(Phillips) $8,060

A Pinxton teacup and saucer each painted with a rural view and inscribed *Matlock Bath* and *Bonsall-dale*, circa 1800.
(Phillips) $517

A Pinxton mug of cylindrical form with angular handle, painted in the manner of William Billingsley, with a band of pink roses, 10cm., circa 1798.
(Phillips) $1,094

A pair of English porcelain beakers, possibly Pinxton, painted with floral swags suspended from a wide salmon-pink and gilt scrolled border, 10cm high.
(Phillips) $961

A Pinxton yellow ground sucrier and cover of oval form with applied ring handles, painted with a river view, reserved on a yellow ground, 9.5cm., circa 1798.
(Phillips) $790

PLYMOUTH

The first pottery in England to make hard paste porcelain was William Cookworthy's factory at Plymouth, where production started in 1768. There were enormous technical difficulties to overcome, with a huge amount of kiln wastage, and this made it difficult to turn the project into a commercial success.

The Plymouth paste was very hard and white, and the glaze tended to be heavily smoked. Spiral wreathing, a pattern of fine grooves which appeared on the surface of the vessels as they twisted in the kiln, is also common. However, some quite elaborate shapes were achieved, such as large vases and intricate shell salts. More common are the useful tablewares, with pickle leaf dishes, for example, often painted in underglaze blue and overglaze iron red. The decoration was often in the Chinese Mandarin or famille verte style. Most successful of all were the bird decorated mugs by the French painter Mons Saqui.

Most of the polychrome production was unmarked, and is often difficult to distinguish from early Bristol. With the blue and white output, however, this is easier, as Plymouth produced a very blackish underglaze blue, due to the high temperature at which it was fired. It is rarer than the polychrome, but a greater proportion is marked.

Marks usually comprised the chemical sign for tin with a combined 2 and 4 in underglaze blue, and naturally add greatly to the value of a piece.

After less than three years, Cookworthy transferred the whole operation to Bristol in 1770.

Two Plymouth porcelain figure groups by William Cookworthy's factory, each of two scantily-draped putti before flowering bocages, enriched in colors, 7³⁄₄in. high, circa 1770. (Christie's) **$1,172**

A Plymouth cream jug, painted in underglaze faded sepia or blue with flowers, trees and rocks, 9cm. (Lawrence Fine Arts) **$720**

A set of four Plymouth figures, emblematic of the Seasons, each in the form of a putto and decorated in colored enamels, circa 1768-70, 14cm. high. (Dreweatt Neate) **$2,718**

A rare Plymouth figure of 'Winter' in the form of a naked boy with a robe, in mint condition. **$1,360**

A pair of Plymouth figures of musicians wearing pale clothes, he playing the recorder and his companion the mandolin, Wm. Cookworthy's factory, circa 1770, 14.5cm. high. (Christie's) **$1,200**

A Plymouth group of two putti emblematic of Spring, 14.5cm. high, impressed letters S & D (flower festoon R). (Phillips) **$640**

POOLE POTTERY

The firm of Carter & Co was established in Poole, Dorset in 1873 to manufacture earthenware and tiles. The latter it often supplied for subsequent decoration, by, among others, William De Morgan. In 1895 they took over the nearby Architectural Tile Co.

Their range of earthenware, notably ornamental pottery, was developed principally by Owen Carter, the son of the proprietor. His experiments with glazes led to the creation of the matt, cream glaze which came to be associated with Carter Stabler and Adams. This amalgamation took place in 1921, when Owen Carter went into partnership with Harold Stabler and John and Truda Adams.

It was out of this partnership that the Poole Pottery, as it was renamed in 1963, grew. Poole Pottery products from all periods are much in vogue as collectibles today.

A pottery charger painted by Nellie Blackmore with a view of the ship the Harry Paye, by Arthur Bradbury, 15in. diam. (Christie's S. Ken) $1,000

A pair of pottery doves designed by John Adams, and modeled by Harry Brown, impressed *Poole, England*, 8¼in. high. (Christie's S. Ken) $480

A pair of pottery bookends each modeled in full relief as leaping gazelles, impressed *Poole* and incised *831*, 8in. high. (Christie's S. Ken) $720

A pottery candelabra, molded with fruit and foliage and covered in a light blue glaze, impressed *Poole England* mark, 8½in. high. (Christie's S. Ken) $120

A Phoebe Stabler 'Piping Faun' roundel, modeled as a young faun with pan pipes tripping through a circular garland of flowers and reeds, 40cm. diameter. (Phillips) $780

A terracotta sculpture of a fully rigged galleon, modeled by Harry Stabler, glazed in shades of blue, green, yellow and white, 20½in. high. (Christie's S. Ken) $1,250

A terracotta two-handled oviform vase shape No. 973, painted with flowers and foliage below geometric border, impressed *CSA Ltd.* mark, 7in. high. (Christie's S. Ken) $720

POOLE POTTERY

A Poole Pottery deep dish, made to commemorate the sail ship, drawn by Arthur Bradbury, painted by Ruth Pavely, impressed mark and *528*, 15in. diameter.
(Woolley & Wallis) $433

A pottery wall decoration modeled as a yacht in full sail, glazed in yellow on gray base, impressed *Poole England* mark, 4in. high.
(Christie's S. Ken) $80

A pottery biscuit barrel and cover with wicker handle painted by Sylvia Penney, with stylized flowers and foliage, impressed *Poole*, 5½in. high.
(Christie's S. Ken)   £140 $225

A pottery nursery rhyme jug, designed by Dora Batty and painted by Ruth Pavely, depicting a scene from 'Ride a Cock Horse to Banbury Cross', impressed *Poole England* mark, 7½in. high.
(Christie's S. Ken) $145

A pair of Pheobe Stabler earthenware figures modeled as a boy and girl, each draped with a garland of flowers, impressed *Hammersmith Bridge* mark, 7in. high.
(Christie's S. Ken) $920

A pottery vase, shape No. 466, painted by Rene Hayes with a band of geometric pattern in typical colors on a white ground, impressed *CSA Ltd* mark and painted insignia, 5½in. high.
(Christie's S. Ken) $160

'Buster Boy', a pottery figure by Phoebe Stabler of a putto seated on a rock with floral garland draped around his body, incised *Stabler Hammersmith London 1916*, 7in. high.
(Christie's S. Ken) $320

A terracotta shallow bowl, decorated by Anne Hatchard painted with a deer in an open landscape, impressed *CSA* mark, painted insignia and *RG*, 9½in. diameter.
(Christie's S. Ken) $400

A Phoebe Stabler plaster bust of a young girl with pigtails, painted yellow, inscribed *Phoebe Stabler 1911*, 15in. high. (Christie's) $440

POTSCHAPPEL

The porcelain made at Meissen must surely be one of the most forged and copied artefacts of all time. One of the host of factories which sprang up in the 19th century precisely to do this, was situated at Potschappel near Dresden, the major center for Meissen copies.

The Potschappel factory was established in 1875 and traded as the Sächsische Porzellanfabrik Carl Thieme. It produced exclusively Meissen type pieces, such as the crinoline groups which had been made from the mid 18th century. Carl Thieme, the founder, was also the chief designer.

Various marks were used. Some pieces were clearly marked *Dresden* or *Potschappel*, while others have simply a cross and a *T*. Crossed *Ls* with a coronet and a flower with leaves or a bee on a hive are further variations.

A Carl Thieme Potschappel porcelain table centerpiece, the shaped base with an 18th century lady with two suitors, 55cm. high. (Henry Spencer) **$1,600**

Potschappel porcelain cabinet cup and saucer by Carl Thieme, with a pink ground with a landscape decoration. (G. A. Key) **$160**

A pair of Carl Thieme blue ground baluster vases and covers painted with riders hunting, 46cm. high, late 19th century. (Christie's) **$1,735**

A pair of Potschappel (Carl Thieme) baluster vases, covers and stands, enriched with gilt caillouté and on footed shaped-square stands applied and painted with bouquets and edged with molded scrolls and shells, late 19th century, 32³/₄in. high. (Christie's) **$11,869**

A pair of Potschappel porcelain jars and covers with scroll handles terminating in female heads, set on rectangular stands, 47cm. high. (Bearne's) **$1,937**

A Carl Thieme Potschappel pierced centerpiece applied with flowers, the base with four figures, 12¹/₂in. high. (Christie's S. Ken) **$640**

PRATTWARE

Blue printed ware proved enormously popular in the early 19th century, with just about every English pottery turning out vast quantities of the stuff.

In the 1840s however the firm of F & R Pratt of Fenton achieved a breakthrough when they introduced multi-color printing. This they did by engraving each color, using a palette of red, blue, yellow, black or brown, on a separate copper plate. When carefully arranged and engraved in stipple, the result was a full range of colors, which decoration was sometimes further enhanced with gilding.

Initially this was used mainly for decorating potlids, where even great paintings by famous artists were sometimes reproduced. Soon everyone was imitating Prattware, and the range of wares so decorated extended to include tea and dessert services, vases, ceramic picture frames and bread plates.

Pratt was blessed with a highly skilled engraver, Jesse Austin, who sometimes signed or initialed his work. His mark adds great cachet to a piece.

Pratt's pieces usually carry the mark *F & R Pratt Fenton* impressed, or more rarely, a crown with *Manufacturers to HRH Prince Albert/F & R Pratt.*

A 'Pratt' creamware cow creamer, sponged and painted in black and ocher, set on a green shaped base, 14cm. high.
(Bearne's) $634

A Prattware group of Saint George slaying a dragon, flanked by two female figures in ocher dress, 25cm.
(Phillips) $960

Pair of Prattware figures of Elijah and the Widow of Zarephath, England, late 18th century, 9¹/₂in. high.
(Skinner Inc.) $660

A creamware model of an owl, circa 1785, of Pratt type, with alert expression and incised plumage and splashed in ocher, green and brown spots, 5½in. high.
(Christie's) $5,280

A Prattware George IV commemorative plate with a profile head of the King wearing a laurel wreath and naval uniform, 22cm.
(Phillips) $640

A Prattware cider jug, circa 1800, molded with exotic barnyard fowl within an oval reserve edged with stiff leaf-tips, 7³/₄in. high.
(Christie's) $1,430

PRATTWARE

A Prattware flask of circular form with a portrait of The Duke of York and the reverse Louis XVI and Marie Antoinette, 5in. high, circa 1794. $200

A pair of Pratt type small figures of birds, 3½in. high. (Dreweatt Neate) $1,365

18th century Pratt figure of a cat with blue, green and ocher splashed decoration, 3in. high. (Prudential) $440

An amusing Staffordshire Pratt Ware teapot and cover modeled in the form of a brown bear, seated upright with a white crabstock spout, 17cm. high.(Phillips) $950

Two rare Prattware elephant money boxes, decorated with blue sponging and yellow and green pheasant's eyes, 20.5cm. high. (Phillips) $20,156

An English pearlware Pratt-type jug, circa 1810, the barrel-shaped body painted in yellow, ocher, green, brown and blue, 7¼in. high. (Sotheby's) $1,035

A fine Prattware toby jug, the ruddy-faced toper firmly grasping his jug and goblet, his pipe of coiled snake type resting against his chest, 9¾in. high, circa 1800–20. (Tennants) $1,395

A pair of Prattware oval plaques molded in relief with classical profile heads of a man and a woman, 26.5cm. (Phillips London) $1,750

A Pratt-type portrait mug of Lord Rodney, typically modeled facing forward, his eyes looking upward, 6½in. high, late 18th century. (Christie's) $354

QIANLONG

The Emperor Ch'ien Lung held sway for 60 years between 1736–95 and his peaceful reign marked a high point in the history of Chinese ceramics. T'ang Ying had supreme control of the Imperial Porcelain Manufactory from 1743 and he brought the Imperial wares to a peak of perfection, introducing to them many new 'foreign' colors, and the use of double glazes.

Blue and white was still made; the vases were often of archaic bronze forms decorated with bronze patterns or a pattern of floral scrolls. The blue, however, was usually a dullish indigo in tone, and the character of Kangxi ware is lacking.

On-glaze painting in famille rose enamels was widely extended in the Qianlong period, and tints were now mixed to produce the European effect of shading. Designs were taken from nature or copied from the antique, featuring brocade designs etc.

Much Qianlong ware was exported, notably 'Mandarin' wares, ewers, punch bowls and vases painted with panels of figure subjects with the surrounding space filled with composite designs of blue and white with passages of pink scale diaper or scrolls broken by small vignettes. Table ware often has elaborately molded and pierced ornament in famille rose colors. Gilding, too, was freely employed.

In Ch'ien Lung's time the art of porcelain reaches a technical apogee, but later in the period it is already beginning to lose freshness and spontaneity. The pieces are marvellous examples of neatness and finish, but there is a cold sophistication about them, and they lack the fire and vigor which characterised the Ming and Kangxi periods.

An exceedingly fine, very large christening bowl, early Qianlong, painted in overglaze enamels of rose, jaune, vermilion, aubergine, blue, iron red and orange, 22in. (Greenslade Hunt)
$18,420

A Chinese armorial oval plate, the center painted in famille rose enamels with the coat of arms for John Rowsewell impaling Colthurst, 26.4cm. wide, Qianlong. (Bearne's) $1,162

A pair of Chinese porcelain, double gourd reticulated vases, the alternate pierced panels in turquoise and red enamel, 14.3cm. high, Qianlong. (Bearne's) $428

A Chinese 'cherry pickers' tea caddy, of arched form, enameled and gilt with European figures, iron red borders, 11cm. high, Qianlong. (Tennants) $918

An ormolu-mounted Chinese blue and white porcelain tankard and cover, the domed-lid with spreading husk-trails and fluting, the porcelain Qianlong, 8¼in. high. (Christie's) $1,794

One of a pair of Chinese blue and white porcelain circular plates, each centered by a pagoda lakeland landscape, 18in. diameter, Qianlong, circa 1760. (Tennants) (Two) $454

QIANLONG

A Qianlong famille rose and gilt edged barber's bowl, decorated with peonies, 30.4cm. long. (Stockholms Auktionsverk)
$886

A matching pair of Mandarin pattern vases and covers, Qianlong. (Greenslade Hunt)
$3,714

A Chinese blue and white porcelain tureen and cover, with paired animal mask handles, 13in. wide, Qianlong, circa 1760. (Tennants)
$1,377

A fine celadon-glazed globular vase, Hu, Qianlong archaistic seal mark and of the period, the globular body molded with three horizontal ribs, all under an even pale celadon glaze, 16¹/₈in. high. (Christie's)
$39,742

A pair of Chinese porcelain spaniels, Qianlong period, with heads turned to one side in alert expression, 9¹/₈in. high. (Christie's)
$20,700

A fine celadon-glazed moulded vase, Meiping, impressed Qianlong seal mark and of the period, relief molded on the body with sprays of the sanduo, fruiting peach, finger citrus and pomegranate, 9in. high. (Christie's)
$36,903

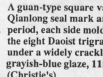

A fine robin's-egg-glazed oviform vase, impressed Qianlong seal mark and of the period, covered overall with a mottled glaze of turquoise and rich blue tone, 9¹/₄in. high, box. (Christie's)
$24,179

A pair of Chinese baluster jars, each brightly painted with birds, chrysanthemums and peonies in a rocky garden, 30.5cm. high, Qianlong, covers missing. (Bearne's)
$1,401

A guan-type square vase, Cong, Qianlong seal mark and of the period, each side molded with the eight Daoist trigrams, all under a widely crackled pale grayish-blue glaze, 11in. high. (Christie's)
$17,772

QUIMPER

Faience has been made at Quimper, in the Finisterre area of Brittany, since 1690, with three main factories in operation. These were Pierre-Paul Caussy (1743-82), Antoine de la Hubaudière from 1782 onwards, and in the 19th century the Fougeray factory also produced items in imitation of 18th century wares.

Stoneware, too, was made there in the 19th century. Quimper ware is very like delft in its decorative style, which often features peasant figures and bold floral designs.

Quimper standish containing two inkwells with Breton male decoration and orange border, 5¾in. x 4¼in.
(Eldred's) $231

HR Quimper platter with female decoration, 12 x 9¼in.
(Eldred's) $143

Large three-piece Quimper lavabo with floral decoration on a yellow ground, marked *Henriot Quimper France,* **height of dispenser 14¾in.**
(Eldred's) $248

Pair of Henriot Quimper plates, male and female central decoration with unusual border and modified star/waffle edge, 9¾in. diameter.
(Eldred's) $495

Four Quimper plates with scalloped edges and salmon loop border, three with central Breton male decoration and one with female, marked *HR Quimper,* **10in. diameter.**
(Eldred's) $1,595

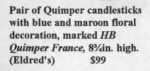

Pair of Quimper candlesticks with blue and maroon floral decoration, marked *HB Quimper France,* **8¾in. high.**
(Eldred's) $99

Covered Quimper coffeepot with Breton female decoration, marked *Henriot Quimper France 744 ter.,* **10in. high.**
(Eldred's) $209

Pair of conical Quimper wall vases, one with male decoration and one with female, marked *HR Quimper France,* **10¾in. long.**
(Eldred's) $770

REDWARE

Redware is the original pottery of the American colonies. Its manufacture began in the early 1600s, lasting well into the 19th century, with a potshop in just about every village.

Redware was cheap and easy to make. Its basic color came from the presence of iron oxide in the clay, which, when fired produced various red tones. It could however be given various other colors by additions to the glaze. While imperfections in the clay often provided interesting natural decorations, the prevalent form of intentional decoration was the use of slip.

One of the earliest recorded potteries was at Jamestown, Virginia, which was operating in 1625. Carolina and Georgia were other states with a strong pottery tradition. Most important of all, however, was Pennsylvania, where the Amish carried slip decoration one stage further to make intricate sgrafitto designs.

The disadvantages of redware are that is brittle, easily broken, and porous, making it unsuitable for a number of domestic uses.

A very fine and rare glazed redware standing dog, attributed to John Bell, Pennsylvania, mid 19th century, 9in. high.
(Sotheby's) $26,450

A glazed redware covered bowl, Adams County, Pennsylvania, 19th century, the circular lid with full-figured bird and handle, 6¼in. high.
(Christie's) $5,520

A green glazed redware flower pot, stamped *John Bell*, Pennsylvania, 1860–1870, cylindrical tapering, with everted brim and applied saucer, 7in. high.
(Christie's) $1,725

A slip decorated redware plate, Smith Pottery, Norwalk, Connecticut, 1825–1880, with coggle wheel rim embellished with pretzels decorated in yellow slip, 12½in. diameter.
(Christie's) $2,070

A redware sgraffito decorated mug, signed *W. Roth*, possibly Berks or Mongomery County, Pennsylvania, dated *1821*, with German inscriptions and decorated with distlefink, 5in. high.
(Christie's) $4,025

A sgraffitto decorated redware plate, attributed to Conrad Mumbouer, Pennsylvania, dated *1802*, the surface decorated with an inscribed potted heart issuing stylized flowers and notched tulips, 11½in. diameter.
(Christie's) $21,850

A glazed redware face jug, signed *Lanier Meaders*, Georgia, circa 1970, modeled with flaring ears, protruding eyebrows and lips and a crooked nose, 10¼in. high.
(Sotheby's) $1,000

REDWARE

A glazed redware handled cheese mold, Pennsylvania, 19th century, cylindrical with applied handle, molded rim and body, 4¹/₂in. diameter. (Christie's) $575

A figural redware whistle, attributed to Jesiah Shorb, Pennsylvania, 19th century, molded in the form of a barking Dachshund with whistle in tail, 4⁵/₈in. high. (Christie's) $3,680

A glazed redware creamer, Pennsylvania, 19th century, daubed with manganese on a red body with a clear lead glaze, 3¹/₂in. high. (Christie's) $1,093

An unglazed redware wall pocket, stamped *George S. Freshley*, 1856–1922, Lebanon, Pennsylvania, circa 1883, with punch decorated rim and large applied medallions, 10¹/₂in. high. (Christie's) $748

A glazed redware flowerpot and saucer, probably Lebanon or Berks County, Pennsylvania, 19th century, the coggle rim above applied ovoid decorations, 8¹/₂in. high. (Christie's) $288

A yellow glazed redware food mold, stamped *John Bell*, 1800–1880, Waynesboro, Pennsylvania, 1830–1880, glazed in yellow with manganese decorated brim, 8¹/₄in. diameter. (Christie's) $920

A glazed redware pipe holder, possibly George A. Wagner Pottery, Weissport, Carbon County, Pennsylvania, 1875–1896, cylindrical with perforated lid and four pipe stands, 4in. high. (Christie's) $2,760

An extremely fine and rare sgraffito-decorated redware pie plate, attributed to Johannes Neesz, Tyler's Port, Montgomery County, Pennsylvania, circa 1800, 10⁵/₈in. diameter. (Sotheby's) $24,150

A glazed redware mantle ornament, Pennsylvania, initialed *M M* and dated *1798*, in the form of a pelican pecking its breast, mounted on a molded plinth, 6¹/₂in. high. (Christie's) $24,150

REDWARE

A slip decorated redware dish, Pennsylvania, 19th century, with coggle wheel rim embellished with criss-cross decoration, 13in. diameter.
(Christie's) $3,220

A molded redware figural group, attributed to the 'Master Hobo Potter', Pennsylvania, 19th century, depicting a dog resting on an alligator atop a turtle, 5in. high.
(Christie's) $13,800

A rare slip-decorated redware pie plate, Pennsylvania, 19th century, of circular form with crimped edge, 12¹/₈in. diameter.
(Sotheby's) $1,955

A glazed redware fancy presentation flower pot, attributed to Enos Smedley, 1805–1892, Pennsylvania, dated 1827, body inscribed *Earl Pell L. C. Leah Connell/5th moth, 18th dy, 1827*, 9³/₄in. high.
(Christie's) $18,400

A double walled pierced glazed redware covered bowl, possibly Henry Grady, 1812–1880, Shanksville, Somerset County, Pennsylvania, 1843–1880, yellow glazed cylindrical body.
(Christie's) $12,650

A glazed redware flowerpot and saucer, attributed to Henry Fahr, b. 1821, Pennsylvania, with ruffled rim and saucer and pressed ruffled bands, 8¹/₄in. high.
(Christie's) $253

A glazed redware mug, stamped *Solomon Bell*, 1817–1882, Winchester or Strausburg, Virginia, 1843–1882, glazed yellow with green daubs, 5in. high.
(Christie's) $2,990

A scroddle-glazed redware bank, probably Philadelphia, circa 1840, in the form of a miniature chest of drawers, with all over yellow and brown scroddle decoration, 6¹/₂in. high.
(Christie's) $460

A redware field jug, Pennsylvania, 19th century, baluster form, with applied handle, straight spout and dripped manganese glaze, 11in. high.
(Christie's) $403

REDWARE, STAFFORDSHIRE

Redware is simply red clay pottery, and wares also tend to be simple in form, lead-glazed with a soft, porous body, ranging in color from a pinkish-buff to red and brown.

It was much used in 18th century Staffordshire, particularly for tea and coffee pots.

Pieces are generally unmarked, though pseudo Chinese seal marks are sometimes found.

A Staffordshire redware hexagonal teapot and cover, circa 1760, molded with panels of Chinese figures, 4³/₄in. high. (Christie's) $2,300

A Staffordshire glazed redware small teapot and cover, circa 1755, of barrel-shape, with faceted spout and dolphin handle, 3¹/₂in. high. (Christie's) $483

A Staffordshire glazed red stoneware coffee pot and cover, 1765–70, the tapering cylindrical body engine-turned all over with a diamond and chevron pattern, 9¹/₁₆in. high. (Sotheby's) $2,645

A Staffordshire red stoneware milk jug and a cover, 1765–70, the pear-shaped body and spout engine-turned in 'rose', diamond and chevron patterns above a flared and fluted foot, impressed pseudo-Chinese seal mark, 6¹/₄in. high. (Sotheby's) $345

A Staffordshire red stoneware coffee pot and cover, circa 1765, the pear-shaped body decorated on either side with mold-applied reliefs of a moustachioed 'Drama' mask, 7⁵/₁₆in. high. (Sotheby's) $862

A Staffordshire glazed redware small teapot and cover, circa 1745, of Astbury type, with dolphin handle and serpent spout, 4¹/₄in. high. (Christie's) $3,520

An English redware coffee pot and cover, the body with engine-turned decoration, the ribbed cover with acorn finial, 23cm., pseudo Chinese seal mark. (Phillips) $640

A Staffordshire redware pecten-shell-molded teapot and cover with scroll handle, the snake spout molded with flowering foliage, circa 1755, 12.5cm. high. (Christie's) $6,940

LUCIE RIE

Lucie Rie (b.1902) is an Austrian artist potter who trained under Powolny in Vienna. In 1938 she came to the UK as a refugee from Nazism and opened a button factory in a London mews, where she was joined by fellow refugee Hans Coper.

Her early pre-war work had consisted of simple, thinly potted stoneware, sometimes polished or covered with rough textured glazes, her style influenced both by functionalist ideals and by Roman pottery. Her mark at this time was a painted *LRG* over *Wien*.

After the war she made porcelain decorated with unglazed bands of cross-hatched decoration colored with manganese oxide, and stoneware in elegant simple shapes.

She used color sparingly, and developed a number of glazes, notably a yellow one containing uranium. Others were characterised by their rough uneven texture.

The significance of her work was recognised when she was made a Dame of the British Empire and she still flourishes today. Her mark now is an impressed monogram *LR* within a rectangle.

A white stoneware teapot by Dame Lucie Rie, the lid with brown rim, the tip of spout repaired, circa 1957, 9in. wide. (Bonhams) $1,376

A dramatic stoneware open bowl by Dame Lucie Rie, the white bowl flecked with dark brown, circa 1960, 12⅝in. diameter. (Bonhams) $7,707

A fine stoneware vase by Dame Lucie Rie, the body with diagonal fluting, covered by a lightly pitted mustard glaze with a bluish hue, 8in. high. (Bonhams) $4,771

An outstanding oval vessel by Dame Lucie Rie, the shoulder with a band of impressed hollows heightened turquoise, impressed *LR* seal, 7in. wide. (Bonhams) $14,986

An impressive stoneware jardinière by Dame Lucie Rie, yellow and beige pitted glaze, impressed *LR* seal, circa 1960, 8½in. high. (Bonhams) $4,771

A white stoneware milk jug by Dame Lucie Rie, with bronzed feathered rim, impressed *LR* seal, circa 1958, 3⅝in. high. (Bonhams) $404

An exquisite white porcelain vase by Dame Lucie Rie, with inlaid lines running around the body, impressed *LR* seal, circa 1980, 7in. high. (Bonhams) $3,670

A fine stoneware 'knitted' bowl by Lucie Rie, inlaid with concentric dark circles from the well, impressed LR seal, circa 1982, 9in. diameter.
(Bonhams) $4,800

A Lucie Rie stoneware bowl, with straight sides covered with an off-white glaze having faint brown speckling, 13.5cm. diam. (Phillips London) $3,200

A cobalt blue stoneware bowl by Dame Lucie Rie, the rim speckled with a darker blue, impressed LR seal, circa 1970, 8¼in. diameter.
(Bonhams) $4,037

A lime-yellow stoneware bowl by Dame Lucie Rie, with feathered bronzed band, impressed LR seal, circa 1975, 5¾in. diameter.
(Bonhams) $2,753

A porcelain footed bowl by Lucie Rie, 'American' yellow glaze, impressed LR seal, circa 1970, 6⅛in. diameter.
(Bonhams) $2,160

A fine stoneware bowl by Dame Lucie Rie, on shallow foot, slate-gray ground covered in thick white pitted glaze, circa 1960, 24cm. diameter.
(Christie's) $10,527

A stoneware bowl by Lucie Rie with compressed flared sides, the exterior carved with fluted decoration, impressed LR seal 14cm. high. (Christie's) $3,200

A stoneware coffee pot by Lucie Rie, brown with cane handle, impressed LR seal, circa 1952, 7¼in. high.
(Bonhams) $225

A rare porcelain bowl by Lucie Rie, the white glazed exterior inlaid with small brown circles each with a dot, circa 1968, 5in. diam.
(Bonhams) $6,400

A lovely oval earthenware bowl by Dame Lucie Rie, the exterior burnished, the interior white with painted brown lines and a yellow band, circa 1947, 8¼in. wide.
(Bonhams) $5,505

A stoneware pouring vessel by Lucie Rie, white with pulled handle, impressed LR seal, circa 1957, 3¼in. high.
(Bonhams) $680

A fine porcelain golden bronze bowl by Lucie Rie, the deep terracotta foot and well surrounded by a circular ring of turquoise, circa 1986, 9¼in. diam. (Bonhams) $7,200

RIE

A rare porcelain bowl by Lucie Rie, bronze with a sloping white band inlaid with diagonal lines, circa 1958, 4³/₈ in. diam. (Bonhams) $2,900

A rare stoneware 'spinach' bowl by Dame Lucie Rie, covered in a thick cratered glaze with a golden bronze band at the rim, circa 1986, 7in. diameter. (Bonhams) $4,037

A stoneware salad bowl by Lucie Rie, white with speckling and unglazed ring within, circa 1955, 9¹/₂in. wide. (Bonhams) $1,160

A superb porcelain bowl by Lucie Rie, uranium yellow with deep bronze running band at rim, impressed seal, circa 1975, 7in. diameter. (Bonhams) $9,600

A stoneware salad bowl with pulled lip by Lucie Rie, covered in a finely pitted bluish-white glaze with iron-brown flecks, circa 1954, 14.3cm. high. (Christie's) $1,160

A porcelain bowl by Dame Lucie Rie, covered in a translucent finely crackled yellow glaze with lustrous bronze run and fluxed glaze to rim, circa 1980, 16.6cm. diam. (Christie's) $2,922

A small stoneware bowl by Lucie Rie, covered in a mirror-black manganese glaze with white rim, circa 1953, 10cm. diam. (Christie's) $800

A porcelain inlaid sgraffito bowl by Lucie Rie, covered in a pink glaze between two bands of turquoise, the rim and foot covered in a lustrous bronze glaze, circa 1980, 18.2cm. diameter. (Christie's) $4,800

A rare stoneware bowl by Lucie Rie, covered in a translucent white glaze with a bronze rim running into the white body, impressed LR seal, circa 1955, 4¹/₄in. high. (Bonhams) $1,250

A fine bronze and white porcelain bowl by Dame Lucie Rie, sgraffito radiating lines inside and contrasting inlaid lines to exterior, circa 1980, 8in. diameter. (Bonhams) $5,505

A stoneware cream pot by Lucie Rie, covered in an unusual yellow glaze with running bronze rim, circa 1960, 2³/₄ in. high. (Bonhams) $760

A fine stoneware flared bowl by Lucie Rie, covered in a pale lemon, olive green and speckled pink spiral glaze, impressed LR seal, circa 1960, 32cm. diam. $9,600

ROBJ

Robj was a French dealer who in the 1920s and early 30s commissioned small decorative porcelain items, such as inkwells, ashtrays, preserve pots etc, for sale in his Paris showroom. Lamps, bottles and incense burners often in the form of the human figure were popular as were Cubist inspired statuettes in cream colored porcelain with a crackle glaze. Robj sponsored annual competitions until 1931, and winning designs were sometimes produced in limited editions at the Sevres factory.

Robj French porcelain inkwell, figural blackamoor in gold trimmed white turban and costume, 6¹⁄₄in. high. (Skinner Inc.) $275

French porcelain perfume burner by Robj, white robed Oriental gentleman sitting cross-legged on gold accented stepped platform, 8¹⁄₄in. high. (Skinner Inc.) $550

A Robj figural nightlight, fashioned as a semi-naked girl in green dress and white cloak, clasping a bunch of flowers, marked *Robj Made in Paris*, 26cm. high. (Phillips) $542

Robj, twelve polychrome-decorated figural ceramic bottles and stoppers, each representing a different person, marked *Robj Paris*, 26.5cm. high. (Sotheby's) $3,755

A Robj porcelain decanter and stopper, the pear shaped decanter modeled as a Scotsman playing bagpipes, printed *Robj, Paris, Made in France*, 27cm. high. (Bonhams) $320

A Robj spirit flask and stopper in the form of a Breton girl wearing national dress, 25.7cm. high. (Phillips London) $440

A Robj earthenware bowl and cover, formed as a Red Indian's head, with dark red glazed feather headdress, 20cm. high. (Christie's) $675

A Robj porcelain jug, modeled as a rotund lady wearing a plum colored dress, the spout modeled as an apron, 19.5cm. high. (Phillips) $382

ROCKINGHAM

American Rockingham ware has a yellow earthenware body, covered with a mottled brown glaze containing manganese. It was much used for household wares and dates from around 1840 onwards. East Liverpool, Ohio, emerged as the principal center of manufacture, while Taylor & Speeler set up a production unit at Trenton in 1852. Animal figures and toby jugs with Rockingham glazes were also produced by the Bennington factory.

Antique Rockingham barrel-shaped pitcher, possibly Bennington, 6in. high.
(Eldreds) $60

Antique Rockingham batter jug with single spout, raised decoration, 9¾in. diameter.
(Eldreds) $44

Antique Rockingham pitcher with raised floral decoration, 7½in. high.
(Eldreds) $75

Two Rockingham glazed pottery spaniels, possibly Ohio, 19th century, 12in. high.
(Skinner) $920

A Rockingham flint enamel hot water urn, Bennington, Vermont, 1849, baluster-form, with domed faceted cover with acorn finial, 21in. high.
(Christie's) $9,200

Antique Rockingham covered ice water pitcher with raised tavern scene, 9in. diameter.
(Eldreds) $150

Rockingham glazed mantel ornament, possibly midwestern United States, 19th century, in the form of a recumbent lion, 15in. wide.
(Skinner Inc.) $950

Antique Rockingham pitcher with raised hunting scene.
(Eldreds) $100

ROCKINGHAM

Pottery manufacture began at the Rockingham factory near Swinton in Yorkshire in the mid 18th century. During the early 19th century high quality pottery was produced mainly for export to Russia. From 1826-42, however, when the factory was run by the brothers Thomas, George and John Brameld, its porcelain became highly acclaimed at home. In quality, Rockingham's output was second only to Nantgarw, while its superior strength meant that it could be used for an astonishing diversity of forms.

It is perhaps most famous for its brown glazed ware. This glaze was applied very thickly, the object being dipped three times, to give a streaked chocolate coloration. It was used for such objects as toby jugs, tea and coffee pots, as well as the famous Cadogan pots. These were teapots shaped as a peach with foliage and fruit decoration. They were lidless, the liquid being poured in through a hole at the bottom to which was attached a tapering, slightly spiraled tube which finished just short of the top. They were thus unspillable.

Blue and white ware was also produced in the common Willow pattern and some designs peculiar to Rockingham. Rarer are green glazed and cane colored wares, the latter often decorated with raised classical or floral ornament in blue, white, chocolate or green.

Rockingham also produced a staggering diversity of ornamental ware, from baskets and scent bottles and toys down to bedknobs and door handles – the list is virtually endless, and some outstanding artists were engaged to decorate these.

Their useful ware

A Rockingham dated claret-ground cylindrical mug, painted with a horse with jockey up, inscribed in gilt *First Year of WATH RACES, MDCCCXXXI*, 1831, 13cm. high. (Christie's) $7,482

A Rockingham polychrome porcelain figure of a girl feeding a lamb, seated in puce bodice and white skirt, circa 1830. (Tennants) $866

A rare and fine pair of Rockingham vases of distinctive shape with flattened bodies rising from leaf molded bases, probably painted by Edwin Steele, 12cm. (Phillips) $4,340

A very rare Rockingham empire-style coffee-pot and cover, the ovoid body enameled in colors on either side with a bouquet of flowers, 7³/₄ in. high, 1826–30. (Tennants) $731

A pair of Rockingham porcelain small spill vases, each decorated with a continuous scene of a spoonbill and other birds, 3¹/₄ in. high, circa 1830. (Tennants) $3,726

An important Rockingham Royal Service plate, from the service made for William IV, the light blue border gilt with oak leaves with acorns, 24cm. (Phillips) $5,760

ROCKINGHAM

comprised dinner and dessert services, which fall into two basic designs, one featuring coronet knobs and scrolled handles and the other rustic handles and twig finials. Several famous services were made for the nobility and royalty – William IV paid £5,000 for a Rockingham dinner service. The company, however, lost money on virtually all of these commissions, and with their huge diversity of output the factory was never really on a sound financial footing. The Bramelds relied heavily on their patron Earl Fitzwilliam, whose successor in 1841, in justifiable exasperation, refused to plow any more money into the enterprise. By the next year the factory had closed.

There is a diversity too of Rockingham marks. On pottery *Brameld* is generally found together with a + and a numeral. On cane ware this is usually in an oval plaquette. After 1826 *Rockingham* becomes more common, most often found on brown ware, and until 1830 the Earl Fitzwilliam griffin arms are found with *Rockingham Works Brameld*. After 1830 the color of the mark changes to puce.

An attractive pair of Rockingham models of pugs, both seated on oval maroon scrolled bases, 6.5cm., impressed marks.
(Phillips) $1,532

A Rockingham flower encrusted circular basket with overhead handle, the exterior applied with flower heads, circa 1830, 11.2cm.
(Bearne's) $760

A Rockingham porcelain neo rococo style teapot and sucrier and covers, painted in colors probably by John Randall with exotic birds.
(Spencer's) $1,450

A Rockingham green-ground hexagonal baluster vase and cover, painted with bouquets and scattered flowers and insects, circa 1826-30, 46cm. high. (Christie's)
                    $2,000

Pair of Rockingham figures of a young boy and a girl, inscribed no. 36, 4¾in. high. $720

A Rockingham Cadogan teapot, of peach shape, 4½in. high, impressed Brameld.
(Dreweatt Neate) $160

ROCKINGHAM

A very large Rockingham armorial soup tureen, cover and stand, painted with fruit, probably by Thomas Steele, and exotic birds and butterflies, 43cm.
(Phillips) $4,000

Rockingham-type brown glazed figure of a lion, England, mid 19th century, (chips under base rim), 11in. wide.
(Skinner Inc) $320

A Rockingham miniature lavender-ground teapot and cover, applied with trailing white flowers, Puce Griffin mark and Cl. 2 in red, circa 1835, 6.5cm. high. (Christie's) $720

A Rockingham porcelain octagonal plate, decorated in famille verte enamels, 35cm. diam. (H. Spencer & Sons) $440

A Rockingham porcelain figure of John Liston as 'Lubin Log', wearing a lilac jacket and holding a hat box, umbrella, striped bag and coat, 18cm. high.
(Tennants) $4,284

One of a pair of early Rockingham primrose leaf molded plates, painted with flowers in vases on marble tables, probably by Edwin Steele, 24.5cm.
(Phillips) $1,600

A Rockingham cabinet cup and stand with two gilt scroll handles, circa 1835, the stand 11.5cm. diam., the cup 10cm. high.
(Christie's) $880

A Rockingham miniature plate encrusted with three flower-sprays, Puce Griffin mark, circa 1835, 9.5cm. diam.
(Christie's) $400

A Rockingham bulbous pot pourri two handled jar, painted in colored enamels with a view in Cumberland, 25cm. high.
(Tennants) $4,590

ROOKWOOD

The foundation of the Rookwood pottery in 1880 received enormous publicity because it was established by a Cincinnati society lady, Maria Longworth Nichols. Its initial aim was to produce a better art pottery rather than commercial success, but in 1883 William Taylor, a friend of Mrs Nichols, was appointed manager, and he both extended the range of designs and organized a distribution network on sound commercial lines.

Though some utility wares were made in the early years, the emphasis was mainly on art pottery which was made using various techniques. The results were often characterized by carved, incised or impressed designs in high relief, often with gilt decoration and overglaze painting or slip painting under the glaze. This last, in which rich warm colors were airbrushed to give an evenly blended background, became known as 'Standard' Rookwood.

Tinted glazes and colored bodies were introduced and in 1884 an aventurine glaze was developed by accident, in which bright gold crystals appeared deep under the surface. This became known as 'Tiger Eye'.

When Mrs Nichols remarried in 1886, her interest in the pottery waned, and in 1889 she transferred the ownership to Taylor. Under his direction, floral decoration on rich brown, orange and yellow backgrounds and on pink and white 'Cameo' pieces predominates. He moved the business to larger premises at Mount Adams, Cincinnati in 1892, and 'Iris' 'Sea Green' and 'Aeriel blue' designs appeared.

Besides floral decoration, Rookwood pieces now were also adorned with portraits of

Rookwood bookends, William P. MacDonald, 1922, Art Deco Oriental figural, with black comb highlighted in red, 8in. high.
(Skinner) $825

A Rookwood pottery basket, by artist Artus Van Briggle, decorated in slip underglaze with blossoms, berries and leaves, 6½in. high.
(Skinner) $700

Rookwood Pottery tea set, 1900, by Caroline Steinle, yellow and brown pansies with green stems under a green-brown standard glaze.
(Skinner) $173

Rookwood Pottery beer tankard for Cincinnati Cooperage Company, raised ribbon mark, no. 1333 S, 7¾in. high.
(Skinner) $230

Pair of Rookwood crow bookends, 1926, oversize weighted set of mauve molded rooks in William McDonald's design, 6½in. high.
(Skinner) $413

Rookwood Pottery bisque finished reversible, lidded pot-pourri jar, Cincinnati, Artus Van Briggle, 1887, decorated with morning-glories, 6¼in. diameter.
(Skinner) $690

ROOKWOOD

American Indians, Negroes, animals, and figures from Old Master paintings.

The pottery was outward looking in that it sent several of its leading designers to study in Europe. Among these was Artus van Briggle, who came back with the idea of a matt glaze, and this was incorporated into regular production from 1901. Following this, the production of architectural ware, tiles and medallions etc. began.

Taylor died in 1913, and the factory continued to live on its reputation for almost thirty years. Its earlier successes were never repeated, however, and it closed through bankruptcy in 1941.

Early Rookwood art pottery was confined to pieces individually decorated by the artist, and they commonly signed or initialed their works. Often, too these were dated. From 1886 a reversed *R-P* was officially adopted, with a flame point added for each year up to 1900. A Roman numeral was then added after the new century.

Rookwood Pottery sage green standard glaze bowl and creamer, Cincinnati, Mary A. Taylor, 1886, decorated with chrysanthemum in salmon, cream and beige, 2¾in. high. (Skinner) $374

One of a pair of Rookwood stoneware bookends, modeled as sphinx holding books, light brown glaze, 18cm. high. $480

Three Rookwood pottery standard glaze mouse plates, Cincinnati, Ohio, circa 1893, each depicting a mischievous mouse, 7in. diam. (Skinner) $570

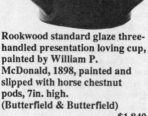

Rookwood standard glaze three-handled presentation loving cup, painted by William P. McDonald, 1898, painted and slipped with horse chestnut pods, 7in. high. (Butterfield & Butterfield) $1,840

Rookwood Pottery high glaze jar, Cincinnati, 1946, decorated with low relief medial band of stylised flowers, 6in. high. (Skinner) $230

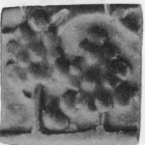

Rookwood faience grape tile, Cincinnati, high relief grapes on the vine, matt glaze decorated in pale purple, teal green and oatmeal, 6in. wide. (Skinner) $345

A Rookwood pottery jardinière, the oviform creamware body enameled in black and white with bats flying over fields, dated *1882*, 21cm. high. (Christie's) $496

ROOKWOOD, JUGS

Rookwood pitcher in a standard glaze with floral decoration, mark of Albert R. Valentine, 1888, 8in. high.
(Eldreds) $715

Rookwood pottery Spanish water jug, Cincinnati, Ohio, 1882, cobalt blue glaze on strap handled, double spout round pitcher, 10in. high.
(Skinner) $440

A Rookwood pottery decorated pitcher, artist's initials MLN for Maria Longworth Nichols, 1882, 6in. high.
(Skinner) $720

Large Rookwood Pottery standard glaze pitcher, Cincinnati, Kataro Shirayamadani, 1890, decorated with floral branch in shades of yellow, orange, green and brown, 12¾in. high.
(Skinner) $3,000

Rookwood Pottery Limoges style jug, Cincinnati, Albert R. Valentien, 1882, with underglaze slip decoration depicting birds in bamboo and clouds in grey, 4¾in. high.
(Skinner) $489

Rookwood pottery vase standard glaze ewer, Cincinnati, Ohio, 1896, by Matthew Daly, underglaze decoration of open petaled white roses against shaded brown green ground, 9¾in. high.
(Skinner Inc.) $400

Rookwood Pottery standard glaze ewer, initialed *M.L.N.,* Maria Longworth Nichols, no. 499 W, decorated with leaves and nuts, 7¼in. high,
(Skinner) $515

Rookwood Pottery sterling silver overlaid standard glaze claret jug, Sallie Toohey, 1896, decorated with stylised leafy twig, 7in. high.
(Skinner) $1,955

Rookwood large corn jug, Sallie Toohey, 1896, standard glaze with four ears of corn, conforming stopper with cork insert, impressed marks, total height 13in.
(Skinner) $1,210

ROOKWOOD, SCENIC PLAQUES

Rookwood Pottery scenic vellum plaque, Cincinnati, Carl Schmidt, 'The Trossachs, Loch Katrine', 10¼in. wide. (Skinner) $4,312

Rookwood pottery scenic vellum plaque, Frederick Rothenbusch, 1915, "Late Autumn" woodland with light snowfall, 10 x 14in. (Skinner Inc.) $1,760

Rookwood scenic vellum plaque, Sara Sax, 1916, 'The Top of the Hill', snow covered landscape, impressed marks, 7³/₈ x 9³/₈in. (Skinner) $4,070

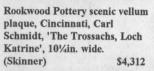

Rookwood pottery scenic plaque, 'The End of Winter', Cincinnati, Ohio, 1918, original frame, 12¼in. x 9¼in. (Skinner Inc.) $2,800

Rookwood Pottery scenic vellum plaque, Cincinnati, E. T. Hurley, woodland pond with birches in shades of blue and salmon with ivory and brown, 14½in. high. (Skinner) $8,625

Rookwood Pottery scenic vellum plaque, signed C. Schmidt, 1921, 12½ x 8½in. $1,600

Rookwood Pottery scenic vellum plaque, Cincinnati, E. T. Hurley, 1913, 'Sunset Through the Birches', dark green foliage against blue/gray foreground, 8¾in. wide. (Skinner) $3,656

Rookwood Pottery scenic vellum plaque, Cincinnati, Fred Rothenbusch, 1912, shoreline windmills and landscape in shades of blue and green, 14¼in. wide. (Skinner) $8,050

Rookwood Pottery scenic vellum plaque, Cincinnati, Ohio, 1914, executed by Edward George Diers, (1896–1931), 10³/₄in. high. (Skinner Inc.) $1,900

ROOKWOOD, VASES

Rookwood Pottery standard glaze vase, Cincinnati, Howard Altman, 1903, decorated with poppies, 6¾in. high.
(Skinner) $518

Rookwood Pottery standard glaze vase dated *1892*, initialed by Harriet Strafer, no. 612 W, 6in. high, 6in. wide.
(Skinner) $400

Rookwood Pottery standard glaze vase, Cincinnati, 1903, decorated with nasturtiums in yellow, rust and green, 8in. high.
(Skinner) $518

Rookwood Pottery wax resist vase, Cincinnati, Ohio, 1928, executed by Elizabeth Neave Lingenfelter Lincoln (1892–1931), 11in. high.
(Skinner Inc.) $300

Rookwood Pottery vase, signed *Elizabeth Neave Lingenfelter Lincoln*, dated *1904*, having chocolate brown to moss green ground, 7in. high.
(Du Mouchelles) $300

Rookwood Pottery matt glaze vase, Cincinnati, Elizabeth N. Lincoln, 1929, with stylised floral decoration in olive green, 4¾in. high.
(Skinner) $403

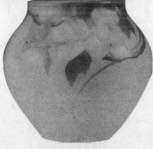

Rookwood Pottery standard glaze vase, Cincinnati, Artus Van Briggle, 1891, two-handle form decorated with daisies, 5¾in. diameter.
(Skinner) $805

Rookwood Pottery vellum vase, 1907, by Edward Diers, decorated with white, yellow and pink Dogwood on a blue-green ground, 6½in. high.
(Skinner) $1,380

Rookwood butterfly handle goose vase, 1891, standard glaze with three geese in flight, blue green areas, impressed marks, 6½in. high.
(Skinner) $825

ROOKWOOD, VASES

Rookwood pottery vase, Cincinnati, Ohio, 1915, with incised line and petal decoration in matte brown glaze, impressed mark 12½in. high. (Skinner Inc.) $400

A Rookwood pottery standard glaze portrait vase, decorated with portrait of a black African with a cap, 1897, 12in. high. (Skinner) $2,400

Rookwood Pottery standard glaze vase, Cincinnati, Geneva O. Reed, 1893, decorated with fern in shades of green, rust and sand, 9¾in. high. (Skinner) $805

A Rookwood standard glaze pottery Indian portrait vase, decorated by Grace Young, date cypher for 1905, 30.5cm. high. $5,200

Two Rookwood Pottery tiger eye vases, Kataro Shirayamadani, Cincinnati, Ohio, (1887–1915 and 1925–1948), 14½in. high. (Skinner Inc.) $2,600

Rookwood Pottery iris glaze vase, Cincinnati, Ohio, 1906, executed by Charles Schmidt (1896–1927), 9⅝in. high. (Skinner Inc.) $3,850

Rookwood Pottery scenic vellum glaze vase, Cincinnati, E. T. Hurley, 1938, red sky sunset, foreground trees in blue, green and pale yellow, 10½in. high. (Skinner) $3,220

Rookwood Pottery porcelain vase, Cincinnati, Ohio, 1925, executed by Kataro Shirayamadani (1865–1948), 8in. high. (Skinner Inc.) $1,000

Rookwood pottery scenic vellum vase, Cincinnati, 1913, decorated with landscape scene in gray-blue on shaded yellow to peach background, 13⅝in. high. (Skinner Inc) $2,000

ROSENTHAL

Philip Rosenthal opened his porcelain factory in 1879 in Selb, Bavaria. It was noted from the first for the high quality of its products. He designed three major services, Darmstadt (1905), Donatello (1907) and Isolde (1910) which at first were left undecorated, but later painted under the glaze in various styles.

From the 1920s figures in Art Deco style were also produced, including theatrical characters and subjects in modern dress, many of which were signed by the artist. Philip Rosenthal died in 1937 and was succeeded by his son, also Philip, who appointed independent artists to work in studios in Selb on pieces which were sold in the Rosenthal studio houses. The firm continues in business today.

Marks include a crown over crossed lines and *Rosenthal*, or over crossed roses.

A Rosenthal figure of a postillon by T. Kärner, 1920–21. (Arnold Frankfurt) $211

A Rosenthal figure 'Merry March' of a woman in carnival costume, circa 1920, 36cm. high. (Kunsthaus am Museum) $746

'Fright'. A Rosenthal porcelain bust of a faun by Ferdinand Liebermann, modeled as a young bare-chested faun holding a set of pan pipes, 39.4cm. high. (Phillips) $1,350

A Rosenthal ceramic sculpture by Gerhard Schliepstein, circa 1930, 50.8cm. high. $2,130

A Rosenthal figure of a female tennis player, striding out on an oval base, by Fritz Klimsch, 1936, 51cm. high. (Kunsthaus am Museum) $743

Rosenthal polychrome figure 'Girl Drinking', signed Ernst Wenck, 1865–1929. (Arnold) $294

A Rosenthal guitar playing pierrot with poodle, seated on a mound, by Rudolf Marcuse, 1913, 33cm. high. (Kunsthaus am Museum) $805

ROSEVILLE

The Roseville Pottery was established in 1892 in Roseville, Ohio, but moved in 1898 to Zanesville, where the general manager, George F Young, began making art pottery in 1900.

Their early Rozane ware was characterised by slip painting on a dark ground, finished with a high glaze, and closely resembled other art pottery being made in Zanesville at the time by the Weller and Owens pottery companies. It was renamed Rozane Royal to distinguish it from subsequent styles.

With competitors in such close proximity, however, it was necessary to develop new styles very quickly, and Roseville soon had a wide and rapidly changing range, which tended more and more towards matt glazing over relief modeling.

Roseville pottery hanging basket, with scalloped edge around the rim, matte green glaze, early-mid 20th century, 8in. diameter.
(Du Mouchelles) $110

Roseville Pottery ewer, circa 1939-1953, of dusty rose glaze with yellow flowers and teal wash, 10in. high.
(Du Mouchelles) $200

Roseville Magnolia cookie jar, 1943-44, urn form with double handles, tan to green rough ground decorated with white and pink magnolia blossoms, 10½in. high.
(Du Mouchelles) $140

Roseville pottery Peony vase, urn form with double handles, having rough shaded aqua green with relief decorated peony, circa 1942, 7¼in. high.
(Du Mouchelles) $85

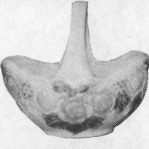

Roseville pottery Bittersweet basket, shaded green ground decorated in low relief with bittersweet with orange berries, circa 1951, 8in. high.
(Du Mouchelles) $85

Roseville pottery jardinière, circa 1915, Donatello pattern with upper band in orange with green and cream ribs below , 8in. high.
(Du Mouchelles) $250

Roseville pottery Rozane Ware basket, circa 1917, stippled light green ground decorated with yellow and lavender roses, 6½in. high.
(Du Mouchelles) $90

ROYAL CAULDON POTTERIES

Cauldon Potteries were born out of Brown, Westhead, Moore & Co. who had been operating at the Cauldon Place Works in Hanley since 1858. From 1904, they traded as Cauldon Ltd., and then, when granted the royal warrant in 1924, they became Royal Cauldon.

Their wide range of products included, during the Art Deco period, several tube-lined types, including their popular Poppy design by Edith Gater, which was used on a number of shapes.

Royal Cauldon ware "Chang" design wall plaque, 1930s, 17¹/₂in. diameter.
(Muir Hewitt) $420

Royal Cauldon Chang pattern jug, 8in. high.
(Muir Hewitt) $90

Royal Cauldon Chang pattern vase, 8in. high.
(Muir Hewitt) $85

A pair of Brown-Westhead Moore & Co. porcelain square jardinières, molded and gilt with masks and strapwork, mark for 1872, 10¾in. high.
(Christie's) $1,693

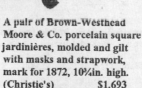

A Brown-Westhead Moore & Co. pottery umbrella stand of hexagonal section, with flared rim and pierced japonaiserie base, painted mark for Cauldon Place Art Studio, late 19th century, 70cm. high.
(Christie's) $775

A Brown-Westhead Moore & Co. pottery charger painted with lions fighting over a lioness, signed and dated 1874?, 63.5cm. high.
(Christie's) $682

A pair of Brown-Westhead Moore & Co. majolica vases, each modeled as three cranes standing around bullrushes, circa 1880, 21cm. high.
(Christie's) $1,350

A good Brown-Westhead & Moore porcelain urn vase, circa 1890, the squat globular body molded with a foliate scrolled band, 10in. high.
(Bonhams) $1,410

ROYAL COPENHAGEN

As its name suggests, the Royal Copenhagen Porcelain Factory was established under the auspices of the Danish Royal family in 1775, and continued under their patronage until it was bought by Aluminia in 1867. In 1884 it was moved to the Aluminia works in the city, under the direction of Philip Schou.

A number of notable artists worked for the company, including G Rode and C F Liisburg, who painted in colored porcelain slip from the 1880s. The factory was notable for its smooth shaped figures decorated in pale colors under a smooth glaze. In the 1890s some abstract elements emerged, but naturalism reasserted itself again later in the work of G Henning and A Malinowski.

There was some experimentation with glazes, with sang-de-boeuf and crystalline glazes being introduced in the 1880s.

From the 1930s figures were almost exclusively of stoneware and relief decorated stoneware vases were also produced. Some styles and decorations also show a strong Chinese influence.

Marks are generally a crown and motif over three waves, sometimes in conjunction with *Denmark, Danmark* or *Royal Copenhagen.*

A Copenhagen snuff box and cover modeled as a pug's head, circa 1780, contemporary silver reeded mount, marked for Hamburg, 6cm. wide. (Christie's Geneva) $5,000

Royal Copenhagen poly-chromed porcelain fairytale group, marked June 10, 1955, 8in. high.
(Skinner) $1,000

An impressive Royal Copenhagen 'Flora Danica' dessert dish and cover, with dentate edge, the bell-shaped cover with pierced basketwork sides, 29cm., printed marks, 20th century.
(Phillips) $3,800

Royal Copenhagen figure in the form of one child reading a book to another child, 7½in. high. (Eldred's) $165

A fine Copenhagen botanical campana vase brilliantly painted with a broad register of specimen flowers, roses, dahlias, asters and lilies, blue wave mark, circa 1810, 43.5cm. high. (Christie's) $45,000

Carl Hallier and Knud Andersen for the Royal Copenhagen Porcelain Manufactory Ltd., vase and cover, with base, 1937, the patinated bronze cover with spherical knop, 8½in.
(Sotheby's) $2,725

ROYAL DUX

Royal Dux is the tradename of the Duxer Prozellanmanufaktur, which was established in 1860 in Dux, Bohemia, now Duchov, Czechoslovakia. It was noted at first for its portrait busts and extravagantly decorated vases, many of which were destined for the American market. From the 1920s onwards it produced Art Deco style figure, of single ladies, dancing couples etc. Marks include an *E* (for the proprietor Eichler) in an oval surrounded by Royal Dux Bohemia set on an embossed pink triangle.

A Royal Dux ceramic centerpiece, with two classical maidens modeled in full relief, 15½in. high. (Christie's S. Ken) $1,087

A Royal Dux ceramic centerpiece modeled as a young maiden draped on a conch shell, 15in. high. (Christie's) $697

A Bretby pottery centerpiece in the style of Royal Dux, modeled as a young maiden in flowing robes perched between conch shells, 15¼in. high. (Christie's) $547

A Royal Dux twin-handled porcelain urn, on square pedestal base, the cylindrical body molded in full relief with two infants embracing above the head of an old man, 14½in. high. (Christie's) $510

A Royal Dux ceramic centerpiece, the base modeled as roots and foliage supporting maiden in flowing robes perched between two shells forming the bowls, 16¼in high. (Christie's) $1,335

A Royal Dux figure of a naked female dancer poised on one leg with a robe draped over her thigh, 14½in. high. (Christie's) $930

A whimsical Royal Dux porcelain group modeled as a small boy in swimming costume squatting down to fondle his devoted pet dog, 6¼in. high. (Christie's) $172

A Royal Dux ceramic figure of a Greek youth wearing a toga and sandals, painted in shades of green sepia and gilt, 17½in. high. (Christie's) $330

ROYAL DUX

Royal Dux porcelain ornament of a conch shell with a nymph attendant, on a rock formed and lily leaf base, 15in. tall. (G. A. Key) $600

A pair of Royal Dux figures, one of a goat-herd wearing a bear skin over his tunic, his companion feeding a lamb from flowers, 52cm. (Bearne's) $1,600

A. Royal Dux figure group, boy in tunic and breeches with setter type dog, on rustic plinth, 13in. wide, pink triangle mark. (Russell Baldwin & Bright) $931

Royal Dux porcelain figural vase, early 20th century, with two Art Nouveau maidens clinging to the sides, 21¹/₂in. high. (Butterfield & Butterfield) $1,955

A pair of Royal Dux book ends in the form of clowns, cream, green and brown designs with gilt work. (G. A. Key) $560

Royal Dux, Art Nouveau porcelain simulated marble bust of a girl wearing a floral bonnet and dress, with applied pink seal mark, 20in. high. (Lawrences) $2,720

Royal Dux, Art Nouveau centerpiece, circa 1900, porcelain glazed in shades of green, brown and rust, 13¹/₂in. high. (Sotheby's) $1,278

A pair of Royal Dux bisque porcelain figures of a rustic boy and girl, the young boy wearing a green hat, the girl wearing a décolleté pink blouse, 17in. high. (Spencer's) $800

A Royal Dux group in the form of Pierrot kissing the hand of a young woman wearing a flowing ball gown, after a design by Schaff, 28.5cm. (Bearne's) $950

ROYAL DUX

A Royal Dux pottery group in the form of a brown and white cow, feeding from a bundle of greenery, 46cm. high.
(Bearne's) **$477**

A pair of Royal Dux figures, in the form of a gardener, his lady companion holding a posy, 40.5cm. high.
(Bearne's) **$1,101**

A Royal Dux porcelain figure group of a Roman charioteer, the chariot drawn by two rearing horses, 46cm. overall.
(Henry Spencer) **$1,600**

A Royal Dux group in the form of a camel, with its rider leaning over in conversation, 50cm. high.
(Bearne's) **$1,932**

'At the Masquerade Ball', a large Royal Dux group, modeled as an elaborately costumed couple dancing, 49cm. high.
(Phillips) **$960**

A Royal Dux bisque porcelain Art Nouveau style flower holder, as a maiden draped in a brown robe seated upon a rocky outcrop, 27cm. high.
(Spencer's) **$856**

A Royal Dux equestrian group, as an elegantly dressed horseman talking to a young peasant girl, impressed pink triangle mark, 16in. high.
(Spencer's) **$1,287**

A pair of Royal Dux figures of a near eastern desert dweller and fishergirl, both wearing green and apricot rustic dress, pink triangle pad mark, 20th century, 24¼in. high.
(Christie's) **$1,425**

A Royal Dux Art Nouveau conch shell group with three water nymphs in relief, 17½in. high.
(Reeds Rains) **$950**

ROYAL DUX

Royal Dux style centerpiece designed as a young lady holding water lily, impress mark 8335, 12in. high. **$320**

A Royal Dux figural dish modeled with a boy and two puppies by a poll, impressed *2106*, 22cm. wide. **$320**

A Royal Dux porcelain group of a dancing couple in blue glazed and gilt Eastern costume, 12¼in. high. **$800**

A Royal Dux Bohemia figural vase modeled as a nude maiden standing leaning against a rocky outcrop, in shades of sepia, green and brown, 39cm. high. (Christie's) **$1,041**

A pair of Royal Dux Bohemia figures of troubadours, in fin de siècle dress, the man with guitar, his companion with mandolin, 80cm. high. (Christie's) **$4,862**

A Royal Dux Bohemia figure of a young woman in Edwardian dress standing leaning against a shell, 17.5cm. high. (Christie's) **$302**

A Royal Dux pottery group modeled as male and female figures in classical garb, 48.5cm. (Phillips) **$470**

A Royal Dux centerpiece, the trefoil base with column modeled as three bare breasted girls kneeling and supporting lily-form bowl, 6½in. high. **$512**

A Royal Dux polychrome wallmask of a young woman wearing a blue floral bonnet and gazing at a butterfly, 20cm. high. (Christie's) **$356**

ROYAL DUX

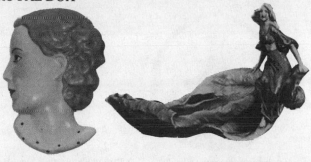

Royal Dux wall mask, 7in. high,
1930s.
(Muir Hewitt) $300

A Royal Dux figure of a maiden
perched on a large leaf,
impressed *855*, 24cm. long.
$400

A large Royal Dux group in
the form of a scantily clad
female welcoming the
returning hunter, 70 cm. high.
(Bearne's) $1,888

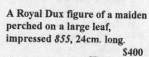

A pair of Royal Dux figures of
water carriers in shades of
sepia green and brown, 70cm.
high. $1,200

A Royal Dux Bohemia Group,
modeled as a Grecian youth
riding a horse and leading
another, 34.5cm. high.
(Christie's) $609

A pair of Royal Dux figures
in the form of a shepherd
and his companion, 49 cm. high.
(Bearne's) $1,661

A Royal Dux bust of a fin de
siècle lady, dressed in ornate
'Lace' bonnet, in pastel shades
of pink, white and blue.
(Phillips) $729

A Royal Dux Bohemia group of
a retriever carrying a
pheasant, painted in shades of
sepia, green and gilt, 41cm.
long.
(Christie's) $313

A Royal Dux Bohemia figure
of a young woman in classical
dress, standing holding a
tambourine, 33cm. high.
(Christie's) $278

ROZENBURG

The Rozenburg factory was established at The Hague in 1885. They produced an extremely thin earthenware with a delicate, translucent body, overglaze painted with patterns of birds and plants inspired by the batik designs of the Dutch East Indies. Enameling in shades of mauve, ocher, orange and green was applied to a clear white ground.

The first Art Director was T. Colenbrander, and another noted designer was J.J. Kok, who juxtaposed flat and curved surfaces to good effect, and favored elongated handles and spouts. The painter J. Schellink contributed decorations of stylized flowers in black, red, purple, green and yellow on a dark green ground.

Earthenware vase with basket handle, by J.L. Verhoog, manufactured at the Hague by Rozenburg, date-coded 1898, 13in. high.
(Skinner Inc.) $1,600

A Rozenburg eggshell porcelain vase painted by R. Schenken, painted in shades of red, green, brown, lilac and yellow, 31.5cm. high, 1902.
(Phillips) $4,420

Unusual pair of Rozenburg pottery vases, the Hague, date coded 1898, decorated with polychrome floral and dragon motif on brown ground, 9¹/₂in. high.
(Skinner Inc.) $1,300

A Rozenburg glazed earthenware vase, painted with flowering creeper and butterflies, circa 1900, 43cm. high.
$517

A Rozenburg pottery vase decorated in mauve, brown, green, blue and yellow, with an elaborate pattern of fleshy flowers, 30cm. high.
(Phillips) $495

Rozenburg thistle wall plate, the Hague, date coded 1898, hand painted with stylized thistle flowers in earthy tones brown, rust and lavender-gray, 10¾in. diameter.
(Skinner Inc.) $700

Large earthenware two-handled vase, Rozenburg, produced at the Hague, date coded 1903, decorated by H.G.A. Huyvehaar, bold polychrome designs of flowers and foliage, 13¹/₂in. high.
(Skinner Inc.) $1,400

RUSKIN

The Ruskin Pottery was founded at West Smethwick, Birmingham, in 1898 by William Howson Taylor (1876–1935) who had trained at the Birmingham School of Art. Throughout his career he was constantly experimenting with glazes and it is these which give his work its principal interest.

Initially, he made 'Soufflé' ware, where the predominant colors were blues, greens, purples, grays and celadons with a glaze in a single color or mottled, clouded or shaded with a harmonising tone.

Luster wares were also made in a wide range of colors and shades, and a pearl luster was introduced, sometimes with a blistered texture and often with a kingfisher blue glaze. Flambé glazes with scattered viridian spots derived from the use of copper salts were produced, and after 1929 matt and crystalline glazes were added to the range. Taylor's High Fired wares featured dramatic color contrasts, for example purple and black streaking on sea green, or black and green on cream.

With regard to the wares produced, many vases were made, some of which could be heavily potted and covered with blue, green, orange or crystalline blue with a frosted effect. The shapes were often based on Chinese styles. Other products included useful tableware, buttons, hatpins and cufflinks, some silver mounted.

Unfortunately Taylor took the secrets of his glazes with him to his grave, determined that his work should not be imitated. Production stopped at the factory in 1933.

Marks include Taylor's name up to 1903, after which *Ruskin* becomes usual, and the pieces are often dated.

A Ruskin high-fired egg-shell stoneware bowl, with dark mottled red glaze clouding to green and purple towards the foot, 21cm. diameter. (Christie's) $2,134

A Ruskin high-fired stoneware vase, the oatmeal ground clouded with green and speckled with irregular areas of purple and blue, 1915, 21.cm. high. (Christie's) $2,134

A Ruskin Pottery high-fired stoneware vase, with matt white ground, mottled purple beneath fragmented duck egg speckled with green-black, impressed pottery seal *Ruskin Pottery West Smethwick*, dated *1908*, 31.6cm. high. (Christie's) $2,363

A Ruskin high-fired stoneware bowl, the exterior glazed in deep red clouding over gray the interior red speckled with purple and green, 1933, 24.5cm. diameter. (Christie's) $1,450

A Ruskin high-fired stoneware bowl, the oatmeal ground mottled overall in dove-gray overlaid with red and purple clouding, with green speckling, 31cm. diameter. (Christie's) $3,200

A Ruskin high-fired stoneware vase, pale ground mottled overall in purples and greens fragmented with random 'snake-skin' patterning, 1914, 32.3cm. high. (Christie's) $3,201

RUSKIN

A Ruskin Pottery high-fired stoneware vase, with tall cylindrical neck, gray ground with mottled liver-red and mauve, 1924, 29cm. high. (Christie's) $766

A Ruskin Pottery high-fired stoneware bowl, the white exterior with mottled gray, the interior with mottled liver red and purple with speckled well, impressed *Ruskin England, 1927*, 24.2cm. diameter. (Christie's) $1,378

A rare Ruskin Pottery high-fired stoneware vase, tall mallet-shaped, mottled gray ground with areas of cloudy and mottled blue, impressed *Ruskin England, 1924*, 37cm. high. (Christie's) $3,544

A Ruskin Pottery high-fired stoneware vase, with flared cylindrical neck, white ground beneath mottled green with slight red veining, impressed *Ruskin England 1914*, 17.6cm. high. (Christie's) $1,477

A Ruskin Pottery high-fired eggshell stoneware bowl, the interior covered in a mottled jade green glaze, the exterior mottled liver red speckled with green, 17cm. diameter. (Christie's) $2,757

A Ruskin Pottery high-fired stoneware vase, white ground covered in mottled greenish buff glaze beneath clouds of dark maroon and blue, impressed *Ruskin England 1922*, 22.5cm. high. (Christie's) $2,363

A Ruskin Pottery high-fired ginger jar on stand, with domed cover, on tripod stand, covered in a gray with mottled liver and purple-red and green-black speckling, 11.2cm. high. (Christie's) $1,378

A small Ruskin Pottery high-fired bowl, with flared circular foot, gray ground with mottled liver red and purple glaze speckled with green, 8.6cm. high. (Christie's) $788

A Ruskin Pottery high-fired vase, with tapering neck and flared rim, band of molded floral decoration, covered in a mottled oatmeal glaze, 27cm. high. (Christie's) $591

RUSKIN

A Ruskin high fired lamp base, of tapering cylindrical form with bulbous neck, impressed factory marks, 8¾in. high.
(Christie's) $763

A Ruskin Pottery high-fired stoneware bowl, with three pulled notches, gray ground beneath mottled liver red with cloudy purple and turquoise and pitted green-black speckles, 21cm. high.
(Christie's) $1,969

A Ruskin high fired stoneware bottle vase covered in a mottled pink glaze flecked with blue and jade green, 1924, 6½in. high.
(Christie's) $497

A large Ruskin Pottery high-fired stoneware vase on stand, the white ground mottled with liver red, blue and purple beneath speckled green, on ornate tripod stand, impressed *Ruskin, 1914*, 44.5cm. high.
(Christie's) $6,301

A Ruskin Pottery high-fired eggshell stoneware bowl, pierced with floral roundels, red-purple glaze fading to mottled mauve and green towards the well, impressed *Ruskin England 1924*, 15cm. diameter.
(Christie's) $1,378

A Ruskin Pottery high-fired stoneware vase and cover, with short cylindrical neck, the domed cover with knopped finial, dove gray ground fragmented with random gray and green 'snake-skin' patterning.
(Christie's) $9,845

A Ruskin Pottery high-fired stoneware vase, with everted rim, white ground beneath liver red and dove gray streaked glaze, 23.6cm. high.
(Christie's) $1,969

A Ruskin Pottery high-fired stoneware vase, swollen form tapering to cylindrical neck, covered in a mottled gray glaze, impressed *Ruskin England 1927*, 9.5cm. high.
(Christie's) $236

A Ruskin Pottery high-fired stoneware vase, with flared rim, covered in a mottled dove gray speckled glaze, impressed *Ruskin*, 24cm. high.
(Christie's) $1,969

SALTGLAZE WARE

A saltglaze effect is achieved by glazing during the firing with salt thrown into the kiln at a temperature above 2,000°F, where it combines chemically with the silicate in the clays to form a durable sodium silicate glaze which has the orange-peel appearance associated with Chinese porcelain.

Most early saltglaze ware is coarse and brown, but after the 1740s, when Staffordshire potters had achieved a light white stoneware body comparable in delicacy and durability with Chinese porcelain, the process was also used very successfully with this.

A Staffordshire saltglaze bear-jug and cover of conventional type, covered in chippings and clasping a dog, circa 1750, 26.5cm. high.
(Christie's) $6,400

A Staffordshire saltglaze solid-agate model of a cat, circa 1750, modeled to the right with brown and buff clays, brown slip eyes and splashed with blue on the ears and back, 5in. high.
(Christie's) $1,610

A Staffordshire saltglaze small cream-jug, circa 1745, of pear shape, with reeded strap handle and enameled in colors with a gardener in blue jacket, 3⅛ in.
(Christie's) $1,495

A pair of Staffordshire saltglaze white cornucopia wall vases, circa 1750, each with a spirally-fluted body beneath a valanced rim molded with a naked boy amongst fruiting vines, 9in. high.
(Sotheby's) $2,185

A Staffordshire saltglaze balu-ster coffee pot and cover, pain-ted with loose bouquets and flower-sprays within puce and iron-red loop and foliage rims circa 1755.
(Christie's) $8,800

A Staffordshire saltglaze globular teapot and cover, circa 1760, with pierced waisted knop, foliate-molded spout and crabstock handle and enameled in colors with cupid shooting an arrow at a maiden seated beside an arbor, 4½in. high.
(Christie's) $5,750

A Staffordshire saltglaze flaring cylindrical coffee-pot and cover, circa 1760, with flattened spire finial, dome cover, scroll spout and handle, the front and back painted in iron-red with a still life of fruit, baskets, cornucopia and butterflies, 8⅞in. high.
(Christie's) $18,400

A Staffordshire saltglaze quatrefoil teapot and cover, circa 1745, the domed cover molded with four shells and enameled in the famille rose style with half flowerheads and a band of trellis broken by floral panels, 5in. high.
(Christie's) $2,185

A Staffordshire saltglaze teapot and cover with loop handle and the spout molded with a maskhead and a serpent, 14.5cm. high.
(Phillips) $782

An English saltglazed coffee pot and cover, with a bird spout and a strap handle with pinched terminal, 8¼in. high, circa 1740.
(Bonhams) $4,480

A Staffordshire saltglaze teapot and cover with crabstock spout and handle, painted in colors with panels of flowers on a mulberry ground, 13cm. high.
(Phillips) $442

A Nottingham brown saltglaze small bulbous tankard, circa 1700, possibly by John Morley, pierced with scrolling flowering foliage, 3⅞in. high.
(Christie's) $2,990

A rare pair of Brampton saltglazed stoneware King Charles spaniels, on oval bases applied with a fruiting vine, circa 1830, 14¾in. high.
(Neales) $3,360

A documentary Staffordshire saltglaze 'scratch blue' inkstand, circa 1761, cylindrical, the upper surface with four pen holes and a central well, inscribed 'WM 1761', 2in. high.
(Christie's) $2,185

A Staffordshire brown saltglaze teapot and cover, circa 1745, possibly Joshua Twyford, with crabstock finial, spout and handle and applied allover with scrolling fruiting vine and flowers, 3½in. high.
(Christie's) $690

A rare Staffordshire saltglaze yellow-ground teapot and a cover, circa 1750, the hexagonal body molded on each side within a recessed oval panel with a chinoiserie scene, 5⅛in. high.
(Sotheby's) $1,265

A Staffordshire saltglaze quatrefoil teapot and cover circa 1745, probably by Thomas and John Wedgwood, 'Big House', Burslem, with acorn finial, scaled serpent scroll spout and notched loop handle, 4⅝in. high.
(Christie's) $3,220

A fine white saltglaze sauceboat, circa 1745-50, following a silver shape with barbed rim and wishbone handle, 13.5cm. long. (Phillips) $1,575

A Staffordshire saltglaze two-handled cup, circa 1765, enameled in colors with a Chinaman seated in a garden and a Turk seated at a table, 4³/₄in. high. (Christie's) $2,420

A Staffordshire saltglaze sauceboat, circa 1760, the spout molded with a leaf and enameled in colors with a lady playing the harpsichord, 7⁷/₈in. wide. (Christie's) $3,850

A salt-glazed stoneware tankard of cylindrical form incised with simple foliage enclosing royal cypher of George III, circa 1780, 12in. high. (Christie's) $320

A Staffordshire saltglaze scratch blue teabowl and saucer, circa 1765, with stylized lollipop flowers and chevron border. (Christie's) $1,035

A Staffordshire saltglaze small mug or cup, circa 1750, of bell shape with grooved strap handle, 7.2cm. (Phillips) $1,450

A Staffordshire saltglaze solid-agate model of a seated cat, circa 1745, in dark-brown and buff clays with blue ears and splashed in blue, 4in. high. (Christie's) $4,950

A Staffordshire saltglaze documentary two-handled footed cup, inscribed H/RE 1762, 14.3cm. high. (Christie's) $6,325

A Staffordshire saltglaze arbor group, circa 1760, modeled as a couple seated beneath an arbor, his hand on her bare knee, 6in. high. (Christie's) $60,500

SALTGLAZE

A Staffordshire white saltglaze footed globular teapot and cover, circa 1750, with acorn finial and loop handle, 4½in. high.
(Christie's) $805

A Staffordshire saltglaze solid-agate model of a cat, circa 1750, in buff and brown clays, splashed in blue, 11.8cm. high.
(Christie's) $2,530

A Staffordshire saltglaze teapot and cover, circa 1760, of globular shape with a straight spout and plain handle, 9.5cm. high.
(Phillips) $1,716

A Staffordshire saltglaze scratch blue puzzle jug, circa 1760, with scroll handle and rim applied with shells and berries, 21.6cm. high.
(Christie's) $1,725

A Staffordshire saltglaze Jacobite quatrefoil teapot and cover, circa 1760, enameled in colors with Charles II in the branches above the shells, 5¼in. high.
(Christie's) $8,250

A large Staffordshire saltglaze candlestick group, circa 1755, modeled as two cranes, each standing on either side of a bamboo candle-holder, 11¾in. high.
(Christie's) $110,000

A Staffordshire saltglaze scratch blue documentary cylindrical tea canister, inscribed *Grace Leigh 1754*, 8.9cm. high overall.
(Christie's) $1,495

A Staffordshire saltglaze documentary shaped inkwell, dated *1745*, the base inscribed *Alex: Ready Esq.r 1745*, 6.2cm. high.
(Christie's) $2,300

A Staffordshire saltglaze scratch blue teabowl and saucer, circa 1750, with very stylized flowering branches beneath a band of swags.
(Christie's) $460

SAMSON

Edmé Samson set up his porcelain factory in Paris in 1845 with the intention of making reproductions of the most popular pieces produced by other makers in both China and Europe.

Samson's pieces were made mainly from a grayish-hued hard paste porcelain, even where the originals had been in soft paste, and a bluish tinged glaze is found particularly on Chinese inspired examples. In fact, it can be very difficult to tell these Chinese reproductions from the originals. The body used is very similar, though Samson's wares have a smooth finish as opposed to the 'orange-peel' texture of Chinese porcelain. In the main, the Chinese wares which were imitated were 'Export' pieces decorated in the European style in famille rose and famille verte palettes, and they often featured armorial decoration. English production was not so popular on the Continent at the time. Bow, Chelsea and Derby figures were, however, produced in considerable numbers.

Reproductions of St Cloud and Chantilly pieces were very popular however, in particular their celebrated cachepots, the originals of which were already beyond most purses. Meissen was another favorite source on inspiration, and here again it is sometimes difficult to tell the original from the copy, although the Samson pieces tend to have a light speckling on the body and a blackening of the base. Their appearance overall is somewhat glassier, and the colors harsher. Strangely, Italian porcelain escaped Samson's attentions almost entirely, though many copies of tin-glazed earthenwares such as Deruta and Gubbio were made. Iznik pottery was another prime target.

A pair of ormolu-mounted famille rose Samson porcelain vases and lids, each with domed hexagonal lid, the porcelain late 19th century, 17in. high. (Christie's) $3,229

Pair of Samson porcelain busts, Princess De Lambrell and Henry IV, 5in., French, 19th century. (G. A. Key) $278

Pair of Samson porcelain figure ornaments, 'Presentation of Ribbons' and 'The Hairdresser', 7in. high. (G. A. Key) $680

A Samson armorial plate in the Compagnie des Indes style, painted with a central coat-of-arms, circa 1880, 16¼in. diameter. (Christie's) $497

Pair of French gilt-bronze-mounted Samson porcelain three light candelabra, signed *Leverrier, Paris*, circa 1900, the baluster form porcelain bodies decorated in the famille verte palette, height 17in. (Butterfield & Butterfield) $1,610

A pair of Samson white figures of Saints Andrew and John, the former standing before his cross, the latter holding the Book of Revelation, circa 1880, 15½in. high. (Christie's) $2,250

SAMSON

A fine and large pair of French figures of a lady and gentleman in Meissen style, wearing elaborate 18th century costume, 20in. high.
(Spencer's) $1,288

Samson porcelain teapot and cover with fluted molded body, domed lid, shaped handle and spout.
(G. A. Key) $131

Pair of Samson porcelain figures, young boy and girl representative of the Seasons, late 19th century, 5³/₄in.
(G. A. Key) $140

A Samson jar and pierced cover with artichoke finial, applied with shell molded handles, painted in the famille rose style, late 19th century, 12in. high.
(Christie's) $479

A pair of Samson models of Bolognese hounds, after Meissen originals, each modeled seated with gray or brown markings, 9in. high, the largest.
(Christie's) $2,645

Samson porcelain tea caddy of rectangular section form, polychrome decoration with engraved body in the manner of the Worcester factory, 19th century, 4in.
(G. A. Key) $42

A large pair of Samson famille rose baluster jars and domed covers, each painted with shaped panels of figures in fenced gardens, 25in. high.
(Christie's) $3,358

A pair of Samson models of pugs, 19th century, faint blue marks at back, both with pink collars fixed with bells and attached at the back with blue bows, 4¹/₄in. high.
(Christie's) $1,589

A pair of Samson figural candelabra, late 19th century, bearing gold anchor marks, modeled in the Chelsea style with Neptune and Amphitrite, 14³/₄in. high.
(Christie's) $3,738

SATSUMA

From the 16th century pottery was made at Kagoshima (formerly Satsuma) prefecture in Japan. Korean potters provided the early inspiration - the main kilns at Naeshirogawa and Ryumonji were developed under them, and early pieces are notably Korean or Chinese in style.

From the 18th century however, Satsuma ware is essentially a hard, gray-white or vellum colored earthenware with a crackle glaze, which is embellished with extravagant gilding and enameling. It was introduced to the West at the Universal Exhibition in Paris in 1867.

CHINA

A Satsuma rectangular box and cover decorated in various colored enamels with a shaped panel depicting ladies and children in a lakeside landscape in Spring, signed *Ryozan*, late 19th century, 14cm. long. (Christie's) $6,400

A fine Satsuma vase, the body painted with a samurai, women and children under trees in a winter landscape, signed *Seikozan*, 37.4cm. high. (Bearne's) $8,456

A small deep Satsuma bowl, the central hexagonal roundel containing the word renchu (a company), beneath which numerous figures converse merrily, the reverse decorated with dense chrysanthemum blossoms and butterflies, signed Shizan, Meiji period (1868-1912) 9.9cm. diameter. (Christie's) $2,500

A pair of Satsuma vases decorated in various colored enamels and gilt, the tapering cylindrical bodies with a continuous decoration of bijin and children strolling in an extensive landscape, signed *Seikozan zo*, late 19th century, 11.8cm. high. (Christie's) $2,900

A small Satsuma dish decorated in various colored enamels and gilt, the interior with the Takarabune laden with the Seven Gods and their attributes, the rim with overlapping fan design, made by Nakamura Baikei, late 19th century, 12cm. diameter. (Christie's) $3,600

A large Satsuma vase decorated in various colored enamels and gilt with a profusion of chrysanthemums and other flowers and foliage, late 19th century, 46cm. high. (Christie's) $10,000

A globular jar painted and heavily gilt with three roundels enclosing a shishi lion above waves and peonies, 11in. high. (Christie's) $15,286

Satsuma style lidded vase, Meiji Period, finely painted in gilt and polychrome enamels with a kikko-diaper ground, 11½in. high. (Butterfield & Butterfield) $1,100

SATSUMA

An Imperial globular jar with short flaring neck, painted and gilt with panels of peonies and Buddhistic lions, 4½in. high. (Christie's) $800

A Satsuma figure of Kannon, the seated divinity wearing an elaborate necklace and robes decorated with swirling cloud, mon and lozenge design, signed *Yasukyo saku*, late 19th century, 61.5cm. high. (Christie's) $7,200

An Imperial model of Kannon seated on a caparisoned elephant, her hands clasped together, wearing a high cowl and flowing robes, 7¼in. high. (Christie's) $800

A pair of Imperial tapering cylindrical vases with slightly flaring necks, painted and gilt with broad bands of chrysanthemum sprays, signed *Satsuma yaki Masanobu*, 18.5cm. high. (Christie's) $1,280

A Satsuma rectangular vase with panels alternately depicting chrysanthemums beneath bamboo beside a stream among brushwork fences and kimono stands, Satsuma mon, signed Satsuma yaki Tokozan, late 19th century, 24cm. high. (Christie's) $5,600

A pair of ovoid vases painted and gilt with tapering rectangular panels of butterflies amongst chrysanthemums, 9¾in. high. (Christie's) $5,308

A flaring conical teapot and cover with loop handle and angular spout, painted and gilt with a broad band of chrysanthemum sprays, signed *Meizan sei*, 9in. high. (Christie's) $7,200

A pair of bottle vases with lightly flaring knopped necks, the globular bodies painted and gilt with scattered sprays of magnolia, signed *Dai Nippon Taizan sei*, 12in. high. (Christie's) $1,280

An Imperial oviform vase painted and gilt with chrysanthemum sprays and leafy plants issuing from a fenced garden, signed *Shosen*, 6½in. high. (Christie's) $4,000

A large Satsuma two-handled tripod-footed koro and cover decorated with a border of butterflies and flowers, signed *Fujo Satsuma Kinran-toki*, *Tokozanzo* and *Satsuma mon*, 19th century, 48cm. high.
(Christie's) $18,200

Two Satsuma eggcups decorated in various colored enamels and gilt with scenes of threshing, harvesting and other activities, signed *Kinkozan zo*, Meiji Period (1868–1912), 6.5cm. high.
(Christie's) $2,500

A tripod flaring cylindrical koro painted and gilt with chrysanthemums issuing from behind wicker fences, 5¹/₂in. high.
(Christie's) $2,548

A lobed cylindrical vase painted and gilt with raised alternating panels of birds, ladies and children at leisure on a riverbank before a high mountain, 7in. high, signed *Tanimoto Ryozan*.
(Christie's) $2,079

A pair of ovoid vases with molded dragon handles painted and heavily gilt with Buddhist figures and dragons below pavilions and rockwork, 10in. high, signed *Chikuho Ryo zo.*
(Christie's) $1,906

A hexagonal jar and domed cover modeled as a shrine, painted and gilt with panels depicting fishermen before Mount Fuji, 6³/₄in. high, signed *Nambe*.
(Christie's) $1,525

A teapot and domed cover with snake finial and dragon spout, painted and heavily gilt with fan-shaped panels of warriors, 7¹/₂in. high.
(Christie's) $1,274

A pair of ovoid vases painted and gilt with panels of ladies and children at leisure in flower strewn gardens, 12¹/₂in. high, signed *Ryuun Fuzan*.
(Christie's) $1,213

19th century Satsuma porcelain figure of a boy playing a drum, his gilded robe richly decorated in black, red, white and blue, 38cm. high.
(Finarte) $5,726

SATSUMA

A heavily gilt group of Kannon seated on a caparisoned elephant, wearing flowing robes and a high cowl, 12¹/₂in. high, signed *Dai Nihon, Satsuma-yaki Hotoda*. (Christie's) $780

A pair of vases with pierced angular handles painted and gilt with shaped panels of figures at leisure on terraces, 7¹/₂in. high, signed *Satsuma-yaki Gyozan zo*. (Christie's) $554

A tripod koro and pierced domed cover modeled as a lantern, painted and heavily gilt overall with a design of chrysanthemum flowerheads, 5¹/₂in. high, signed *Nikko*. (Christie's) $901

Satsuma covered censer, Meiji period, signed *Shuzan*, well painted in gilt and polychrome enamels with a dense ground of scattered blossoms and diaper patterns surrounding two large reserves, 6¹/₄in. high. (Butterfield & Butterfield) $2,588

A pair of trumpet-shaped Satuma vases and bases, signed *Satsuma Yasui Zo*, 19th century decorated with Bentens Daruma and other legendary figures, 23.5cm. high. (Christie's) $1,200

A large globular lobed koro and domed cover with kiku head finial, painted and richly gilt with a continuous band of wisteria hanging from a fence above chrysanthemum, 13¹/₄in. high, signed and dated *Kizan Tempo V (1834)*. (Christie's) $15,593

A Satsuma tripod koro, 19th century, decorated in various colored enamels and gilt with lobed square panels each filled with two ho-o birds, 12.5cm. high.(Christie's) $2,775

A pair of ovoid vases with short flaring necks, painted and heavily gilt with scenes of the Immortals, 17¹/₂in. high. (Christie's) $17,409

A combination Satsuma mask and bowl, the mask in the form of a chubby face, the jet black hair decorated with flowers, 22.3cm. high. (Bearne's) $2,309

SATSUMA

A bowl painted and heavily gilt to the interior with a central roundel of peonies attached to canes, 5in. diameter, signed *Kinkozan*.
(Christie's) $2,548

A square dish with canted corners painted and heavily gilt with numerous figures and children, 7¹/₂in. wide.
(Christie's) $8,067

A shallow Satsuma dish with foliate rim decorated in various colored enamels and gilt, the well depicting a cockerel and hen, signed *Kizan*, late 19th century, 15.9cm. diameter.
(Christie's) $1,250

A good Japanese Satsuma cricket basket and cover, with looped handle and pierced sides, painted with floral panels, 7in. high.
(John Nicholson) $1,950

A good small pair of Japanese Satsuma vases, with lion ring handles, the body painted with birds and flowers, 7¹/₂in. high.
(John Nicholson) $630

A vase painted and gilt with a cockerel, hen and chicks beside a river bank in a landscape, 8¹/₄in. high.
(Christie's) $2,760

A fine and large Satsuma oviform jar and cover with three shaped panels depicting flowering shoots of peony and chrysanthemum, signed *Nihon Satsuma, Kinran Toki, Tokozan zo*, late 19th century, 52.5cm. high.
(Christie's) $56,000

A small Satsuma lobed bowl, the exterior with a band containing seated figures praying, conversing, arguing, a lower band with various personal items, signed Kaizan sei, late 19th century, 11.1cm. diameter.
(Christie's) $2,400

A Satsuma shallow dish with a lobed rim decorated in various colored enamels, and gilt with a central roundel depicting Tadazumi slaying the nue watched by Yorimasa, signed Kozan, late 19th century, 11.8cm. wide.
(Christie's) $960

SATSUMA

A Satsuma beaker, the exterior with a continuous decoration of three levels from the heavenly to the terrestial, with Kannon, birds, students and bijin, signed *Inkinzan zo*, late 19th century, 8.6cm. high.
(Christie's) $2,160

A good small Japanese Satsuma square dish, with floral gold painted border, the center painted with a lakeland landscape, 6in. wide.
(John Nicholson) $2,325

A Satsuma koro and cover in the shape of a basket tied in a large bag decorated in various colored enamels and gilt, signed *Kinkozan*, late 19th century, 9.9cm. high.
(Christie's) $4,800

A large reticulated koro and pierced domed cover modeled as a kiku head with upright square handles, 14¹/₂in. high.
(Christie's) $13,800

Pair of large Satsuma style vases, Meiji Period, signed *Tulzun*, each with everted rim and pear-shape body, 13¹/₄in. high.
(Butterfield & Butterfield) $1,210

An ovoid ewer and domed cover with a dragon spout, handle and finial, painted and gilt with chrysanthemums, 7¹/₄in. high.
(Christie's) $3,821

A Satsuma shallow dish decorated with a scene of courtiers marveling at the beauty of a lady's kimono within a circle of stylized fungus pattern, signed *Kinkozan zo*, Meiji period (1868–1912), 30.6cm. diameter.
(Christie's) $3,350

A fine reticulated Satsuma vase with four leaf-shaped panels alternately depicting bijin with children in an extensive landscape and river scenes with cranes, blossom and other birds, Satsuma mon, signed Ryozan zo, late 19th century, 17.4cm. high.
(Christie's) $13,600

A Satsuma tripod koro, the body with three irregularly shaped panels depicting civic and military scenes on a ground of massed chrysanthemum heads and other flowers, signed *Hotado*, late 19th century, approx. 7.8cm. high.
(Christie's) $3,600

SATURDAY EVENING GIRLS

This intriguing title (*SEG* is the usual mark) is found on the products of the Paul Revere Pottery, which was set up at the beginning of the 20th century for the purpose of training girls from poor immigrant families in Boston. The profits from the pottery were used to fund the girls' education in other subjects. The output mainly consisted of earthenware, nursery and breakfast bowls and dishes and these were decorated with birds, flowers or mottoes, often around the borders.

Saturday Evening Girls pottery decorated bowl, Boston, 1912, artist initialed *S.G.* for Sara Galner, 10¾in. diam.
(Skinner) $960

Saturday Evening Girls pottery motto plate, Mass., 1914, signed S.G. for Sara Galner, 7½in. diam.
(Skinner) $5,200

Saturday evening girl's decorated cream pitcher, Boston, circa 1910, signed S.E.G., 191-5-10 I.G., 3in. high.
(Skinner) $1,280

Decorated Saturday Evening Girls pottery pitcher and bowl, Boston, 1918, both with rabbit and turtle border.
(Skinner Inc.) $480

Saturday Evening Girl Pottery vase, Boston, Massachusetts, 1922, with incised and painted band of tulip decoration, 6¾in. high.
(Skinner Inc.) $325

Saturday Evening Girls Pottery decorated motto pitcher. Boston, Massachusetts, early 20th century, 9¾in. high.
(Skinner Inc.) $2,200

Saturday Evening Girls pottery bowl, green glazed half-round with sgraffito interior border of yellow nasturtium blossoms, 8½in. diameter.
(Skinner Inc.) $960

Early 20th century Saturday evening girl's decorated pitcher, Boston, signed S.E.G. 276-1-10, 9½in. high.
(Skinner) $5,600

SAVONA

The Ligurian coast thrived as a pottery center from the sixteenth century. Most commonly found today, however, are the wares marked with the arms of Savona or a crudely drawn lighthouse, dating from the seventeenth and eighteenth centuries. These tend to be heavily potted in a baroque style which imitates contemporary silver forms. The decoration is usually in blue, and in Ming style. Sometimes rather crudely painted polychrome pieces also appear.

One of the major workshops was that of Sebastian Falco, whose pieces bear a falcon mark. He specialised in a speckled manganese ground with tiny scenes in reserved panels.

The Borelli family too were making tin-glazed earthenware as early as 1735, in the Castelli style, and the family tradition was maintained into the early nineteenth century. They produced some figures, some painted and some in the biscuit state, and a pleasant butter-colored creamware.

An Italian maiolica wet drug jar named for *Ol. D. Scorp. Sem.* in manganese on a banner above a shield, circa 1721, probably Savona, 8³/₄in. high. (Christie's) $927

A Savona large Jar, painted in blue with a Roman soldier on horseback pursuing a stag, 23.5cm., shield mark. (Phillips) $2,790

A pair of Savona faience figures of a gardener leaning on a watering can, his companion with a hurdy-gurdy, circa 1760, 20cm. high. (Christie's) $4,000

A Savona blue and white oviform wet-drug jar, titled in manganese *S. de Pharfara* between bands of foliage, circa 1720, 7³/₄in. high. (Christie's) $548

An Italian maiolica syrup jar named for *Sy. Viol. Sol* in manganese on a banner on a ground of stylized flowers and foliage, circa 1700, Savona or Nove, 7¹/₄in. high. (Christie's) $927

A Savona blue and white circular stand; the well painted with a bird in flight above fortified buildings within a border of figures and animals in landscape, 18th century, 9in. diameter. (Christie's) $913

A Savona faïence polychrome teapot and cover, Albisola Factory, circa 1765, the bullet-shaped body with a powdered manganese ground reserved on either side with a yellow-edged quatrefoil panel, 5¹/₄in. high. (Sotheby's) $1,265

SÈVRES

Porcelain production began at Sèvres in 1756 when the Vincennes factory was moved there, and the first 14 years of its output are considered by many to be unsurpassed.

At first, a soft paste porcelain was made, with silky glazes and richly ornate decoration. It was hugely expensive to make, however, and had the further disadvantage that it could not be molded into complex shapes, which tended to fracture in the kiln. Nevertheless, it was dear to the heart of Louis XV, who was wholly responsible for funding the operation, and his mistress Mme de Pompadour. He assisted it further by issuing several decrees granting virtual monopolies in favor of Sèvres, and even acted as salesman in chief, holding annual exhibitions at Versailles and selling off the pieces to his court.

Sèvres products are remarkable for their brilliant ground colors and chemists were constantly at work developing new tones. Honey gilding, then a virtually new technique, was also widely used, while a host of flower and figure painters (Louis engaged fan painters for this) added their designs. With regard to form, tableware shapes largely followed those of the delicate lines of contemporary silver. Sèvres was also famous for its soft-paste biscuit models, notably in the period 1757-66, when Etienne Maurice Falconet was chief modeler.

By 1769, Sèvres was moving over to hard paste manufacture, and this period coincided with a change to more severe, neo-Classical forms, while decoration too became very much simpler. On many pieces, indeed, this was reduced to a simple ground color with gilding.

A pair of Sèvres style ormolu-mounted turquoise ground urns and covers, late 19th century, with ring in scroll handles headed by female herms, 16in. high. (Christie's) $6,800

A Sèvres two-handled écuelle, cover and stand painted with alternate garlands of pink roses and berried laurel, date letter *r* for 1770, 26.5cm. wide. (Christie's) $5,917

A pair of Sèvres green-ground pots à fard painted with figures by buildings, strolling and fishing in wooded river landscapes within gilt scroll, date letter E for 1757, 9cm. high. (Christie's) $15,200

A Sèvres bleu celeste milk-jug painted with a bouquet of flowers and fruit reserved within a chased gilt line cartouche, date letter *J* for 1762, incised 4, 12cm. high. (Christie's) $3,000

A pair of gilt-metal-mounted Sèvres-patten dark-blue-ground vases and covers with drum-shaped bodies and tall trumpet necks, circa 1880, 22in. high. (Christie's) $4,968

A Sèvres coffee-can and saucer with blue oeil-de-perdrix on a pale-pink-ground reserved with circular medallions painted with pink roses, circa 1765. (Christie's) $1,250

SÈVRES

Ground colors changed too, not always for the better. Nor did biscuit figures adapt very well, having a grayer cast in hard paste and becoming more classical in form. After the departure of Falconet for the Russian court, various sculptors were employed to produce reduced size copies of their own works, and they sought to reproduce in the new medium, the appearance of marble, but without surface glaze or shine.

On the abolition of the monarchy Sèvres was taken over by the State in 1793. Under Napoleon's appointee Brogniart, soft paste was finally abandoned (it was revived again in the late 1840s) in favor of a new hard paste formula which was particularly suitable for tableware.

Soft paste wares are clearly marked in blue enamel with the usual crossed *Ls* motif and a date letter (doubled after 1777). In hard paste, a crown is placed above the blue mark from 1769-79. After 1793 a date appears instead of the letter.

Fake Sèvres pieces abound, and it is important to be able to distinguish between hard and soft paste wares. This can be done by viewing obliquely so that the light penetrates both the ground color and the painting. If it is soft paste, the transparency will be seen to be consistent throughout. On hard paste the painting will form a slight shadow against the close texture of the paste over which both glaze and color form a thin coating.

Genuine Sèvres soft paste porcelain has a virtually clear glaze, not uneven as found in forgeries. On more recent forgeries too the colors are not blended with the glaze as was the case with the originals.

A pair of gilt-metal-mounted Sèvres-pattern vases and covers, the dark-blue grounds painted with mythological scenes, late 19th century, 39½in. high. (Christie's) $16,434

A Sèvres sucrier and cover painted in colors with Watteauesque scenes of figures in landscapes, 8cm., date letter for 1756. (Phillips) $1,275

A pair of Sèvres style turquoise ground seaux, 19th century, with foliage scroll handles, the bucket shapes painted with reserves of court figures, 5½in. diameter. (Christie's) $1,900

A pair of Sèvres style turquoise ground vases and covers, with gilt entwined serpent handles, the tapering forms painted with wide bands of court figures in classical landscapes, 19in. high. (Christie's) $2,750

A pair of Sèvres-style tapering cylindrical gilt-metal mounted vases and covers, painted in colors with lovers in landscape, circa 1880, 18¾in. high. (Christie's) $3,329

A Sèvres armorial bleu nouveau dessert-plate from the Sudell service, the center painted with a yellow and black bird, 1793, 20.7cm. diameter. (Christie's) $5,410

SEVRES

409

SÈVRES

A Sèvres white biscuit group of La Pêche after the original model by Falconet, formed as two maidens and putti with fish, printed marks for 1886 and 1892, 13in. high.
(Christie's) $2,011

A pair of very large Sèvres style earthenware vases with ovoid bodies painted with rustic lovers in Boucher style, signed *Maglin*, circa 1860.
(Phillips) $45,706

A gilt-metal-mounted Sèvres-pattern vase of broad and squat form, the body painted with figures wearing 18th century dress at a marriage banquet, late 19th century, 28¹/₂in. high.
(Christie's) $8,217

A pair of Sèvres-pattern cylindrical jars and covers painted with narrow blue and gilt vertical stripes entwined with pink ribbon and gilt foliage divided by loose bouquets of flowers, late 19th century, 13.5cm. high.
(Christie's) $680

A Sèvres-pattern dark-blue-ground sugar-bowl and cover of shaped-cylindrical form with a flower finial, painted in the style of Morin with figures on shores, imitation blue interlaced L marks, late 19th century, 5¹/₄in. high.
(Christie's) $673

Pair of 'Sèvres' porcelain covered urns, late 19th century, each ovoid vessel painted with four portraits of members of the 18th century court on a raised oval jeweled 'frame' blue interlaced *L*, height 20¹/₂in.
(Butterfield & Butterfield)
                          $2,875

A Sevres two handled seau a bouteille, painted in colors with large sprays of garden flowers, date letter *H* for 1760, painter's mark for Rosset, 19.5cm. high.
(Christie's London) $6,000

A pair of Sèvres style turquoise ground vases with pointed oviform bodies painted with figures of a lady and gentleman in 18th century costume, 29.5cm.
(Phillips) $880

A fine and rare Sèvres plate from the Service de Départements, commemorating the Département des Basses Pyrenées, painted by A. Poupart, signed and dated *1823*.
(Phillips) $7,440

410

SÈVRES

A Sèvres (later-decorated) bleu celeste trembleuse cup, cover and saucer with a gilt berry and leaf finial and an entwined double handle, painted with vignettes of exotic birds, the porcelain 18th century. (Christie's) $1,682

A pair of gilt-metal-mounted Sèvres-pattern pale-blue-ground oviform vases and covers painted by D.P. Boucher with pastoral scenes of children in idyllic rural landscapes, circa 1895, 35³/₄in. high. (Christie's) $19,900

'Sèvres' gilt-bronze-mounted center bowl, late 19th century, the oval bleu-du-roi-ground bowl reserved on either side with a painted panel, 13¹/₂in. high. (Butterfield & Butterfield) $2,750

A pair of gilt-metal-mounted Sèvres-pattern green-ground vases and covers, painted in muted colors with scenes of medieval knights, one with a warrior knighting another attended by a multitude of spectators before pavilions and a castle, late 19th century, 50¹/₂in. high.(Christie's) $43,824

'Sèvres' gilt-bronze-mounted porcelain centerbowl, late 19th century, painted on one side with a pastoral scene of a man presenting a reclining woman with flowers, 24¹/₂in. high. (Butterfield & Butterfield) $6,050

A pair of gilt-metal-mounted Sèvres-pattern biscuit porcelain vases, the fluted spreading bodies with channeled banks filled with merry-making putti, square plinths, the porcelain with imitation interlaced L mark, late 19th century, 16¹/₂in. high. (Christie's) $1,098

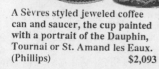

A Sèvres styled jeweled coffee can and saucer, the cup painted with a portrait of the Dauphin, Tournai or St. Amand les Eaux. (Phillips) $2,093

A pair of French 'Sèvres' vases, Louis-Philippe, Paris, circa 1840, each with a painted scene of scènes galantes, 86cm. high. (Sotheby's) $24,685

A Sèvres white porcelain group of Diana the huntress and two other figures on a rocky outcrop, 33cm. total height. (Bearne's) $880

SÈVRES

A Sèvres tray from the Duchess of Bedford service, of lozenge shape, the center painted with fruit and flowers within an oval reserve, 1762, 30cm. wide.
(Christie's) $8,114

A Sèvres vase, 'Cuvette à Fleurs à Tombeau', and brass liner, finely painted with a panel by Bouchet, 7¼in. high.
(Bonhams) $2,560

A Sèvres plate, finely painted with a central spray of summer flowers within a bleu celeste border, 9¼in. diameter.
(Bonhams) $480

A pair of metal-mounted Sèvres-pattern tapering oviform vases and domed covers painted by Tisserand with scenes of Napoléon engaged in his campaigns, imitation Sèvres marks, late 19th century, 44½in. high.
(Christie's) $16,560

A Sèvres bleu lapis orange-tub with gilt vermiculé decoration, painted with bouquets of garden flowers within reserves, date letter H for 1760, painter's mark for Thévenet, 9cm. high.
(Christie's) $1,080

A pair of Sèvres gilt-metal-mounted green-ground tapering-oviform vases and covers with white and gilt solid strap handles, the bodies painted in the style of Boucher, date codes for 1862, 14½in. high.
(Christie's) $3,652

A Sèvres green-trellis-ground small sugar-bowl and cover (pot à sucre calabre) the gilt-edged green trellis ribbons joined by flowerheads, circa 1765, 6.5cm. diameter.
(Christie's) $2,350

A pair of Sèvres plates from the service given by Louis XVI to Archduke Ferdinand of Austria, the centers painted with sprays of pink roses on a purple ground, date letters for 1785, 24cm. diameter.
(Christie's) $7,607

A Sèvres-pattern bleu celeste-ground inverted baluster ewer painted with a gallant paying court to two ladies, circa 1860, 10in. high.
(Christie's) $720

SÈVRES

A Sèvres oval plaque painted by Pauline Laurent after F.X. Winterhalter with a three-quarter length portrait of Queen Victoria in ceremonial regalia, circa 1858, 7½in. high.
(Christie's) $7,669

A Sèvres cuvette à fleurs Courteille of bombé form with two concave aubergine-ground pilasters gilt with entwined trailing foliage, circa 1765, 25cm. wide.
(Christie's) $12,679

A Sèvres rose-ground orange-tub, each side painted with trophies including a horn, hat, tambourine and peacock feathers, painter's mark for *Buteux*, circa 1758, 9cm. high.
(Christie's) $7,200

A pair of gilt-metal-mounted Sèvres-pattern dark-blue-ground oviform vases and covers painted by J. Pascault with Le Mariage, the other after David with Le Sacre, late 19th century, 43¼in. high.
(Christie's) $23,738

A Sèvres ballooning coffee-can and saucer painted with landscape scenes, the saucer with figures watching an airborne balloon, enclosed by gilt, green and yellow bands with puce dashes.
(Christie's) $5,000

A pair of Louis XVI ormolu-mounted Sèvres hard-paste porcelain vases, each painted on one side with Chinese musicians within a drapery cartouche, possibly for Nicolas Schadre, 15½in. high.
(Christie's) $71,060

A Sèvres circular two-handled écuelle, cover and stand, the kidney-shaped panels painted with pastoral landscapes, circa 1765, the stand 19cm. diameter.
(Christie's) $10,143

A Sèvres rose Dèjeuner en Porte-Huilier comprising a Porte Huilier, a teapot and cover and a cup and saucer, date letter *H* for 1760.
(Christie's) $5,071

A Sèvres coffee cup from the Catherine the Great service, painted in colors with a panel of white classical figures on a brown ground.
(Phillips) $476

SÈVRES

'Sèvres' porcelain vase, late 19th century, of goblet form, painted with a continuous frieze of figures in a garden, 19in. high. (William Doyle Galleries) $2,185

A pair of Sèvres biscuit figures of Spring and Autumn, possibly modeled by Falconet, she with incised *F* mark. (Phillips) $1,020

An attractive Sèvres sucrier and cover painted in colors with harbor scenes within ciselé gilt borders, 17cm., date letter for 1778. (Phillips) $1,870

A pair of gilt-metal-mounted Sèvres-pattern slender baluster vases, the dark-blue grounds reserved with tight bouquets of summer flowers within white cartouches circa 1880, converted to table-lamps, 16½in. high. (Christie's) $2,656

Pair of 'Sèvres' cachepots, each of cylinder form, painted with reserves of rustic lovers and floral sprays against a bleu celeste ground, 6¾in. high. (William Doyle) $1,265

A pair of gilt-metal-mounted Sèvres-pattern green-ground vases, the bodies of tapering oviform and each painted with a scene of Amphitrite, attended by nymphs, tritons and cherubs, late 19th century, 43¼in. high. (Christie's) $16,434

A gilt-metal-mounted Sèvres-pattern two-handled oval center-dish, the claret ground painted by Guy with Napoléon rallying his generals before a shadowy army, 20th century, 18½in. wide. (Christie's) $1,900

A Sèvres Empire cabinet-cup and saucer painted with a portrait medallion of Darnalt on a silver ground with foliage swags, circa 1820. (Christie's) $1,750

A Sèvres straight-sided miniature teapot and a cover painted in neoclassical style with a bouquet of flowers within a blue-ground bordered panel, date letter *L* for 1764, painter's mark *f* for Pfeiffer, 3½in. high. (Christie's) $1,306

SÈVRES

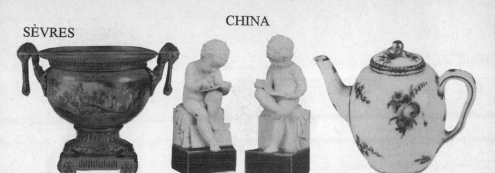

A gilt-metal-mounted Sèvres-pattern two-handled jardinière, the front with six playful putti around a felled tree-trunk, circa 1860.
(Christie's) $4,185

Pair of 'Sèvres' porcelain figures, each depicting a seated putto writing or reading, set on a flambé glazed square base, 17in. overall height.
(William Doyle) $37,950

A Sèvres miniature globular teapot and an associated cover painted in colors with sprays of flowers within blue enamel bands and gilt dentil rims, circa 1765, 4¼in. high.
(Christie's) $513

A good pair of English Sèvres style vases and covers, each painted with a courting couple on a turquoise ground, 14½in. high, interlaced Ls in blue, circa 1870.
(Neales) $3,003

Two Sèvres style 'jeweled' pink ground plates, one painted with a classical scene, 24.5cm. diameter, 19th century.
(Christie's) $1,030

A pair of ormolu-mounted Sèvres-pattern 'jeweled' vases and domed covers, the pale-blue grounds painted by Lecoq Miroy after Boucher with lovers in landscapes, circa 1880, 11½in. high.
(Christie's) $3,769

Sèvres gilt-bronze-mounted porcelain covered urn, late 19th century, painted in pastel tones with a continuous scene of putti in a landscape, 17⅛in. high.
(Butterfield & Butterfield) $4,950

Sèvres porcelain three-piece demitasse set, 1872–99, red circle mark, polychrome decoration, reticulated outer shell, 7⅝in. high.
(Skinner) $2,415

A Sèvres-style 'jeweled' coffee can and saucer painted in two-tone gilt with bands of flowerheads and scrolling foliage, 19th century.
(Christie's) $938

SHELLEY

Since the 1880s the firm of J.B. Wileman had had as a partner J.B. Shelley, and had also employed his son Percy. In 1896 Percy Shelley built a new factory to produce hand painted earthenware art pieces which were marketed as Intarsio ware and were designed by Frederick Rhead. Walter Slater became Art Director in 1901. Hitherto the firm had produced mainly for export to America, but high tariffs were making this increasingly difficult and Slater decided to concentrate on the home market. His American export pieces had been marketed as Foley China, but he could not register the name for use in Britain as it had already been registered by E. Brain. The name Shelley China was therefore registered instead, with a marketing campaign to ensure buyers recognised the company's continuing production. The firm's name was finally changed to Shelley Potteries in 1929. The art ware which Rhead had begun was now developed by the use of glazes which 'ran' together. Thus bright color combinations could be applied with little hand skill and then the chance element in the firing made each piece unique. The results were considered to typify modern art in their individuality and the quality and immediacy of the colors.

When Percy's son, J.K. Shelley, took over the firm's finances, he persuaded his father to pursue an active marketing policy and to use advertisements to create a market identity for the firm. Such conscious marketing was unheard of at the time.

Shelley Art Deco vase with stylized floral decoration. (Muir Hewitt) $85

One of a pair of Shelley Art Deco vases with tulip decoration, 7in. high. (Muir Hewitt)   (Two) $188

A Shelley nursery tea trio designed by Mabel Lucie Attwell, teapot and cover modeled as a duck, jug as a rabbit and sugar bowl as a chicken, teapot 16cm. high. (Christie's) $640

A Shelley ginger jar and cover designed by Walter Slater, painted with a ferocious dragon in shades of blue and green, 23.5cm. high. (Christie's) $640

Shelley "Mode" shape part tea service, 1930s. (Muir Hewitt) $188

Shelley dripware vase 1930s, 9in. high. (Muir Hewitt) $135

SICILIAN

Maiolica was produced in Sicily basically in imitation of the style of the North Italian centers such as Faenze, Venice and Tuscany, though the results tend to be cruder and more rustic than their prototypes. The areas of Caltagirone and Trapani were two major potting centers on the island.

As is often the case with a devolved art, Sicily went on producing this type of maiolica long after the vogue had passed in the north, and most examples date from the 17th century.

Marks are very rare: *SPQP* is occasionally found, indicating Palerman origin.

A Sicilian waisted broad albarello boldly painted in ocher with a draped bust within an oval cartouche, late 17th century, probably Caltagirone, 22cm. high.
(Christie's) $2,033

A Sicilian waisted albarello painted with a stylized flower and foliage in turquoise and ocher and outlined in manganese on a blue ground, first quarter 18th century, 23cm. high.   (Christie's) $1,360

A Sicilian maiolica albarello of waisted form, painted with a half length portrait of a lady in a blue dress, 21.3cm., end 17th century. (Phillips) $1,368

One of a pair of 17th century Sicilian wet-drug jars with scroll handles, 25cm. high.
(Christie's) $2,400

A good Sicilian (Sciacca) drug jar, painted with a circular panel of a Roman soldier in profile, 24cm.
(Phillips) $3,825

SIENA

The Tuscan town of Siena had a flourishing maiolica industry from the 13th century onwards, but reached its heyday from around the early 16th century, when apothecary pots, dishes depicting Biblical characters and tiles, many for the Petrucci palace, were produced in considerable numbers. These show a marked preference for an opaque dark orange tone.

In the 18th century dishes and panels were produced by Ferdinando Maria Campani and Bartolomeo Terchi, which lean towards Castelli in style.

A pair of Siena massive campana-shaped ewers with molded gilt-winged caryatid handles and an applied gilt foliate mask beneath the lip, circa 1730, 63cm. high.
(Christie's) $26,000

A Siena wall-plaque painted in blue with buildings in a rocky wooded landscape, within an ocher and brown marbled pierced frame molded with putti, circa 1740, 46.5cm. high.
(Christie's) $3,200

SITZENDORF

This was one of the many ceramic factories which sprang up in the Thuringian forests, though, established in 1850, it was much later than most.

Sitzendorf produced hard-paste porcelain figures and cabinet ware, which was often flower-encrusted in the late Meissen style.

Their mark is two parallel lines, crossed with a single line.

A Sitzendorf porcelain comport, the pierced bowl supported on a pillar surrounded by children, painted in pale enamel colors, 38.5cm. high.
(Bearne's) $525

A Sitzendorf polychrome painted pottery figure of a bare breasted dancer wearing blue and green skirt, 9½in. high.
(Christie's) $234

Pair of Sitzendorf figurines, depicting flower girl and gardener boy, impress marks to base 'S' 'DEP' '15024', circa 1880. $320

Sitzendorf porcelain figure in white and gilt of a lady standing by a horse on oval base, 9in., German, 19th century.
(G. A. Key) $174

A pair of Sitzendorf porcelain lamp bases, each in the form of a flower encrusted basket weave globe, supported by three cherubs, total height 40.5cm.
(Bearne's) $680

A pair of Sitzendorf porcelain bulbous urns and covers with cherubs-head pattern handles, the whole encrusted with floral garlands, 10¼in. high.
(Canterbury) $486

A Sitzendorf porcelain classical figure group with polychrome decoration, 10in. high. $680

Pair of Sitzendorf figures of 'Gainsborough Blue Boy' and 'Sarah Siddons', he mainly dressed in blue and cream, 11in. and 12in. high.
(G. A. Key) $426

SLIPWARE

Slipware is the earliest characteristically English earthenware, which gets its name from the creamy mixture of clay and water, known as slip, which was used for its decoration. Slip could either be painted on over large areas, trailed in lines or dots from a quill spouted pot, or combed into the surface of a piece.

The medium was taken to America by European settlers. Examples include Pennsylvania Dutch slipware, with flat decoration for domestic and raised for ornamental use.

A Staffordshire slipware press-molded dated 'Man within the Cumpas' charger by Samuel Malkin, 1726, 35cm. diameter. (Christie's) **$14,680**

A good North Devon slipware harvest jug, dated *1748*, the brown-red earthenware body dipped in cream slip and decorated in sgraffito technique, 12in. high. (Sotheby's) **$18,400**

An English slipware chamber pot, late 17th/early 18th century, the swelling circular body applied with a small strap handle and decorated with two rows of chocolate-brown dots, 7¹/₂in. wide. (Sotheby's) **$1,495**

A remarkable Staffordshire slipware owl jug and cover, the head lifting off to form a drinking cup, the body molded in in buff colored clay, 23cm. (Phillips) **$33,660**

A rare slip-decorated glazed redware large pie plate, Pennsylvania, 19th century, the interior with yellow slip inscription *G. W. Rhoads Dealer in Dry goods groceries & cc also Schwitzer Kase*, diameter 13¹/₂in. (Sotheby's) **$3,738**

A very fine and rare slip-decorated redware charger, New England, 19th century, with the inscription *Temperance, Health, Wealth*, 13³/₄in. diameter. (Sotheby's) **$19,550**

A Staffordshire slipware documentary thistle-shaped tankard, dated 1679, with initials *'IT LT 1679'* above combed decoration, 3¹/₄in. high. (Christie's) **$9,200**

A Staffordshire slipware dish, second quarter 18th century, the the center with a four-petaled brown flower with blue edging, 15³/₄in. diameter. (Christie's) **$11,000**

SONG

It was during the Song or Sung period, from 960–1279 AD, that potters became established as respected craftsmen on a par with the bronze worker and the jade carver, and the pieces they produced were strongly impressionistic and naturalistic in style.

Their wares were made in the simplest ways with little painting or embellishment. Most were wholly undecorated or enhanced by molding, stamping, the application of clay reliefs or etching. All these processes were carried out while the clay was still unfired. The glaze was added and the whole was then subjected to a single firing.

Song glazes tend to be thick and hard, and any crackle is positive and well-defined. They consisted basically of two types, a thick, opalescent glaze of pale lavender or turquoise, and a smooth, translucent celadon glaze with a predominantly green tint. Varying color effects were achieved by the use of different oxides, doubtless at first by accident, but they were soon obviously being achieved systematically.

A Cizhou painted stoneware globular jar, Song Dynasty, painted in dark brown on a cream slip with foliate sprays, 4in. high.
(Christie's) $2,300

An important Jiaotan Guanyao bottle vase, southern Song Dynasty, with a rich pale gray-blue glaze with irregular light brown crackles, 4⅝ in. high.
(Christie's) $354,838

A pair of Longquan celadon cups, the exteriors delicately molded in relief with chrysanthemum petals radiating upward, Southern Song Dynasty, 9.2cm. diameter.
(Christie's) $3,542

A Jun Yao tripod censer under a rich lavender glaze thinning to an olive translucency at the rim, Song Dynasty, 6.5cm. diam. $1,600

A Yaozhou celadon moulded bowl, of conical form, molded on the interior with stylised peony blooms, Northern Song Dynasty, 5¾in. diameter.
(Christie's) $3,100

A Henan black-glazed baluster vase, meiping, freely painted, Song Dynasty, 22cm. high.
(Christie's) $5,000

A small Longquan celadon 'twin-fish' dish, moulded to the interior medallion with a pair of scaly fish, Southern Song Dynasty, 8¼in. diameter.
(Christie's) $3,542

SPODE

As early as 1762 Josiah Spode started developing his Staffordshire pottery, which, under his descendants, became the first in England to introduce bone china bodies at the end of the 18th century. Spode's shapes were mostly plain, with correspondingly simple but elegant decoration, or alternatively elaborate Japanese patterns. The bulk of the factory's production consisted of printed pottery and the porcelain was really only a sideline.

The company was bought in 1833 by Thomas Copeland (q.v.). From 1970, however, it has again traded as Spode Ltd.

Most pieces were marked *Spode*, with a pattern number in red. The earliest sometimes have impressed marks.

A rare pair of Spode tapersticks, brightly decorated with the popular Japan pattern, No. 967, on circular bases, 3¹/₈in. high. (Bonhams) $640

An English porcelain tulip vase modeled as a red striped open yellow bloom, perhaps Spode, circa 1820, 15.5cm. high. (Christie's) $3,200

A Spode garniture of three green-ground campana-shaped vases, the seeded green grounds reserved and gilt with stylized foliage, circa 1810, 16cm. and 13.5cm. high. (Christie's) $1,267

A Spode ironstone celadon-ground two-handled flared cylindrical bowl and cover painted in the famille rose palette, 8in. high, circa 1815. (Christie's S. Ken) $480

A Spode blue-ground potpourri-vase of squat form, the pierced rim with four richly gilt grotesque masks, painted with garden flowers on a dark-blue ground, 11cm. high, circa 1820. (Christie's) $1,320

A pair of Spode two-handled pot-pourri vases, pierced covers and stands painted with loose bouquets of luxuriant flowers on dark-blue grounds, circa 1820, the stands 11cm. diameter. (Christie's) $3,200

A Spode blue-ground two-handled oviform vase, painted with loose bouquets of luxuriant flowers and scattered flower-sprays on a dark-blue ground, circa 1820, 15.5cm. high. (Christie's) $1,750

SPODE

A Spode blue and white plate with a shaped rim from the Caramanian series printed with Sarcophaga and Sepulchres, circa 1800, 10in. wide. (Christie's) $450

A pair of Spode porcelain ice pails with gold scroll handles, liners and covers, 30cm. high. (Bearne's) $6,730

A Spode blue and white plate painted with the DEATH OF THE BEAR within a border of wild animals, circa 1800, 9⁷/₈in. wide. (Christie's) $807

An unusual ice pail, attributed to Spode, with two upright loop handles, printed in blue with the 'Greek' pattern, 23.5cm. (Phillips) $680

A Spode Felspar porcelain part tea and coffee service, each piece painted in gold with sprays of barley and garlands of flowers, early 19th century. (Bearne's) $950

A Spode vase and pierced cover, finely painted with groups of flowers on a dark blue and gilt scale pattern ground, 24cm. (Lawrence Fine Arts) $1,600

A Victorian Spode pottery pot-pourri vase, baluster shape with pierced domed cover having bud finial, 12in. high. (Hobbs & Chambers) $360

Rare pair of blue and white Spode covered cache pots, first quarter 19th century, in Tower pattern, two handles, 10in. high. (Eldred's) $1,650

A Spode blue-ground two-handled oviform vase with waisted neck and on a spreading circular foot, circa 1820, 15.5cm. high. (Christie's) $720

ST CLOUD

Although porcelain seems to have been made at Saint Cloud as early as 1667, it was the faience factory of Pierre Chicaneau which first turned out Chinese-style soft-paste porcelain. When Chicaneau died, his widow remarried one Henri-Charles Trou in 1679, but kept the secret of soft-paste manufacture from her new family until her death, when a renewed patent in 1722 mentions the names of Henri and Gabriel Trou. It was this Henri Trou, her stepson, who eventually took over the Paris factory in the rue de la Ville l'Eveque which had been established in 1722 by the widow of Pierre Chicaneau's son!

The factory greatly benefited from the patronage of the Duc d'Orleans (Monsieur) brother of the king, and had as its mark a fleur de lys or a sun face, which latter is much more common. The body of St Cloud porcelain tends to be heavily potted, suggesting it was difficult to work with, and the paste varies in color from blue-white to ivory. Decoration was usually in the style popularised by Rouen faience with lambrequins much in evidence, from designs inspired by contemporary silver. Meissen influence was also strong, particularly in the latter period of the factory's production, though St Cloud designers were not devoid of their own ideas, and it is probable that the first trembleuse saucer came from there.

Most enamel painting was in imitation of Japanese Arita porcelain decorated in the Kakiemon style. The factory closed in 1766.

A St. Cloud white snuff-box modeled as a recumbent cat, its head turned and with a surprised expression, circa 1740, 7cm. wide.
(Christie's) $4,398

A pair of St. Cloud blue and white spice-boxes and covers, each with four compartments and standing on three paw feet, circa 1710, 14cm. wide. (Christie's) $2,974

A St. Cloud white beaker, cover and saucer with silver gilt mounts, circa 1730.
(Christie's)   £1,160

A St. Cloud dolphin-shaped cane-handle with an iron-red mouth and eyes and blue, yellow and green head and fins, circa 1740, 8.5cm. high.
(Christie's) $2,988

Twelve Saint Cloud blue and white knife handles, painted with bands of lambrequin and scrolls, circa 1715, the handles 8cm. long.
(Christie's) $1,223

A St. Cloud snuff box and cover modeled as a Chinese man, circa 1740, 5.5cm. high.
                               $2,000

STAFFORDSHIRE

Devotees of Arnold Bennett's novels about the Five Towns will be aware of the names Fenton, Longton, Hanley, Burslem, Tunstall and Burmantofts – Bennett left one out – which were the center of the great pottery industry of the 19th century. It was there that Staffordshire figures were produced in their thousands and bought with eagerness to adorn chest tops and mantlepieces in homes all over the country. At one time there were over 400 factories going full blast in the area around Stoke on Trent to satisfy the demand.

Staffordshire figures were unsophisticated in their modeling and cast in the shape of popular heroes or characters from stories, plays and poetry. There was an especially popular line in politicians and heroes like Wellington and Nelson. They were press molded and decorated in underglaze blue and black with touches of color in overglaze enamel and gilding. Early examples have closed bases or a small hole in the base while 20th century pieces are usually slip cast in Plaster of Paris molds and are open ended.

A Staffordshire large blue printed meat dish, with a farmer's wife, surrounded by her children, offering food to a blind and lame traveler, 52cm. (Phillips) $800

Bank, modeled as a bank building with double arched doors and rusticated walls, inscribed *Joseph Alsop STAINFORTH 1842*, 7in. high. (William Doyle) $1,092

A historical Staffordshire wash basin and pitcher by Ralph Stevenson, Cobridge, England, circa 1825, with a foliate band over a view of the Deaf and Dumb Asylum, Hartford, Connecticut, 14in. diameter. (Christie's) $3,740

A Staffordshire porcelain D-shaped bulb pot and cover, circa 1805, finely painted on the front with a fashionable couple strolling with their dog near a stream in a deer park, 8¼in. wide. (Sotheby's) $2,415

Staffordshire child's mug for the American market, circa 1820, the cylindrical body transfer-printed with the Great Seal of the United States, 1⅞in. high. (Sotheby's) $805

A Staffordshire pottery Victorian coronation mug, printed in underglaze purple with the Swansea transfer of the young Queen and her dates, 9cm. high. (Spencer's) $1,500

Historic blue Staffordshire plate, Enoch Wood & Sons, England, 19th century, *Boston State House*, marked on base, 10.25in. diameter. (Skinner) $201

STAFFORDSHIRE

A Staffordshire oblong-hexagonal meat-dish, printed with 'At Monk's Rock' within a border of flowers, 18¼in. wide. (Christie's S. Ken) $1,811

A porcelain pastille-burner, modeled as a twin turreted castle, applied with foliage, 3¾in. high, circa 1840. (Christie's) $142

A 19th century Staffordshire blue and white footbath transfer printed with 'Fountains Abbey' landscapes. (Greenslade Hunt) $1,326

An early Staffordshire tea canister, applied with quasi-heraldic roses on trailed stems, 11.5cm. (Phillips) $1,148

A very attractive and rare set of three Staffordshire tea canisters, the sides with a continuous rural landscape with figures, 10cm. high. (Phillips) $4,800

A pastille-burner modeled as a gothic gazebo with pierced windows and doors, circa 1840, 11½in. high. (Christie's S. Ken) $400

A Staffordshire solid-agate cylindrical tankard, circa 1755, with strap handle and mottled brown, ocher, blue and buff clays, 5⅛in. high. (Christie's) $935

A Staffordshire green spatterware 'Schoolhouse' sugar bowl and cover, circa 1840, painted on either side in red with a schoolhouse and trees, 5in. high. (Sotheby's) $1,495

A Staffordshire blue and white cylindrical mug printed with equestrian figures of The Duke of Wellington and Lord Hill, 4¾in. high. $400

STAFFORDSHIRE, ANIMALS

A pair of late Staffordshire cats, seated on rectangular cushion bases painted in green and pink, 7in. high.
(Christie's) $400

A fine pair of Staffordshire models of rabbits, with white bodies with black markings, their floppy back ears with pale apricot interiors, 24.5cm. long.
(Phillips) $4,500

An attractive pair of Staffordshire pottery models of grayhounds, seated with fully modeled fore-legs, the base molded with a dead hare, 21cm. high.
(Spencer's) $472

A Staffordshire group of two grayhounds before a tree stump spill vase, 10½in. high. (vase chipped)
(Christie's) $200

Two rare Staffordshire models of elephants, standing foursquare and with her calf at her side, 14.5cm. and 13.5cm. high.
(Phillips) $918

A figure of a standing camel before a tree stump applied with foliage, painted in colors on a shaped oval base, 6½in. high.
(Christie's S. Ken) $1,250

A pair of Staffordshire white-glazed figures of spaniels, with painted features and baskets of flowers clasped in their mouths, 1860–80, 9¾in. high.
(Christie's) $2,576

An English pottery model of a lion standing with a yellow globe under his front paw and before a flowering tree, 12cm. high.
(Phillips) $714

A pair of Staffordshire cow and calf figure groups, enameled colors, coved base, 8in. high.
(Locke & England) $565

STAFFORDSHIRE, ANIMALS

A pair of Staffordshire models of chickens, circa 1790, modeled as a rooster and a hen, with blue sponged plumage, standing on grassy mound bases, 8³/₄in. high, the rooster.
(Christie's) $1,380

A Staffordshire porcelain spill-vase modeled on the fable of the Fox and the Stork, enriched in colors and gilt, circa 1830, 6¹/₂in. high.
(Christie's) $239

A pair of models of seated spaniels, typically modeled facing left and right, wearing gilt collars and chains, 12¹/₂in. high, 19th century.
(Christie's) $797

A very rare and large Staffordshire model of a cat, seated on oval base with markings sponged in black and beige, on oval base, 26cm.
(Phillips) $1,860

A pair of models of greyhounds, their fur with shaped black patches and with curled forelocks, one with a rabbit in its jaws, circa 1860, 10¹/₄in. high.
(Christie's S. Ken) $1,350

A Staffordshire group, modeled with two spaniels seated flanking a clock face, one with black and white fur, the other with iron-red and white fur, 1860–80, 9¹/₂in. high.
(Christie's) $736

Pair of late 19th century Staffordshire dalmations sitting on cobalt blue oval bases, the collars and chains painted in gold, 5in. high.
(Peter Wilson) $390

An attractive and rare Staffordshire enamel pug dog bonbonnière, the animal with pale, straw-colored body, 5.5cm.
(Phillips) $956

A pair of Staffordshire pottery poodles with clay fragmented coats, separate front legs, 19th century, 8in. high.
(Locke & England) $298

STAFFORDSHIRE, FIGURES & GROUPS

A 19th century Staffordshire pottery group, of a batsman and wicket keeper, 6³/₄in. high. (Bonhams) $594

A pair of Staffordshire equestrian portrait figures, 'King William III and Queen Mary', 10¼in. high. (Bonhams) $314

Staffordshire pottery figure of a man with raised drinking vessel, standing by a spill tree, 9in., English, late 19th century. (G. A. Key) $175

A rare Staffordshire figure of William Macready as 'James V of Scotland', wearing an ermine-edged cloak, tunic and short trunks, 21cm. (Phillips) $484

Four Staffordshire figures of the Apostles, Saints Mark, Matthew, Luke and John, all standing and each with his appropriate emblem, 19cm. high. (Phillips) $1,573

A rare Victorian Staffordshire figure of the Rev. C.H. Spurgeon, standing in black coat and white trousers, 12¼in. high (Tennants) $1,020

19th century Staffordshire pottery watch stand, three maidens standing under a bower of roses, pale coloring, 11½in. high. (Peter Wilson) $133

A pair of Staffordshire pottery figures of a young man and woman, he with a monkey, she with a tambourine, 18cm. (Bearne's) $160

Longton Staffordshire group of 'Tam O'Shanter' and 'Souter Johnny', base incised Samson & Smith, Longton, Staffordshire, England, 1892, 13in. high. (G. A. Key) $230

STAFFORDSHIRE, FIGURES & GROUPS

A Staffordshire group, depicting King John sitting in a tented pavilion signing the Magna Carta, 12¼in. high.
(Bonhams) $200

A rare pair of Staffordshire groups of the flight into and return from Egypt, with Mary riding on a gray ass and Joseph holding the animal's head, 24cm. high.
(Phillips) $2,250

A very large Staffordshire group of Bacchus and Ariadne, after an original marble, on rectangular base, 64cm.
(Phillips) $1,200

A pair of figures of a sailor and a girl, modeled standing beside bollards, 9½in. high, 19th century.
(Christie's) $620

A pair of Staffordshire pugilist figures modeled as the boxers Mollineux and Cribb, circa 1810, 22cm. high.
$3,600

A colorful Staffordshire pottery group, the Prince of Wales and Princess Alexandra of Denmark, 26cm.
(Bearne's) $320

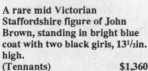

A rare mid Victorian Staffordshire figure of John Brown, standing in bright blue coat with two black girls, 13½in. high.
(Tennants) $1,360

A pair of Salt pottery bocage figures, one inscribed *Sportsman*, his lady companion entitled *Archer*, 17.3cm.
(Bearne's) $880

An early Staffordshire pottery group of a shepherd sitting on a rocky outcrop, playing a flute, his companion standing at his side, 25cm.
(Bearne's) $560

STAFFORDSHIRE, FIGURES & GROUPS

Staffordshire group of a child standing by a zebra with panniers on its back, 19th century, 7in.
(G. A. Key) $248

19th century Staffordshire pottery figure of David Garrick playing Richard III, 26cm.
(Peter Wilson) $226

Large Staffordshire figure of a huntsman on horse with hounds chasing fox, approximately 9in. high.
(G. A. Key) $393

An early Staffordshire equestrian figure of William III astride a trotting gray horse, on a rectangular base, 19.2cm.
(Phillips) $2,741

An Obadiah Sherratt group of Polito's Menagerie, the stage with an organ grinder and companion and five other musicians wearing iron-red, blue and pink clothes, circa 1830, 35cm. wide.
(Christie's) $24,000

A Staffordshire equestrian figure of Sir Robert Peel, wearing a black top hat and dark blue riding jacket, 13½in. high. $6,000

A mid 19th century Staffordshire railway group, as an arch with clock face, flanked by girls in Highland dress, 10½in. high.
(Tennants) $714

A Staffordshire pearlware cow creamer and stopper with a pink lustered border, a milkmaid seated to one side, 14cm.
(Phillips) $800

A theatrical group from the 'Bride of Abidos' modeled as Mr. Barton and Miss Rosa Henry as 'Giaffier & Zuleika', 12½in. high, circa 1847.
(Christie's) $708

STAFFORDSHIRE, FIGURES & GROUPS

A colorful Staffordshire pottery group of Samson killing the lion with his bare hands, 31.5cm. high.
(Bearne's) $134

An Obadiah Sherratt group, entitled 'Grecian and Daughter', 9in. high. $1,120

A clock-face group of Daniel in the lion's den, modeled kneeling, flanked by two rearing lions, 10in. high, circa 1860.
(Christie's) $886

A group of the Queen and Emperor, painted in colours on shaped oval base, named in raised capitals and enriched in gilding, 11½in. high.
(Christie's S. Ken) $400

A rare Staffordshire arbor group of two musicians, the lady and gentleman seated on green stools and the lady playing a mandoline, the man a pipe, 16.5cm.
(Phillips) $2,750

A Staffordshire pottery group in the form of a young Welshman and woman, supporting a bucket on a milestone inscribed *Langolen 1 Mile*, 27cm.
(Bearne's) $480

A rare Staffordshire group of boxers 'Heenan. Sayers' with painted details and molded title, 9½in. high, First Heavyweight Boxing Championship.
(Russell Baldwin & Bright) $1,000

A good Yorkshire cow group, the milkmaid with a high black coiffure, molded bead choker and a high shouldered white dress spotted in blue, 14.5cm. high.
(Spencer's) $1,399

An Obadiah Sherratt group of a Savoyard in crown, red cape with green lining and green striped trousers with a naturalistically painted bear on a leash, 8¼in. high.
(Christie's) $3,217

A Staffordshire jug depicting Wellington at Salamanca, 5½in. high.
(Christie's) $225

A Staffordshire character jug of Stanley Baldwin, shown seated with pipe in hand, 16.5cm.
(Phillips) $560

A Staffordshire jug printed and colored with an equestrian portrait of the Duke of Wellington. $320

A 19th century Staffordshire pottery jug made to commemorate the Coronation of Queen Victoria, 17cm. high.
(Spencer's) $560

Late 19th century Staffordshire jug and basin set with floral decoration. $160

A Staffordshire jug molded as the head of 'Lord Rodney', the rim molded with a flag and cannons, circa 1785, 6¼in. high.
(Christie's S. Ken) $530

A Staffordshire brown and white part glazed Parian jug with portraits of Wellington and Blucher, inscribed Jane Roberte, 7½in. high.
(Christie's) $360

A Staffordshire saltglaze owl jug and cover, circa 1760, with applied ridged plumage enriched with brown slip spots, 8¼in. high.
(Christie's) $55,000

Staffordshire pottery "Boxing" pitcher, England, circa 1825, titled below *Spring and Langan*, and with floral decorated rim and handle, 8½in. high.
(Skinner Inc.) $360

STAFFORDSHIRE, TEA & COFFEE SETS

A Staffordshire solid-agate pectin-shell molded teapot and cover, circa 1760, with dolphin handle, lion finial and serpent spout, 5¹/₂in. high. (Christie's) $6,600

Antique blue and white historical Staffordshire coffee pot, 'Commodore MacDonnough's Victory', 10in. high. (Eldred's) $880

Large Staffordshire barge pot, brown glaze, slip decoration, including impressed name and date, 1896, 13in. high. (G.A. Key) $450

A Staffordshire creamware tapering cylindrical coffee-pot and cover, circa 1755, with crabstock finial, spout and handle with applied molded reliefs of stylized flowering branches, 8¹/₄in. high. (Christie's) $575

Staffordshire Pottery teapot, inscribed 'Nectar Tea', complete with milk jug. (Border Bygones) $160

A Staffordshire coffee-pot and cover, circa 1765, with white flower finial, the domed cover molded with overlapping leaves, 8¹/₈in. high. (Christie's) $4,025

Antique English Staffordshire teapot, in the 'Canova' pattern by Mayer, pink and green decoration on a white ground, 6in. high. (Eldred's) $330

A Staffordshire accession pottery teapot and cover, printed in black on each side with a portrait of the young Queen together with the dates of her birth and proclamation, height 7in., circa 1837. (Bonhams) $560

A Staffordshire yellow-ground teapot and cover, circa 1810, after prints by Adam Buck, the conical cover printed in black with vignettes, 5¹/₂in. high. (Christie's) $276

STONEWARE

Salt glazed stoneware is a very old method of making pottery and there had been workshops producing this sort of ware at Lambeth in South London for many centuries when John Doulton started to work there in 1815. He made salt glazed domestic jars, bottles and barrels in brown with a slip glaze using the same methods as potters had used since the Middle Ages. John's son Henry realised the potential of stoneware when he followed his father into the business. He expanded the firm's operations into architectural stoneware and then the decorative stoneware which was to make the family fortune. In 1866 he encouraged students from the nearby Lambeth School of Art to come to work in a studio he attached to his pottery and allowed them complete licence to experiment and make everything they wanted. He was fortunate in having as protegés gifted people like the famous Barlow family, Frank Butler, George Tinworth and Eliza Simmance. Their work was shown abroad, particularly at Paris in the 1867 Exhibition, where it created a sensation.

A Nottingham type glazed red stoneware posset pot, dated 1791, 9½in. high.
$2,000

A saltglazed stoneware baluster shaped character jug, 4¾in. high, circa 1800.
(Dreweatt Neate) $234

An extremely rare English brown stoneware enameled mug, probably London, 1690–1710, the body thickly enameled on the front with a blue- and black-delineated white hare, 3in. high.
(Sotheby's) $20,700

An English brown stoneware mug, Nottingham or Derbyshire, mid 18th century, the cylindrical body decorated with horizontal ring turnings above a slightly flared foot, 3⅝in. high.
(Sotheby's) $460

A cobalt blue-decorated salt-glazed stoneware pot, impressed *John Remmey, New York,* circa 1795, 9½in. high.
(Sotheby's) $805

A fine Nottingham saltglazed stoneware 'carved' jug, the double walled globular body pierced and incised with stylized plants, circa 1700, 3¾in. high.
(Neales) $2,720

A Bottger polished brown stoneware baluster coffee pot and domed cover, circa 1715, 17.5cm. high.
$16,800

STONEWARE, 19TH CENTURY

A saltglaze stoneware two-handled 'Farmer Giles' mug, the merry man with brown curly hair wearing a hat, 22cm. high.
(Bearne's) $387

A salt glazed and cobalt decorated stoneware lady's spittoon, stamped *Cowden & Wilcox, Harrisburg, Pennsylvania*, 1869–1887, circular, with tapering top opening to a receptacle, 3½in.
(Christie's) $2,070

Two-gallon stoneware jug, inscribed in cobalt *E.A. & H. Hildreth, Southampton*, 14in. high.
(Skinner Inc.) $880

A rare ocher-decorated salt-glazed stoneware double-handled jug, signed by Lyman & Clark, Gardiner, Maine, circa 1830, of bulbous form, 15½in. high.
(Sotheby's) $4,025

An incised and cobalt-decorated stoneware harvest jug, New York, 1805, decorated on the obverse with incised floral vine below a fish, the reverse with a Masonic apron, inscribed and dated *J. Romer, 1805*, 7in. high.
(Christie's) $6,000

A salt glazed stoneware water cooler, attributed to Charles and William Wingender, New Jersey, late 19th century, barrel shaped, with domed lid decorated with concentric bands of blue, 14½in. high.
(Christie's) $863

A very fine and rare incised cobalt-blue-decorated salt-glazed stoneware pitcher, signed by *Richard C. Remmey*, Philadelphia, Pennsylvania, dated *1872*, 7in. high.
(Sotheby's) $17,250

A cobalt-blue decorated salt-glazed stoneware crock, American, 19th century, decorated on the front with a cobalt blue bird perched on a flowering branch, 10¼in. high.
(Sotheby's) $575

Incised and cobalt decorated stoneware planter, probably Pennsylvania/Ohio, 19th century, decorated with masonic and patriotic symbols, 10½in. high.
(Skinner) $13,800

STONEWARE, 19TH CENTURY

Stoneware pitcher, America, 19th century, cobalt applied floral decoration, inscribed *All Life is Brief – What Now is Bud Will Soon be Leaf,* interior Albany glazed, 8in. high. (Skinner) $1,265

A large brown stoneware jug flanked by portraits of Queen Victoria and the Duchess of Kent, 24cm. (Phillips) $240

A salt glazed and cobalt decorated stoneware batter jug, stamped *Cowden & Wilcox, Harrisburg, Pennsylvania,* 1869–1887, baluster form with lid and spout cover, 9¼in. high. (Christie's) $1,610

A salt glazed and cobalt decorated stoneware puzzle jug, attributed to Richard Clinton Remmy, 1835–1904, Philadelphia, 1859–1870, baluster shaped, with circular rim with seven applied spouts and applied strap handle, 6½in. high.(Christie's) $8,625

Pair of English stoneware Japan pattern pot-pourri jars and covers, Samuel Alcock & Co., circa 1869, the sides applied with flanking dragons' masks, 23½in. high. (Butterfield & Butterfield)
$4,400

A salt glazed and cobalt decorated stoneware crock, stamped *Cowden & Wilcox, Harrisburg, Pennsylvania,* 1869–1887, decorated with face of an Amish man and a plume, 12in. high. (Christie's) $20,700

A rare cobalt-blue-decorated saltglaze stoneware barrel-form water keg of impressive size, Pennsylvania, mid 19th century, 24½in. high. (Sotheby's) $3,000

A rare incised and cobalt blue-decorated salt-glazed stoneware crock, Nathan Clark & Co., Lyons, New York, circa 1845, 14½in. high. (Sotheby's) $16,500

A rare cobalt-blue-decorated salt-glazed stoneware water cooler, American, circa 1845, of ovoid form with flared rim, 17¾in. high. (Sotheby's) $1,955

STONEWARE, 20TH CENTURY

A stoneware swollen sack form by Elizabeth Fritsch, the front decorated with aubergine, terracotta, buff and mustard angular panels, over which mid and light blue geometric design, 1983, 41cm. high.
(Christie's) $11,737

A fine Abuja stoneware dish by Michael Cardew, with river pattern, the flared rim with vertical banding, glazed shiny olive and sage green, impressed twice with MC and Abuja seals, 15¼in. diameter.
(Bonhams) $640

An ash-glazed stoneware face-jug, attributed to Evan Javan Brown, Georgia, 20th century, the handle pulled from the back and ceramic chards for eyes and teeth, 6¼in. high.
(Christie's) $2,420

A stoneware oviform vase, by Katharine Pleydell-Bouverie, covered in lavender blue glaze, with olive green glaze at the rim and shoulder, impressed KPB seal, 22.1cm. high.
(Christie's) $1,600

A small stoneware cut-sided bowl by Katharine Pleydell-Bouverie, with incised decoration, covered in a dark brown glaze, impressed KPB, 8cm. diameter.
(Christie's) $158

A stoneware pot by William Staite-Murray, incised with gray-blue floral designs, glazed gray with traces of pale yellow and brown areas, 10in. high.
(Bonhams) $1,120

A St. Ives stoneware pitcher, with pulled lip and applied handle, covered in a pale sage green glaze over iron brown body, impressed with St. Ives seal, England, 20.7cm. high.
(Christie's) $197

A stoneware sculptural form by Ewen Henderson, handbuilt, highly pitted areas of beige, pink and gray, 19in. high.
(Bonhams) $3,232

A large stoneware bottle vase by Janet Leach, the cup-shaped rim applied with lug handles, covered in a pitted matt olive green and brown glaze with translucent olive green running, 48.5cm. high.
(Christie's) $886

A stoneware mug, by
Katharine Pleydell-Bouverie,
impressed Cole, circa 1930,
11.5cm. high. $200

A Bernard Leach stoneware
bottle vase with narrow neck,
the body partially covered with
a running celadon glaze, 13¹/₂in.
high.
(David Lay) $612

A spherical stoneware bowl,
by Val Barry, covered in a
greenish-gray matt glaze,
with brown speckling,
18.7cm. high. $280

A large stoneware footed
circular dish, incised James
Tower 84 and with paper
label inscribed James Tower
No. 167 Reflections, 54.4cm.
diam. $680

Glazed stoneware grotesque jug,
circa 1980, Burlon Craig,
Lincoln County, North
Carolina, impressed mark at
base, 16¹/₂in. high.
(Skinner) $330

A stoneware water pot by
Ladi Kwali, made at Abuja,
circa 1960, 29cm. high.
    $360

A St. Ives stoneware bottle vase
by Bernard Leach, covered in a
translucent crackled cream-
white glaze stopping short of the
foot, circa 1950, 26.8cm. high.
(Christie's) $574

A Bernard Leach stoneware
St Ives four inch tile painted
with a weeping willow tree,
10.2cm. square. (Phillips
London) $400

A fine white stoneware vase by
Bernard Leach, with narrow
neck and vertical indentations,
impressed BL and St. Ives seals,
circa 1960, 10³/₄in. high.
(Bonhams) $1,468

STRASBOURG

The Rococo style is seen at its best in the faience of Strasbourg, which was intended mostly for the German market.

The factory there was established in 1721 by Charles-François Hannong and its wares initially followed the Rouen style. In 1739 however Paul-Antoine Hannong became artistic director and he started making full use of the 'grand feu' colors, as well as gilding.

The arrival of several leading German painters in Strasbourg enabled Hannong by 1750 to become the first faience producer to decorate his wares in the full palette of enamel colors as used on porcelain. Perhaps the most striking of these was a rich crimson.

The monogram initials of Paul Hannong *(PH)* and Joseph Hannong *(JH)* are frequently seen on 19th century reproductions.

A Strasbourg hexafoil plate finely painted in petit feu colors, the center with a tied bouquet, circa 1748, 24.2cm. diameter.
(Christie's) $11,052

A Strassbourg octagonal dish, painted in blue within black outlines, with molded wavy rim, Charles Hannong, mid 18th century, 23.3cm long.
(Lempertz) $534

A Strasbourg rococo oval two-handled tureen, cover and stand, circa 1750, with eagle's head handles, the cover with rose finial, stand 15in. wide.
(Christie's) $17,825

A Strasbourg figure of a huntress after the model by J. W. Lanz, in a large green tricorn hat with a gilt rim and white fringe, 1752–55, 18cm. high.
(Christie's) $3,326

One of a pair of mid 18th century Strasbourg hexafoil plates, 24cm. diam.
(Christie's) $800

A large Strasbourg surtout-de-table, circa 1750, 52cm. high, the plateau 64cm. wide.
                    $6,400

A Strasbourg blue and white octagonal dish, circa 1730, 11½in. wide.
                    $1,750

439

SUNDERLAND

In the 19th century Sunderland became a popular pottery center, where many factories specialised in producing commemorative wares and gifts for sailors. These consisted mainly of jugs, wall plaques and mugs, bearing some painted scene, a motto or doggerel, usually in a pink luster frame, which was 'splashed' to give a blotched appearance.

The pictures which appeared on these are fairly limited in range, common themes being the Wearmouth Bridge, a balloon ascent and the 'Sailor's Return' or 'The Sailor's Farewell', or simply sailing ships.

Many other factories, from nearby Newcastle to far away Swansea, copied Sunderland luster ware, and as most pieces are unmarked, it is often difficult to make a confident attribution, though many genuine Sunderland wares were made as presentation pieces, and the name and date on these can be very useful.

Genuine Sunderland commands a premium among luster wares, and another criterion is the rarity of the scene or verse which appears on a piece. Some were used again and again, while others have survived on only a few pieces.

A Sunderland luster jug, printed with a ship in full sail and inscribed in black *J.T., M.T. & ( ) Owners of the Waterlily of Exeter 1845*, 8¾in. circa 1845. (Christie's) $325

A Sunderland luster jug decorated in colors with scenes and insignia relating to the Alliance of England and France, 17cm.
(Phillips) $735

A large Sunderland luster jug with rare verse 'The Sailor's Tear', the presentation inscription dated *1841*, 9in. (Russell, Baldwin & Bright)
                                          $507

A Staffordshire yellow-ground luster jug, transfer-printed in black and enriched in colors, circa 1815, 7½in. high.
(Christie's) $800

A Sunderland pink lust jug printed in black with a portrait bust of Earl Grey and inscribed *'The Choice of the People and England's Glory'*, 19cm.
(Phillips) $800

One of two Sunderland luster jugs, each inscribed 'Francis & Betsy Taylor', circa 1845, 8¼ and 9¼in. high. $1,200

Queen Caroline: a small luster pottery cream jug, printed in black with portrait and national flora, 8cm. high.
(Phillips) $600

SUSIE COOPER

Susie Cooper was born in Stansfield, near Burslem, in 1902. She attended evening classes at Burslem School of Art and joined A. E. Gray in 1922 to gain the practical experience necessary to qualify for a scholarship at the Royal College of Art. She began as a paintress but became resident designer in 1924. She remained with Gray until 1929 and designed banded ware, nursery ware and hand painted floral and geometric patterns.

In 1929, with the financial backing of her family, she set up on her own as an independent producer.

Harry Wood of Wood & Sons offered her facilities to produce new tableware shapes, and in 1931 she settled at the Crown Works in Burslem.

Cooper's avowed policy was to provide well designed, practical pieces at sensible prices, catering for 'professional people with taste and not much money'. To this end, she was quick to adopt new technologies such as lithography.

Factory production ceased for a year following a disastrous fire in 1942, but was back on its feet again by the early Fifties, following participation in the prestigious Festival of Britain in 1951, and bone china was also added to the range. Following another major fire in 1957, Cooper merged with R.H. & S.L. Plant in 1961, and the new company was taken over by Wedgwood in 1966. Cooper, however, continued to design for her own section within the Wedgwood empire for over 20 years. The last surviving 'Pottery Lady', she died in 1994.

A pair of Susie Cooper slender ovoid vases in the 'Moon and Mountain' pattern, painted in colors, 22.5cm. high.
(Christie's) $2,188

A Gray's Susie Cooper oviform jug, in the 'Cubist' design, painted in colors, 13cm. high.
(Christie's) $353

A Susie Cooper set in the 'Moon and Mountain' pattern, comprising: coffee pot and cover, milk-jug and sugar bowl, five coffee cans and six saucers, 2nd Galleon mark, height of coffee pot 20cm.
(Christie's) $1,010

A Gloria luster pedestal bowl made for the British Empire Exhibition, the interior decorated with putti harvesting fruiting vines, printed British Empire Exhibition marks and Susie Cooper monogram, 23cm. diameter.
(Christie's) $589

A Susie Cooper Crown Works plate painted in silver luster with stylized tulips, with lime green border, 28cm. diameter.
(Christie's) $251

'Skier', a Crown Works Nursery Ware Kestrel cocoa pot and cover, gazelle *SCP* mark, 5in. high.
(Christie's) $1,220

SUSIE COOPER

A Susie Cooper wall mask modeled as the head of a woman with gray streaked black hair, 10¾in. long. (Christie's) $1,500

A Susie Cooper coffee set for six, pattern No. E69, painted with an abstract geometric design in blue, black, brown, yellow and green, height of coffee pot 17cm. (Christie's) $1,515

A cylindrical vase with inverted rim decorated with applied crescent motifs, incised signature, 7¾in. high. (Christie's) $195

A Carved Ware baluster vase, with a continuous frieze of stylized leaves, incised signature and 592, 9¼in. high. (Christie's) $225

A Susie Cooper Kestrel coffee service, decorated with geometric patterning in shades of yellow, black, green and blue, comprising: coffee pot and cover, milk-jug and sugar bowl, five cups and saucers. (Christie's) $2,020

A Gloria luster pear-shaped vase, with scrolling flowers and foliage in gold, printed factory mark, painted Susie Cooper monogram, 7½in. high. (Christie's) $500

A Gloria luster waisted cylindrical vase painted in pink, lilac and gilt, painted Susie Cooper monogram, 12in. high. (Christie's) $1,300

Susie Cooper coffee set with star decoration (coffee pot, sugar bowl, 4 cups and saucers). (Muir Hewitt) $320

A cylindrical biscuit barrel and cover in the 'Seagull' pattern, with a stylized gull above blue and green waves, printed facsimile signature, 5¼in. high. (Christie's) $810

SWANSEA

The history of the Swansea pottery is closely bound up with that of Nantgarw, after the proprietor of the Cambrian pottery in Swansea, L W Dillwyn, brought William Billingsley and Samuel Walker from there in 1814.

Like Nantgarw, Swansea styles show a strong French influence, but it is that of the Empire rather than Sèvres. There is less scroll and ribbon molding and painting is often sparing, with plates often quite plain in shape.

The Swansea body was much stronger than that of Nantgarw, and thus many more upright shapes were produced. Swansea is in fact notable for its wide range of shapes. A few biscuit figures of sheep were even produced in 1817, together with biscuit plaques with applied flowers.

Like Nantgarw, distribution in 1816–7 was mainly through Mortlock in London, but a smaller proportion of pieces was put out for decoration. It was Billingsley who supervised in-house painting at Swansea, with a predilection for flowers and landscapes in very delicate colors. Other flower painters who worked with him there were David Evans, William Pollard and Henry Morris. Outside decoration was also done in Swansea by Thomas Baxter, who was noted for his sentimental figure scenes and single birds in landscapes.

Swansea made wide use of formal patterns and transfer printing before 1817, but these are not found on the later Trident porcelain. Much decoration was carried out at Swansea between the end of production in 1816/7, when the factory was taken over by the Bevingtons, and the final dispersal sale in 1826, for although Billingsley had departed, Evans, Pollard and Morris were still there.

A Swansea porcelain dessert service painted with single flower sprays, circa 1820. (Christie's) $852

A Swansea cup and saucer painted with full-blown pink roses and green leaves, circa 1820. $480

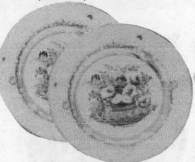

A pair of Swansea decorated porcelain plates, each painted to the center with baskets of flowers reserved in gilt with scroll and diaper border, 23 cm. diameter. (Christie's) (Two) $1,565

A Swansea pot-pourri vase and pierced cover of campana shape, painted by David Evans, with a frieze of garden flowers, circa 1820, 13.5cm. high. (Christie's) $3,350

Pair of Swansea vases, each of elongated campana form, circa 1815, 10in. high. $4,150

A Swansea pottery pearlware mug, circa 1838, commemorating the coronation of Queen Victoria, 8.5cm. high. (Bonhams) $2,400

SYLVAC

The Shaw & Copestake factory at Longton, Stoke, was founded in 1894 by William Shaw, firstly in a short-lived partnership with William Copestake and thereafter with Richard Hull Sr. It was Hull's son, also Richard, who was to coin the name SylvaC in 1935. Early Shaw & Copestake products tended to be very ornate in shape and decoration. They were marked with a distinctive daisy mark. During the 1920s the company made their name as producers of clock sets in many styles, from Gothic columns to Art Nouveau forms. During the 1920s the firm also began to produce a colorful Cellulose Ware. This was cheap and cheerful biscuit ware which was dipped, then hand-painted in vivid colors and left unglazed, though sometimes a light coat of varnish was applied. The content of their range also changed dramatically as they moved to figure production. All sorts of model animals, from rabbits to elephants, were given the cellulose treatment. Concurrently with these developments, matt glazes began to be introduced, and nearly all the items mentioned in the previous paragraph can be found in these, with green by far the most popular color. Blue, on the other hand, is now the most sought after, as it is the rarest. As the 1930s progressed, tableware and novelty items were added to the range and some of the hugely popular prewar dogs and bunnies were still in production when the factory went into voluntary liquidation in 1982.

Sylvac bunny match holder, 4in. high, 1930s.
(Muir Hewitt) $45

Sylvac vase with lamb figure, 4in. high.
(Muir Hewitt) $45

Stylized Art Deco style Sylvac jug, 1930s, 7in. high.
(Muir Hewitt) $105

Sylvac dog, 7in. high, 1930s.
(Muir Hewitt) $45

Sylvac rabbit, 4in. high, 1930s.
(Muir Hewitt) $60

Sylvac dog, 4in. high, 1930s.
(Muir Hewitt) $45

TANG

The ancient custom of burying the dead alongside many of the items which surrounded them in life has contributed greatly to our understanding of earlier times, and most of the pottery which survives from the Tang period (618–906 AD) does in fact come from such burial sites.

These show that Tang potters were able to carve figures with skill and refinement from bodies ranging from soft earthenware to a hard porcelain-like stoneware, which varies in color from light gray and rosy buff to white.

They are usually covered with a thin, finely crackled glaze, either pale yellow or green in color, though some are more richly coated with amber brown or leaf green glazes. Splashing, streaking and mottling are all characteristics of Tang pieces, which presage the Staffordshire Whieldon and agate ware of 1000 years later. Marbling of the ware by blending light and dark clays in the body was also achieved, and again this was to be reproduced much later in the 'solid agate' ware of Staffordshire.

Of all the figures found in Tang pottery, the horse is conspicuous both for its frequency and for the spirit and character with which it is portrayed.

Some Western influences can be seen in Tang pottery, and certainly there were many contacts with the near East at the time. Typical examples are the egg-and-tongue and honeysuckle patterns to be found in border designs, which show clear Graeco-Roman influence.

A Sancai buff pottery globular jar, Tang Dynasty, 16.8cm. high. $5,000

A pottery figure of a horse, T'ang Dynasty, in chestnut glaze, 12½in. high. (Eldreds) $1,045

A fine Sancai glazed buff pottery figure of a hound, standing four-square on an oval pedestal, Tang Dynasty, 17.2cm. high. (Christie's) $19,500

A rare blue-splashed Sancai tripod censer, Tang Dynasty, the body covered with blue, green, orchid and white splashes streaking toward the base, 7½in. diameter. (Christie's) $12,750

A rare Sancai pottery incised tripod dish, supported on three short feet, the interior finely incised with a goose and three stylized clouds in the medallion Tang Dynasty, 29.2cm. diameter. (Christie's) $34,960

A large painted pottery horse standing foursquare on a rectangular base, the saddle draped with a knotted cloth falling in folds above a striped saddle blanket, Tang Dynasty, 41cm. high. (Christie's) $5,600

TANG

A Sancai glazed buff pottery model of a boar standing four-square on a pierced rectangular base, Tang Dynasty, 20cm. long. (Christie's) $4,500

A fine Sancai glazed buff pottery shallow bowl, the exterior applied with quatrefoil florettes on a ground of slip-trailed diagonals, Tang Dynasty, 9.8cm. diam. (Christie's) $10,000

An ocher glazed buff pottery model of a ram standing four-square on a pierced rectangular base, (legs restored) Tang Dynasty, 20cm. long. (Christie's) $2,500

A pair of standing pottery figures of attendants, Tang dynasty (618–906), each wearing formal robes and head-dress, 66cm. high. (Sotheby's) $2,576

An important massive glazed buff pottery figure of a Bactrian camel, extremely well modeled standing four-square on a rectangular plinth, Tang Dynasty, 82cm. high. (Christie's) $246,000

Two painted red pottery figures of standing matrons, both with hands held before their chests, Tang Dynasty, both about 37cm. high. (Christie's) $21,000

A rare brown-glazed ewer of ovoid shape on a short foot, surmounted by a slightly tapered cylindrical neck applied with a molded loop handle and short cabriole spout, Tang Dynasty, 13.5cm. high. (Christie's) $2,685

A red painted pottery standing horse and a groom, the horse with plain saddle and brick-red painted body, the groom with clenched wrists and looking upwards, Tang Dynasty, the groom 28cm. high. (Christie's) $9,845

Sancai glazed vase, Tang Dynasty, the high-shouldered ovoid body curving inward to the small mouth and tapering to a flat foot, 10¼in. high. (Butterfield & Butterfield) $1,210

446

TECO

The Teco pottery operated out of Terra Cotta Illinois in the early years of this century. Its output is characterised by matt green glazes which are frequently used on shapes based on natural forms.

Teco pottery wall pocket, green matt glaze on hanging vase with angular top over molded roundel, 5¹/₄in. wide. (Skinner Inc.) $385

Teco pottery handled vase, decorated by four angular quatriform handles extending to base rim, 13¹/₂in. high. (Skinner Inc.) $1,320

Teco floor vase, Gates Potteries, Terra Cotta, Illinois, circa 1906, green glazed with rolled rim continuing into four squared vertical strap handles, 20⁵/₈in. high. (Skinner) $7,150

Rare and important Teco Pottery vase, Terra Cotta, Illinois, circa 1905, shape 119, designed by Fritz Albert, matt green glaze on ovoid form, 13in. high. (Skinner) $14,950

Teco Pottery vase, designed by Fritz Albert, supported on three molded flaring feet under a green glaze, stamped Teco 115, 9in. high. (Skinner) $2,500

Teco Pottery vase, Terra Cotta, Illinois, designed by Hugh M. G. Garden, gloss mottled pale green glaze, 11¼in. high. (Skinner) $575

A Teco Art pottery fluted vase, Illinois, circa 1905, 10½in. high. (Skinner) $1,250

Teco pottery vase with four handles, Terra Cotta, Illinois, circa 1910, squat, impressed twice, 6½in. high. (Skinner Inc.) $1,300

TERRACOTTA

Terracotta is a red earthenware which has been used in many ages and civilisations for a wide variety of purposes. It is normally unglazed, though for domestic use a thin glaze has to be applied to inside surfaces, since it is slightly porous. Terracotta was very popular in the mid-late 19th century for garden ornaments, vases etc. as well as figures and tableware. English companies which included it in their range were the Minton factory, F & R Pratt, and Doulton.

A pair of polychrome terracotta female busts personifying France and Spain respectively, French, late 19th century, 18in. high.
(Christie's) $742

'Lisetta', an Ernst Wahliss terracotta plaque molded in relief with a profile bust of a young woman surrounded by a garland of flowers, 41cm. high.
(Christie's) $334

A pair of eighteenth century glazed terracotta figures, each in two sections, with detail picked out in purple, in the form of a smiling bewigged footman with neckerchief, late 18th century, probably Italian, 64½in. high.
(Christie's) $96,000

A set of three black glazed terracotta jugs of graduated size, printed in yellow with portraits and vases of enamelled flowers. $320

A Continental painted terracotta group of three boys, German, circa 1900, made in Germany, 11¾in. high.
(Sotheby's) $1,925

George Goudray 'Les Nenuphars', painted terracotta bust of a girl in Art Nouveau style, with incised signature, 23in. high.
(Lawrences) $1,728

A pair of French terracotta figures, by Gossin Frères, Paris, each in 18th century costume, each on a circular naturalistic base, signed, late 19th century.
(Christie's) $13,282

A Continental terracotta bust of General von Steuben, 18th century, wearing a wig tied en queue and with lace cravat, 26½in. high.
(Sotheby's) $3,450

TERRACOTTA

A French terracotta bust probably representing Louis XV, wearing a wig tied en queue, inscribed with date *1739*, 16¼in. high.
(Sotheby's) **$1,150**

An Art Deco terracotta wallmask modeled as a stylized girl with blue hair dressed with flowers, 9in. long.
(Christie's) **$280**

A white glazed terracotta relief of the Madonna and Child, in the manner of the della Robbia workshop, molded in half-length, 27¼in. high.
(Sotheby's) **$2,185**

A fine and rare modeled terra cotta newsboy architectural plaque, H. A. Lewis, South Boston, Massachusetts, 1883–1887 modeled in the half round with the figure of a running newsboy, 61in. wide.
(Sotheby's) **$14,300**

A pair of terracotta garden ornaments in the form of seated grayhounds, each wearing a studded collar, 33in. high, 19th century.
(Bearne's) **$7,144**

A plaster terracotta-look sculpture of a young girl's smiling face with grapes, signed *Géo Verbanck*, and dated *1921*, 33cm. high.
(Hôtel de Ventes Horta) **$537**

A pair of terracotta figures of winged sphinx, with painted finish, one French, 19th century, the other of a later date, 30in. high.
(Christie's) **$3,170**

Portrait medallion of Benjamin Franklin, signed and dated *J. B. Nini 1770*, terracotta, 142mm. diameter.
(Skinner) **$825**

A pair of Watcombe Torquay terracotta portrait busts of Princess Louise and the Marquis of Lorne, circa 1871, 12½in. and 12¼in. high.
(Christie's) **$219**

THURINGIA

In the 18th century Thuringia was a region of dense forests with unlimited fuel and plentiful clay, and it is therefore hardly surprising that it boasted a host both of faience and porcelain factories.

Apart from some fine baroque tureens, however, most of the faience output was not particularly distinguished or even distinguishable, one factory from another. Dutch influence was very evident in the vast amount of blue and white and chinoiserie decoration, and a large part of their production consisted of beer mugs.

The typical Thuringian high temperature palette consisted mainly of cobalt and manganese used over a muddy yellow, a green achieved by mixing yellow and blue, and a dry red which lies atop the glaze. The decoration on the mugs is usually boldly drawn, with thick manganese outlines of trees in olive green, their stylised leaves outlined in dark manganese. Overall, their general appearance is fairly rustic.

Most Thuringian porcelain factories were born out of the misfortunes that befell Meissen during the Seven Years War, but their existence seldom outlasted the founders' personal interest.

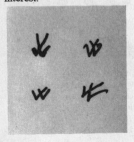

A German porcelain cylindrical coffee-pot and cover painted with figures in landscapes within gilt borders, circa 1800, probably Thuringian, 5¹/₂in. high. (Christie's) $836

A Thuringian figure of a lady, possibly Wallendorf, holding her black apron in one hand, wearing a lace collar, a red bodice and a floral skirt, 13cm. (Phillips) $825

A pair of Thuringian figures of a shepherd and shepherdess, he in a long coat, she in a black and red hat, white bodice with a purple edge, circa 1770, 14cm. high. (Christie's) $2,166

A Thuringian pear-shaped coffee-pot and cover with scroll handle and shell-molded spout one side painted with a huntsman and companion and a hound, circa 1770, 24.5cm. high. (Christie's) $8,446

A Thuringian eye bath modelled as the head of a man wearing a yellow hat, last quarter of the 18th century, 8cm. long. $800

A Thuringian figure of Provender for the Monastery, circa 1775, 11.5cm. high. (Christie's) $1,200

TIFFANY

Pottery was a comparative latecomer to the Tiffany range, being first exhibited at the St. Louis World Fair in 1904. Commercial sales began the following year. Their ware comprised a fine white clay fired at high temperature, on occasion with high relief or pierced decoration.

There was, as might be expected from the period and the source, a strong Art Nouveau influence both on shape and decoration, the former often emerging from the latter, for example, vase lips formed by leaves. Mossy green, yellow and ivory glazes were much used, and more simple vase forms were often covered in rich eastern glazes.

Most pieces were marketed under the trade name Favrile, and were usually cast, rather than hand-thrown.

When Tiffany left Tiffany Studios in 1919, production ceased.

A Tiffany pottery molded vase, New York, the mottled dark green and blue glaze on white ground, 7½in. diam., circa 1908.
(Skinner) $650

Tiffany pottery vase, with mottled earth tone brown-tan-amber glaze overall, 9½in. high.
(Skinner Inc.) $1,980

Pair of early 20th century Tiffany bronze dore and opalene jewel pricket candlesticks, 12.4in. high.
(Skinner) $3,200

One of a set of twelve Mintons pâte-sur-pâte service plates, decorated by R. Bradbury, retailed by Tiffany & Co., New York, 1937, 10⅝in. diameter.
(Butterfield & Butterfield)
                              $4,400

Tiffany pottery bowl, raised rim bulbed pot of white clay fired with amber, blue, gray and green drip glaze overall, 6in. high.
(Skinner Inc.) $600

A Tiffany Art pottery vase, New York, 1906, of cylindrical form with repeating molded lady slippers on stems, 12¼in. high. $3,850

Tiffany pottery flower bowl, heavy walled jardinière form of white clay decorated in blue, 5¼in. high.
(Skinner Inc.) $1,650

TOURNAI

The Tournai porcelain factory opened in 1751 when Joseph Peterinck was granted a patent by the Empress Maria Theresa. A soft paste porcelain was manufactured, at first with a slightly grayish hue, but after 1765 it became much creamier.

The decoration owed much to Meissen styles, and commonly depicted flowers, landscapes, castle scenes etc. Much of the finest bird and flower painting is attributed to Henri-Joseph Duvivier, who was chief painter at Tournai between 1763–71.

A blue enamel ground is common on Tournai pieces and later bird painting from Buffon's *Histoire Naturelle des Oiseaux* was done by Jean-Ghislain-Joseph Mayer, who became head painter in 1774.

Many English potters and painters were employed at Tournai during the early period and much of their output bears a strong resemblance to Derby, Worcester and Chelsea pieces of the period. Groups and figures were produced by Nicholas-Joseph Gavron and by Joseph Willems, a sculptor from the Chelsea factory, and, after his death in 1766, by Antoine Gillis and Nicholas Lecreux. Groups were often left white, but sometimes painted in strong enamels.

When Peterinck died his son took over for a short time, before leaving to establish his own factory in the town in 1800. The original factory was bought by the de Bettignies family who kept it until it was taken over by the Boch brothers in 1850. It was during the de Bettignies period that many flagrant forgeries of Sèvres, Chelsea and Worcester pieces were produced.

Early marks include a tower either in enamels or gold.

A Tournai spirally molded blue and white part coffee service with floral decoration, circa 1770.
$1,344

A pair of Tournai white glazed vase groups, each baluster vase with pierced neck and applied with trailing plants, 18cm. high, late 18th century.
(Bearne's) $1,344

Pair of Tournai faience figures of pug dogs, after the Meissen models by J. J. Kandler, circa 1765, 15cm. high.
(Christie's) $16,000

One of a pair of Tournai two-handled seaux a glace covers and liners with molded Ozier borders, circa 1770, 25cm. wide. $480

A Tournai fable teacup and saucer painted in the manner of Duvivier with 'The Fox and The Crane', gilt castle marks, circa 1765.
(Christie's) $2,000

A Tournai ornithological oviform jar and cover from the Duc d'Orleans service, circa 1787, 18.5cm. high.
$1,750

URBINO

Urbino, the capital of the Duchy of the same name, became a maiolica center only in 1520, when "Guido da Castello Durante" established a workshop there. Guido was the son of Nicola Pellipario, who had worked at Castel Durante, and his father joined him at Urbino in 1527. It was Nicola Pellipario who popularised the istoriato style, with which Urbino came to be especially associated.

Their Fontana workshop produced many pieces, including large wine coolers, salvers, pilgrim bottles and stands, with a characteristic decoration of arabesques and grotesques painted in color on a white ground edged in yellow and picked out in orange. Guido's son Orazio Fontana, started up his own workshop next door in 1565, and where pieces are unsigned, it is difficult to tell whose workmanship they are.

The work of the painter Francesco Xanto Avelli is fairly easy to distinguish, however, for he specialised in crowded scenes, almost like stage settings, featuring characters with very rounded limbs and his favorite tones were bright yellows and orange.

There are many recent imitations of the Urbino grotesque-arabesque style, but these can usually be distinguished by the pen-like draughtsmanship of the painting, which indicates that the white tin-glaze ground had been fired first to make painting easier. Beware too a pinkish purple tone which the 16th century artist did not possess.

An Urbino tazza on low foot, painted in the center with a figure of Medusa standing and wearing a green and amber dress, 26cm., probably Fontana workshop.
(Phillips) $1,920

An istoriato charger, Urbino, circa 1535, painted by Nicola da Urbino, painted in strong colors with The Rape of Helen, the underside undecorated, 20³/₈in. diameter.
(Christie's) $134,500

An armorial salt, Urbino, circa 1575, workshop of the Patanazzi, the central salt resting on the backs of four putti kneeling on the rim of a boat-shaped salt raised on four scroll feet, 9¹/₈in. high.
(Christie's) $13,800

An Urbino maiolica accouchement bowl painted inside the deep bowl with an expectant mother and child, 15.5cm. diameter, Patanazzi workshop, last quarter 16th century. $3,200

A finely painted Urbino Istoriato dated dish with The Adoration of the Magi, a mountainous landscape in the background with hill-top towns, 29cm. diameter.
(Phillips) $8,840

An Urbino Istoriato dish of shallow Cardinal's hat form, painted in the workshop of Guido Durantino with Joshua slaying the thirty-one kings, circa 1550, 27cm. diameter.
(Christie's) $31,671

·Ƭ Urbino·

URBINO

An Urbino Istoriato low tazza painted by Francesco Durantino with the birth of Adonis, with Lucina nursing the infant, circa 1545, 27cm. diameter.
(Christie's) $21,114

An Urbino tin-glazed earthenware inkstand, from the Patanazzi workshop, circa 1570, in the form of a large pipe organ with putti above, 17½in. high.
(Sotheby's) $28,750

An Urbino Istoriato dated tazza painted by Francesco Xanto Avelli with a scene from the martyrdom of St. Ursula, 1541, 27cm. diameter.
(Christie's) $31,671

A rare Urbino maiolica accouchement shallow bowl painted with an interesting interior scene of the expectant mother seated on a stool surrounded by three attendants, 16.5cm., circa 1570.
(Phillips) $4,560

An istoriato vasque, Urbino, circa 1550, workshop of Orazio Fontana, the trefoil bowl applied with grotesque masks, the interior of the basin painted with The Contest Between The Muses and the Pierides, 19¼in. wide.
(Christie's) $178,500

An Urbino istoriato tondino of Cardinal's hat form painted in the workshop of Guido Durantino, the broad flat rim painted with a warrior holding a halberd and standing beside a flaming altar, circa 1535, 26.5cm. wide.
(Christie's) $12,765

An Urbino istoriato dish, painted with a standing figure of Venus with Cupid beside her, a central figure of Jupiter holding a thunderbolt and with his eagle at his side, 26.5cm.
(Phillips) $10,556

An Urbino maiolica wet drug or syrup jar, workshop of Orazio Fontana, 1565-70, 34cm. high.
(Phillips) $19,200

An Urbino istoriato dated documentary large circular dish painted by Francesco Xanto Avelli da Rovigo with The Rape of Helen, 1535, 46.5cm. diameter.
(Christie's) $75,000

VAN BRIGGLE

Artus van Briggle was born in Felicity, Ohio in 1869. He studied painting in Cincinnati, where he also worked as a decorator of dolls' heads and vases. Around 1887 he became Director of the Rookwood Pottery, where he decorated vases with flowers in underglaze colors. It was part of Rookwood's enlightened philosophy to send talented decorators on scholarships abroad, and van Briggle benefited under this scheme with a period at the Académie Julien in Paris in 1893. On his return to Cincinnati he continued at Rookwood, while experimenting at home with the production of Chinese matt glazes.

He fell ill with tuberculosis and moved to Colorado in 1895, where he established the van Briggle Pottery Co in 1902. There he produced vases and plates decorated with stylized animal and flower forms in the Art Nouveau style. These were often relief decorated and covered in soft-colored glazes. Until his death in 1904, the pieces were entirely glazed, but later only partial glazing was introduced.

Van Briggle pottery copper clad vase, Colorado, 5½in. high. $1,275

Van Briggle pottery vase, caramel glaze with moss green mottling, inscribed mark and *1913*, 6in. high. (Skinner) $467

Early Van Briggle vase, 1904, broad shoulder with two handles under a green glaze, incised *AA, 242, Van Briggle, 1904*, 5in. high. (Skinner) $600

Van Briggle Pottery vase, Colorado Springs, 1915, semi-matt glazed green at rim and shoulder shading to mottled olive/brown, 7¾in. high. (Skinner) $578

Van Briggle pottery vase, Colorado Springs, Colorado, after 1920, relief decorated with cranes in turquoise matte glaze, 16¾in. high. (Skinner Inc.) $550

A Van Briggle pottery bowl, the underside formed as a large shell, with the reclining figure of a mermaid to one side, 39cm. diameter. (Christie's) $1,550

Van Briggle Pottery vase, Colorado Springs, circa 1904, with molded floral design, yellow and ocher semi-matte glaze, 8½in. high. (Skinner Inc.) $850

VENICE

Though some pieces of Venetian faience can be dated back to 1520, production did not begin in any quantity until the middle of the century. As a major trading port, Venice was obviously open to Middle and Far Eastern influences and this is reflected in the pottery which was produced there.

Ground colors are often stained to a lavender blue, with the decoration painted in strong cobalt, relieved only occasionally with a little opaque white or yellow.

A Venice Istoriato saucer dish painted with Apollo slaying the children of Niobe, circa 1560, 29.5cm. diam. (Christie's) $28,000

A small Venetian wet drug jar, painted beneath the spout with a full-face head of a boy with white frilled collar, 20cm. (Phillips) $5,278

A Venice wet drug jar, painted with a profile bust portrait of a soldier in blue helmet, under the spout, 21.5cm.
(Phillips) $1,319

A Venice vaso a palla with the portrait heads of two saints in cartouches, circa 1550, 28cm. high.
(Christie's) $9,200

A Venice drug bottle, painted on one side with a head and shoulders portrait of a man wearing blue tunic and hat, 22cm.
(Phillips) $5,278

VENICE: VEZZI

The first hard-paste porcelain factory was established in Venice in 1720 by Francesco Vezzi (1651–1740), a wealthy goldsmith. In this he enlisted the assistance of the dubious Christoph Konrad Hunger, who had already deserted Meissen in 1717, claiming to be able to help duPaquier in Vienna. He had at least learned enough there to enable him to help Vezzi produce true porcelain, but he then reverted to type and quit Venice for Meissen again in 1727. He promptly disclosed that Vezzi was reliant on Saxon clays, whereupon their export was promptly banned, forcing the factory to close.

A Venice (Vezzi) blue and white teabowl painted in a gray-blue with two birds in flight among plants and flowering shrubs flanked by buildings between blue line rims, circa 1725, 7.3cm. diameter.
(Christie's) $9,600

A Venice (Vezzi) teapot and a cover with colored chinoiserie figures in panels at various pursuits including swinging on a rope, playing a horn and carrying a snail, incised Z mark circa 1725, 16.5cm. wide.
(Christie's) $18,400

VIENNA

The porcelain factory of Claude Innocent Du Paquier was established in Vienna during the early years of the 18th century. Though it received no state patronage, the Emperor granted it many privileges and it became the second factory in Europe to commence hard paste porcelain manufacture, following the defection of the Meissen arcanist Stölzel in 1719 and Böttger's half-brother, Tiemann who brought the kiln designs from that factory.

Early Vienna porcelain can be distinguished from Meissen by the flatness of the glaze, which becomes greenish when thickly applied, and footrims tend to be rough and unglazed. Like Meissen, the early designs owe much to silver shapes.

Apart from adopting architectural features in their forms, such as gadrooning and fluting, Viennese designers also borrowed shapes from Dutch delftware. Three features which became highly characteristic of Viennese decoration were plastic decoration, baroque scrollwork and Japanese 'sprigs'.

There was some copying of figures from Meissen originals, and many fine pieces were made as gifts for the Russian court. By 1725 iron red, green, purple, pink, yellow and blue enamels were being used, and these were softer in tone than the brilliance of their Meissen counterparts. Schwarzlot, black enamel painting with a brush or point, was much in evidence to depict putti, animals, mythological or hunting scenes. Tableware bearing this last decoration are known as Jagd services.

The factory's output was set firmly in the Baroque tradition, as reflected in the Laub and Bandelwerk (scroll and foliage) and naturalistic

A Vienna (Du Paquier) two-handled circular écuelle and cover molded and colored with prunus, circa 1730, 12cm. (Christie's) $1,181

A Vienna figure of a dwarf 'Die Walper Hollriglin' modeled by J. L. C. Lück, advancing, her arms outstretched and her mouth open, circa 1755, 11cm. high. (Christie's) $18,925

A gilt-metal-mounted Vienna (Franz Dörfl) tea-kettle and cover of globular form, the burnished gilt ground tooled with C-scrolls and painted by A. Wenz with two scenes of classical figures, circa 1900, 8¼in. high. (Christie's) $2,763

A Vienna-style circular dish painted with Esther seated on red drapery beside a banquet-table before a sacrificial urn among columns, King Ahaseurus standing beside her ordering the seizure of Haman, circa 1880, 21¼in. diameter. (Christie's) $6,044

A finely painted and exceedingly large Vienna dish, painted by and signed D. Wagner, Wien, after Titian, entitled Une Allegorie, 55cm., shield mark in blue. (Phillips) $5,202

A Vienna figure of a young 18th century courtier modeled on bended knee, his right hand outstretched in entreaty, impressed beehive mark, date code for 1848, 6in. high. (Christie's) $445

VIENNA

deutsche Blumen decorations which are much used. The period ends with Du Paquier offering the factory to the archduchess Maria Theresa, who bought it in 1744. Du Paquier continued as director, but retired the same year and died in 1751.

During the state-owned period from 1744 there was a noticeable improvement in the quality of the color of the clay, which became whiter. Pieces were decorated now rather in Rococo style and many decorators were persuaded to come from Meissen, among them the flower painters Johann Klinger and J G Richter. From about 1760 there was a large output of Meissen-type figures, under the direction of the chief modeler from 1747–1784, J J Niedermayer. The bases of these assist in their dating, beginning as a mound with a little scrollwork, before becoming more like a flat slab and finally adopting a Neo Classical high base with vertical edging with molded and gilt designs.

The factory was again in difficulties in 1784, when a successful wool merchant, Konrad von Sorgenthal, took over as manager. The restoration of its fortunes which he brought about lasted well into the 19th century, and it did not close until 1866.

In the Sorgenthal period, neo-Classicism asserted itself, as the pieces tried to recapture the forms of classical antiquity in much the same way as Wedgwood did in England, though sometimes the decoration could become too elaborate.

A useful guide to dating post 1783 Vienna is that, in addition to the impressed shield, two or three numbers are also impressed as date marks, eg. 89 = 1789, 808 = 1808.

A pair of large Vienna vases on square bases, finely painted with panels of classical figures, 30in. high.
(Bonhams) $12,800

A Vienna circular wall plaque, painted by H. Reldas, signed, after Rubens, with 'The Rape of the Sabine Women', 45.5cm.
(Phillips) $2,400

Two 'Vienna' porcelain cabinet plates, circa 1900, the first entitled Epheu, painted with a portrait of a maiden, signed *Wagner*, the other entitled Flora n. Vasselon, showing a maiden in a himation, signed *Schütz*, diameter 9¹/₂in.
(Butterfield & Butterfield) $1,725

A Vienna-style claret-ground two-handled baluster vase, painted by Wagner with Schmiede des Vulcan, the god seated among clouds, draped in a red robe and with his sword swathed in green ribbon, France mark, circa 1900, 13in. high.
(Christie's) $2,418

A pair of Vienna-style two-handled tapering oviform vases, covers and square stands, painted by Wagner, late 19th century, 30in. high.
(Christie's) $8,289

A Vienna porcelain plate, the painted reserve depicting figures at an easel, on gilded and jeweled deep blue ground, 9¹/₂in. wide.
(Andrew Hartley) $623

VIENNA

A Vienna-style plate painted by Wagner with a portrait of a young girl with long fair hair, signed, blue beehive mark, circa 1890, 9¹/₂in. diameter.
(Christie's) $1,239

A pair of Vienna-style dark-blue-ground tapering oviform vases, covers and waisted stands, painted in a bright palette by W. Pfohl, circa 1900, 38¹/₂in. high.
(Christie's) $40,986

A Vienna style plate painted in the center with Ruth after Landelle, signed *Deliuror*, within a lime green border, 24.5cm.
(Phillips) $419

'Vienna' porcelain vase, late 19th century, the tall ovoid vase with two branch-molded handles, painted with an oval three-quarter portrait of a woman in a long pink loose-fitting gown, height 15in.
(Butterfield & Butterfield)
                                $1,380

Two 'Vienna' porcelain cabinet plates, late 19th century, the first with a half-length portrait of the Empress Elizabeth of Austria, the other entitled Schifflied, with the figure of a maiden holding a lyre, diameter 9⁵/₈ and 8³/₄in.
(Butterfield & Butterfield)
                                $1,265

A Vienna-style three-handled loving-cup, the exterior printed and painted with a continuous frieze of mythological figures, the gilt scroll handles with leaf terminals, on three paw feet, blue beehive mark, circa 1900, 7¹/₂in. high.
(Christie's) $920

A Vienna-style circular dish painted with a goddess and a maiden among billowing clouds with attendant cherubs, within a gilt-line rim, blue beehive mark, circa 1890, 10³/₄in. diameter.
(Christie's) $2,125

Extremely fine pair of Continental porcelain vases, bearing the Vienna beehive mark, 18¹/₂in. high, early 19th century.
(G.A. Key) $4,779

A Vienna-style plate painted by Scholz with Diana and Venus reclining on furs and drapery beside a pond in a woodland glade attended by Cupids, circa 1880, 9¹/₂in. diameter.
(Christie's) $723

VINCENNES

Vincennes may be said to be the birthplace of the famous Sèvres factory, whither it was removed in 1756 on the orders of King Louis XV.

The entire operation began however at Vincennes between 1738–40, when two financiers, Orry de Vignory and Orry de Fulvy were granted a permit by Louis to use the chateau there for experiments in porcelain manufacture. Their first managers, the brothers Dubois, proved unreliable and were sacked in 1741. Their assistant, François Gravant, took over and his efforts were more successful.

In 1745, with the king increasingly interested, a group of prominent figures was brought together to run the factory with the Orrys and Gravant, its capital was greatly increased, it received a 'privilege' from the king, and the period of its true greatness really began. Vincennes was something of an anachronism in that it set out only to produce soft paste porcelain. Perhaps its backers were wedded to the French traditions that had served well enough at Rouen, Chantilly and Mennecy, or perhaps it just lacked adequate supplies of kaolin, but the result was that it remained hampered by a process that was both costly and increasingly obsolete.

No such conservatism was seen in its decoration however. A new range of colors were developed, with an original range of forms and much use of gilding. Vincennes set out to compete with Meissen, but unlike Meissen pieces, the colors in the Vincennes palette were absorbed into the glaze, which on the usual white ground gave a wonderfully jewel like effect. By 1753 colored grounds were becoming increasingly popular and this led to many

A pair of Vincennes figures of 'La Petite Fille a Tablier' and 'Le Jeune Suppliant', circa 1753, the girl with her hair tied in a headscarf, 8in. high. (Christie's) $9,614

A Vincennes bleu celeste two-handled vase (vase Duplessis à fleurs) of campana form with elaborate foliage-scroll handles, each side painted with bouquets of flowers and fruit within cartouches, circa 1755, 15cm. high.
(Christie's) $13,196

A Vincennes cup and saucer, of 'Gobelet Hébert' shape modeled with five lobes and with a double twisted handle, date letter C for 1755, painter's mark of Denis Levé. (Phillips) $2,945

A Vincennes circular baluster sugar-bowl and cover painted with sprays of flowers including pink roses, date letter for 1754, 8cm. diameter.
(Christie's) $800

A Vincennes bleu lapis coffee-cup and saucer (gobelet à la reine) with loop handle, each side of the cup and the center of the saucer painted with two birds. (Christie's) $2,800

A Vincennes blue celeste sugar-bowl and cover (pot à sucre du roy) painted with figures walking by buildings in wooded landscapes, date letter B for 1754, 8.5cm. diameter.
(Christie's) $5,600

VINCENNES

pieces being covered in lapis blue, jonquil yellow and apple green. These grounds were often supplied with white reserves, which were embellished with superb miniature paintings of landscapes, dallying couples, birds, and an abundance of floral motifs. Gilding was lavish, sometimes enhanced with engraving or, in some cases, two tones of gold were used to give an even richer effect.

While much of the production consisted of tableware, Vincennes, being so closely involved with the Crown, had to maintain French international prestige, and many highly ornamental pieces, vases, urns, jardinières etc. were also produced and these were often used as Royal gifts.

Vincennes also set out to rival Meissen's figure production, and some wonderfully refined sculptures were made. Most were left in the white, but what made the essential difference was a decision in 1749 not to glaze them. The resulting biscuit had a texture akin to the finest marble and immediately became immensely popular.

After the death of the Orrys in the early 1750s, some reorganisation was urgently necessary. The King more or less took over and decreed in 1754 that the factory should remove to Sèvres. It did so in 1756, bringing the Vincennes period to a close.

Dating early Vincennes is extremely difficult. Some pieces are unmarked, others carry only crossed Ls. From 1753 an alphabetical date code was introduced with A for 1753 and so on. These dates were usually placed within the crossed Ls.

A Vincennes bleu celeste teacup and saucer (gobelet Hébert) with gilt entwined branch handle, painted with trailing flowers from cornucopia-shaped bleu celeste borders, date letter B for 1754. (Christie's) **$4,350**

A Vincennes figure of 'Le Porteur de Mouton', circa 1755, modeled as a young man kneeling and offering a beribboned sheep in a basket, 8½in. high. (Christie's) **$3,146**

An ormolu encrier with two wells contained in a gabled niched summerhouse framing a turquoise-glazed Vincennes porcelain model of a pug with a puppy, the pug, circa 1750, 7in. high. (Christie's) **$5,000**

A Vincennes two-handled seau à verre painted en camaieu rose one side with a boy flying a kite before a thatched cottage in a pastoral scene, circa 1752, 11cm. high. (Christie's) **$5,914**

A Vincennes tureen, cover and stand of oval form, gilt with panels of birds in flight within scrolling gilt cartouches, 25.5cm. wide. (Phillips) **$7,820**

A Vincennes partly glazed white biscuit figure of a sleeping putto resting on a bale of hay, circa 1753, 11cm. high. **$1,600**

VYSE

Charles Vyse was an English sculptor and potter who studied at Hanley Art School before moving to London where he opened his studio in Chelsea in 1919. With his wife Nell, he experimented with wood ash glazes on stoneware, and also during the 1920s successfully reproduced Chinese Sung vases.

His figure groups, realistically modeled and sometimes colored, are very sought after. His work is usually marked with initials or a signature. Charles Vyse died in 1968.

A Charles Vyse figure of a Shire horse, on rectangular base, 28.5cm. high.
$465

A Charles Vyse stoneware jug, inscribed *'Fishing's a dry job'* in a band around the rim, above a sceptical fish, 17cm. high. (Phillips)
$560

'The Balloon Woman', Chelsea pottery figure designed by Charles Vyse, painted in colors, painted factory mark, dated *1922*, 22cm. high. (Christie's)
$502

A stoneware globular vase by Charles Vyse, covered in a lustrous mottled khaki and brown glaze with areas of crimson, incised *CV 1933*, 13cm. high. (Christie's)
$1,500

'Fantasy', a Charles Vyse pottery group, of a woman seated cross-legged on a grassy base, scantily clad with a turquoise and mauve robe, 21.50cm. high. (Phillips)
$555

'The Lavender Girl', a Chelsea Cheyne pottery figure by Charles Vyse, painted in colors, 22cm. high. (Christie's)
$468

A stoneware oviform jar by Charles Vyse, 1928, 17cm. high. (Christie's)
$320

A Charles Vyse pottery figure of The Piccadilly Rose Woman modeled as a plump lady, 10in. high.
$840

WAIN

Louis Wain (1860–1931) was an English illustrator and designer who is best remembered for his illustrations of cats engaged in human pursuits. In the early 1900s he designed series of postcards, the A-Mewsing Write-away Series, on this theme for Raphael Tuck. Between 1910–20 he also designed pottery figures of cats in the Cubist style and brightly colored in eg. green, orange and black. His work became increasingly eccentric, however, and he died in an asylum in 1931.

The Laughing Cat designed by Louis Wain made by Wilkinsons, a seated kitten with gray glaze and green ribbon, 7³/₄in. high.
(David Lay) $133

'Felix the Futurist Cat', an Amphora pottery vase designed by Louis Wain, the body incised with *Miaow Miaow* notes, 9¹/₂in. high.
(Christie's) $3,115

A Louis Wain 'Haw Haw' cat, the pottery spill holder modeled as a caricature of Lord Haw Haw, 13.5cm. high.
(Christie's) $502

A large Louis Wain pottery vase modeled as a seated cat, 25.4cm. high.
                    $1,800

A Louis Wain porcelain animal vase, the stylized figure of a dog bearing a shield, with shaped aperture on its back, 14.2cm. high. (Christie's) $1,500

A Louis Wain porcelain lion vase, decorated in black, yellow, green and russet enamels, 11.8cm. high. (Christie's) $1,410

A Louis Wain pottery spill holder in the form of a standing bulldog, the yellow body painted with black scrolls, 9cm. high. (Christie's) $502

A Louis Wain porcelain pig vase, decorated in green, yellow, russet and black enamels, with impressed and painted marks, 12.4cm. high. (Christie's) $2,325

WALLEY ART

The Walley Pottery flourished around the turn of the century in the town of Sterling, Massachusetts.

Its output consisted mainly of simple forms, vases, mugs etc, designed in equally simple shapes. Decoration was often confined to the glazes, which could be mottled or streaked, and used in combinations of color such as a green drip on a brown ground. Occasionally pieces were simply molded with stylized plant and leaf forms. Grotesque mugs with molded mask faces were also produced.

WALRATH

Frederick Walrath (c1880–c1920) was an American artist potter who studied under Charles Binns. He also taught at Rochester and Columbia University, New York. His production consisted of earthenware vases and jars, decorated with linear motifs and stylized plant forms, covered in matt glazes. He exhibited in 1904 at the St Louis World Fair, and in later life worked for two years at the Newcomb College Pottery (q.v.), New Orleans. His mark consists of *Walrath Pottery*, incised, with a device of four arrows.

WALTON

John Walton (c. 1780- post 1835) worked out of Burslem, where by 1818 he was owner of a color works and an earthenware factory. His output included a variety of earthenware figures in imitation of contemporary porcelain originals, and these are characterised by their streaky, opaque coloring and the fact that they are usually in a tree or bocage setting. His figures include soldiers, religious groups, classical subjects, rustic subjects and animals.

A green-glazed grotesque jug, American, 20th century, the bulbous form with applied strap-handles above applied articulated ears flanking a human face, 16in. high. (Christie's) $1,150

Walley Pottery vase, Sterling, Massachusetts, early 20th century, in green drip glaze on brown ground, 9½in. high. (Skinner Inc.) $600

A Walrath pottery pitcher and five mugs, circa 1910, pitcher 6½in. high $1,600

Walrath Pottery vase, Rochester, New York, circa 1910, matt glazed with repeating foliate band in pale blue and mustard against blue ground, 4¾in. high. (Skinner) $920

A Walton model of the royal lion seated, with naturalistically colored body, wearing a crown above its curly mane, 14cm. high. (Phillips) $1,445

A Walton group, 'Songsters' modeled as a boy and girl musicians on a rocky base with bocage behind, circa 1820, 9in. high. (Bonhams) $882

WEDGWOOD

Josiah Wedgwood founded his pottery at Burslem in 1759. It operated there until 1774, by which time he had already opened his Etruria factory, and the business continues in the family until the present day.

Wedgwood products were noted from the first for their high quality, and the company was always in the forefront of pioneering new techniques. One of their early successes, achieved as early as 1761, was the cream colored earthenware, durable and reasonably priced, which was known as creamware. In 1765 came a commission to supply a 60-piece tea service to Queen Charlotte, and this met with such royal satisfaction, that Wedgwood was allowed to call his recent invention Queensware, which name it has borne ever since.

In response to a call for a whiter earthenware, Wedgwood set to work again to develop pearlware, which contained more white clay and flint and was fired at a higher temperature to give a bluish white body. This again proved hugely popular and sold in great quantities between 1790-1820. Production continued until 1846.

Bone porcelain production was attempted from 1812 and successfully resumed in 1878. With Copeland and Minton, Wedgwood was in the vanguard of parian production and parian ware, notably portrait busts, were being produced from 1848 onwards.

Majolica was produced between 1860–1910 for such items as umbrella stands, plaques, comports etc., often using émaux ombrants for decoration. Tiles were also made, and usually transfer printed.

In the 1870s came other developments, such as

A Wedgewood bicolor Jasper dip coffee-can and saucer, the pale-green-ground applied with oval mauve-ground medallions within white relief-molded garlands, 19th century. (Christie's) $707

A Wedgwood black and white oval portrait medallion of Richard, first Earl Howe, modeled by John de Vaere, 12cm. high., 19th century. (Christie's) $376

An unusual Wedgwood Baguley type three piece coffee service, each piece 'incised' with ferns and flowers. (Spencer's) $354

A Wedgwood pearlware jelly mold, circa 1790, of cone shape, enameled with blue and iron-red flowers on green branches, 8½in. high. (Christie's) $2,875

A garniture of two Wedgwood crocus pots and covers and a small flower vase each colored in cream and brown, with relief molded cream ribbon- tied swags, 14cm. to 16cm. (Phillips) $460

A Wedgwood white-jasper anti-slavery medallion, relief decorated in black with a kneeling figure of a black slave, beneath the words *Am I not a man and a brother*, 3.5cm. (Phillips) $832

WEDGWOOD

Victoria ware, with a body midway between bone porcelain and Queensware. From 1880, decoration with printed and painted landscapes and commemorative wares, often at first for the American market, began.

Jasperware had been in Wedgwood's range from the beginning. In the early years of the 20th century it began to be relief decorated not only now in lilac and green but also olive, crimson, buff, black and turquoise. At this time too luster ware production began, notably the Dragon and Fairyland luster series designed by Daisy Makeig-Jones.

Traditional designs continued – particularly at the end of the 19th century there was much harking back to earlier styles – but innovations were, at the same time, constantly being introduced. In 1940 the factory moved to Barlaston.

Marks include *Wedgwood* and from 1891 *Made in England*. Bone porcelain from 1878 is marked with a replica of the Portland Vase. Various designers also signed their works.

A Wedgwood caneware cream jug and cover, the cover with recumbent lion finial, circa 1790, 11.5cm. high.
(Christie's) $450

A Wedgwood 'Queens ware' teapot, painted in colors with a cockerel amongst paeony and chrysanthemum, 5¹/₂in. high.
(Bonhams) $275

A Wedgwood yellow-ground wash basin set printed in black with vignettes of Classical ruins, Italianate boating view and figures before lakes.
(Christie's) $1,364

A Wedgwood black-ground shouldered oviform vase with loop handles, applied with decoration of ladies in classical dress, 19th century, 15in. high.
(Christie's) $1,184

A Wedgwood bone china onion vase with a flared trumpet neck, molded gilt and silvered with two herons amongst bulrushes and lily pads, circa 1890, 8¹/₄in. high.
(Bonhams) $370

A pair of Wedgwood earthenware scalloped dishes painted with putto symbolic of the elements fire and water, 9in. wide.
(Bonhams) $740

A Wedgwood baluster jug, painted on the front with the Arms of the Company in blue, the supporters bearing banners with red crosses, 21.5cm.
$1,750

WEDGWOOD

'Ferdinand the Bull' a Wedgwood figure of a bull modeled by Arnold Machin 12½in. long.
(Christie's) $392

A rare Wedgwood creamware teapot and cover, depicting on one side the Jeremiah Meyer portrait of George III reversed with the Thomas Frye portrait of Queen Charlotte, height 4½in.
(Bonhams) $6,800

An Art Deco Wedgwood animal figure, modeled as a fallow deer, designed by J. Skeaping, 21.5cm. high.
$580

A green-dip Jasper two-handled biscuit barrel and cover, the handles scrolling, decorated with the 'Dancing Hours' below swags of flowers, the interior glazed, impressed marks, inscribed *McVITIE AND PRICE 1906*, 8in. high.
(Christie's) $685

A Wedgwood redware teapot, cover with crocodile finial and **stand, molded in black with** Egyptian motifs, a two-handled sugar-bowl and cover, and a milk-jug, impressed mark.
(Christie's) $593

Wedgwood pottery jug, cream glazed, commemorating Thomas Carlysle with portrait and verse, dated for the 30th April, 1881, 9in. high.
(G. A. Key) $228

A Wedgwood pearlware bough-pot and pierced cover of D-shape, molded, incised and washed in dark brown to simulate a barrel, impressed mark, circa 1790, 7½in. wide.
(Christie's) $538

A Wedgwood ceramic ewer and basin designed by George Logan, covered in a lilac glaze and decorated with stylized yellow floral designs, 29.6cm. height of ewer. (Christie's) $1,250

A Wedgwood pottery charger designed by Keith Murray, covered in a matt straw yellow glaze, printed facsimile signature *Keith Murray,* and *Wedgwood, Made in England,* 35.5cm. diam. (Christie's) $800

WEDGWOOD, BLACK BASALT

Wedgwood basalt figure "Nymph at Well", England, circa 1840, modeled as a female figure holding a shell, 11in. high.
(Skinner Inc.) $1,045

A pair of Wedgwood black basalt griffin candlesticks, circa 1795, 34cm. high.
(Christie's) $2,400

'Bull', a Wedgwood black basalt figure designed by John Skeaping, impressed factory marks and facsimile signature, 5¼in. high.
(Christie's) $941

A Wedgwood black basaltes and rosso antico cylindrical spill vase, circa 1820, applied with figures of 'Springtime' and 'The Spinner', 4½in. high.
(Christie's) $437

Pair of Wedgwood black basalt encaustic decorated oviform two-handled vases and one cover, circa 1800, 37.5cm. high.
(Christie's) $6,400

A Wedgwood black basaltes encaustic decorated pelike, circa 1820, enameled en grisaille with a muse and two youths, 8⅝in. high.
(Christie's) $3,450

A Wedgwood black basaltes encaustic-decorated hydria, circa 1830, enameled in orange, black and white with a classical maiden in a horse-drawn chariot 10¼in. high.
(Christie's) $2,760

Two of four Wedgwood black basalt column candlesticks, carved in gilt with stiff leaves to the tops and spiralling bands of foliage, circa 1900, 11½in. high.
$5,200

A Wedgwood black basalt copy of the Portland vase, the oviform body applied in white with classical figures at various pursuits, circa 1880, 25.5cm. high.
(Christie's) $3,565

WEDGWOOD, BLACK BASALT

A Wedgwood black basalt coffee biggin and cover enameled in famille-rose style enamels with sprays of chrysanthemums and paeonies, 18.5cm.
(Phillips) $512

Two Wedgwood black basalt miniature busts of Homer and Aristophanes, circa 1785, 11cm. and 10cm. high.
(Christie's) $2,400

A Wedgwood black basaltes cylindrical teapot and cover, circa 1790, with sibyl finial and in relief with 'Infants Playing' above a band of engine-turned stripes, 4¹/₂in. high.
(Christie's) $978

A Wedgwood black basalt encaustic-decorated oviform vase and cover, the shoulder with upright loop handles, painted with Classical figures at various pursuits, circa 1820, 24cm. high.
(Christie's) $1,160

A pair of Wedgwood black-and-white jasper two-handled urns, each molded in high relief with classical figures above a fluted tapering stem and square-shaped foot, 11in. high.
(Christie's) $753

A Wedgwood black basalt library bust of Cicero turned slightly to the right and named on the reverse, on a waisted circular socle, late 18th century, 51cm. high.
(Christie's) $2,213

A Wedgwood encaustic decorated basalt vase, decorated with a classical figure of a winged maiden, above a band of anthemion leaves, 23cm.
(Phillips) $1,218

A pair of mid 19th century Wedgwood black basalt triton candlesticks of conventional type, 28cm. high.
(Christie's) $1,450

A Wedgwood black basalt encaustic-decorated oviform two-handled vase painted with Jupiter, circa 1800, 30cm. high. (Christie's) $1,300

WEDGWOOD, BLUE JASPER

Wedgwood jasperware bowl on standard with raised figures on an olive green ground, 5¹/₂in. high.
(Eldred's) $77

Wedgwood blue and white jasperware teapot, 20th century, with classical sprigging, English silver rim, 5¹/₂in. high.
(Eldred's) $132

19th century blue and white Jasperware Stilton cheese dish and cover, possibly Wedgwood.
(G. A. Key) $360

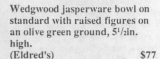

A Wedgwood blue and white jasper bulb pot and cover, impressed mark and V, circa 1785, 24cm. high.
(Christie's) $2,250

A Wedgwood blue and white jasper 'ruined column' vase, the white fluted columns molded with lichen supported on a solid-blue rectangular base, circa 1795, 21cm. wide.
(Christie's) $8,800

A Wedgwood gilt-copper mounted blue and white jasper octagonal scent-bottle, circa 1790, decorated with two putti dancing beneath a tree, 2⁵/₈in. high.
(Christie's) $1,495

A Wedgwood blue dip jasper 'Staites Patent' pipe-bowl of baluster form, fitting a terminal formed as an acorn, 8.8cm. high, circa 1849.
(Christie's) $155

A pair of Wedgwood blue jasper urns and covers, with mask handles and decorated with classical maidens, on square bases, 16.5cm. high.
(Allen & Harris) $306

A large Wedgwood blue jasperware dip two-handled campana-shaped pot-pourri jar, 41.5cm.
(Bearne's) $640

WEDGWOOD, BLUE JASPER

A Wedgwood blue and white jasper dip oval plaque, circa 1790, decorated with 'Sportive Love' modeled by William Hackwood, 4⁵/₈in. high. (Christie's) **$483**

A Wedgwood blue and white jasper dip cylindrical teapot and cover, circa 1785, with figures from 'Domestic Employment' by Elizabeth, Lady Templetown, 4¹/₈in. high. (Christie's) **$920**

Wedgwood dark blue jasper Stilton cheese dish and cover, England, late 19th century, with continuous classical scene, 11⁵/₈in. diameter. (Skinner Inc.) **$360**

Late 19th century Wedgwood blue ground jasper jardiniere, 10in. diam. (Peter Wilson) **$280**

A pair of Wedgwood 'Victoria' ware blue-ground ovIform vases applied with pink and white decoration of classical devices between swags of flowers suspended, circa 1880, 7¹/₈in. high. (Christie's) **$505**

A Wedgwood solid pale-blue and white jasper cylindrical sugar bowl and cover, circa 1785, 10.5cm. diam. (Christie's) **$760**

One of a pair of Wedgwood blue and white jasper cylindrical altar vases, circa 1785, 13.5cm. high. (Christie's) **$1,200**

A rare Wedgwood teapot and cover, with unusual ovoid body decorated in white relief with 'Bacchanalian Boys', 13cm. (Phillips) **$1,377**

A Wedgwood blue and white jasper portrait medallion of William Pitt The Younger, circa 1790, 9.5cm. high. (Christie's) **$800**

WEDGWOOD, CREAMWARE

A Wedgwood creamware chintz-pattern globular teapot and cover, circa 1770, enameled at the David Rhodes workshop, 5in. high.
(Christie's) $2,530

19th century Wedgwood creamware covered tureen with green fern decorated borders, 17in. long.
(Eldred's) $825

A Wedgwood Creamware oviform teapot and a cover, painted in the manner of David Rhodes in iron-red, green and black, circa 1768, 14.5cm. high overall.
(Christie's) $1,480

A Wedgwood creamware oval sauce tureen, cover and pierced stand, painted in the manner of James Bakewell, circa 1770, the stand 26.5cm. wide.
(Christie's) $3,200

Pair of Wedgwood gold embossed creamware covered vases, having four sculpted heads of Bacchus at shoulders, 11¹/₂in. high, circa 1795.
(Schrager) $1,200

A Wedgwood creamware crested large oval settling pan and skimming spoon, circa 1790, the shallow dish with a spout at one end, and printed in brown on one side of the well with the crest of the Palk family of Haldon House.
(Sotheby's) $1,380

A Wedgwood creamware oviform teapot and cover painted in the manner of David Rhodes with vertical bands of stylized ornament, circa 1768, 14cm. high.
(Christie's) $3,347

An interesting Wedgwood creamware veilleuse, the upper section containing an inverted cone, with two spouts, 43cm. high.
(Henry Spencer) $600

A Wedgwood creamware teapot and cover, circa 1770, probably enameled by David Rhodes, enameled in colors with a man standing in a landscape, 6¹/₄in. high.
(Christie's) $6,697

WEDGWOOD, FAIRYLAND

A good Wedgwood Fairyland luster bowl, decorated with numerous figures on a waterside, printed mark in brown, circa 1920, 8¾in. diam. (Tennants) $2,000

A rare Wedgwood flame Fairyland luster 'Fairy Slide' Malfrey pot and cover, 7⅛in. high. (Bonhams) $14,950

Wedgwood porcelain Fairyland luster footed punch bowl, 1920's, decorated on the exterior with the 'Poplar Trees' pattern of trees before buildings, bridges, and fairies, 11in. diameter. (Butterfield & Butterfield) $2,200

A Wedgwood Fairyland luster charger, designed by Daisy Makeig Jones, in the Ghostly Wood pattern, printed and painted in colors and gilt printed factory marks, 38cm. diameter. (Christie's) $23,400

A pair of Wedgwood Fairyland luster Torches' vases, printed in gold and painted on the exterior in Flame Fairyland tones with 'Torches', 28.5cm. high. (Phillips) $3,500

A Wedgwood Fairyland luster plate, the center painted in predominant shades of blue, purple, claret and green and enriched in gilding with goblins crossing a bridge, 1920's, 27.5cm. diameter. (Christie's) $1,965

A Wedgwood Fairyland luster octagonal bowl decorated with 'Dana' pattern, the interior with fairies, rainbows and long-tailed birds, 18cm., Portland Vase mark and no. Z5125. (Phillips) $1,827

A fine and rare Wedgwood Fairyland luster 'Ghostly Wood' ginger jar and cover, designed by Daisy Makeig-Jones, 12¾in. high. (Bonhams) $24,667

A Wedgwood Fairyland luster octagonal bowl, the 'drake neck green' ground painted in dark blue and gold with Firbolgs, 3¼in. high. (Bonhams) $550

WEDGWOOD, FAIRYLAND

A Wedgwood Fairyland luster bowl, the exterior decorated with a midnight-blue ground gilt with trees and flowerheads flanking panels of flying fairies against a flame sky, 27cm. (Phillips) $4,699

A rare Wedgwood Fairyland luster 'White Pagodas' Daventry bowl, designed by Daisy Makeig-Jones, 10^{1}/8in. diameter. (Bonhams) $7,475

A Wedgwood Fairyland luster punch bowl, the interior decorated with The Woodland Bridge pattern, 28.5cm. diameter. (Bearne's) $2,595

A Wedgwood Fairyland luster vase decorated with the 'Imps on a Bridge' pattern, with the brown boy and blue Rock bird, 23cm. (Bearne's) $2,400

A pair of Wedgwood Fairyland luster square vases decorated with panels of the 'Dana' pattern, 19.5cm. (Phillips) $4,400

A Wedgwood Fairyland luster slender baluster vase and cover, the iridescent black ground printed in gold and colored with three fairies, 1920s, 21.5cm. high. $4,000

A Wedgwood Fairyland luster ovoid vase decorated in purple, green, black, yellow and gilt, with the 'Candlemas' pattern, 18.5cm. (Phillips) $2,800

A Wedgwood Fairyland luster 'Melba Cup', the ogee bowl externally painted with dancing fairies and goblins, 3in. high. (Bonhams) $1,100

A Wedgwood Fairyland luster oviform vase, painted with three panels of fairies, elves and birds before river landscapes, 8^{1}/2in. high. (Christie's) $1,378

WEDGWOOD, MAJOLICA

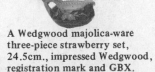

A Wedgwood majolica oval fish-platter, molded in relief on a pale-turquoise ground with a salmon lying on a bed of green ferns with ocher tips, circa 1876, 25¼in. wide.
(Christie's) $694

A Wedgwood majolica-ware three-piece strawberry set, 24.5cm., impressed Wedgwood, registration mark and GBX.
(Phillips) $520

Wedgwood majolica game pie dish, England, 1868, complete with Queensware liner, 11in. wide.
(Skinner Inc.) $3,575

A Wedgwood majolica figure of a young merman, possibly a lamp or tazza base, garlanded with seaweed upholding a branch of coral, impressed marks, date code for 1871, 15in. high.
(Christie's) $762

A good and unusual EPNS mounted Wedgwood tortoiseshell majolica three piece tea service, of tapering cylindrical form.
(Spencer's) $506

A 19th century Wedgwood majolica centerpiece, the pierced basket glazed in brown, green, and yellow, the branchiform pedestal surrounded by three putti, impressed date code CBX for 1869, 16in.
(Michael Dowman) $1,323

A Wedgwood majolica-ware 'Kate Greenaway' jardiniere, modeled as a lady's straw bonnet, 16.5cm., impressed *Wedgwood* and molded registration mark.
(Phillips) $370

Rare Wedgwood Etruscan majolica milk pitcher, with raised decoration of two baseball and two soccer players, 7½in. high.
(Eldred's) $1,320

A Wedgwood majolica teapot and cover of squat bulbous form and with an overhead loop handle, the body glazed in mottled manganese, date code for 1872, 6in. high.
(Christie's) $415

WEDGWOOD & BENTLEY

In around 1770 Josiah Wedgwood arranged with Thomas Bentley for the latter to open a workshop in Cheyne Row Chelsea, where painters would be engaged in decorating creamware. Their partnership lasted for a number of years, and their catalog of 1779 shows that they were producing biscuit ware, jasperware and pearlware.

A Wedgwood & Bentley black basalt hare's head stirrup cup, circa 1775, 16cm. high. $15,000

A black basalt encaustic-decorated teapot and cover, Wedgwood & Bentley, the oval body painted with drapery swags with two pendant medallions, circa 1775. (Christie's) $7,200

A Wedgwood & Bentley variegated oviform caryatid vase, circa 1775, the creamware body with marbleized surface crystalline agate decoration in mottled black and brown slips, 9¾in. high.
(Christie's) $3,450

A pair of Wedgwood and Bentley black basalt urn-shaped vases and covers, the latter with Sybil finials, 28cm. high.
(Phillips) $4,500

A large Wedgwood and Bentley black basalt vase of shouldered ovoid form, with Bacchus head terminals with their horns forming handles, 36cm. high.
(Phillips) $2,650

A Wedgwood and Bentley black basalt oval portrait medallion of Minerva in high relief, circa 1775, 20cm. high.
(Christie's) $1,120

A Wedgwood & Bentley black basalt encaustic-decorated circular sugar bowl and cover, circa 1775, 11.5cm. diam.
(Christie's) $2,800

An oval black basalt plaque of Josiah Wedgwood, modeled by William Hackwood, attributed to Wedgwood and Bentley, circa 1782, 9cm. long.
(Christie's) $450

476

WEDGWOOD WHIELDON

Thomas Whieldon (1719-95) was perhaps the last and greatest of the traditional Staffordshire potters using traditional potting methods. He also had an eye for talent and in 1754 took as his apprentice and then partner Josiah Wedgwood. Together they developed earthenware figures characterised by their dripping colored glazes. Whieldon is particularly associated with a tortoiseshell glaze, made by the use of a limited range of high temperature oxides. The partnership lasted until 1759, when Wedgwood struck out on his own.

A creamware double rectangular tea caddy of Wedgwood/Whieldon type, circa 1760, 14.5cm. wide.
(Christie's) $2,750

A Wedgwood/Whieldon lobed hexagonal teapot and cover with scrolling handle, in green with ocher streaks, 12cm.
(Phillips London) $2,900

A Wedgwood/Whieldon cauliflower molded coffee pot and domed cover, of pear shape, 25.5cm.
(Phillips) $2,500

A Wedgwood/Whieldon cauliflower teapot and cover in shaded green colors.
(A. J. Cobern) $1,250

A mid-18th century Wedgwood Whieldon type cauliflower molded coffee pot and cover, 24.5cm. high.
(Spencer's) $2,500

A Wedgwood Whieldon pineapple teapot and cover, 10cm. high.
(Phillips) $1,600

A Wedgwood/Whieldon cauliflower teapot and cover, 11.6cm. high. $1,000

A Wedgwood/Whieldon hexagonal teapot and cover in chinoiserie style, 16cm. high. $2,500

WELLER

Samuel Weller (1851–1925) acquired the Lonhuda pottery at Steubenville, Ohio in the early 1890s, and moved production to his own pottery which he had established in 1882 at Zanesville. There, he continued to produce pottery in the Lonhuda style, which was now called Louwelsa. This was very like Rookwood Standard ware in appearance, and Weller continued to imitate subsequent Rookwood innovations.

A French potter, Jacques Sicard, joined the business in 1901 and produced Sicardo ware, on which a luster decoration was applied to an iridescent ground in shades of purple, green and brown. Later, a variation, Lasa ware, was introduced with landscape decoration.

Weller worked too in imitation of French Art Nouveau styles, with relief decorations of flowers, foliage and female figures. Aurelia ware was introduced by 1904, having a brushed ground, also Jap Birdimal, with stylized natural forms as decoration.

At its height the business employed some 600 workers and by 1925 Weller owned three factories producing art pottery, garden and kitchen wares. He was succeeded by his nephew Herbert, who died in 1932, and the factory finally closed in 1949.

Marks include impressed *Weller* with the name of the style, and incised *Weller Faience*.

CHINA

Weller Pottery Louwelsa ewer, Zanesville, Ohio, circa 1905, decorated with an oak twig in shades of green with brown and beige.
(Skinner) $100

Weller Pottery Etna pot, Zanesville, Ohio, high gloss glazed and decorated with low relief flowers in rose, yellow, white and green, 4½in. high.
(Skinner) $100

Weller Sicardo Pottery tile, Zanesville, Ohio, Henri Gellee, circa 1905, iridescent green glazed cross and border with incised outline, 7½in. wide.
(Skinner) $600

Weller Pottery 'Wild Rose' pattern vase, circa 1930, peach matt glaze decorated with ivory and pink flowers and a light green wash, 6½in. high.
(Du Mouchelles) $200

Exceptional and rare Weller glossy Hudson vase, signed *Timberlake*, decorated with orchids, Weller Pottery half-kiln mark, artist signature, 27in. high.
(Skinner) $21,185

A Weller Sicard twisted pottery vase, iridescent purples and greens with snails in the design, circa 1907, unsigned, 7½in. high.
(Skinner) $640

WELLER

Weller pottery vase, Zanesville, Ohio, circa 1914, "Camelot" funnel shape neck on squat bulbous body, 7¾in. high. (Skinner Inc.) **$275**

Weller Jap Birdimal vase, decorated by Hattie Ross, decorated with bands of birds in white, green and brown, 5¼in. high. (Skinner) **$316**

Louwelsa Weller pottery Indian portrait vase, Ohio, circa 1915, 10¾in. high. (Skinner) **$560**

Weller Pottery Sicardo vase, Zanesville, Ohio, circa 1905, iridescent glaze in rose, blue and platinum with stylised peacock feather decoration, 5¼in. high. (Skinner) **$633**

Weller silvertone vase, exquisite floral modeling on bulbous body with swirling handles and ruffled rim, 8in. high. (Skinner) **$460**

Weller Sicardo glazed pottery vase, early 20th century, decorated in green, blue, fuchsia and gold iridescence, 6½in. high. (Butterfield & Butterfield) **$690**

Weller Pottery Hudson vase, Zanesville, Ohio, Edith Hood, circa 1920, matt wax glaze over underglaze slip, yellow rose decoration, 8¾in. high. (Skinner) **$403**

Weller Dickensware art pottery mantel clock, housed in elaborated pottery frame decorated with yellow pansies, 10in. high. (Skinner Inc.) **$440**

Weller Pottery Jap-Birdimal vase, Zanesville, Ohio, gloss glazed and decorated with stylized Japanese woman, 10¼in. high. (Skinner) **$863**

WEMYSS

Wemyss Ware is the most distinctive product of the Scottish potteries. Its trademarks are free flowing designs on white of roses, cherries and apples.

The pottery of Robert Heron & Sons was based at Kirkcaldy in Fife and its fame really began when a young Bohemian decorator called Karl Nekola joined the staff in 1883. He became Art Director and by the time he died in 1915 he had made Wemyss Ware famous. The name was taken from nearby Wemyss Castle, the home of the Grosvenor family who did much to popularise the pottery with their upper class friends in London. Thomas Goode and Co, the Mayfair china shop, became the sole outlet for Wemyss Ware in London and sent up special orders for individual customers.

Nekola trained other artists and also his own two sons in the work of ceramic decoration and though no pieces were signed, it is possible to identify different artists by their style. Wemyss was produced in a vast range of shapes and sizes from buttons to garden seats and the washstand sets were particularly well designed.

A Wemyss Ware three-handled loving cup painted with sweet-peas, two impressed Wemyss marks, 9¹/₂in. high. (Christie's) $810

A Wemyss (Bovey Tracey) model of a pig, seated on its haunches, decorated with large black patches, 28cm. high. (Phillips) $1,850

Two Bovey Tracey Wemyss Ware models of pigs, mid 20th century, green printed *Plichta, London England* to both, both signed Nekola Pinxt, 18¾in. and 12in. long. (Christie's) $1,955

A Wemyss (Bovey Tracey) model of a cat after a Gallé original, seated upright, with green glass eyes and a smug expression, 32cm. high, mark *Wemyss* in dark green. (Phillips) $2,625

A Wemyss preserve jar and cover painted with grapes and vine leaves in green and purple, impressed *WEMYSS* to underside, 4.75in. high. (Morphets) $628

Carnations, a combé flower pot, 17.2cm. high, impressed *Wemyss* mark. (Phillips) $1,480

A rare Wemyss jar and cover, circa 1900, painted with a band of strawberries above a leaf border, the cover painted with strawberries, impressed mark, 17cm. (Sotheby's) $1,327

WEMYSS

A Wemyss Ware globular teapot and cover painted with cabbage roses painted Wemyss mark, 8in. wide.
(Christie's) $330

A Wemyss Ware Audley bowl-on-stand, painted with cabbage roses, impressed and painted Wemyss marks, 6½in. high.
(Christie's) $695

A Wemyss Ware pink-glazed model of a pig, impressed *Wemyss Ware R.H.&S.*, circa 1900, 6in. wide.
(Christie's) $616

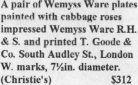

A Wemyss ware commemorative goblet printed with *V R* below a crown and flanked by thistles, roses and shamrock, the reverse dated *1897*, 5¹/₂in. high.
(Christie's) $783

A pair of Wemyss Ware plates painted with cabbage roses impressed Wemyss Ware R.H. & S. and printed T. Goode & Co. South Audley St., London W. marks, 7½in. diameter.
(Christie's) $312

A Wemyss Ware pear-shaped jug, painted with cabbage roses, impressed Wemyss and printed T. Goode & Co., Audley St. London W. marks, 5in. high.
(Christie's) $260

A Wemyss Ware slop-bucket painted with two black cocks and five black hens, impressed Wemyss mark and printed T. Goode & Co. mark, 11¹/₈in. high.
(Christie's) $1,815

A small Wemyss model of a pig, its coat decorated with shamrocks, the ears, snout and trotters in pink, 10cm. high.
(Phillips) $630

A Wemyss Ware preserve jar and cover painted with pink roses and foliage within green dentil rims, circa 1900, 4³/₄in. high.
(Christie's) $154

WEMYSS

A Wemyss Ware three-handled loving cup painted with branches of apples, impressed Wemyss Ware, 9¼in. high. (Christie's) $591

A Wemyss Ware ewer and basin painted with cabbage roses, impressed Wemyss Ware R, H & S marks, the basin 15½in. diameter. (Christie's) $1,270

A Wemyss 'Bute' vase, circa 1900, painted with pink roses, impressed and script marks, 19cm. (Sotheby's) $567

An attractive Wemyss (Bovey Tracey) model of a pig in the usual squatting pose, with ears pricked, painted all over the back and ears with sprays of flowering clover, 46cm. (Phillips) $3,200

A pair of Wemyss candlesticks painted with the rose-pattern, impressed marks, 12in. high, circa 1900. (Christie's) $352

A Wemyss Ware teacup and saucer, painted with cabbage roses and a sugar bowl ensuite impressed Wemyss and printed T. Goode & Co., South Audley St., London W. marks (Christie's) $225

Wemyss china tankard, decorated with flowering tulips, 5½in. high. (G. A. Key) $442

A Wemyss Ware chamber candlestick, painted with cabbage roses, with scroll handle, painted Wemyss mark, 5½in. high. (Christie's) $660

A Wemyss Ware slop-bucket painted with cabbage roses, impressed Wemyss Ware R, H & S mark, 11in. high. (Christie's) $304

WESTERWALD

The Westerwald was one of the great stoneware centers of Germany, though little of value is recorded until the late 16th century. Jugs and Krugs were made in great numbers, often with initials and small decorations such as rosettes, lion masks and angel heads until the late 17th century. Thereafter, greater use was made of incised and combed lines which acted as barriers to contain the cobalt blue and manganese purple colors. Production of these wares continues to the present day.

A Westerwald stoneware Schraubflasche (screw-neck flask) of square shape, molded with horned ogre masks on the shoulders, 30cm.
(Phillips) $512

A Westerwald globular jug glazed in blue and manganese and molded with a royal equestrian portrait medallion, circa 1690, 28cm. high.
(Christie's) $2,367

A Westerwald stoneware globular jug with loop handle, the mottled blue ground applied with navette shaped molded medallions of stylized masks and grasses, late 17th century, 26cm. high.
(Christie's) $1,000

A Westerwald stoneware spirit-barrel of ribbed form, the blue ground incised with bands of scrolling stylized foliage, the ends with winged cherubs' heads and flowers, 18th century, 33cm. long.
(Christie's) $1,530

A Westerwald desk-set modeled as two gallants in incised perukes, their companion holding a shallow circular container and wearing a pleated dress, early 18th century, 23cm. high.
(Christie's) $5,544

A Westerwald jug of globular shape with a grooved neck and foot, applied with panels of wheel motifs and small bosses in gray and black, 21cm. late 17th century.
(Phillips) $136

A German saltglazed stoneware font-shaped salt cellar, probably Westerwald, 18th century, the compressed spherical bowl applied with spiraling borders of boss-molded gadrooning, 3¹/₂in. high.
(Sotheby's) $1,725

A good Westerwald jug, the front with an oval armorial medallion and the inscription *Francisc:Al...and:Pr:Na. .Ov.C: Catti N:Viand:Et.Deci. D.I. Beils.T*, 25cm.
(Phillips) $589

CHINA

A gray and blue painted bellied jug, applied with marguerites, pewter cover, Westerwald, circa 1700.
(Kunsthaus am Museum)
$1,632

A Westerwald salt modeled as a roaring lion, clasping a shallow bowl in its fore-paws, on a heart-shaped foliage base, early 18th century, 17cm. high.
(Christie's) $2,033

A Westerwald Krug, the short cylindrical neck applied with masks and birds, the globular body with The Crucifixion, 17th/18th century, 22.5cm. high.
(Christie's) $2,772

A Westerwald stoneware globular jug with loop handle, applied with an octagonal portrait medallion of William III flanked by scrolling flowers enriched in manganese and with incised stems, late 17th century, 13.5cm. (Christie's) $800

A Westerwald stoneware silver-mounted cylindrical mug with loop handle, the body incised and enriched in blue with stylized foliage flanked by two flowerhead medallions, mid-18th century, 19cm. high.
(Christie's) $1,000

An unusual Westerwald William III Krug with ovoid body, cylindrical neck molded with horizontal ribbing and a ribbed loop handle, 18.55cm., end 17th century.
(Phillips) $760

A Westerwald gray stoneware oviform armorial jug applied with molded crowned coat-of-arms accollé on an octagonal panel, late 17th century, 17.5cm. high.
(Christie's) $845

A Westerwald salt modeled as a gentleman in an elaborate peruke, his pleated frock-coat with flared sleeves, holding a shallow bowl before him, early 18th century, 22cm. high.
(Christie's) $2,772

A Westerwald buff stoneware jug of large globular shape with cylindrical grooved neck and loop handle, circa 1700, 22cm. high.
(Christie's) $800

WHIELDON

Thomas Whieldon (1719-95) was an English potter working out of Fenton Low, or Little Fenton, in Staffordshire, between 1740-80. He produced lead-glazed earthenware and stoneware, and his products included teaware, cutlery handles and agate-ware salad bowls colored in a mixture of brown, cream, and blue and green. He also became well-known for his tortoiseshell-ware.

A number of noted ceramicists were sometime employees of Whieldon, among them Aaron Wood, Josiah Spode I and Josiah Wedgwood.

A Staffordshire creamware model of a water-buffalo of Whieldon type naturally modeled and covered in a streaked manganese glaze, probably 18th century, 25.5cm. long.
(Christie's) $7,482

A rare early Staffordshire teapot of Whieldon type, after a Chinese original, with a replacement cover, 14.5cm.
(Phillips) $480

A Staffordshire creamware baluster cream jug and cover of Whieldon type, applied with trailing fruiting branches, circa 1760, 12cm. high.
(Christie's) $2,000

A pair of creamware Arbour figures of Whieldon type, modeled as a musician playing the fiddle in streaked gray topcoat and yellow waistcoat, his companion in a green splashed crinoline and holding a pug dog on her lap, circa 1750, 15cm. high. (Christie's) $56,000

A creamware cauliflower-molded baluster coffee-pot and cover of Whieldon type, the upper part with cream florettes and the lower part with crisply molded overlapping green leaves, circa 1765, 24¼in. high.
(Christie's) $7,200

A Staffordshire creamware pineapple molded rectangular tea-caddy of Wedgwood/Whieldon type with canted angles, circa 1760, 10.5cm. high.
(Christie's) $1,477

A creamware arbor group of Whieldon type, modeled as a garden shelter, a woman in a crinoline sitting on either side of the curved seat, 14.5cm. high.
(Bearne's) $27,750

A Staffordshire creamware pear-shaped milk-jug, circa 1760, of Whieldon type, on three animal paw feet headed by lion masks (cracked), 5½in. high.
(Christie's) $1,760

WIENER WERKSTÄTTE

The Wiener Werkstätte or Vienna Workshops, were, as the name suggests, an association of Austrian artists and craftsmen after the style of C.R. Ashbee's Guild of Handicraft. Their commercial director was F. Warndörfer, and such notables as Koloman Moser and Josef Hoffmann were the first art directors. The aim of the association was to apply artistic principles and designs to the widest possible range of items, from textiles to architecture, and they became, in the succeeding decades, a driving force in European design.

Their ceramics are notable for their stark simplicity of design. Many of their designs were produced by the Wiener Keramik workshop, which was established in 1905 under Michael Powolny and Bertold Löffler. One of their most characteristic items was black and white majolica, painted with geometric patterns in the Cubist style. Powolny and Löffler also modeled figures. The Wiener Werkstätte themselves finally closed in 1932.

A Wiener Keramik figure of a putto, designed by M. Powolny, 40.5cm. high. (Christie's) $4,000

A Gmundner Keramik covered box, designed by Dagobert Peche for the Wiener Werkstaette in 1912, of octagonal section with domed lid, 16cm. high. (Phillips) $584

A Wiener Werkstätte terracotta figurative mirror by Vally Wieselthier, square, the frame with three masks and assorted stylized fruit in high relief, 1928, 40 x 28cm. (Christie's) $8,754

Phyllis, a female terracotta head by Vally Wieselthier, of a young girl with blushing cheeks and wearing a hat decorated with flowers, with painted Wiener Werkstätte monogram, 1919, 35.5cm. high. (Christie's) $10,155

A Wiener Keramik ceramic wall-mask, molded as a girl's head with a hat, painted in polychrome glazes, 24cm. high. (Christie's) $1,120

A Wiener Werkstätte terracotta polo player by Gudrun Baudisch, on rectangular base, polychrome glazes, 1927, 18.5cm. high. (Christie's) $1,137

A Weimar ceramic porcelain oviform chocolate jug, 19cm. high, printed factory mark Leuchtenburg. (Phillips) $130

WILKINSON

This Staffordshire pottery firm operated several factories in the Burslem area from the late 19th century. In 1894, Arthur Wilkinson's brother-in-law, Arthur Shorter, took over, keeping the name of Royal Staffordshire Pottery. His son, John took charge of the family's other pottery, Shorter & Son, while his other son Colley remained with his father.

Wilkinson's had produced many Art Nouveau pieces in the early years of the century, such as Oriflamme and Rubaiyat, but demand for these was waning in the early 1920s. In 1920 they bought the adjoining Newport Pottery, and it was here that they employed Clarice Cliff and allowed her to experiment on some undecorated shapes in the works. At this time she was also attending evening classes at Burslem under Gordon Forsyth. Forsyth did not approve of her work, believing it represented the superficial use of aspects of what he called 'modern art', without any understanding of the principles.

Her experiments attracted more favorable attention from Colley Shorter, who decided to try them on the market. Her Bizarre and Crocus ranges met with such acclaim that the whole factory was soon turned over to producing her designs. The rest, as they say, in history, with Colley Shorter marrying Clarice Cliff in 1940.

A Wilkinson Ltd matchstriker, formed as a seated dog with painted yellow, black and purple patches, the base titled *Do Scratch my Back*, 12.5cm. long. (Bristol Auction Rooms)
$125

A Wilkinson Ltd. toby jug, designed by Sir F. Carruthers Gould, in the form of Marshal Joffre, sitting with a shell on his knee, 26.3cm. high. (Bearne's)
$563

A Wilkinson Ltd. toby jug of Winston Churchill modeled by Clarice Cliff, seated on a bulldog draped with a Union Jack, 30.5cm. (Phillips)
$1,000

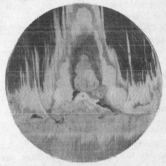

A Wilkinson Bizarre pottery circular charger, by Clarice Cliff, 18¼in. diam. (Andrew Hartley)
$2,500

A Wilkinson Pottery wall mask from the Bizarre series by Clarice Cliff, printed factory marks, 8in. high, 1930's. (Muir Hewitt)
$690

An A. J. Wilkinson toby jug of Neville Chamberlain, his hands folded in front of him, the chamfered base inscribed *Justice, Peace, Truth, Happiness*, 29.5cm. (Phillips)
$384

WOOD

The Wood family of Burslem are famous to collectors because of their high quality pottery figures made by two, if not by three, generations of Ralph Woods. Ralph Wood Senior, who died in 1772, and his brother Aaron developed an individual style for their productions which they passed onto their respective sons. Ralph's son, also named Ralph, lived between 1748 and 1795, and worked as a potter of model figures in Burslem with his cousin Enoch (died 1840). Their products were particularly noted for delicate coloring. Ralph Wood III succeeded his father Ralph but died at the early age of 27 in 1801. Some earthenware figures that bear the name mark *Ra Wood* may have been his handiwork as may also be porcelain examples. Enoch Wood started his own factory in 1784 and in 1790 went into partnership with James Caldwell, making tableware marked *Wood & Caldwell* which was shipped to America in vast quantities.

A Staffordshire figure of a doe of Ralph Wood type, circa 1770, 15.5cm. wide. (Christie's) $1,350

Ralph Wood jug, modeled by Jean Voysey, circa 1788, 25cm. high. $800

A pair of Staffordshire creamware wall pockets, circa 1780, of Ralph Wood type, molded with putti holding a jug of wine and grapes and the other with a flaming brazier, emblematic of Autumn and Winter respectively, 9³/₄in. high. (Christie's) $1,955

A Ralph Wood figure of an old woman feeding birds, wearing a pale-brown dress and with a white shawl over her head, three birds feeding from a circular green bowl at her feet, circa 1780, 20cm. high. (Christie's) $3,300

A well modeled and brightly glazed Enoch Wood bust of Wesley, the head and hair in white, 32cm. (Phillips London) $1,900

A Ralph Wood figure of s recumbent ram, on an oval green rockwork base molded with foliage, circa 1770, 18.5cm. wide. (Christie's) $5,500

A Ralph Wood group of St. George and the Dragon, the helmeted warrior wearing pale-yellow tunic, seated astride a manganese stallion, circa 1785, 29cm. high. (Christie's) $2,317

WOOD

A Ralph Wood Bacchus mask jug, circa 1775, 23.5cm. high. (Christie's) $1,000

A pair of Staffordshire figures of a gardener and companion of Ralph Wood type, circa 1780, 19.5cm. high. (Christie's) $4,400

A Ralph Wood Toby jug of conventional type, circa 1770, 25.5cm. high. (Christie's) $3,200

A pair of Wood style pearlware groups, titled 'Rualer and Pastime', the brightly colored figures seated before flowering bocage, circa 1815, 8in. high. (Bonhams) $333

A Ralph Wood group of the Vicar and Moses of conventional type, circa 1770, 21.5cm. high. (Christie's) $1,500

A pair of Ralph Wood figures of a shepherd and shepherdess, he standing beside a brown tree-stump, his companion standing placing a flower in her corsage, circa 1785, about 23cm. high. (Christie's) $3,387

A Ralph Wood oval plaque portrait of a woman, perhaps Charlotte Corday, circa 1780, 20cm. high. (Christie's) $1,500

A creamware model of a fox of Ralph Wood type, naturally modeled to the right with brown coat, a bird beneath his right forepaw, circa 1780, 9.5cm. high. (Christie's) $2,800

A Ralph Wood equestrian figure of King William III in the guise of a Roman Emperor seated on a rearing dun stallion, circa 1785, 40cm. high. (Christie's) $11,586

WORCESTER

The history of porcelain making in Worcester is a complex one, involving a number of principal factories. The process began around 1751, when the Worcester Tonquin Manufactory was set up by a consortium of 15 local businessmen. The leading figures in the group were a local surgeon, John Wall, and an apothecary, William Davis. During this earliest, or 'Dr Wall' period, a soaprock body was perfected from experiments at Bristol. The wares were decorated both in blue and white and a colorful polychrome, in a manner which amalgamated both oriental and European influences to form a highly distinctive style of their own. The shapes of these were graceful and the painting very fine.

During the ten years from 1755, decoration became increasingly subtle, derived mainly from Meissen or Chinese ideas, and while oriental figure painting was fairly naive, flower painting reached surprising heights of sophistication.

No factory marks were used until after 1765. Between then and 1776, which is generally seen as the end of the First Period, there was an enormous output of all the standard forms in a huge range of patterns. Both potting and painting continued to be of a high standard.

Between 1757-76 transfer printing in overglaze jet black became common and took the form of either European scenes or commemorative prints, of which the most common is Frederick of Prussia. Most were engraved by Robert Hancock.

Wall retired in 1775, and Davis struggled to keep the factory going in the face of increasing competition, in particular from the Caughley

A very rare Worcester teabowl and saucer, delicately painted in blue with the 'Heron on a Floral Spray' pattern after a Chinese original, the saucer 11.8cm. (Phillips) $2,170

A rare early Bristol/Worcester cream pot and cover of globular shape, painted in blue in 'Three Dot' painter style with an Oriental landscape, 7.5cm. high. (Phillips) $9,350

A pair of Worcester oviform vases with short waisted necks, painted with exotic birds and with birds, butterflies and insects in flight, circa 1755, 12.5cm. high. (Christie's) $15,752

A very fine early Worcester 'Scratch Cross' mug, painted with a version of the 'Willow Root' pattern with a Long Eliza figure standing between fences, 9.1cm. (Phillips) $8,060

A Worcester baluster sparrow beak jug with a grooved loop handle, painted in colors with three chinoiserie figures and a boy in a landscape with a tree and house, 8cm. high. (Phillips) $630

A fine Worcester 'fable' plate, painted in the center with a fox reclining on a tree trunk, the scalloped rim gilt with trellis and flowers, 21.5cm., crescent mark. (Phillips) $2,325

WORCESTER

factory, which, under Thomas Turner, had by then more or less cornered the market for blue and white.

In 1783, Davis was joined by John Flight, and after that they managed to produce some blue and white to compete with Caughley, but most was by now of an inferior quality. By the time a further new partner, Martin Barr, joined in 1793, blue and white production had ceased.

The factory had received a further blow in 1787, when Turner had persuaded Flight's chief decorators, Robert and Humphrey Chamberlain, to set up on their own as painters and decorators. The partners now decided to concentrate their efforts of producing high quality, though not always very expensive pieces, for the top end of the market. Flight improved the soaprock body with the result that tea services were now of unsurpassed thinness and translucence. They also rediscovered fine gilding.

By 1790 Chamberlain's had severed their links with the Caughley factory and were now making their own products. Because of their common backgrounds perhaps, the products which they and Flight's turned out over the next decade were very similar. Both, for example produced tea services in spiral, fluted shapes, decorated in underglaze blue with gold, or simple gold sprigs. Flight's however continued to play more for the upper end of the market, and their quality was unsurpassed.

They did, however, have to find new painters. Of these, John Pennington was the only one capable of reproducing the cabinet pieces of Sèvres. Zachariah Boreman and Joseph Hill specialised in landscapes. Between 1808–13, William

A Worcester circular basket, the spreading sides pierced with interlaced circles applied with puce and green florettes, 21cm., square mark.
(Phillips) $918

A pair of rare Worcester scale pink vases, each painted with Chinese figures in fenced gardens, 21cm., the porcelain circa 1770, the decoration probably later.
(Phillips) $4,060

A Worcester cup and saucer painted in the kakiemon palette with underglaze blue, iron-red, green and gilt with sprays of prunus and chrysanthemum, circa 1760, 2¾in. high.
(Christie's) $538

A Worcester small baluster mug with grooved loop handle, painted with a loose bouquet and scattered flowers, circa 1760, 8.5cm. high.
(Christie's) $886

A rare Worcester dessert plate with lobed edge, decorated with an unusual design of fanciful flowers and acanthus leaves on a blue ground, 21.5cm.
(Phillips) $279

A Worcester apple-green ground cabbage-leaf molded mask-jug painted with exotic birds perched and in flight among shrubs in landscape vignettes, circa 1770, 20.5cm.
(Christie's) $3,064

WORCESTER

Billingsley, the greatest flower painter of the age, also worked for Flight before leaving for Swansea and Nantgarw.

By now a third Worcester factory had been opened by Thomas Grainger, who had been a manager at Chamberlains. For the next 80 years Graingers were to rival the two main factories, for while their wares were generally cheaper and aimed at the more modest end of the market, at their best they could produce pieces quite equal in quality to Flights and Chamberlains.

After the Neo-Classical period of the early 1800s, the 1820s and 30s saw a revival of a fussier, almost neo-rococo taste. Richness and extravagance were called for both in terms of shapes and decoration. Graingers and Chamberlains both answered this demand with hundreds of different, complicated designs, with each fancy border available in a selection of coordinating colors. Flights, however, failed to adjust and this failure ended in their near bankruptcy and merger with Chamberlains in 1840, when the company became known as Chamberlain & Co.

Times were getting harder for everyone, however, and the new company was failing to compete with the bigger Staffordshire factories. It was bought by Kerr & Binns in 1851 and became the Worcester Royal Porcelain Co in 1862.

The popularity of parian had prompted a renewed interest in figure making, and Worcester became the most important maker of colored figures when these became popular in the 1870s and 80s. Their success was due in no small measure to the modeling skills of James Hadley, who though largely untutored, was able to design

An unusual Chaffers octagonal dish painted in blue with the 'Jumping Boy' pattern, within an alternating border of diaper and floral panels, 10.5cm.
(Phillips) $2,233

A Worcester mask-jug, the oviform body molded with leaves enriched in yellow, puce and purple, circa 1770, 19cm. high.
(Christie's) $1,969

A rare pair of Worcester pot-pourri vases and covers, with pierced lattice work bands to the rims, the covers with four pierced lattice work panels, unmarked, circa 1775, 10½in.
(Woolley & Wallis)
                                $17,460

A Worcester plate from the Duke of Gloucester service, the center luxuriantly painted with peaches, plums, cherries and blackcurrants and with a ladybird and an insect, gold crescent mark, circa 1775, 22.5cm. diameter.
(Christie's) $15,836

One of a set of twelve dessert plates of square shape, seven painted by Ricketts and five by Sebright, 20.5cm., date codes for 1918.
(Phillips)   (Twelve)
                                $1,530

A fine and early Worcester tankard of cylindrical 'Scratch Cross' form, with grooved strap handle, painted in vivid palette with the 'Beckoning Chinaman' pattern, 9cm.
(Phillips) $8,526

WORCESTER

and model in any required style. Also very popular at the time were ivory carvings which were being brought over from Japan and India. Most porcelain factories tried to reproduce these tones, but Worcester was by far the most successful with their 'Old Ivory' and 'Blush Ivory' bodies, which were widely copied and used on most of Hadley's figures, as well as vases and teawares.

After the death of their director R W Binns in 1900 and Hadley in 1903, the Worcester factory, which had bought out Graingers in 1889, continued to rely on the popularity of their designs, and little new or very exciting was produced for the next twenty years.

During the later first period a crescent or square mark was used on pieces decorated with underglaze blue, then incised *B* marks were used from 1792 till 1800. Thereafter the name of the factory usually appears, with date codes below the factory mark from 1862.

A Worcester partridge tureen and cover sitting on a rest, with natural colored plumage in shades of brown, red and black, the head in red, 14.5cm.
(Phillips) $2,639

A Worcester 'Hop Trellis' chocolate cup and saucer, of reeded form with entwined twig handles, painted with red berried festoons, 9cm.
(Phillips) $713

A pair of Worcester shagreen-ground Imari pattern tapering hexagonal vases and domed covers, painted with fabulous winged beasts sinuously en-twined about flowering shrubs, circa 1770, 30.5cm. high.
(Christie's) $42,000

A Worcester globular teapot and cover painted in a pale famille rose palette with flowering peony and chrysanthemum issuing from rockwork, circa 1755, 13cm. high.
(Christie's) $2,757

An attractive Worcester 'Hop Trellis' teacup and saucer, painted with festoons of red berried festoons, above a turquoise and 'pearl' border.
(Phillips) $1,008

A richly decorated Worcester scale blue dish, painted in the center with butterflies and insects and on the rim with exotic birds in colors, 24.5cm.
(Phillips) $3,857

WORCESTER BARR, FLIGHT & BARR

This is one of the more important convolutions of the complex and changing relationships between the Flight & Barr families at Worcester and as a period it lasted from 1807-13.

It is characterised by pieces reflecting the neo-classical taste of the period, and there was much use of marbling and figures in panels, the best of which were painted by Thomas Billingsley.

A Barr, Flight & Barr, Worcester shaped oval dessert dish, painted with a Japanese design, 28cm. wide.
(Bearne's) $477

A Barr, Flight & Barr inkstand with two ear-shaped holders at the side flanking a loop handle with gilt mask, 14cm.
(Phillips) $1,120

A Worcester (Barr, Flight & Barr) marbled-ground vase of urn shape, the richly gilt angular handles with Bacchus-mask terminals, painted in the manner of Thomas Baxter, circa 1810, 36.5cm. high.
(Christie's) $14,000

A Barr, Flight and Barr coffee can and saucer, finely painted with shell panels probably by Samuel Smith.
(Phillips) $2,258

A magnificent Barr, Flight & Barr vase, the full front panel painted with a study of tropical shells including a glorious strombus, a murex and limpet, 33cm.
(Phillips) $16,000

A Barr, Flight & Barr plate, decorated probably in London and in the manner of the Baxter workshop, 23.5cm. diam. (Phillips)
$520

A Barr, Flight & Barr inkwell painted with a shell attributed to Samuel Smith, painted with a whelk-type shell and seaweed, 7cm.
(Phillips) $5,000

A Barr, Flight & Barr porcelain circular tureen and stand, the painted panel attributed to Thos. Baxter, 7in. high, 7½in. wide overall, circa 1810-15.
(Andrew Hartley) $6,750

WORCESTER, CHAMBERLAINS

A Chamberlain's Worcester shallow bowl and cover, the center to the interior painted with a loose bouquet within a gilt scroll well, circa 1840, 16cm. diameter.
(Christie's) $2,559

A rare Chamberlain cottage pastille burner and cover also formed as a thatched house, of square shape with brick walls, 8cm. high.
(Phillips) $442

An English porcelain pen-stand and stopper, modeled as a winged putto, leaning on a shell molded bowl with three apertures, circa 1825, probably Chamberlain's, Worcester, 5in. wide.
(Christie's) $303

A rare Chamberlain's Worcester lilac-ground jug, with a large oblong octagonal panel painted in the manner of Humphrey Chamberlain, 10in. high.
(Christie's) $8,364

A pair of Chamberlain's Worcester sauce-tureens and covers, circa 1811, puce printed marks, each with dolphin finial and pierced gallery, 9¹/₈in. high.
(Christie's) $3,450

A Chamberlains Worcester jug, spirally fluted, painted sepia view of Worcester from a garden with figures in the foreground, 7in.
(Russell, Baldwin & Bright) $1,010

A Chamberlain's Worcester mug, the cylindrical body brightly painted with a Japan pattern in iron red, blue and gold, 13.3cm. high.
(Bearne's) $745

A Chamberlain soup tureen, cover and stand, decorated in a rich Imari palette with the so-called 'Tree of Life' pattern, stand 30.5cm.
(Phillips) $1,440

A large Chamberlain jug, finely gilt with bands of hops and foliage on alternating blue and white grounds, 19.5cm.
(Phillips) $1,400

WORCESTER, FIRST PERIOD

A Worcester hop-trellis fluted teapot, cover and stand of barrel shape, painted with red berried foliage-swags, circa 1770, the teapot 12.5cm. high. (Christie's) **$7,253**

An early Worcester quatrelobed cup, painted in famille rose palette with flowering plants and scattered insects, 6.5cm. (Phillips) **$3,468**

A Worcester outside-decorated globular teapot and cover painted in black with two quail flanked by a brightly colored flower-spray, circa 1770, 13.5cm. high. (Christie's) **$2,418**

A Worcester blue-ground fable-decorated plate painted in the manner of Jefferyes Hammett O'Neale, circa 1768, 19cm. diameter. (Christie's) **$4,836**

A Worcester milk jug of barrel shape, painted in blue with the 'Barrel Jug Scroll' pattern, 8cm. crescent mark, circa 1765. (Phillips) **$456**

A First Period Worcester junket dish, painted with three classical vases adorned with flower branches, 23cm., cracked. (Lawrence Fine Arts) **$480**

WORCESTER, FLIGHT & BARR

A Worcester, Flight & Barr, canary-yellow ground flared flower pot with fixed gilt ring handles, circa 1805, 16cm. high. (Christie's) **$2,400**

A pair of Worcester (Flight & Barr) oviform vases, painted with The Queen Charlotte pattern, with short flared necks and on spreading circular stems, circa 1800, 51cm. high. (Christie's) **$9,845**

A Worcester Flight & Barr oviform jug, with central medallion painted by John Pennington in grisaille with a portrait of King George III, height 6$^{1}/_{2}$in., circa 1790. (Bonhams) **$2,800**

A Worcester, Flight, Barr & Barr urn-shaped two-handled vase and cover, circa 1820, 46cm. high. $2,800

A pair of Worcester (Flight, Barr & Barr) magenta-ground pot-pourri vases, covers and liners, circa 1817, impressed marks, 15½in. high.
(Christie's) $7,475

A Flight, Barr & Barr Worcester armorial vase and cover, attributed to Thos. Baxter, 19cm. high. $5,200

Flight Barr & Barr Worcester plate, the center painted with a crest and motto, within a floral border in colors, printed and impressed marks, circa 1813/40.
(G. A. Key) $231

A pair of Worcester (Flight, Barr & Barr) centerpiece bowls, circa 1815, on three fluted tapering legs headed by lion masks, 8½in. high.
(Christie's) $4,025

A rare Flight, Barr and Barr cottage pastille burner and nightlight in the form of a rustic half-timbered house with a gabled thatched roof, 17cm. high.
(Phillips) $578

WORCESTER, GRAINGER

A Grainger's Worcester porcelain tankard with boldly gilded borders, scrolling and handle, 5¼in. high, circa 1812-20.
(Andrew Hartley) $2,000

A Grainger Lee & Co. garniture of three campana pot-pourri vases, finely painted with titled views, 13½in. and 11¼in. high.
(Bonhams) $4,000

An English ivory porcelain trout's head stirrup-cup naturalistically modeled with gills and scales and painted in tawny shades with darker brown spots, perhaps Worcester (Grainger & Co.), circa 1860, 4in. high.
(Christie's) $672

WORCESTER, ROYAL

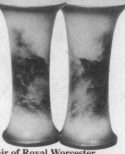

A pair of Royal Worcester vases, oviform with tall slender necks and twin-handled, the handle terminals modeled as swanheads, painted by Sedgley, signed, 14in. high.
(Christie's) $3,427

Richard Sebright, a good Royal Worcester oval plaque painted with a basket overflowing with apples, grapes, peaches, pears and strawberries, signed, 15cm. x 21cm. date code for 1913.
(Phillips) $5,472

A pair of Royal Worcester porcelain beaker vases signed *H Stinton*, the ivory ground painted with highland cattle, cypher mark for 1913.
(Morphets) $1,382

James Hadley, a fine large pair of figures of eastern water carriers, the lady holding the vase on her shoulder, the man with a large jug slung over his right shoulder, 43cm. high, date code for 1911.
(Phillips) $1,575

Harry Stinton: a pair of vases with unusual pierced necks and scroll handles shaded in 'blush ivory', signed, 11.7cm., date code for 1908.
(Phillips) $1,628

A pair of Royal Worcester parian figures of Morning Dew and Evening Dew, partially glazed and modeled as nymphs wearing loose flowing robes, impressed marks, circa 1860, 16¹/₂in. high.
(Christie's) $1,036

A pair of Royal Worcester vases and covers, painted with two Highland cattle on misty mountainsides, signed *John Stinton*, 24cm., date code for 1903.
(Phillips) $2,639

A pair of Royal Worcester spirally molded candlesticks of squat form, the shaded yellow and apricot bodies with knopped stems and circular feet, 1892, 4¹/₄in. high.
(Christie's) $402

A pair of Royal Worcester cylindrical vases painted in colors with scenes of Highland cattle in mountainous landscapes, signed *J. Stinton*, 26.5cm., date codes for 1921.
(Phillips) $4,060

WORCESTER, ROYAL

A pair of Royal Worcester figures modeled as a lady and gentleman, 14in. high, circa 1887.   **$1,600**

A 19th century Royal Worcester porcelain figure of an elephant, wearing a blanket and howdah, 7½in. high.   **$480**

A pair of Royal Worcester vases and covers painted with swans by C. H. C. Baldwyn, signed, 12¹/₂in. high, 1903. (Tennants)   **$2,456**

A pair of Royal Worcester porcelain pot pourri vases and covers, of slender inverted baluster form, painted in colors by J. Lander with full blown crimson and yellow roses, 33cm. high. (Spencer's)   **$2,320**

A pair of Royal Worcester figures of children, the girl skipping and wearing a pink short tunic and yellow skirt, her hair uplifted by the breeze, the boy aiming to strike a striped football, circa 1870, 12¹/₂in. high. (Christie's)   **$1,036**

A pair of Royal Worcester tapering oviform ewers with trefoil lips, painted by G. Johnson on an azure ground with four swans in flight, date codes for circa 1909, 10¹/₂in. high. (Christie's)   **$9,950**

A pair of Royal Worcester two-handled oviform vases, painted in colors and gilding enriched in white with sprays of pink and mauve clover, date code for 1898, 8¹/₄in. high. (Christie's)   **$730**

A Royal Worcester model of George Washington on a dappled charger, modeled by Bernard Winskill, 45cm. high, No. 150 of an edition limited to 750 copies. (Bearne's)   **$2,142**

A pair of Royal Worcester vases, decorated with aquilegia in soft shades, within green scale molded borders and with double gilt and coral handles, 28.5cm., date code for 1903. (Phillips)   **$1,218**

WORCESTER, ROYAL

A Royal Worcester 'Aesthetic' teapot and cover, circa 1882, polychrome decorated in 'greenery yallery' colors 6¹/₈in. high.
(Sotheby's) $3,410

Pair of Royal Worcester ornaments, formed as hands, predominantly white glazed with a jeweled and green band base, 6in. high.
(G. A. Key) $420

Doris Lindner, a very rare model of Chanticleer, the cockerel lightly colored with gilt highlights, 26cm, date code for 1959.
(Phillips) $374

George Owen: a rare Royal Worcester reticulated campana-shaped vase with double upswept scroll handles, finely pierced, 15cm. high, date code for 1912.
(Phillips) $8,525

A pair of Royal Worcester large moon-flask vases with short waisted necks and bronzed and gilt loop handles, painted with large sprays of pink and yellow orchids and overlapping leaves, date codes for 1878, 18¹/₂in. high.
(Christie's) $973

A Royal Worcester box and cover possibly after an original model by James Hadley modeled as a child falling backwards into a drum, late 19th century, 3³/₄in. high.
(Christie's) $474

Royal Worcester circular porcelain plaque, 1912, painted with highland cattle, signed *H. Stinton*, in a silver frame, Birmingham 1912, 4in. diameter.
(Peter Wilson) $483

A pair of Royal Worcester vases, each spirally molded body painted with leaves and ferns in autumn tints and gold, 27.3cm. high.
(Bearne's) $493

Royal Worcester porcelain jardinière by James Hadleigh, reticulated top, circular base with leaf formed and molded feet, 8in. tall.
(G. A. Key) $937

CHINA

A Royal Worcester figure, Nursery Rhyme series, "Little Jack Horner", 4in. high, and with date code for 1952. (Canterbury)   **$339**

Two rare Royal Worcester models of ladies' shoes, decorated with gilded dots on a matt gold ground, pink pierced laces, 15.5cm., date codes for 1879. (Phillips)   **$1,473**

A Royal Worcester model of Napoleon Bonaparte, by Bernard Winskill, No. 23 of an edition limited to 750 copies. (Bearne's)   **$1,478**

A large earthenware jar and cover, printed and painted with panels of pheasants and highland cattle in the manner of John and Harry Stinton, 14in. high. (Spencer's)   **$1,020**

Very fine pair of Royal Worcester two handled vases, the deep blue grounds decorated in gilt, dated code for 1898, 9in. high, decorator's mark Charlie Deakins. (Ewbank)   **$4,223**

A rare Royal Worcester porcelain 'Persian' pierced vase modeled by James Hadley, with gilded decoration by Samuel Ranford, of birds amongst scrolling foliage, 7in. high. (Spencer's)   **$1,600**

William Ricketts, a Royal Worcester pot pourri vase and pierced cover, painted in colors with a cluster of ripe fruits, 17cm., date code for 1926. (Phillips)   **$853**

A pair of Royal Worcester figures in the form of Eastern water carriers, each on one knee pouring the contents from a large jar, 25.5cm., printed mark, circa 1891. (Bearne's)   **$1,450**

Dog Toby, a very rare Royal Worcester extinguisher, the dog wearing an orange Tyrolean hat with a white feather, 7.5cm., probably 1882. (Phillips)   **$7,038**

WORCESTER, ROYAL

George Owen: a rare Royal Worcester reticulated cup and saucer, the double walled cup with gilt loop handle and supported on three gilt lion paw feet, date code for 1927. (Phillips) $3,060

A pair of Royal Worcester ring-necked pheasants, modeled by R. Van Ruyckevelt. (Bearne's) $1,267

George Moseley, a teapot and cover of globular shape with gilt scroll handle and finial, painted with apples and blackberries,, 13.5cm., date code for 1930. (Phillips) $805

A Royal Worcester figure of Mary Queen of Scots standing wearing a crucifix, a black-trimmed gilt snood, holding a handkerchief and 'jeweled' rosary, date code for 1917, 8¼in. high. (Christie's) $475

Three Royal Worcester wall-brackets allegorical of the Seasons after models by James Hadley and formed as maidens seated in grottoes, pierced for suspension, circa 1870, 9½in. high. (Christie's) $949

A fine and attractive Royal Worcester china pot pourri vase and covers, painted in colors by Harry Ayrton with a still life of peaches, blackberries and a cob nut on a mossy banking, 34cm. high. (Spencer's) $1,255

Salamander on Tree Stump: a very rare Royal Worcester extinguisher, the salamander with tail coiled around a tree stump, 10cm., date code for 1880. (Phillips) $8,525

A Royal Worcester blue-ground three-piece garniture, decorated by Thomas Bott, the largest with *TB* monogram and *63*, gilded by Josiah Davis, the largest 16in. high. (Christie's) $7,542

A Royal Worcester blush porcelain figure of a man sharpening a scythe, wearing a hat, open neck shirt and breeches, on rustic base, 8½in. high. (Andrew Hartley) $534

YI

This was a Korean period lasting from 1392-1910 which was largely Chinese dominated, although in the 18th century a more characteristic Korean style began to emerge.

The Japanese had invaded in the 16th century and many Korean artists had been deported to encourage the arts in Japan. Bereft of their best craftsmen, it was the rustic arts which continued to flourish in Korea, e.g. Ido bowls. Among the best works of the period are rough blue and white porcelain pieces.

YONGZENG

Yongzeng was an Emperor (1723-35) of the Ching dynasty. In his reign more factories at Ching-te-chen came under Imperial control. From 1728 the noted potter Tang Ying was employed and under his aegis archaistic copying of earlier wares was encouraged, particularly Sung celadons, blue and white Ming and the styles and nien hao of K'angxi.

YUAN

The irresistible onslaught of Genghis Khan resulted in the establishment of the Mongol Yuan dynasty (1279-1368) by his almost equally well-known descendant Kublai. Generally speaking the Mongols showed little interest in the arts. Wares on the whole were more thickly potted and many large dishes and wine jars were made for the Indian and Middle Eastern markets.

One of the most important developments of the period, however, was shu fu porcelain (Privy Council ware), which had a slightly opaque, bluish glaze covering molded, low relief designs.

Blue and white decorated jar, Yi Dynasty, the body freely painted in underglaze blue with a pair of sparrows perched on a branch of flowering prunus, 5⅝in. high. (Butterfield & Butterfield) $1,540

Underglaze blue decorated vase, Yi Dynasty, the body decorated in underglaze blue with leafy blossoming branches and hovering bats on a white ground, 10¾in. high. (Butterfield & Butterfield) $27,500

A fine and rare 'Green dragon' baluster jar and cover, encircled Yongzheng six-character mark and of the period, crisply painted in underglaze-blue around the body with two five-clawed dragons, 8¾in. high. (Christie's) $63,871

A blue and white saucer-dish, encircled Yongzheng six-character mark and of the period, painted at the center in vivid blue tones with a ferocious four-clawed dragon writhing amongst clouds and fire scrolls, 6in. diameter. (Christie's) $3,690

A Yuan blue and white dish, the interior painted with a central medallion of phoenixes in flight amid scrolling clouds, below a chrysanthemum scroll around the well, Yuan dynasty, 28.5cm. (Christie's) $15,752

A very rare blue and white vase, Yuhuchun, Yuan dynasty, freely painted to the body in deep purplish tone with two figures within a rocky landscape divided by a willow tree, 9¾in. high.(Christie's) $133,283

ZSOLNAY

The Zsolnay earthenware pottery was established in 1862 at Pécs in Hungary by Vilmos Zsolnay, with the aim of shaping a characteristic national style.

Most of the output consisted of practical ware for everyday use, though some ornamental pieces were produced, often with Persian inspired motifs. Vases and bowls were made in Art Nouveau style with boldly colored glazes and luster decoration.

A Zsolnay Pecs luster group modeled as two polar bears on a large rock in a green and golden luster, 4½in. high.
(Christie's) $430

A Zsolnay Pecs green luster pottery figure of a stylized fish, printed factory marks, 4¹/₂in. high.
(Christie's) $58

A small Zsolnay figural luster vase decorated on the shoulders with the partially clad Orpheus with his lyre beside him and an amorous mermaid, 13cm. high.
(Phillips) $1,050

A large Zsolnay luster group, of two men possibly Cain and Abel, one lying prostrate on a domed rocky base with the other towering above him, 37.5cm. high.
(Phillips) $930

A Zsolnay vase of ovoid form with everted rim, painted in shades of pink and green on a cream ground with hummingbirds amongst waterlilies, late 19th century, 41cm. high.
(Christie's) $789

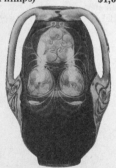

A Zsolnay Pecs pottery two-handled vase of ovoid form swelling towards the base, decorated with stylized floral motifs, 22.5cm. high.
(Christie's) $830

A Zsolnay Persian ewer, the globular body painted in shades of pink, blue, green and gilt with two cranes teasing a tortoise, 23cm. high.
(Christie's) $347

A Zsolnay Pecs green luster jug, the handle modeled as a nude maiden gazing over the rim, 16in. high.
(Christie's S. Ken) $1,200

ZURICH

The Zurich porcelain factory was begun by a group of business men in 1763, under the direction of Adam Spengler, a skilled faiencier. At first, soft paste porcelain was produced, but later production changed to hard paste, using clays from near Limoges.

The early years were very productive, with a thriving export trade. Small individual pieces of tableware were made, as well as great services. From about 1780 vases in the Sèvres style were produced in simple forms with painted rural scenes, often inspired by Nilson engravings.

1775–9 saw the finest period of figure production. Many of these were by Johann Valentin Sonnenschein, whose work followed German models, depicting peasants, soldiers etc. in contemporary dress. Towards the end of his career he also designed some larger table centerpieces. Spengler's son, John James, also spent a short while making figures at Zürich before going to Derby.

The smoky brown hue of Zürich porcelain can often look rather like Ludwigsburg, and there was little originality of form. The best known painter at the factory was the poet Salomon Gessner, who signed his work, and specialized in rather tedious Swiss landscapes.

After Spengler's death in 1790 porcelain production ceased, and faience only was produced thereafter.

The usual mark is a Z with a stroke through it, in underglaze blue.

Zurich sugar bowl and cover with gilt fruit knop and floral decoration, circa 1765, 10cm. high. $2,500

A Zurich figure of a shepherd modeled by J. J. Meyer, 20cm. high, incised mark N I. (Phillips) $7,200

A Zurich ornithological teapot and a cover of bullet shape, painted in colors, one side with an owl and a woodpecker, the other with an eagle and a snipe, circa 1770, 17cm. wide. (Christie's) $3,200

A Zürich cup and galleried saucer with a wishbone handle, painted with loose sprays of flowers among scattered sprigs, circa 1770. (Christie's) $403

A Zurich oval dish with pierced border, painted in colors with a parrot perching on a branch, incised Z, blue Z and two dots, circa 1770, 12.3cm. wide. (Christie's) $4,200

A Zürich figure of a lady, circa 1770, blue Z mark, in white, red trimmed skirt and bodice, holding a lamb, modeled by Josef Nees, 5¼in. high. (Christie's) $1,240

INDEX